CHRISTIAN FAITH
AND
MODERN THEOLOGY

Edited by CARL F. H. HENRY

CONTEMPORARY EVANGELICAL THOUGHT

CHRISTIAN FAITH AND MODERN THEOLOGY

CONTEMPORARY EVANGELICAL THOUGHT

CHRISTIAN FAITH
AND
MODERN THEOLOGY

✝

J. OLIVER BUSWELL, JR. GORDON H. CLARK
JOHN H. GERSTNER VERNON C. GROUNDS
CARL F. H. HENRY FRED H. KLOOSTER
ROBERT D. KNUDSEN HAROLD B. KUHN
GEORGE E. LADD ROGER NICOLE
M. EUGENE OSTERHAVEN JAMES I. PACKER
LORMAN PETERSEN ROBERT D. PREUS
WILLIAM CHILDS ROBINSON ROBERT PAUL ROTH
HERMANN SASSE C. GREGG SINGER
BASTIAAN VAN ELDEREN, JR. WARREN C. YOUNG

Edited by

CARL F. H. HENRY

CHANNEL PRESS
New York

Affiliate of
MEREDITH PRESS
Des Moines & New York

LIBRARY OF CONGRESS CATALOGUE CARD NUMBER: 63-23360

MANUFACTURED IN THE UNITED STATES OF AMERICA FOR MEREDITH PRESS

VAN REES PRESS • NEW YORK

CONTENTS

✝

INTRODUCTION

✝

I T WAS MY privilege in 1960 to address Protestant ministers in Germany and Switzerland on theological issues. The spirited and challenging discussions we shared made it quite clear that the Continent once again is experiencing the strain of spiritual slump and doctrinal uncertainty. Fascination with the theological lodestars that shone in the period between the Wars is lessening; in the Christian community the horoscope-watchers are more engrossed now with the stellar prominence of Bultmann than with that of Barth or Brunner. At his home in Zurich Brunner himself conceded to me that "Bultmann is king" among the younger intellectuals, and in Basel Barth dolefully portended a future either of Bultmannism or resurgent Lutheran confessionalism.

This opportunity came in connection with the Graham evangelistic crusades. In Berne, Zurich, Basel, Lausanne, Essen, Hamburg, and West Berlin people in general had shown mounting curiosity and interest in the projected meetings. Despite the low church attendance that characterized these cities for the most part, the people seemed to sense, nonetheless, that in the clash of contemporary ideals Christianity still offers some a power which they could appropriate if they would. The clergy, however, were more preoccupied with theological and philosophical problems, and the question of the larger doctrinal implications of Billy Graham's ministry kept obtruding itself.

Leaders of the German Evangelical Alliance therefore arranged precrusade lectures for ministers that should investigate the special relevance of evangelical theology for the problems of modern life. These lectures, together with subsequent discussion periods, became my assignment. A personal acquaintance since college days, and a moving spirit in the founding of "Christianity Today," Mr. Graham shared my approach to these special meetings. After hearing the historic Christian emphases in the lectures, all attending ministers were to have full opportunity for interaction and for open dialogue concerning the contemporary theological dilemma.

So it was that, in possibly the first gathering of this kind in a generation, ministers from all theological traditions met on the Continent across denominational lines for an aggressive presentation of the conservative viewpoint. For several hours they then engaged in spirited debate with each other, and with the speaker, in a doctrinal confrontation in which historic Christian emphases (rather than modern alternatives) occupied the center of discussion.

I had faced this responsibility with some measure of Niebuhrian anxiety (I use the phrase as a perverse sort of shorthand for post-Adamic apprehensiveness). As the crusades drew near, certain evangelical leaders—in keeping with their pietistic heritage—questioned the wisdom of any special theological emphasis; doctrinal debate, they contended, might dissipate interest in evangelism. While Mr. Graham and I had already agreed that the theological discussions for the clergy and the evangelistic crusades should not be wholly identified, we both felt that theological concerns should be fully probed. As matters developed, even ministers who fell into spirited disagreement on doctrinal issues were drawn all the more by curiosity to attend the evangelistic enterprise; even where they themselves stayed away, their church people came.

No two situations were wholly alike. The evangelical ministers, often a woeful minority, did not know quite what to expect, and so at times risked only the route of least resistance. In Switzerland the theological lectures suffered almost everywhere except in Basel, because the sponsoring committee insisted that Dr. Graham address these meetings also. Because of Dr. Graham's world prominence, the committee then was unable to rule out attendance by lay workers and their families who had energetically prepared for the crusades. As a result, ten to twelve hundred workers appeared for lectures presumably geared to the specialized needs of one to two hundred ministers. In Lausanne, for example, many of the listeners must have been tempted to remark: "We had not so much as heard that there is a Bultmann"; or, if they had heard, there was little more some cared to hear along that line.

In Basel, on the other hand, the meeting was restricted to ministers, and proved to be the most rewarding of the Swiss pre-crusade meetings. I had resolved, come what may, I would venture a running critique of neo-orthodoxy in Basel. For one thing, Continental theologians apparently had not even seen the scholarly evangelical criticisms of neo-orthodoxy that some of their former doctoral students from America had published. It would be an evasion, if not a lack of courage, simply to exchange pleasantries. It was essential to express the deep discontent of American evangelicals with specific tenets of neo-orthodoxy; it was important to ask whether Barth and Brunner had not themselves unwittingly prepared the way for Bultmann's seizure of theological initiative. That Thurneyson, Eichrodt and other prominent churchmen, long associated with crisis-theology, participated was gratifying. But most remarkable of all was an existential turn in the question period in Basel that dramatically reinforced the evangelical desire to hold theology and evangelism together in scriptural dimensions. A divinity student now at Heidelberg for graduate work, but who had studied under some of the professors here in attendance, had come to the Basel crusade the previous night. There he heard once more the old message and the old call to personal faith in the Saviour's atonement and resurrection. Mostly out of curiosity, he said, he joined those who went forward during the invitation, but to his astonishment, and by the grace of God, he told the ministers' group, he could now confidently say as a divinity student that he had actually been "born again." He illustrated anew that evangelistic theology and theological evangelism complement each other ideally.

In Hamburg, the moderator of the ministerial meetings insisted that, despite the ever-changing theological fads, German churches as a whole are characterizable neither as Bultmannian, Barthian, nor anything else; at grass roots, he claimed, they are still devoted to the simple and devout preaching of the Gospel. Somewhat similar statements were made a century ago about the majority of churches in the lean liberal era when Schleiermacher's and Ritschl's views were regnant. Yet the formative theological centers—strategic university chairs, university pulpits, influential religious presses, ecclesiastical representation in study conferences and so on—were in that case disproportionately assigned to the nonevangelical community. Moreover, academic recognition or preferment was given to those open to the newer emphases.

The experience of evangelicals in the United States has not been much different. The political promotion of new theological fashions by influential ecclesiastical leaders is, in fact, directly responsible for many reservations among the membership of numerous denominational churches. The force and vigor of evangelical impact grow dull when enterprises generated by evangelical loyalties are deliberately placed into the service of alien convictions and conservative forces are politically restrained and penalized. As recently as 1961 a scientific survey by the Opinion Research Bureau of Princeton, New Jersey, indicated that the Protestant clergy in America designate their theological perspectives as follows: fundamentalist or conservative, 74 per cent; liberal, 14 per cent; neo-orthodox, 12 per cent. While dialectical and existential theologies may have registered some gains in the past few years, the great divergence between the positions of Tillich and Bultmann from those of Barth and Brunner, and the fragmentation of positions among Bultmann's disciples themselves, may sug-

gest no forthcoming substantial change in these figures. While Barth's
1962 visit to America rallied large audiences, many liberals were openly
disappointed that he had brought along no acceptable "ecumenical theology" (whatever that may be!).

Meanwhile signs remain of a renewed interest in conservative Protestant theology. No one expects therefrom the sudden emergence of a Christian world; to erase the distinction between church and world is, after all,
a speculative fallacy. Even if the notion of a wholly converted earth had
biblical warrant (which it assuredly does not), the present era of rampant
antichrist philosophies, or ever-increasing multitudes being propelled into
the lap of paganism, and of apostasy in the churches themselves is hardly
suited to millennial expectations except on an apocalyptic basis. What
we do see, however, is a new attestation of the enduring relevance of
evangelism wherever and on whatever continent sinners accept the call to
decision for Christ. We see, too, a fresh searching of Scripture for light
on man's madness; larger appreciation of the theological vigor of historic
Christianity; the emergence of expository and doctrinal literature from a
reverent biblical perspective and of periodicals that rival and challenge
the erstwhile influential liberal journals.

There are soft spots in the evangelical vanguard, however. For one
thing, the Christian-college movement has not challenged the world of
secular thought aggressively but has viewed itself, rather, as an evangelical
holding operation. Further, the concept of Christian vocation has not
permeated the nonprofessional classes identified with the churches; interest in jurisprudence and problems of social justice lags behind that in
evangelism and education. In respect to biblical inspiration and man's
uniqueness by creation, one, unfortunately, may discern unnecessary toler-
ances in certain evangelically dedicated institutions.

These problems notwithstanding, the evangelical movement is distinctive and distinct from the modern theologies for such uniform emphases
as the rational and propositional nature of divine revelation; the final
authority of the Bible; man's fall from a condition of original righteousness, and involvement of the race in the sin and guilt of the first Adam;
the divine promise of redemption and provision thereof through the coming of Jesus Christ in a series of supernatural acts that climax Old Testament prophecy. Evangelical Christianity asserts Jesus of Nazareth to be
the supreme revelation of the Godhead: born of a virgin, sinless in life,
atoning by his death for the sin of the world, and triumphant in bodily
resurrection from the grave, He is the life-giving Head of the Church and
returning, regnant Lord.

Today the Christian faith is contradicted at assorted levels by assorted
systems of speculation. One such threat was discussed in the summer of
1961 by a group of evangelical scholars. For most of a week they met at
Union Theological Seminary in New York City to discuss the teachings

and influence of Rudolf Bultmann. From this seminar came plans for the present symposium on *Christian Faith and Modern Theology;* many of the volume's contributors, in fact, attended and participated in the discussions. It was felt that an exposition of evangelical perspectives over against one or another of the modern alternatives would fill a definite need, even if such an exposition were but a partial doctrinal overview and concerned itself with the schematic investigation of but one or another contemporary nonevangelical scholar at special points of interest. Funds to underwrite the seminar and to implement this symposium were a personal gesture of recognition by Evangelist Billy Graham for the theological lectures that supplemented his European crusades. Appreciation is expressed also to others who gave supplementary support to the effort, among them Mrs. Dorothy M. Bisbee. My wife, Helga Bender Henry, gave herself cheerfully to much of the manuscript preparation, and my secretary, Irma Peterson, devoted countless hours to project-related typing and correspondence.

Christian Faith and Modern Theology is the fourth in a series of volumes initiated under the title *Contemporary Evangelical Thought* (1957); volumes two and three, *Revelation and the Bible* (1958) and *Basic Christian Doctrines* (1962), like the present volume four, carry this series designation by way of subtitle. The introductory surveys of twentieth-century theology on the Continent, in Great Britain and in the United States are among the valuable features of this effort. These delineations form an important background for studying particular themes. A selective bibliography of related reading is appended.

CARL F. H. HENRY

Editor, "Christianity Today"
Washington, D.C.

EUROPEAN THEOLOGY
IN THE
TWENTIETH CENTURY

Hermann Sasse

Hermann Sasse taught Church History and Symbolics at Erlangen University from 1933-48, when he joined the Lutheran Free Church in Germany. Since then he has taught at Immanuel Theological Seminary, North Adelaide, Australia. For ten years he was active in the World Conference on Faith and Order, serving in 1927 as a delegate to the World Conference of Lausanne and later as a member of the Continuation and of the Executive Committees. He has written many books, among them Die Weltkonferenz fuer Glauben und Kirchenverfassung *(1929).*

EUROPEAN THEOLOGY
IN THE
TWENTIETH CENTURY

NOT TO have lived before 1914 is not to know how happy life can be. Applying Talleyrand's famous dictum [1] on the year 1789 to the great watershed of our century, we might well ask, Have the nations of Europe ever experienced happier years than those from the turn of the century to the outbreak of World War I? This was a period of unprecedented wealth, the result of industrial progress, of world trade, and of vast colonial expansion. The Western civilization of Europe and America seemed rapidly to be conquering the whole world and to be outstripping all mankind on the road of unlimited progress. There were political tensions and even wars in various parts of the world. There was social unrest, too, and the name "Bolshewiki" was born. But no human eye could possibly foresee the immense catastrophes foreshadowed by such events. For those who remember, these years linger on like a late summer day whose golden brightness betrays nothing of the impending devastating gales of autumn and winter.

I. THEOLOGY AT THE TURN OF THE CENTURY

The happiness of those years is reflected also in the prevailing theology. A great missionary who saw the tragedy of the Armenian people and predicted that the greatest persecutions of the Christian faith would occur in the twentieth century was laughed at. How could persecutions occur in our

---

[1] He who has not lived before 1789 has not known the sweetness of life.

3

civilized world? Was not the Kingdom of God visibly growing on the mission fields of the entire world? Said John Mott in the closing address of the World Missionary Conference of Edinburgh in 1910: "God grant that we all of us may in these next moments solemnly resolve so to plan and so to act, so to live and so to sacrifice, that our spirit of reality may become contagious among those to whom we go: and it may well be that the words of the Archbishop shall prove to be a splendid prophecy, and that before many of us taste death we shall see the Kingdom of God come with power" (Report, Vol. IX, p. 351). These were the last words of that Conference, and in them Mott referred to the opening-day address by the Archbishop of Canterbury (Dr. Davidson), which ended with the application of Mark 9:1 to the momentous assembly: ". . . it may well be that if that come true, 'there be some standing here tonight who shall not taste of death till they see'—here on earth, in a way we know not now—'the Kingdom of God come with power' " (Report, Vol. IX, p. 150). Significantly, the great American leader of world mission and the great English churchman were agreed in this hope. This unwarranted optimism characterized Western Christendom at that time.

At the turn of the century the life of all European churches was at extremely low ebb. On the Continent the masses of the working class had been practically lost to the Church. And the growing socialist parties not only were hostile to the Church, but also openly espoused atheism. In this respect the socialists found support even among their political opponents in the liberal middle classes. In Germany, professors of science and philosophy had attacked Christianity since 1906. "Jesus never lived" was among the topics they discussed in mass meetings where they propounded a modern, scientific, and even atheistic view of the world. Of those who did not share such a radical viewpoint many were satisfied with a liberal view of God and man, of the world and society; the majority of the middle class had no use for the Bible and the dogma of the Church. The Protestant Church was merely an organization maintained by the state and controlled by the ruling political powers. Within this aggregation of nominal church members was a small minority of souls who remained loyal to the faith once delivered and defended it against both the radicals and the liberals.

II. GREAT GERMAN CONSERVATIVE THEOLOGIANS

As everywhere in Christendom, a conservative, confessional or "positive" theology had to maintain itself against the "liberals" and also against a merely historical theology which could not appreciate the dogma of the Church. It is, however, characteristic of German conservative theology at the turn of the century that just its greatest representatives tried to maintain the authority of Holy Writ without the traditional doctrine of inspiration. This doctrine, which had been lost in the age of Rationalism, had not been regained in the great revival of dogmatic theology in the nineteenth century, probably because the dogmaticians also were too much under the spell of that historism which was prevalent in Germany. Hence we find in European Protestantism no parallel to the Fundamentalist movement which at the turn of the century (see S. J. Andrews, *Christianity and Anti-Christianity in Their Final Conflict*, 1898; *The Fundamentals*, 1909-1915) arose in conservative churches and groups in America as a necessary reaction against a church-destroying crude Modernism. While Fundamentalism at once exercised an influence on the British churches, it did not become known in Germany before 1924 and then only in its excessive forms. Its great theological leaders, men like J. Gresham Machen and B. B. Warfield, have never become really known in Germany. Only in our own day, when the devastating consequences of Bultmannism are becoming manifest, the question arises anew whether the authority of Holy Scripture can be maintained without realizing what the Bible teaches about the nature of its inspiration.

As outstanding representatives of conservative biblical theology in Germany we mention Hermann Cremer (1835-1903), Martin Kähler (1835-1912), Theodor Zahn (1838-1933), and Adolf Schlatter (1852-1936). Cremer founded modern theological lexicography of the New Testament. Kähler became widely known because of his participation in the debate concerning the historical Jesus. As G. Lagrange, the founder of modern Roman Catholic biblical scholarship, told those who wanted to write the life of the historic Jesus, the only way to do that would be to write the four Gospels over again, so Kähler in a famous book tried to show that "the so-called historic Jesus" of modern scholarship is a figment of the imagination; the real Jesus of history, said Kähler, is the historic Christ of the Bible (*"der geschichtliche biblische Christus"*). Theodor Zahn, the last great exegete of the Erlangen school of Lutheran theology, has re-established, with his amazing command of Patristic scholarship, the reliability of the New Testament writings as historical sources. Adolf Schlatter, an independent thinker of Swiss Reformed background, has influenced several generations of theologians both as an outstanding teacher and as author of New Testament commentaries which must be regarded as masterpieces of biblical scholarship.

The work of these great theologians cannot be overestimated. Together with like-minded teachers of systematic theology as, for example, L. Ihmels (1858-1933), E. Schaeder (1861-1936), K. Heim (1874-1960), they upheld the authority of the Scriptures and the Christ of the Bible, the crucified and risen Lord, the Saviour of sinners. Their theology, however, was not at home in an age of optimism with its idealistic view of man. Their fight for the old Gospel was a defensive war not only against a superficial liberalism, but also against a very stringent theology that understood the

Bible and the dogma of the Church from merely or mainly an historical
point of view. We shall survey this theology by discussing briefly three
of its prominent representatives: Adolf von Harnack, Ernst Troeltsch and
Albert Schweitzer.

III. HARNACK: THE HISTORICAL INTERPRETATION OF CHRISTIANITY

In 1888 Harnack wrote an important memorandum on the place of the
history of the ancient Church in the theological curriculum. A quotation
he records here from Cardinal Manning sheds light on a basic problem of
modern theology. Certain Roman Catholic theologians had refused to
accept the Vatican's dogmatic statement on the papacy because of its
false assertions about the early history of the Church. Archbishop Manning (later Cardinal), the great champion of papal infallibility, withstood
them by saying: "One must overcome history with the dogma." Harnack
called this a frivolous word and such it is indeed, if it means that the
Church can abolish historical facts simply by a dogmatic decree or
can declare something that never happened to be an actual historical
event. Harnack tried to define the true relationship between dogma and
history by declaring "one must purify the dogma by history"; that is,
historical research must tell the Church what can or cannot be dogma.
He was unlike Ferdinand Christian Baur, founder of the Tübingen
school of historical criticism, in whose theology the dogma was lost
because it considered the history of Christianity as simply the development of the idea that underlies the Christian religion. Like Ritschl,
Harnack wanted to help the Church understand and, where necessary,
reform its doctrine. This practical aim is the basis of Harnack's *History
of Dogma* and explains, at least partly, the success of this magnum opus
in circles beyond those of historical research. It found powerful expression in Harnack's famous lectures on "Das Wesen des Christentums"
("What is Christianity?") which he delivered in the winter of 1899-1900
to the students of all faculties at Berlin University. Speaking—sometimes
one is tempted to say preaching—only from brief notes, he shared the
results of his scholarship in the form, as it were, of a personal confession.
When the lectures were printed in 1901, the book (soon translated into
many languages) influenced the public in a measure comparable only to
that engendered by the "Discourses on Religion" with which, in 1799,
Schleiermacher had inaugurated the theology of the nineteenth century.

Harnack's thesis is that the dogma, properly speaking, does not belong
to the essence of Christianity. As the ancient Church developed it, mainly
in regard to the doctrines of the Trinity and of the Person of Christ,
the dogma was a necessary product of the history of the Church and a
necessary means of protecting the Gospel from dissolving into ancient

syncretism. The idea of Harnack is that the dogma was just as necessary for the preservation of the Gospel in the ancient world as the constitutional forms of the Church, such as episcopacy and synods. Greek philosophy, so Harnack thought, became the vehicle for expressing the content of the Gospel. The original Gospel is nothing else but the religion of love for God and neighbor, the glad tidings of the fatherhood of God and the brotherhood of man, to use the terms of Anglo-Saxon Protestantism. "The Gospel as Jesus proclaimed it," said Harnack, "has to do with the Father only, and not with the Son. This is not a paradox nor, on the other hand, is it rationalism, but the simple expression of the actual fact as the evangelists give it" (*What is Christianity?,* Translated by T. B. Saunders, 1901, p. 144). While admitting that Jesus regarded Himself as the Messiah, Harnack says: "The sentence 'I am the Son of God' was not inserted in the Gospel by Jesus himself, and to put this sentence side by side with the others is to make an addition to the Gospel" (*loc. cit.*). What, then, is meant when the Church calls Him the "Son of God"? "No one who accepts the Gospel and tries to understand Him who gave it to us can fail to affirm that here the divine appeared in as pure a form as it can appear on earth" (p. 145 f.). It is certainly no accident that Harnack here quotes Goethe who, in his last conversation, used these words to express his reverence for Jesus ("... *wie nur je auf Erden das Göttliche erschienen ist*"). He designated "the divine" with a neuter term, thereby avoiding any reference to personality and to the personal "God." Harnack does not deny that Jesus spoke of Himself as the Son of His heavenly Father. On the basis of Matthew 11:27 he interprets this association to mean: "It is 'knowledge of God' that makes the sphere of Divine Sonship.... The consciousness which he possessed of being the Son of God is, therefore, nothing but the practical consequence of knowing God as the Father and as His Father. Rightly understood, the name of Son means nothing but the knowledge of God" (p. 128). Here we recognize the influence of Ritschl, who rejected what he considered metaphysics in Christian doctrine and tried, rather, to understand the Sonship of Christ in ethical categories. Ritschl's ethical thinking determines also Harnack's concept of Christ's significance for the world, and for civilization. " 'The image of Christ,' as a modern historian justly says, 'remains the sole basis of all moral culture, and in the measure in which it succeeds in making its light penetrate is the moral culture of the nations increased or diminished' " (p. 123). This quotation from Houston Stewart Chamberlain also echoes the spirit of Goethe's words. We can see how these thoughts found ready response in England and in America where the new "social gospel," based in part on Ritschl's ethical understanding of the Kingdom of God, was coming into vogue.

Did Harnack really succeed in "purifying" the dogma with his historical research, or did he not rather destroy it? If the latter is the case, does not the Gospel disappear along with dogma? This is the question opponents persisted in asking. As leading representative of this new historical theology, Harnack several times found himself involved in doctrinal controversies between "orthodox" and "liberal" groups in the Church. The issue at stake was whether the Apostles' Creed should be retained as an obligatory confession to be recited in the liturgy. Harnack's position satisfied neither side. He agreed with the liberals in rejecting such doctrines as the virgin birth and the bodily resurrection of Jesus. The old dogma retained by the Reformers, although it did not fully express the faith of the Gospel, he believed should be replaced by some better confessional formula. Because of these views the conservatives considered Harnack an enemy of the Christian faith; the liberals, on the other hand, were disappointed with the great historian's moderation in discussing the practical outworkings of their position. Not "abolition of the Creed" was required, said Harnack, but rather, patient work in formulating a new theological expression of the faith.

Meanwhile those who could not accept certain portions of the Creed which, according to Harnack, had no bearing on the essential core of the faith, were encouraged to continue their use of the Creed in a broad sense without surrendering their true connotations. This same approach Harnack practiced on later similar occasions. He approved, for example, of instituting a court in the Church of Prussia to deal with pastors who deviated from its doctrine. He recognized that a Church legally founded on the confessions of the Reformation and whose membership included both conservatives and liberals could not permit unlimited freedom in teaching; rather, such a Church must somehow, in a decent and Christian way, be able to dismiss those radicals whose offensive doctrine could endanger the structure of the Church. However, when this Prussian court dismissed a pastor whose pantheistic denial of God's personality had given serious offense, Harnack objected to his dismissal because the man had been a successful minister. What was the basis for his decision therefore? Harnack's conservative opponents as well as his liberal friends regarded his attitude as an untenable compromise. The latter recognized, and properly so, that if Harnack was right, that the ancient creeds were inadequate and contained errors, and that the evangelical Church must eventually replace them with something better, then their use today could not be made compulsory. Either the creeds are true or they are false. But this simple alternative did not exist for the great historian. The tragic relativism of his historical theology becomes quite clear in his great book on Marcion which in 1921 crowned his lifelong studies on the ancient Church. Concerning Marcion's rejection of the Old Testament, Harnack says: "To reject the Old Testament in the 2nd century was a mistake which the ancient Church has rightly rejected; to retain it in the 16th century was a destiny which the Reformation was not yet able to escape; to preserve it as canonical document in Protestantism since the 19th century is the consequence of a religious and ecclesiastical paralysis" (*Marcion,* pp. 247 ff.).

The theological question is whether the Old Testament is God's Word, God's true revelation. If so, it is valid for all time. If not, its canonization was wrong from the very first, and the Church was guilty of a monstrous lie. But since it acknowledges no absolute truth, Harnack's historical relativism allows no such questions. What should the Church do, then, amid this relativistic theology? "One only can wish that in the choir of the seekers for God there might be found even today Marcionites" (p. 265). What kind of Church would we have if it included people who denied what Jesus Christ regarded as Holy Scripture to be the Word of God? Harnack viewed the future evangelical Church simply as a visible organization "which comprises everything which among us is regarded as religion as far as it is not Catholic or Jewish" (A. von Zahn-Harnack: *Adolf von Harnack,* p. 598). He could hardly anticipate how soon Hitler's Marcionites would take over the evangelical Church of Prussia and try to realize this ideal.

IV. TROELTSCH: THEOLOGY OF RELATIVISM

The outcome of Harnack's system is the tragedy of all merely historical theology. Fr. Meinecke's words about Ernst Troeltsch, the other great representative of historical relativism, could be spoken of Harnack, too: "His friends, who were devoted to him in admiration and love, and who have lost in him one of the most affluent sources of light for their life, have nevertheless when they exchanged their impressions of him among themselves, been driven to confess that his positive leading ideas and aims stood in a certain disproportion to the amazing riches of his speculative historical outlook; and that his weighty speech would often curiously ebb away when, at the end of impressive reproductions of the life and thought of others, he was put to develop his own position in a firm, clear, and unambiguous manner" (quoted from Baron von Hügel's introduction to the posthumous book by Ernst Troeltsch: *Christian Thought. Its History and Application,* by Ernst Troeltsch, edited with an introduction by Baron F. von Hügel; a Living Age Book, published by Meridian Books, The World Publishing Company, Cleveland and New York, 1957, p. 23 f.). While Harnack was the great church historian, Troeltsch was the philosopher and systematic theologian, the dogmatician, so to speak, of the religio-historical school that succeeded Harnack's. The religio-historical school tried to find the essence of Christianity by comparing it with other religions and sought to explain the Bible from the history of oriental religions. It was Troeltsch who in a special way won the respect and approval of the English-speaking world, partly, perhaps, because of his great sociological treatise, *The Social Teachings of the Christian Churches and Groups,* and partly because of what historians must consider a great weakness of this book, namely, a misrepresentation of Luther and of the Lutheran Reformation which underlies Troeltsch's evaluation of the importance of the English and American "sects" for the modern world. Troeltsch discovered that the "sects" of the Reformation, like the Anabaptists and the Enthusiasts, were instrumental in bringing forth what he called "modern culture," that is, civilization since the Enlightenment. They represent for him the real progressives, while Luther's and Calvin's theology seem to him something which belongs still to the Middle Ages. Hence the love of modern Americans, especially the theologians of the social gospel, for Troeltsch.

The major problem of his theological system is that of "the place of Christianity among the world religions" and forms the title of a lecture which he was to deliver at Oxford in 1923. His death, however, prevented his giving an oral and personal statement of what was nothing less than a revocation of what he had offered in 1905 as the solution to the great problem of Christianity's absolute validity. Christianity for Troeltsch had been the true religion, not because the other religions are not true—already in those years he taught that truth is always polymorphous—but because Christianity's claim to truth is different from the claims of other religions: "If we examine any of the great world religions we shall find that all of them, Judaism, Islam, Zoroastrianism, Buddhism, Christianity, even Confucianism, indeed claim absolute validity, but quite naively, and that in a very different manner in each case, the differences being illustrative of differences in their inner structure." While the claims of these other religions are bound to certain nationalities, cultures, and philosophies, Christianity has no such restrictions. The absence of such limitations "illustrates the purely human character of its religious ideal, which appeals only to the simplest, the most general, the most personal and spiritual needs of mankind. Moreover, it does not depend in any way upon human reflection or a laborious process of reasoning, but upon an overwhelming manifestation of God in the persons and lives of the great prophets. Thus it was not a theory but a life—not a social order but a power. It owes its claim to universal validity not to the correctness of its reasoning nor to the conclusiveness of its proofs, but to God's revelation of Himself in human hearts and lives. Thus the naive claim to absolute validity of Christianity is as unique as its conception of God. . . . It possesses the highest claim to universality of all the religions, for this its claim is based upon the deepest foundations, the nature of God and of man" (*op. cit.,* pp. 49 f.).

In this manner Troeltsch presents his earlier convictions. These he proceeds to criticize with great sincerity, however, in view of what a deeper study of world religions taught him and perhaps—although he does not say so—in view of what the breakdown of Christian civilization during World War I revealed to him. Says Troeltsch: "I found Buddhism and Brahmanism especially to be really humane and spiritual religions, capable of appealing in precisely the same way to the inner certitude and devotion of their followers as Christianity" (*ibid.*, p. 52). Moreover, he had learned to understand how closely religion is related to the political, social, ethical, aesthetic and scientific ideas of a given civilization. "Christianity has become the religion of all Europe," he notes. "It stands and falls with European civilization" (p. 54). To determine the relative value of the great religions "it is not the religions alone that we must compare," he says further, "but always only the civilizations of which the religion in each case constitutes a part incapable of severance from the rest. But who will presume to make a really final pronouncement here? Only God Himself, who has determined these differences, can do that" (pp. 56 f.). Thus Troeltsch makes his final conclusions in regard to the doctrine of polymorphous truth. Christianity is true *for us* in the West, just as other religions are "true" for other civilizations having their own standards. "In our earthly experience the Divine Life is not One, but Many," he says. "But to apprehend the One in the Many constitutes the special character of love" (p. 63).

This represents the last great attempt of modern theology to understand Christianity from the vantage point of the historian and to "purify the dogma by history." Gone is the dogma, the doctrinal content of the Gospel. But how can the soul survive in the thin atmosphere of such relativism? It cannot. One must visualize Harnack standing at the graveside of one of his children and praying from the old doctrinally dogmatic hymns of the Lutheran Church to recognize the holding power of the old faith which his reason could no longer comprehend. Or one must read what the Roman Catholic philosopher Peter Wust writes of his conversation with Troeltsch in October of 1918. They discussed the breakdown of Germany. Troeltsch explained it as the final outcome of Germany's intellectual decline in the nineteenth century due to the loss of idealistic belief in *"den Geist."* Troeltsch then admonished Wust, who had given up the Catholic faith many years ago: "You are still young. If you want to do something for the rebirth of our nation, go back to the old faith of the Fathers and as a philosopher strive to restore metaphysics from the weary skepticism of a fruitless epistemology" (Peter Wust, *Gestalten und Gedanken*, 1940, p. 218).

V. SCHWEITZER: THE END OF CHRISTOLOGY

Before enlarging on the new development which comes to prominence in 1918, we must return to those happy pre-war years to meet another theologian of more than passing significance, namely, Albert Schweitzer,

the prophet of what he called "consistent eschatology." Just when
European optimism was first being challenged by what in France was
called the *"fin de siècle"* mood, optimistic theology, too, came under
questioning because of the rediscovery of the New Testament doctrine
of *"finis saeculi."* New Testament scholars challenged the concept that
the Kingdom of God is a state of perfection in this world that will come
through moral and social progress. Harnack's image of Jesus as defined
in *What is Christianity?* now was replaced by that of the eschatological
prophet whose message of the approaching end of the world, of the Last
Judgment and the coming Kingdom could be translated into terms that
satisfied the religious needs of modern man. Harnack's Jesus, the prophet
of the Gospel of God's infinite love, appealed to everyone. But what could
Albert Schweitzer's Jesus signify, that prophet whose words, deeds, and
entire life predicted events to be imminent which have never occurred?
What can this Jesus mean to us? Who was He? The names attributed to
Jesus, such as "Messiah," "Son of Man," "Son of God," says Schweitzer at
the close of his *The Quest for the Historical Jesus* (New York, The Macmillan Co., reprint 1961), have become merely historical symbols. If
Jesus referred these titles to His own person, He was simply expressing
His own consciousness of being a ruler or a commander. We have no name
that adequately expresses what He means to us. "As one unknown and
nameless He comes to us," says Schweitzer, "just as on the shore of the
lake He approached those men who knew not who He was. His words are
the same: 'Follow thou me,' and He puts us to the tasks which He has to
carry out in our age. He commands. And to those who obey, be they wise
or simple, He will reveal Himself through all that they are privileged to
experience in His fellowship of peace and activity, of struggle and
suffering, till they come to know, as an inexpressible secret, who He is . . ."
(Albert Schweitzer, *My Life and Thought, an Autobiography,* tr. by C. T.
Campion, London, George Allen & Unwin, 1933, pp. 71 f.). Here, too, a
great man has uttered the last words of a great theology. Another attempt
to understand Jesus and to interpret Him to modern man by means of
historical research has failed. Since we do not know who Jesus was,
nothing remains then but to follow Him in silent obedience. It is with
deepest respect that one must look at Schweitzer's decision to abandon his
theological lectureship to study medicine and to go as a medical doctor
to the mission field. Whatever the psychological reasons for Schweitzer's
great decision may have been, the deepest, the metaphysical reason—if
we may put it this way—is contained in the closing sentence of his book.
In *The Quest for the Historical Jesus* he sets forth in amazing fashion
the final deductions of two centuries of European scholarship concerning
the historical Jesus. Only a great man like Schweitzer could have stepped
from Strassburg, one of the truly European universities, into the primitive
forests of Africa to serve One whom he did not know.

VI.   THE TURNING TIDE IN EUROPE

Schweitzer arrived in Africa in 1913; in 1917 he returned to war-torn Europe as a prisoner of war. The turning point in the history of the Old Continent had come: that was the year America entered and decided the War and the year of the Russian Revolution, which ended with the victory of Bolshevism. Among those powers which henceforth would determine the history of Europe was the modern Roman Church, whose political revival was accompanied by what has been called "the awakening of the Church in the souls" of European mankind. The Codex Juris was finalized and Eugen Pacelli, the man who was to become the greatest of the modern popes, entered his political career as nuncio in Munich. Mainly because of the rising liturgical movement which soon exercised a strong influence also on the Protestant churches, the era of religious individualism in the Roman Catholic Church drew to an end. The great turn from subjectivism to objectivism became apparent in all spheres of life.

On the occasion of the 400th anniversary of the Reformation on October 31, 1917, the Protestant churches of Germany began to re-examine the nature of the Christian faith. On this day at a solemn observance at the University of Berlin, Karl Holl, who had been appointed to assist Harnack, delivered his famous lecture, "What did Luther Understand by Religion?" An outstanding scholar in all areas of Church History and superior to Harnack as a theologian, Holl had tried to show already before the War what the Reformation's message concerning justification of the sinner could mean to modern man.

But in the "happy years" he had had no response. Now, however, the time suddenly had come for a new understanding of Luther's theology and of Lutheran doctrine. The carefree optimism of the pre-war years lay buried on the battlefields. The idealistic view of man, and of his ability to find God by his own efforts, was shaken. The words sin, death and devil that had become more or less meaningless now were cruel realities. From Luther, men once again began to learn that man is nothing in himself, that he must learn to despair of himself and must hope in Christ. But it was many years before this generation rediscovered the meaning of sin and forgiveness, of judgment and justification. Even Holl's great lecture of 1917 did not encompass full understanding of the *"sola fide,"* but took the untenable position that we are declared righteous on account of what we are to be in the future. The teaching of the New Testament and of the Reformation that we have no righteousness except that imputed by Christ—this insight which presupposes complete despair not only of man, but also of pious man, even of my own pious ego—could not be expected to be restored in a short time.

As demonstrated by the history of theology, it is the deep needs of the human soul that stir up theological research. So, too, in this instance. Without this practical, existential approach one cannot understand the research on Luther during the last decades. Where this motivation declined, the new theology of the Reformation seemed to decay into mere historical scholarship or into a kind of scholasticism. While it is true that the "Luther Renaissance," as the movement was first called, failed to renew the Lutheran Church in Germany and the Scandinavian countries, yet it must be said that all Lutheran churches benefited considerably from it. In the churches of the Augsburg Confession there has been a new consciousness of the greatness of the Lutheran heritage. Even outside the orbit of Lutheranism a new interest in Luther is noticeable (for example, in England among Methodists and Evangelical Anglicans) and indicates that the movement must not be underestimated. Although it started with a new study of the doctrine of justification, problems of ecclesiology, of the Scriptures, and of the sacraments soon gained new attention.

The revival of Lutheran theology has been impeded, however, by the anticonfessionalism of the modern ecumenical movement, especially in Sweden, and by that of the Barthian theology in Germany. But we can expect that Lutheran doctrine will gain growing interest in connection with a development now in process in many quarters of Christendom; a new concept of the dogma of the Church has arisen as a reaction against an ecumenicity which threatened to destroy the doctrinal substance of Christianity.

VII. BARTH: A CHANGE OF DIRECTION

More than any other theologian Karl Barth represents the great change that has taken place in continental theology. He himself doubts, and his friend and co-worker Thurneysen rejects, the idea that the new theology stems from the great disillusionment following World War I. It cannot be denied, however, that the collapse of optimism concerning man and the world paved the way for new attention to the Word of God. It is significant that the new theology did not issue from some university but rather from the manse and the pulpit. Instead of the homiletician's query *"How* shall I preach to modern man?" Barth and his friends once again posed the preacher's primary question: *"What* shall I cry?" Once again they saw that the preacher's task is not to teach religion, nor to arouse religious sentiments, nor to proclaim human wisdom, but rather faithfully to deliver the message entrusted to him by God, to preach the Word, the whole Word and nothing but the Word, that Word of the Cross which is foolishness to the world. Here was the crucial shift from subject to object, from the thoughts, sentiments, desires, and needs of pious man, to the Word which God has given us in the Bible.

The object of "modern" theology had been the Christian religion, that is, the experiences, convictions, and theological ideas of the Christian *man.* In the new theology the object was God's revelation, the Word of God. But can "revelation" be an object of scientific observation? Harnack's objection was that the concept of "revelation" is not a scientific concept; scientific theology cannot explain the prophets' consciousness of God nor the experiences of God that religious men claim as "revelation" (see Karl Barth, *Theologische Fragen und Antworten, Gesammelte Vorträge,* Bd. III, p. 31). Nothing reveals more clearly the theological situation created by the appearance of Barth's *The Epistle to the Romans* (1918, new edition 1922) than the discussion between Barth and Harnack. Barth, the son of a conservative Swiss professor of New Testament, had studied for the most part with Harnack in Berlin and with W. Herrmann in Marburg. In 1923 Harnack published the "Fifteen Questions Addressed to the Theologians Who Despised Scientific Theology." Here he expresses personal disappointment with the new theology that issued from those who had been trained in a more or less "liberal" theology. The foremost theologian of that time, he vents his grave concern over the future of that Protestant theology which he himself had helped bring to full recognition in the German universities as a science. The correspondence between Professor Harnack and his most illustrious student unlocks in a unique way the past forty years of continental theology.

In this controversy Barth showed himself to be a theologian of great stature. He was not ashamed of a theology whose task he regarded not unlike the task of preaching—a quite horrible idea for a "scientific" theologian. Yet he was able to construct a system of theology based on the axiom that God has spoken, a theology which was different indeed from what the previous centuries had understood by a "scientific" theology; it shared with the Reformers, however, and with the great theologians of all ages the presupposition of a divine revelation given to us in Holy Scripture. If this is an axiomatic presupposition, then it is a necessary presupposition; without it there would be no theology at all.

In this essay we cannot possibly outline Barth's theology in its various phases from the time of his first writings to the last volumes of his *Kirchliche Dogmatik.* Barth has never been ashamed of changing his view where a deeper insight so necessitated. He has never been a "Barthian"; he is a thinker, rather, who followed his own way even if it led him to unsuspected conclusions. With the exception of Thurneysen, early companions like E. Brunner, Gogarten and Bultmann parted from him at certain junctures for various reasons. His academic work at Göttingen, Muenster, Bonn, and later at Basel earned him the respect even of those who opposed him. It is significant that even Roman Catholic theologians have always paid tribute to him. There is a growing conviction that he has had no equal among the theological thinkers of the last century. It may well be that his influence will surpass even that of Schleiermacher, another of the outstanding sons of the manse (Ritschl and Harnack were pastors' sons also, as are Bultmann and Tillich) who for some inscrutable reason seem to have the gift of making themselves heard and of altering the course of church history.

We can mention only briefly the great problems inherent in Barth's theology. The first is that of revelation. He was the first Protestant theologian to see the importance of the Constitution "On the Catholic Faith" in which Rome established her doctrine on natural revelation at the Vatican Council of 1878. Discussion of the problem of the *"analogia entis"* with Catholic, Reformed (Emil Brunner) and Lutheran (Althaus, Elert) theologians and historical investigation of Anselm's ontological proof of the existence of God play a major part in Barth's life work. His doctrine of the Word of God has opened deliberations on the relationship between Scripture and the Word of God which will occupy at least the next generation. The main topic of his theology, as G. C. Berkouwer has described it, is "The Triumph of Grace." Although he rejects the classical Calvinistic dogma of predestination, Barth has opened new vistas concerning this doctrine. The most controversial parts of his work pertain to the sacraments, especially his attitude toward infant baptism, which he regards as a wrong practice that should be abolished by the Church. Also controversial is his concept of the relation between law and Gospel.

Barth's great weakness lies in applying his theological doctrines to the practical problems of Church and society. In matters of church policy and in his judgment and attitudes in the application of Christian ethics to political problems, Barth fails to match the level of his theological pursuits. Even those who admire him as a profound thinker wonder if Meinecke's evaluation of Troeltsch must not be applied also to Karl Barth. Only the future can sift the great from the lesser in the life and work of this world-renowned theologian and churchman, Karl Barth. Reared in a small church and in a small nation, he never seems able to lose entirely the perspective of a Swiss citizen who from a more or less neutral point of view tries to help the great outside world with his counsel.

VIII. THE REBIRTH OF DOGMATIC THEOLOGY

What has Barth contributed to the matter of "dogma and history" in Continental theology? In brief, he rediscovered the meaning of the Protestant dogma. Under the influence of a "historistic" view of the world, modern Protestant theology had lost its understanding of the "dogma." Historism or Historisticism is that view of man and society which interprets human life exclusively or predominantly from the perspective of history and historical research so that man becomes essentially an historical phenomenon. It is a world view that has grown out of the development of modern historical research and scientific historiography. Theology can never surrender the methods and results of true historical research which have helped to shed light on the Bible and on the history of the Church. But theology must beware of thinking that the historical approach to the Scriptures and the Church is the only possible and legitimate one. Such "historism" would be just as incorrect as the "naturalism" of certain scientists in the early twentieth century who tried to understand man and human history exclusively from the standpoint of natural science. Man is certainly a phenomenon of nature and can and must be understood as such. But no natural science can ever probe man's innermost being. So, too, man is a phenomenon of history and must be understood as such. But no historical investigation of man's life and history will ever uncover his innermost being. Historical research can investigate the phenomena of the history of religion. The historian as historian can draw a picture of Buddha, or of Jesus, and he can try to reconstruct their doctrines. But he dare not say who is right and who is wrong or in what respect one or the other may be correct or incorrect in his claims. For such a judgment is a judgment of faith. If a historian does so, he does so as a believer. Historical research can describe prophets like Jeremiah and Ezekiel as true and those whom they called false it can call impostors. But it is never the province of the historian as historian to declare who are the true and who are the false prophets. Harnack was quite right when he said that only what men have thought and said about revelation and not "revelation" itself can be an object of historical research. Yet, for the believer revelation is far more real than what we otherwise experience as reality. Barth was right in telling Harnack that exactly what the Christian faith calls revelation is the true object of theology. All theology presupposes an act of faith, a concrete decision that involves the whole of life. With deep interest the religious historian examines the various claims for absolute validity made by the various religions. While he can compare them, he is unable with the means of his sciences to make a definite decision between them. This was the mistake of Harnack and of Troeltsch. It is the theologian who makes this decision. He does so because he is not only a scholar, an historian who applies scientific methods and standards to the phenomena at hand; he does so because he is also a believing Christian. David Friedrich Strauss has coined the phrase of a *"voraussetzungslose Wissenschaft,"* a science which approaches its subject matter without prejudicial presuppositions. Whether such science exists in any sphere of human thought and knowledge is very doubtful. Not only Thomas and Luther, but also Plato and Kant approached their areas of searching with preconceived ideas. And we certainly know with what massive dogmatism scientists like Haeckel and Ostwald tried to interpret the phenomena of Christianity. We ask, then, what are the assumed presuppositions of Harnack's and Troeltsch's historical theology? Both were deeply rooted in German idealistic philosophy. This heritage they tried to combine with the heritage of the Church. But can the idealistic view of man as an essentially good creature be reconciled with the Christian view of man as a lost sinner? This Barth doubted and for this reason Harnack and he could never agree. In the last analysis it was Harnack's philosophy which made it impossible for him to accept "revelation" in the sense of a work and word of God which cannot be experienced, but must be believed.

Why did people who had not accepted the witness of the Church listen to Barth? True, conservative scholars of the first decades of this century had insisted that the Bible is not only a collection of documents of an important religious history, but the Word of God. Why, then, did those who had been unwilling to listen to a man like Schlatter now give ear to Barth? In the first place, Barth represented a generation that had gone through the "liberal" theology. As a young theologian he had really lived by what he learned from Harnack and Herrmann and had experienced the bankruptcy of this theology. He had experienced what might be called a theological conversion, and his message was interpreted by his generation as a "metanoeite," a powerful call to repentance. In the second place, Barth saw the close relationship between what was called "liberal" and "positive" theology. Unfortunately, the conservative theology of the nineteenth century had been a strange mixture of orthodox and pietistic elements and had also worshiped the strange gods of the modern world. As a prominent example we quote Hofmann, a leading protagonist of Lutheranism at Erlangen, who said of theology: "I, the Christian, am to me, the theologian, the proper object of my science." Under Schleiermacher's influence these men had learned to interpret theology as the science of man, even if the Christian man, the dogma as the content of the experiences which this man has made or can make. Even the Orthodox, whether Lutheran or Reformed, were far removed from the teachings of Luther and Calvin and the great church theologians of former ages; for these leaders the object of theology always had been God and not man, had been God's revelation in His Word and not man-made religion.

It was the dawning of a theological springtime when in the mid-twentieth century the new theology began to captivate the younger theologians of Switzerland and Germany and then, spreading to the Reformed churches on the Continent, began to influence the rest of continental Protestantism as well. In Holland it was opposed not only by the Liberals, but also by the strict Calvinists who are stronger in Holland than in any other part of Western Europe. It took a long time until these circles recognized Barth's importance, and G. C. Berkouwer of Amsterdam, the theological leader of the Gereformeerde Kerken and himself a Reformed dogmatician of the first rank, wrote an approving yet critical analysis of Barth's theology. In Scandinavia, with the exception of Denmark, the homeland of Kierkegaard, Lutheranism was very reluctant to accept Barth. Perhaps nothing is more significant about the challenge which Barth's theology brought to all churches than the reception it has found among Roman Catholics like Urs Von Balthasar and Hans Küng.

Barth's influence upon British and American theology is beyond the scope of this article. Basically it was Emil Brunner who became the messenger of the new theology for the churches of the English-speaking world. He became known in Europe through *The Mediator,* a work which appeared in 1927 at the same time as Barth's first volume of *Christliche Dogmatik* (replaced since 1932 by *Die Kirchliche Dogmatik*). Of considerable influence in Germany, Brunner nonetheless appealed to the British and American churches more than Barth, partly because he knew English-speaking Christendom, partly because his theology was less offensive to the Liberalism which attaches to Western Protestantism. The contrast between the two men is nowhere more apparent than in their attitude towards the Virgin Birth. While Brunner rejected the doctrine, Barth, to the amazement of many of his followers, defended it. Barth's chapter, "The Miracle of Christmas," as it appeared in his *Kirchliche Dogmatik* in 1938 (Vol. I, II; in English, *Church Dogmatics,* New York, Charles Scribner's Sons, 1956, Vol. I/2, pp. 172-202), is among the best discussions of the subject in print.

IX. THE THEOLOGICAL TASK OF TODAY

Whatever the lasting effects of the rebirth of dogmatic theology after the First World War may have been, one thing was already clear at the beginning of World War II. The great problem of "dogma and history" had not found a definite solution. The disintegration of "Dialectical Theology" and the parting of Barth, Brunner, Bultmann and Gogarten resulted from their differing views of divine revelation that had developed across the years. More than the question of general revelation was at stake when in 1933 ethical and political decisions had to be made on the basis of deepest theological convictions. More than anticipated, it was also the question of God's revelation in the Bible which separated these men. This became quite obvious when R. Bultmann's demythologization of the New Testament met with unexpected success during the years of World War II. Students who in earlier years had gone from Harnack's lecture hall to the battlefields of Flanders returned with a hunger and thirst for Biblical theology and for the dogma of the Church. The

generation however, which went to war in 1939 with the theology of the
"Confessing Church" came back as adherents of Bultmann. What attracted
them to this change was not only theological Existentialism which tried
to explain their own human existence, but obviously also what they felt
were deficiencies in the theology in which they had been reared. Dietrich
Bonhoeffer's development during his years of imprisonment shows a
noticeable turning away from the churchly atmosphere of the "Confessing
Church" toward a more secular theology which seeks out and finds man
in the everyday world. Bonhoeffer, who was one of Harnack's last students,
might have become the leader of a new school of theology had he been
spared. It is one of the features of the history of twentieth-century
European theology that from the nations at war two generations of
young theologians were decimated. Is this one reason why in our time
aged men like Bultmann and Tillich have exercised an influence on
youth which would have been unthinkable thirty years ago? But even
in Karl Barth, whose thinking has undergone so many changes, there
must be some trait or feature which stems from his early exposure to
liberal theology. He has always tried to maintain the authority of the
Bible with great seriousness. But as a dogmatician whose thinking was
centered in the Bible, as he feels, he has deviated extensively from the
dogma of his Reformed Church; in his old age he has not only become
more broad-minded in his judgment of nineteenth-century theologians,
but he has developed also a rather strange antipathy toward anything
that might be labeled "confessionalism." He who in the "Barmen
Declaration" of 1934 had so strongly rejected what he regarded as the
church-destroying heresy of the "German Christians," [2] that is, the view
that there are other sources of God's revelation than Christ alone as
He is witnessed to in the Bible, could live peacefully in Basel, after his
expulsion from Germany, with all sorts of heretics, including those who
rejected the divinity of Christ and were teaching a natural theology.
Nor has he ever clearly rejected those powers which after the war continued the politics of enslaving the Church under a totalitarian state in
the East. We do not mean to disparage the great theologian. We simply
wish to indicate certain limitations of his theology which, contrary to
his own intentions, helped prepare the way for a revival of that very
relativism and liberalism which he has fought so forcefully for over
forty years.

The old liberalism of the early twentieth century is dead. Based on
a belief in man's essential goodness and in his ability to control life, this
liberalism collapsed in the face of this century's wars and revolutions.

[2] The "German Christians" were traitors who surrendered the Church to the
totalitarian state. Barth paid them undeserved honor by ascribing to them any
theological convictions.

But some essential element thereof has remained and seems to be developing in the churches into a new liberalism or Modernism. Even Rome is experiencing something of this development, as evidenced by the condemnation of certain outgrowths of the new biblical scholarship in Catholic theology.

Bultmann's preface to the 1951 reprint of Harnack's *What is Christianity?* gives a clear picture of the present situation. It is significant that this book should be printed again in our time and that it is Bultmann who should present it to the public. Rejecting what he feels must be rejected of Harnack's views, Bultmann tries to point up the proper questions which Harnack placed not only before his generation but before ours as well, questions which are still without sufficient answers. "In view of the present danger of a neo-Orthodoxy, of the repristination of a narrow-minded Confessionalism" we must again listen to Harnack but without "repristinating" his system of theology. What this neoliberalism (Bultmann considers it a reaction against the renewal of orthodoxy in the form of "Confessionalism" and "Barthianism") has in common with the old liberalism of 1900 is the rejection of what Bultmann calls "myth." He refuses to believe the great miracles connected with the person and work of Christ. The danger of this neoliberalism is the fact that its champions use the old dogmatic terms like "incarnation," "resurrection," "justification," but with totally different meanings. The "demythologization" of the New Testament is actually a "redogmatization" of the Christian faith.

It is wrong to say that the new theology is simply the radical application of the principles of historical research to the Gospels. To declare, for example, that the report of the empty grave is mere legend is not a historical but a dogmatic statement. The arbitrary way in which modern New Testament scholars deal with the sayings of Jesus raises the suspicion that behind the modern "kerygmatic theology" there is really no historical method at all. What was recorded after Easter they assumed must be understood as shaped by the *kerygma* of the Church. The individual scholars are unable to agree on what in a particular case should be regarded as historic; at the same time each is convinced that only his hypothesis is correct. Often dogmatic doubt hides behind historical criticism. The whole movement shows, however, that the revival of dogmatic theology has not succeeded in giving the Church a satisfactory answer to the great question of "dogma and history." Such an answer can come only through a new understanding of Holy Scripture as the Word of God which is both divine and human and must be understood, therefore, dogmatically and at the same time historically. This is the great task with which Protestant theology must wrestle during the remainder of the twentieth century.

DUTCH AND SWEDISH THEOLOGY

Since it is impossible to discuss all of continental theology within the framework of this essay, we mention only briefly Holland and Sweden, the two countries outside the German-speaking Continent which have made significant contributions.

In *Holland* the "Gereformeerde Kerken," the largest continental Free Church which in 1892 grew out of the separations of 1834 and 1886, has become the guardian of orthodox Reformed theology. This "Neocalvinism" goes back to A. Kuyper (1837-1921) and Herman Bavink (1854-1921). With its center in the Free University of Amsterdam it has defended the classical doctrine of the inspiration of Holy Scripture not only against the modernism that prevailed in the (National) "Hervormde Kerk," but also against Karl Barth. In view of Barth's growing influence in both groups, the contrast seems to be lessening. This is apparent from the fact that the present leader in theology at the Free University of Amsterdam, G. C. Berkouwer, could write not only his great *Dogmatic Studies,* but also a book like *The Triumph of Grace in the Theology of Karl Barth,* which might more forcefully have assailed Barth's doctrine of Scripture (Grand Rapids, Wm. B. Eerdmans Publishing Co., 1956).

Since the dissolution of the union between Sweden and Norway in 1905, *Swedish Lutheranism* has been influenced by a revival of nationalism ("Sweden's people God's people"). This spirit went hand in hand with the ecumenical movement that arose before World War I under the impact of the Student Christian Movement. Both tendencies deterred the confessional substance of the Church which at the turn of the century was still very strong. Swedish scholarship has contributed greatly to the history of religion (Soederblom) and to Luther research (Nygren, Bring, Wingren and others). But a predominantly historical approach to the Bible and to the Christian faith has prevented a renewal of dogmatics. Even the greatest Swedish theologian of our time, Anders Nygren (born 1890, Professor in Lund 1924-58, Bishop 1948-58), shows these limitations despite his understanding (Commentary on Romans) of the doctrine of justification. The Lutheran substance seems to have been better preserved in Norway (Leiv Aalen, successor to O. Hallesby in the Free Faculty at Oslo), and even in Denmark where Regin Prenter (Aarhus) has written a Dogmatics which could possibly revive Lutheran doctrine. Like the German Lutheran dogmaticians Elert (1885-1954) and Althaus, however, Prenter has not yet reached Luther's understanding of the written Word of God.

BRITISH THEOLOGY
IN THE
TWENTIETH CENTURY

✝

James I. Packer

James I. Packer is Lecturer and Librarian at Latimer House, Oxford, a post to which he was called in 1961 after serving from 1955-1960 as Tutor at Tyndale Hall, Bristol, England. He received the B.A. from Oxford in 1948 in classical studies, and in 1950 in theology; the M.A. in 1952; and D.Phil. in 1954 for a thesis on the soteriology of Richard Baxter. An Anglican clergyman, he is author of Fundamentalism and the Word of God *(1958) and a contributor to many religious journals.*

BRITISH THEOLOGY
IN THE
TWENTIETH CENTURY

IT IS NOT British theology that has led the world during the twentieth century. The real epoch-makers, those whose work has actually become a theological watershed for Protestantism generally, have been, rather, men like Schweitzer, Barth, and Bultmann—none of them British. Of the greatest British theologians of this century—by common consent, Bishop Charles Gore (d. 1932), Peter Taylor Forsyth (d. 1921), and Archbishop William Temple (d. 1944)—the most that can be said is that they influenced some people inside and outside their immediate circle but few beyond the bounds of the British Isles.

I. INTRODUCTION

British theology last led the world in the seventeenth century when Puritan teaching on the Christian life was the envy of Lutheran and Reformed divines and the stock-in-trade of the New England pulpit. Since then, however, British theology has been consistently insular, occupied with its own internal dialogue, viewing continental and, in this century, transatlantic developments with a sense of detachment, learning from them rather tardily, and contributing little of importance to their discussion. This situation reflects, in part, a difference of cultural and theological background: British theology as a whole, having mainly historical interests and caring nothing for Kant, has never, like German theology, been haunted by the spectre of nihilism nor, like American theology, been infected with the fever of relativism. Also, the British distaste for extremism prompts prejudice against antithetical thinking—such as marks German and American theology—as necessarily unbalanced. Aloofness is a British national characteristic, moreover, that manifests itself in other realms as well. British theology thus stands apart. It lacks insight into the existentialist *Angst* and Kantian phenomenalism which mold German theology, and it does not sympathize with the American habit of treating symbol and myth, rather than truth and fact, as the basic theological categories. British theology, accordingly, has contributed little to the central debates of twentieth-century Protestantism.

It has not been without significance, however, for it has contributed much to the thought of the ecumenical movement. Being conciliatory and pacific, it has preferred a "both-and" over "either-or" formula, and synthesis over antithesis. Continuity, comprehensiveness, and flexibility have been its ideals. Most modern British theologians see themselves as either conservative liberals or (in the case of High Anglicans) liberal Catholics. Many, by latching on to Alec Vidler's distinction between liberalism, a set of nineteenth-century opinions, and liberality, a temper of inquiry and intellectual generosity ("the opposite not of conservative, but of fanatical or bigoted or intransigent": Vidler, *Essays in Liberality*, London, S.C.M. Press, 1957, p. 21), have made clear their espousal of the latter rather than the former. W. M. Horton's phrase, "adaptive traditionalism," well describes the present British theological temper.

II. CHARACTERISTICS OF MODERN BRITISH THEOLOGY

Three constant features have marked British theological work during this century: its historical orientation, its ideal of rationality, and its churchly consciousness.

1. Its historical orientation. Anglicans are sometimes accused by non-Anglicans of knowing no theology but historical theology, and, although exaggerated, the charge has some validity. But British theologians as a whole tend to prefer an historical to a strictly local or dogmatic method of investigation. While continental writers produce systematic theologies, British divines ponder on the history of doctrine, seeking to adapt and modify traditional views in a way that commends itself to the "modern mind" (the unacknowledged hero of much modern British theology in this century). And the inevitable danger that arises of compromising opportunism and unprincipled relativism is not always avoided. Yet this approach in modern British theology has produced some of the most scholarly and useful studies of particular doctrines—works, for example, by H. R. Mackintosh, *The Person of Jesus Christ* (Presbyterian, 1912); J. K. Mozley, *The Doctrine of the Atonement* (Anglican, 1916); N. P. Williams, *Ideas of the Fall and Original Sin* (Anglican, 1927); K. E. Kirk, *The Vision of God* (Anglican, 1931); R. Newton Flew, *The Idea of Perfection in Christian Theology* (Methodist, 1934).

The penchant of British divines for the historical approach reflects an instinct for tradition and a sense of history which are as British as they are Christian—perhaps more so! British apologetics, too, are historically slanted: the argument regularly proceeds as if the historicity of the Christian facts is the main thing in dispute, and once their historicity is granted no serious question about their meaning can arise. This naïveté perhaps reflects the fact that British intellectual life is still largely nourished by Christian ideas: secularism has not yet gone so far in Britain as in some other places.

2. *Its ideal of rationality.* Rationality here does not mean rationalism, that spirit which refuses to grant the existence of mystery and the supernatural, and which admits the reality of only what it can comprehend to its own satisfaction; rather, rationality here signifies coherence, both metaphysical and moral. This is the real point of the characteristic "appeal to reason" in British theology. It is one expression of the above mentioned love of synthesis. The purpose of this "appeal to reason" is to show how theology fits in with, illuminates, and perfects the rest of knowledge, and how it integrates and gives meaning to all the experiences of life. The feeling that theological work should have apologetic value in an age of wide defection from Christianity has strengthened this purpose. The quest for rationality has marked British theology in this century in at least the following ways:

(1) It has led theologians to seek a concordat with philosophy, and for nearly forty years to ally themselves with idealism which, first in its monistic form and then as "personal idealism" (a pluralistic version which replaced Hegel's universal spirit with finite individual spirits), dominated Oxford and the Scottish universities until the 1930's. The theologians embraced idealism because, as a "spiritual" philosophy which found in personality its highest categories of valuation and interpretation, it seemed to favor theism, and certainly opposed materialism. In 1912 one Anglican enthusiast, R. C. Moberly, called the idealist notion of God as the Absolute "at once the most irrefutable and the most religious view of God that has ever been framed." But this was really inept. Hegelianism means pantheism, and makes a biblical view of creation and sin impossible. Personal idealism implies a finite God in the image of an ideal man. Immanence, taken as an ultimate category of theological explanation, as it is by all forms of idealist theology, implies continuity and correspondence between God and man and leaves no room for anything else. Thus it points away from Incarnation to a divinity in every man, away from reconciliation and atonement to the moral and spiritual evolution of the race, away from special revelation to a universal religious consciousness, away from faith in a historical Christ to naturalistic mysti-

cism ("in tune with the Infinite"). Idealism could not, therefore, be other than a systematically distorting factor in all thought about God and the world, man and sin, revelation, miracles, Christology, and the Gospel. But this distortion was not seen at first.

Between the two World Wars the needed lessons were learned—but slowly. This learning process William Temple reveals in his theological pilgrimage of over thirty years. Starting from idealism, with a weak Christology (essay in *Foundations,* a volume sub-titled "A statement of Christian Beliefs in terms of Modern Thought," 1912), and seeking a philosophical unification of experience under theological auspices (*Mens Creatrix,* 1917), he was driven over the years to a sort of realism by a growing concern to stress features of Christianity which idealism obscures— God's transcendence, the gravity of sin, and hence the rationality of a particular redemptive revelation, and of a personal Incarnation as that revelation (*Christus Veritas,* 1924; *Nature, Man, and God,* 1934). It was a triumph of Christian instinct over philosophical conditioning, a triumph which, by Temple's own admission, the Johannine writings did most to bring about. By 1937 Temple was insisting that sin is an irrational factor in God's world which precludes explanatory syntheses, and in that year he called theologians to "renewed devotion of their labour to the themes of Redemption, Justification, and Conversion," as the realm where "our need lies now and will lie in the future" (Introduction to the Report, *Doctrine in the Church of England,* p. 17). In 1942, in a private letter, he explained how through deeper appreciation of the biblical outlook his approach to the ideal of synthesis had been transformed:

> "What we must completely get away from is the notion that the world as it now exists is a rational whole; we must think of its unity not by the analogy of a picture, of which all the parts exist at once, but by the analogy of a drama where ... the full meaning of the first scene only becomes apparent with the final curtain; and we are in the middle of this. Consequently the world as we see it is strictly unintelligible. We can only have faith that it will become intelligible when the divine purpose, which is the explanation of it, is accomplished.
> "Theologically, this is a greater emphasis on eschatology ..."
> (F. A. Iremonger, *William Temple,* London, Oxford University Press, 1948, p. 537 f.).

Temple's words effectively mark the end of the idealist epoch in British theology. British theologians as a body are not now committed to immanentism in any form. Yet they retain their rational temper and synthetic instincts, and would never indulge in anything like the Barthian polemic against natural theology (which polemic, indeed, they tend to regard as a sign of shallowness!). Antitheses between theology and particular philosophies they regretfully recognize, but that there is a necessary opposition between theology and philosophy as such they would not admit. (Of course, there are one or two Barthians in Britain, but there are one or two neo-Thomists too!—and at this point they tend to cancel each other out.)

(2) The quest for rationality has led Anglican divines in particular to explore the "incarnational" approach pioneered in the liberal Catholic manifesto *Lux Mundi* (1889; subtitled "A series of studies in the religion of the Incarnation"). In this book, Gore and his colleagues used the Alexandrian identification of the incarnate Son with the cosmic Logos, ever active in all nature and all men, as grounds for claiming as Christian such current trends of thought as evolution and socialism. Since *Lux Mundi,* liberal Catholics generally have maintained that it is the Incarnation, the taking of manhood into God, rather than the Atonement, which throws most light on the meaning of human life, for the Incarnation crowned the creative work of the Logos by bringing human nature to the height of its perfection, unattainable otherwise, and demonstrated how, through union with the Incarnate One, our humanity may be perfected also. This consciously anti-Protestant, pro-patristic line of thought has led some Anglo-Catholics to view the Church as the extension of the Incarnation and to analyze salvation not as forgiveness and co-resurrection with Christ through faith, but as a progressive divinizing of nature through the sacraments. This "incarnational" approach fascinated Anglicans for more than a generation because of its seeming possibilities for synthesis (supernaturalizing the natural). The chief monuments to its influence are Temple's *Christus Veritas,* which argues "from the emerging series Matter, Life, Mind, Spirit, to the Incarnation as the grade of reality in which humanity is fulfilled" (A. M. Ramsey, *From Gore to Temple,* London, Longmans, Green and Company, 1960, p. 148), and Lionel Thornton's *The Incarnate Lord* (London, Longmans, Green and Company, 1928), which uses Whitehead's philosophy of organism to present the Incarnation, Scotist-fashion, as the climax of creation. Einar Molland points picturesquely to this "incarnational" interest when he comments that if the Orthodox is the "Church of Easter" and the Lutheran the "Church of Good Friday," the Anglican is the "Church of Christmas" (*Christendom,* London, A. R. Mowbray Company, 1959, p. 148).

(3) Since reason operates in the moral no less than in the metaphysical realm, the quest for rationality has prompted much reflection on the moral coherence of God's ways with man. The desire for a moral rationale of revelation for apologetic purposes goes back through Butler at least to Anselm. But the suggestion that dogmatics itself should consciously follow a moral method of inquiry and exposition was not made until Forsyth put in his famous plea for a "moralising of dogma," that is, for reconstructing theology as a "metaphysic of the conscious" which "starts with the conviction that for life and history the moral is the real,

and that the movements of the Great Reality must be morally construed as they are morally revealed" (*The Person and Place of Jesus Christ*, 1909, p. 222 f.). No doubt the background of this plea was the anti-metaphysical bias which Forsyth learned from Ritschl; but the actual warrant for it (so Forsyth claimed) is just the Christian revelation itself, which discloses not an impersonal cosmic principle, but a living God who is holy love. Moreover (Forsyth argued), this method is of great importance for commending Christianity to a generation for whom the notion of truth guaranteed by external authority (Church or Bible) has become unconvincing: the Gospel must be trained on the conscience, and then by its own moral power will evidence itself as truth. In all this Forsyth was voicing something which modern British theologians in general have felt. The moral as well as the metaphysical coherence of the Christian revelation must be shown. Much British doctrinal exposition in recent years has been consciously "moralized," but none, perhaps, as successfully as Forsyth's own work.

(4) The ideal of rationality has predisposed British theologians against all dialectical modes of theological thought. The appeal to paradox as an ultimate category finds no response among them, and teaching which multiplies paradoxes finds no favor. The thought of Barth, Niebuhr, and even Brunner (the one neo-orthodox theologian who is widely read in Britain) has made little direct impact in England and not much more in Scotland. The ideal of rationality at the same time prompts British theologians to impute irrational obscurantism to any who are content to be naively biblical, who state and apply what the Bible says simply on the grounds that the Bible says it. This, it seems, rather than any particular doctrinal quarrel, explains why British theologians as a body remain doubtful about Billy Graham, and why the resurgent British evangelicalism of the post-war years, which by and large is content with naive biblicism, is not much respected in theological circles.

3. Its churchly consciousness. Neither in England nor in Scotland is modern theology in any potent sense confessional; yet modern British theologians of all churches and schools have shown a deep awareness that they speak to the Church from within the Church, and with a responsibility towards the Church. This sober awareness has marked not only Anglo-Catholics, with their deep sense of the Church's organic life; it has manifested itself also to quite a remarkable degree among liberal thinkers. Between the wars, Schleiermacher's program of distilling doctrine from the Church's corporate experience, although out of fashion elsewhere, was widely taken up by British liberal theology. This approach, it was held, was the way to rehabilitate Christianity. In their editorial preface to the volumes of the liberal *Library of Constructive Theology* (New York, London, Harper and Brothers, 1928–), W. R. Matthews and

H. Wheeler Robinson wrote: "The authors (in the series) have a common mind . . . with regard to the starting-point of reconstruction. They desire to lay stress on the value and validity of religious experience and to develop their theology on the basis of the religious consciousness. In so doing they claim to be in harmony with modern thought. . . ." The dangers of subjectivism and relativism in such a method are obvious, yet most of the liberals of this period, because of their strong sense of unity with the universal Church, were kept from leaving conventional paths very far. Their aim, like Schleiermacher's own, was to reconstruct the old faith from within, and not to recast it into something new from without.

These facts show why British theology during this century, as compared with its German and American counterparts, has been so remarkably stable. Despite weakened conceptions of revelation and inspiration, and persistent shakiness in handling the central doctrines of the Gospel—the atonement, justification, faith, the Holy Spirit, the Lord's return—it has remained steady, and potentially disruptive continental developments (in the areas, for instance, of Gospel eschatology and form-criticism) have been neutralized before being swallowed. The conservatism of British liberalism, by and large, has been astonishing. There were some extremists, of course, and the limelight they enjoyed sometimes conveyed the impression that the older theology was about to collapse. Since almost all of the most powerful British theologians of the century have been on the side of the creeds, however, such fears have not been well-founded at any time. Conservative evangelicals, often oblivious to everything but the place of Scripture, have sometimes been puzzled that, with the prop of an infallible Bible removed, British theology has not collapsed into complete unbelief. But twentieth-century British theology has at no point been a monolithic structure. By its own constant claim, made by all schools of thought (except the conservatives themselves), it has rested on a threefold appeal: (1) to Scripture (as at least a record of revelation, if not a revelation in itself), (2) to the Church (creeds, traditions, and corporate experience, however interrelated), and (3) to reason (the mind's eye for coherence and congruity). In this broad-based and nicely balanced structure, the weakening of one buttress has not sufficed to topple British theology. Indeed, the eclipse of idealism, the "biblical theology" movement, and the growth of an apologetic for special revelation based on the inner coherence of Scripture, plus a growing sense that an evangelical theology focused on grace is at the present time more necessary than a theological philosophy focused on nature, have brought British theology today closer to the faith of the Reformation than it was at the beginning of the century.

Let us now examine some of the changes that have taken place.

III. MOVEMENTS IN MODERN BRITISH THEOLOGY

For our purposes, the British theological scene at the turn of the last century may be described as follows:

First, Old Testament higher criticism (that is, Wellhausenism) had clearly come to stay. In an age when idealism and Darwinism joined hands to affirm evolution as the only valid category for scientific and philosophical explanation, the scientific status of an evolutionary account of Old Testament theology and religion seemed beyond question. Wellhausenism had captured the British universities and most of the theological colleges, and was rapidly being embodied in standard commentaries and reference books (the *International Critical* and *Westminster Commentaries,* the *Cambridge Bible* and *Century Bible* series, Hastings' series of Bible dictionaries, and so forth). The magic names in Old Testament study were S. R. Driver, Regius Professor of Hebrew at Oxford, and W. Robertson Smith (d. 1894), higher criticism's martyr, who after losing his Aberdeen chair for heresy became Professor of Arabic at Cambridge, and whose *Religion of the Semites,* according to a first-hand observer, "was regarded almost as a sort of Bible in itself" by Oxford theological students in the early nineteen-hundreds (J. W. C. Wand, *Anglicanism in History and Today,* New York, London, Thomas Nelson and Sons, 1961, p. 122). The only major attempt to turn the higher critical flank was James Orr's *Problem of the Old Testament* (1906), which won respect for its scholarship but not assent to its argument. In 1907 Orr himself wrote wryly that critical scholarship "is for the present so settled on its lees in its confidence in its immovable results that little anyone can say will make any impression on it" (*The Bible Under Trial,* 1907, p. 54).

In the New Testament field, however, historical conservatism was the order of the day. It was generally held that the work of the Cambridge Three, B. F. Westcott (d. 1901), J. B. Lightfoot (d. 1889), and F. J. A. Hort (d. 1892), had conclusively vindicated the main outlines of the Gospel story. "Their lasting contribution," wrote Alan Richardson (his adjective is empirically justified), "was to show that the Church's ancient faith in Christ Incarnate, Crucified, Risen and Ascended, was in no way imperilled by the most scrupulous employment of critical historical methods but was rather established by it" (*The Bible in the Age of Science,* Philadelphia, Westminster Press, 1961, p. 63). Confidence in the substantial historicity of the Gospel narrative has persisted throughout this century. Rationalistic Gospel criticism, still a live issue in other places, has really been a dead issue in Britain since the century opened. The opinions of Harnack, Schmiedel, Bultmann, and others who oppose the "Jesus of history" to the "Christ of faith" have been respectfully noted and considered; but though their skepticism about the virgin birth, miracles, and bodily resurrection of Jesus has been taken up by some able scholars, the main body of British theologians and New Testament scholars have always opposed them. Before the Second World War, while the Fourth Gospel was somewhat suspect, the reliability of the "artless" synoptics was steadily maintained; today, the synoptics are suspected of being more midrashic than was once thought, but the historicity of John is affirmed with more conviction than for many years. One British book after another on the Gospels has used the tools of the critical trade to modify skeptical continental extremes. It is this persistent confidence in the essential factuality of the Gospel story which largely explains why, on the one hand, British theologians still value historical apologetics, and why, on the other, they do not feel closely involved in the apologetic problems besetting those who, with Bultmann, think that the historical Jesus was totally unlike the Christ of the New Testament.

The main theological question at hand when the century began concerned the nature and status of the Bible. Wellhausenism rules out inerrancy. What, then, becomes of biblical inspiration and authority? Can they be retained, if inerrancy is given up? Scholars labored to show that they could. Following William Sanday (*Inspiration,* 1894), they remodeled the idea of inspiration by arguing that not the words of Scripture but its authors were inspired. Inspiration (or revelation, for, according to this view, the two words were synonymous) means moral and spiritual illumination, or religious insight. This God gave to the biblical writers as they were able to bear it; they received it more or less faithfully, and verbalized it as best they could. The Bible is thus the record of God's progressive self-disclosure to their conscience and consciousness, and of their own apprehension of Him, evolving correlatively. Although not verbally inspired, the Bible may be called the Word of God inasmuch as it contains a record of revelation as given in history. It is the only record of this revelation that we have, and as such is indispensable.

But if the Bible is not all true, how can it be authoritative? This question was answered in terms of the principle that authority in religion has the nature of a moral claim, and does not require for its reality the bestowal of inerrant factual information. The traditional polemic against Roman belief in an infallible Church was turned against the doctrine of the infallible book. The true authority of the Bible, it was said, is known in the experience of being "found" by that in the Bible which evidences itself to us as having the nature of the ethically highest. This experience of moral and spiritual authority should satisfy us. The desire for an infallible Bible, we are told, is just as improper and irreligious as the belief that we have one is false.

To stop there, as the liberals usually did, leaves unanswered two questions of some urgency. First, different things "find" different people: how

may we know what ought to "find" us? Second, what is the relation
between the moral and spiritual insight enjoyed by the biblical writers
and the beliefs about matters of fact with which, to their thinking, all
knowledge of God—be it theirs or anyone else's—was bound up? How far
may we sit loose to the latter without imperiling our receptiveness to the
former? To these questions liberal Protestantism really has no answer.
Gore, the liberal Catholic, had one, however. He held that the authority
of Scripture, moral and spiritual as it is, is mediated to us, and the necessary area of factual belief circumscribed for us, by the normative witness
to essential Christianity which was given by the early Church's corporate
life and in particular by the ecumenical creeds. On this basis, Gore contended tirelessly and with good effect against those who queried the virgin
birth, the dominical miracles, and the resurrection. Critics were quick
to point out the peculiarity of a view which ascribes an infallibility to
the creeds which it denies to the Scriptures; yet Gore's position was
clearly more satisfying to the spirit than the liberal alternative. It is not
surprising that in the vacuum created by the rejection of biblical infallibility, and by the liberal failure to offer any certainty in matters of faith,
or even to see that man's cry for certainty was any more than weakness
of the flesh, Gore's point of view made great headway in the Church of
England.

Other features of the situation may be more briefly described.

In Christology, two opposite trends were in evidence: the one, hu-
manitarian (Jesus was a God-indwelt man), the other, kenotic (Jesus was
God the Son, who, in becoming man, renounced His omniscience, omnipotence, and omnipresence, for the period of His earthly life). The latter
view was more than an apologetic device for explaining why Jesus' view
of the Old Testament differed from Wellhausen's, although it was in this
connection that Gore introduced it to England (in *Lux Mundi*). The
deepest motive of the kenotic trend was to do justice to Jesus' humanity,
and to the moral grandeur of His life and death as man, something which
(it was held) classical Christology, concentrating on His deity and ignoring His human limitations, had never done. This motivation is obvious
in the three major expositions of the kenotic theme produced in the early
years of the century by Frank Weston (*The One Christ,* 1907), H. R.
Mackintosh (*The Person of Jesus Christ,* 1912), and P. T. Forsyth (*The
Person and Place of Jesus Christ,* 1909). It is in Forsyth, according to
Ramsey, that "kenotic doctrine comes nearest to vindicating itself" (Ramsey, *op. cit.,* p. 40). Perhaps it is significant that this very un-Johannine
Christology, which divides the indivisible Trinity and changes the un-
changeable Word, should have flourished in England just at the time
when the Fourth Gospel was under a cloud; that its sternest critic should
have been that most Johannine thinker, William Temple (*Christus
Veritas,* chap. VIII); and that during the past twenty-five years, when the

Fourth Gospel has been better appreciated, little has been heard of the kenotic theory.

On the atonement, Ritschlian and immanentist influences were inclining men to abandon objective theories for Abelardianism. The chief monuments to this tendency, which began to be reversed soon after the First World War, are H. Rashdall's *The Idea of Atonement in Christian Theology* (1918) and R. S. Franks' two books, *History of the Doctrine of the Work of Christ* (1918) and *The Atonement* (1934).

Eschatology was not seriously studied, except as a biblical curiosity. Universal progress until the Kingdom of God had come on earth as assumed by all except the evangelicals. (Most of these were premillennialists, and some held, following J. N. Darby, that the pre-parousia apostasy had already begun; these views had no influence outside evangelical circles, however.)

From the standpoint of our present concern, the main movements in British theology during this century may be pinpointed under three heads:

1. The eclipse of evangelicalism. While the word "evangelical" may be variously applied, its meaning in Britain was quite definite at the beginning of the twentieth century. It denoted the position of those in all the churches who, in opposition to rationalism on the one hand and sacramentalism (Roman and Anglo-Catholic) on the other, maintained the theory of the Reformation, the piety of the Puritans, and the evangelistic ideals of the eighteenth-century Revival, basing these tenets on a robust belief in the plenary inspiration, entire truth, final authority, and vitalizing power of Holy Scripture as "God's word written" (Thirty-nine Articles, XX). In the mid-nineteenth century, evangelicalism was the norm in all British churches except the Church of England, where latitudinarians ruled and Tractarian "catholics" crusaded. But before the century ended most non-Anglican evangelicals had accepted higher criticism. This proved disastrous, for evangelical theology had been conscientiously monolithic, seeking to be wholly Bible-based and Bible-controlled, and to judge everything by the biblical standard. As a result, when the formal principle of the divine truth of biblical teaching, as such, was given up, evangelical theology literally fell to pieces. Its sharply defined traditional tenets—verbal inspiration, total depravity, sovereign grace, penal substitution, imputed righteousness, final perseverance—dropped from the picture and its doctrinal outlines were blurred beyond recognition. Within a generation, the classic evangelical theology, at least at the ministerial level, had almost vanished. The strongest resistance occurred in the Church of England, where many evangelicals rejected the higher criticism and preserved their historic position intact. Throughout the first half of the century men like H. C. G. Moule, W. H. Griffith Thomas, and T. C. Hammond maintained a theological testimony to the old paths which, to say the least, was very respectable. But they had little influence on Anglican theological life. J. K. Mozley makes a fair and perceptive comment on this situation:

> The Anglican Evangelicals have had a far more distinguished record in theology than is apt to be recognised. But their influence on the general thought of the Church suffered from, among other causes, their attitude on the subject of the Bible and their inattention to the problems arising in connexion with the philosophy of religion. They were far more rigid in face of the results which were claimed to follow from the methods of Higher Criticism than were ... the *Lux Mundi* school, while they made no attempt to construct a Christian philosophy of religion, which could appeal on purely intellectual grounds to minds conversant with modern movements in science and metaphysics. It is, of course, possible to hold that in both these respects the Evangelical theologians were in the right; but it can hardly be doubted that their doctrinal appeal was lessened owing to what seemed to many to be a narrowness in their outlook (*Some Tendencies in British Theology*, New York, The Macmillan Company, London, S.P.C.K., 1951, pp. 26 f.).

Does this seeming "narrowness" deserve praise or blame? If praise, perhaps it should be qualified. The evangelicals must certainly be praised for seeing that Wellhausenism cut across Christ's teaching about Scripture, and also for refusing the kenotic explanation thereof, which, as they realized, completely undermines our Lord's authority as a teacher. And they can hardly be blamed for thinking it more important to continue in the evangelistic and pastoral work to which they had given themselves continuously since the awakening of 1859 than to construct religious philosophies. On the other hand, there is no denying that the cultural isolationism into which evangelicals had been falling for half a century was now coming home to roost; they were simply not equipped for the kind of philosophical as well as critical counter-attack that the situation required. Even if they had been—if, shall we say, there had been twenty James Orrs to do battle instead of just one—it is doubtful whether the evangelical impact on an evolution-fixated age would have been any greater than in fact it was.

Just as the first liberal Catholics had wedded Tractarian tradition to current secular trends in *Lux Mundi,* so some Anglican evangelicals left their conservative moorings to champion a parallel synthesis in a book entitled *Liberal Evangelicalism* (1923). They embraced higher criticism and renounced inerrancy; also, they "sat loose" to the substitutionary doctrine of the atonement. They held that the "evangelical experience" could be conserved independent of the precise view of Scripture and the Cross that historically had produced it. This contention was wrong, as forty years' trial has shown. The idea is in fact self-contradictory, since "evangelical experience," if it means anything at all, means specifically experience which is generated and fed by evangelical doctrine. While liberal Catholicism prospered, liberal evangelicalism languished theologically and, like other mediating theologies, proved to be barren and unstable, or, to use Archbishop Ramsey's polite phrase, "somewhat viable to the superficial liberal and progressive ideas of the time" (*op. cit.,* p. 156). It is not hard to see why this should have been so. Liberal Catholicism is a comparatively stable structure; it has a fixed credal minimum and also a characteristic theological method—a sustained dialectic between the Bible and ecumenical tradition, and between these and current philosophy as well. This approach gives continuity to liberal Catholicism through all its reassessments and reshapings of detail. But liberal evangelicalism was simply an opportunist compromise. Unlike liberal Catholicism, and the older evangelicalism with its biblical method, it had no methodological basis of its own; it merely offered on a pietistic basis an enlarged area for intellectual license. This, perhaps, is the best explanation for what puzzled Mozley, namely, that the liberal evangelicals have made no distinctive contribution to theology at all (Mozley, *op. cit.,* pp. 78-83).

So far, evangelicalism has been discussed purely from the standpoint of its view of Scripture. But in one sense, of course, even if their view of the Bible is unsatisfactory, all who affirm man's helplessness in sin, and salvation by faith in Christ and His atonement are evangelicals. Two such evangelicals, both Scotsmen, must be cited here: Principal James Denney, of Glasgow, and Principal P. T. Forsyth, of Hackney College, London. They were Britain's greatest theologians of the Cross in this century. Both were self-consciously "modern men," committed to biblical criticism and sharing Ritschl's prejudice against "metaphysical" theology.

But both had revolted as adults against current immanentist, sacramentalist, and un- or anti-dogmatic fashions in theology and religion, and both sought in all that they did to recall men from these barren wastes to the apostolic message of faith in a crucified Saviour. Forsyth had been converted out of liberalism while in the ministry; Denney (so his friend W. R. Nicoll tells us) had been led by his wife to study Spurgeon, whence came "the great decision of his life," namely, to center his ministry wholly on the cross of Christ (*Letters of Principal James Denney to W. Robertson Nicoll,* 1920, p. xvi). Both Denney and Forsyth had the spirit of crusaders, and valued each other as comrades in arms. Denney wrote of Forsyth: "He has more true and important things to say, in my opinion, than anyone at present writing on theology." And Forsyth called Denney "the greatest thinker we have on our side" (*Letters of Principal James Denney to His Family and Friends,* 1921, pp. 154, 153). Their cast of mind differed, however. Denney, the New Testament exegete, excelled in exact analysis, and his writing was lucidity itself, whereas Forsyth, the theological prophet, used a method of synthetic impressionism and had a written style once unkindly described as "fireworks in a fog." But their aims were the same, and their views substantially identical, as their books on the atonement show (J. Denney, *The Death of Christ*, 1902, with supplement, *The Atonement and the Modern Mind*, 1903; *The Christian Doctrine of Reconciliation*, 1917; P. T. Forsyth, *The Person and Place of Jesus Christ*, 1909; *The Cruciality of the Cross*, 1909; *The Work of Christ*, 1909, these three forming a trilogy; also, *The Justification of God*, 1916).

In the first place, both saw the word of the Cross as itself the solution to the problem of authority. Both affirmed that it is simply and precisely the apostolic Gospel, and the God and the Christ of that Gospel, that are authoritative. What humbles and compels assent and response, they say, is and must be the grace of God in the apostolic apprehension and expression of it, that is, God Himself coming to men in Christ, summoning and moving them to faith in the Reconciler and in His finished work. Both thus explain the authority of the Bible in terms, not of the formal factor of inspiration (divine origin) but of its material content and of prevenient grace.

Both stress that, as the Gospel is the heart of the Bible, so the atonement is the heart of the Gospel. Both point to Calvary for the solution of all spiritual and theological problems. Both view Calvary as the act of a holy God who judges sin, and who saves men from sin through His act of judging it. Both Denney and Forsyth were wary of the forensic categories of an older orthodoxy (which, perhaps, they understood in too external a way). Forsyth, stressing Christ's solidarity with His people as their representative and surety, called the atonement penal (since Christ bore what our sins deserved) but not substitutionary; Denney, on similar grounds, called the atonement substitutionary but not penal. But the difference here was merely verbal. Finally, both emphasized the finished character of Christ's reconciling work, and invoked the resurrection as proof of it.

It is true that their method of analyzing Christianity in terms of the apostolic religious consciousness, and reading the New Testament as an expression of this rather than as a written revelation from God, cast such a rationalistic and ultimately agnostic haze over their theology that no amount of stress on the witness of the apostolic consciousness to the objectivity of the atonement and the prevenience of grace could dispel it. Their method was evidently intended to secure the status of the Cross as a redemptive revelation of God, and to establish the normative character of the apostolic preaching, without ever raising the question of whether or not God has *spoken* (verbally, propositionally). What they considered to be the strength of their method might more truly be judged its weakness. Nonetheless, their reassertion of the Gospel of atoning grace was one of the finest things that twentieth-century British theology has seen.

But these men were swimming against the stream. While they had many admirers in their lifetime, they had few disciples and no one to carry forward their emphasis. The New Testament Gospel was as much out of fashion as biblical inerrancy, and evangelicalism was heavily eclipsed.

2. *The retreat from immanentism.* When this century began, divine immanence, as we saw, was the accepted key-feature for any account of the relations between God and man. But, as indicated above, this immanentist incubus had been shaken off before the middle of the century by a development due to several converging factors.

First, strongly criticized by Cambridge realists (G. E. Moore, B. Russell) in the twenties, and by Oxford logical empiricists (G. Ryle, A. J. Ayer) in the thirties, idealism lost its standing in the universities as a respectable philosophy.

Second, immanentists provoked reaction by running their favorite idea to death, and by putting it to heterodox use in Christology. Thus, in 1907, in a swashbuckling manifesto, *The New Theology,* R. J. Campbell explicitly reduced the Incarnation to an instance of immanence, or divine indwelling. Similarly in the early twenties, the leaders of the Modern Churchmen's Union (Anglican) proclaimed a Christology of mere immanence, and claimed a measure of such immanence Incarnation) in every man. "It is impossible to maintain that God is fully incarnate in Christ, and not incarnate at all in anyone else," said H. Rashdall in 1921. Gore, who had previously criticized Campbell in *The New Theology and the Old Religion* (1908), saw that the root of the trouble in both cases was immanentism pushed to its logical conclusion, that is, the assimilating of divine to human, and human to divine. H. D. A. Major blandly admitted Gore's charge as follows: "Dr. Gore is correct in affirming that we believe that there is only one substance of the Godhead and the Manhood, and that our conception of the difference between Deity and Humanity is one of degree. The distinction between Creator and creature, upon which Dr. Gore and the older theologians place so much emphasis, seems to us to be a minor distinction. . . . It is not a moral distinction at all" (*Modern Churchman,* October, 1921, p. 357). But, according to J. W. C. Wand, a first-hand observer, when once the Modernists (as they were called, although their movement had no links with Roman modernism) brought their views into the open, "public opinion was revolted by the revelation. The movement . . . dwindled . . . to a position of comparative insignificance" (*op. cit.,* p. 126). Immanentism was thus discredited.

Third, the category of transcendence was re-established as fundamental to that of immanence. By their own method (analysis of the religious consciousness) philosophical theologians were driven to stress the "otherness" of the Immanent, and Its felt discontinuity, as well as continuity, with man. Otto's *Idea of the Holy* (1917; English translation, 1923) was influential here. John Oman labored impressively to vindicate the idea of a personal Supernatural (*The Natural and the Supernatural*, 1931). Temple's work, as we saw, tended in a similar direction. Gore's remarkable apologetic trilogy, *The Reconstruction of Belief* (*Belief in God; Belief in Christ; The Holy Spirit and the Church* 1921-5), complemented these developments. Gore's appeal was to divine revelation in history, in the prophets and in Christ, and not at any point to the religious consciousness. (Among the *Lux Mundi* group he was really the least affected by immanentism.) His running fight with immanentism, as he built up an orthodox account of God transcendent and Triune from biblical history, helped to lead thinkers away from immanentist theory to a different mental method and set of conclusions. The immanentist tide was running out.

Fourth, the Barthianism and Neo-Thomism of the thirties, both stressing God's transcendence, knocked further nails into the coffin of immanentism.

Fifth, there was more and more stress on the principle that biblical categories must control the theologian's use of philosophical concepts (such as immanence), and not vice versa. This emphasis was a direct result of the "biblical theology" movement.

3. *The rise of "biblical theology."* Like the discovery of penicillin, the "biblical theology" movement was in a sense accidental, that is, it was merely the by-product of some other research, in this case Gospel study by a Cambridge college chaplain, Sir Edwyn Hoskyns. Pursuing "the quest of the historical Jesus" as all students of the Gospels had been doing for decades, Hoskyns was led to challenge the liberal Protestant reading of the evidence in a more radical way than had been done for some time. Men like Harnack had presented the historical Jesus as an ethical teacher whose followers deified Him and onto His teaching had grafted a mystery cult. But, Hoskyns argued, all the identifiable literary strata of the synoptic Gospels deal with the same themes: the presence of the Messianic kingdom in Jesus' words and works; the divine necessity of Jesus' death and future return in glory, according to Old Testament prophecy; and the calling of His disciples to share His humiliation now, that they might share His glory hereafter. Denney had anticipated these conclusions in *Jesus and the Gospel* (1908), but without making much impact. When Hoskyns published them, however (most fully in *The Riddle of the New Testament*, with F. N. Davey, 1931), their importance was seen at once. They were valued as closing three troublesome gaps which the liberal view had opened.

First, they closed the gap between the Jesus of history and the Christ of faith. The contrast which underlies the synoptic tradition at this point, Hoskyns argued, is not between the Jesus of history and the Christ of faith, but between the Christ humiliated and the Christ returning in glory ("The Christ of the Synoptic Gospels," in *Essays Catholic and Critical,* ed. E. G. Selwyn, 1926, p. 177). The Christ of apostolic faith is indeed the Jesus of history, risen and exalted as foretold.

Second, Hoskyns' conclusions closed the gap between Palestinian discipleship and the developed churchmanship of the apostolic age. The contrast which the evidence offers us here, Hoskyns wrote, is "not between the disciples of a Jewish prophet and the members of an ecclesiastically ordered sacramental cultus, but between the disciples of Jesus who are as yet ignorant of His claims and of the significance of their own conversion, and the same disciples, initiated into the mystery of His Person and of His life and death, leading the mission to the world" *(loc. cit.).* The faith of the apostolic Church is thus a "spontaneous Christian development" (p. 178) out of Palestinian discipleship. What caused the development was not Hellenism, but Pentecost.

Third, Hoskyns' conclusions closed the gap between the two Testaments. Christ and His disciples read the Old Testament as a Christian book, as part one of the story of the acts of God, that looks prophetically toward part two, toward the events which formed the theme of the apostolic witness. The two Testaments, therefore, belong together. Since the New depends on the Old, the two must be read as a theological unity, and read "from within," not as records of fitful insights garnered by religious adepts, but as believing testimony to the action of God in fulfilling His plan of history.

Hoskyns' work began a new era in British theology. For a generation now British biblical and theological study has proceeded on his principles, and seems likely to continue to do so. Of *The Riddle of the New Testament,* Professor C. F. D. Moule, of Cambridge, wrote in 1961: "The general direction in which the argument moved was ahead of its time then and seems to be more than ever coming into its own now" *(Theology,* April 1961, p. 146). Few would disagree. Never, since Hoskyns gave them an approach to the New Testament which shows it to be coherent both internally, part with part, and externally, with the Old Testament, have British biblical scholars as a whole been attracted to views which would divide one part of Scripture from another. Here, as elsewhere, the British theologian holds that the most coherent view is the one most likely to be right. And it is against this background of Hoskyns' solution to the problems of the historical Jesus, and to the unity of the Bible, that British theologians do their work today.

IV. BRITISH THEOLOGY TODAY

Because of its complex dialectical method, and its motivating passion for coherence and continuity, modern British theology is not likely to become seriously unsteady in the foreseeable future. With the Anglicized neo-Thomism of E. L. Mascall and the Scotticized Barthianism of T. F. Torrance as lookouts, no return to immanentism is to be expected. Today everyone stresses the reality of revelation; revelation by divine action is universally affirmed, and room is slowly being made again for its biblical and necessary presupposition, that is, revelation by speech. Although plenary biblical inspiration is not generally admitted, it is a matter of common consent that the Bible is a record of revelation, a witness and response to revelation, and a revealing medium. Many books have been written in recent years expounding its inner unity. That authority belongs extensively to the total biblical interpretation of the total biblical narrative, and within this, supremely to the Gospel would be axiomatic with most British theologians today, although the value of this admission must remain problematic so long as biblical facts like the Fall are begrudged factual status. Man's guiltiness and perversity in God's sight is, however, recognized by all, at any rate in general terms. The influential "social" Trinitarianism of Leonard Hodgson (*The Doctrine of the Trinity*, New York, Charles Scribner's Sons, 1944, London, James Nisbet & Co., 1943) has displaced the implicit Sabellianism of the idealist era. The two-nature Chalcedonian Christology, long maligned by persons who disliked the "metaphysical" categories of nature and substance, is now widely accepted again, chiefly through Anglo-Catholic advocacy. Kenoticism smoulders, but it has been some time since its ashes were stirred. Abelardianism has virtually vanished: that Christ died as man's representative, that His death was a sacrifice offered on man's behalf and changed man's situation for the better would be generally agreed. There would be disagreement as to how this was accomplished, however, most theologians shying away from the ideas of penalty and substitution. Against a broad ecumenical background the Church and the sacraments are themes for sustained debate between "catholics" and "protestants."

This situation, and the conservative tendencies which still operate within British theology, offer some encouragement for evangelicals. Things are better, or at least less bad. Nevertheless, British theology still has two great weaknesses. First, its typical idea of biblical authority (dialectically related to that of church and conscience) lacks the precision which a clear grasp of inspiration, inerrancy, and the relationship between the Spirit and the Word would give. Hence, subjectivist impressionism and unreformed traditionalism frequently mar British discussion of the details of doctrines; also, as long as doubts remain as to whether biblical assurances, purporting to be divine promises, really are so, the door is barred against an entrance, theological or experimental, into the biblical view of the life of faith as a matter of "standing on the promises of God." Second, British theology is not evangelical enough in its interests. The concentration on redemption, justification, and conversion, for which Temple called in 1937, has not been forthcoming. Tomorrow's theologians will evaluate today's work on the atonement as undistinguished; and for more than a century no British theologian has written a treatise on justification or regeneration. When asked "What is the Gospel?" the trumpets of British theology give a very uncertain sound. But this is no wonder, when those who walk in the old paths of evangelical faith have been out of the British theological conversation for so long. It is greatly to be hoped that they will regain their place in this conversation, for the indicated weaknesses in British theology are such as only evangelicals themselves are ever likely to correct.

AMERICAN THEOLOGY
IN THE
TWENTIETH CENTURY

✝

M. Eugene Osterhaven

*M. Eugene Osterhaven is Albertus C. Van Raalte Professor of System-
atic Theology in Western Theological Seminary (Reformed Church in
America) in Holland, Michigan. In the chair of theology he has, since
1952, succeeded to a post long identified with such names as John E.
Kuizenga and John R. Mulder. He is author of* What Is Christian
Baptism? *(1956). He holds the A.B. degree from Hope College, B.D.
from Western Theological Seminary, and Th.D. from Princeton Theological Seminary. He has taken post-doctoral studies at Basel, Göttingen
and Utrecht universities.*

3. M. Eugene Osterhaven

AMERICAN THEOLOGY
IN THE
TWENTIETH CENTURY

DRAWING the curtain from American theology at the turn of the twentieth century disclosed a far different setting from that of two decades earlier. In 1880 the older theology still prevailed in almost all of the theological schools. Before the end of the century, however, a significant change had taken place. The oldest institutions, those in New England, and their daughter seminaries farther west had replaced their earlier theologians with men of a different spirit. The New England theology which, more than any other single factor, had molded American religious thought for generations, suddenly disappeared, "As it were, in a night," an historian of the period writes, the New England theology "perished from off the face of the earth" (Frank Hugh Foster, *A Genetic History of the New England Theology,* Chicago, The University of Chicago Press, 1907, p. 543). Commenting on this significant break with the Reformation tradition, another avers that "if Calvinism survived this break, as it did at Princeton and other conservative schools, it was no longer the aggressive, forward-looking Calvinism of Edwards and Finney, but a defensive, armor-clad system, beset with 'fightings and fears, within, without'" (Walter M. Horton, "Systematic Theology," in *Protestant Thought in the Twentieth Century,* ed. by Arnold S. Nash, New York, The Macmillan Company, 1951).

What happened to American theology, and in particular to that of New England, between 1880 and 1900 is similar in nature and importance to a transition which occurred in Great Britain two hundred years earlier. Then, to use the title of a study on the subject, it was *From Puritanism to the Age of Reason* (G. R. Cragg, Cambridge, The University Press, 1950). Now, broadly speaking, the transition was from a later form of Calvinism to German idealistic philosophy. As in the closing decades of the seventeenth century when new streams of thought—of the Cambridge Platonists, the Latitudinarians, John Locke, the Deists, and the new science—overwhelmed the earlier British Christian tradition, so in the closing decades of the nineteenth century a flood of ideas that had gathered strength and prestige throughout several generations swept from Germany to inundate the convictions of many American theologians. Among these ideas was a skepticism, based largely on Kantian episte- mology, with respect to the possibility of any real knowledge of God. Another was the acceptance of philosophical monism that brought antipathy to supernaturalism as a consequence. Too, there was openness to the doctrine of naturalistic evolution as well as disparagement of certain cardinal Christian doctrines. Moreover, as Ritschlian theology made its full impact by the turn of the century, a tendency developed to resolve theology into history, sociology and ethics, or even into psychology or a philosophy of religion. By 1900 the transition had been virtually completed and the "liberal" era in American theology had arrived.

I. THE LIBERAL EPOCH

Theological liberalism can best be defined in a threefold manner: it is a method, a spirit, and a body of doctrine. Moreover, the expression covers so wide a range of opinion, attitude, and practice that one could very well be liberal in one respect but not in others. Certain American the- ologians were liberal because of their method of inquiry; although bound to creeds and conclusions based on prior assumptions, they boasted of open-minded and free inquiry. The older theological method was largely dogmatic and deductive, drawing its conclusions from a given revelation. The new method, on the other hand, extolled inductive investigation as harmonious with science and as the only sure basis for an enlightened faith.

As already suggested, liberalism was open, inquiring and unrestrained in spirit. "Theological liberalism," it has been said, "is a comparatively late resultant of a wider liberal trend which, conscious of its kinship with the classical liberalism of Greece and Rome, emerged as the Italian Renaissance in the latter half of the fifteenth century, and which has ever since been seeking with varying success to express itself in literature, in art, in politics, in philosophy, and in culture generally. The common feature is humanism. When the opposition of which it is most conscious is religious, or theological or ecclesiastical, its tendency is atheistic; when its opposition is animalism or 'jungleism,' it seeks alliance with religion; when its opposition is ignorance, it becomes enlightenment; when its opposition is human tyranny, it becomes constitutional democracy or revolutionary Marxism. Theological liberalism could not be completely naturalistic or fully humanistic. But that which distinguishes it from a theology which is not liberal is nevertheless the large measure of control over its spirit, method, and conclusions exercised by naturalistic humanism" (Andrew K. Rule, "Liberalism," in *Twentieth Century Encyclopedia of Religious Knowledge,* Grand Rapids, Baker Book House, 1955, p. 660).

If not consciously or openly, the doctrine of theological liberalism was nonetheless related to philosophical naturalism. Man was the crown of nature and all else was arranged with reference to him. Since human experience was considered the source of doctrine, reason would assign it a proper place in man's theological structure. According to Edward Caldwell Moore (Adolph Harnack's first American pupil and Parkman professor of theology at Harvard), spokesman for those who had embraced the liberal American theological tradition, it is therefore "axiomatic that doctrine has only relative truth," that it changes from age to age, and that "the heresy of one generation is the orthodoxy of the next." There is truth, moreover, in the maxim "that the true Church, in any age, is to be found with those who have just been excommunicated from the actual Church" (Edward Caldwell Moore, *An Outline of the History of Christian Thought Since Kant,* New York, Charles Scribner's Sons, 1912, p. 7. Cf. Gerald Birney Smith, "The Task and Method of Systematic Theology," in *The American Journal of Theology,* Vol. XIV, 1910, pp. 221 f.). The position tended to blur the distinction between the natural and the supernatural, between man and God.

Based on this fundamental weakness, the remaining doctrine of liberalism would necessarily be likewise inadequate. Its God was no longer the Holy One who revealed Himself to Abraham, Isaac, and Jacob, and finally in Jesus Christ, the eternal Word made flesh. Revelation was conceived more as a human achievement than as a divine gift; the Bible as a collection of human insights and opinions than as a message from God. Since liberalism rejected all miracle, it believed Christ to be only human; salvation meant self-improvement, and the Church was interpreted in sociological or ethical terms. Liberalism's optimism concerning the possibilities of human nature was matched only by its repudiation of the traditional doctrine of human sin and the Fall.

The liberal attitude toward Scripture has already been mentioned. The battle that ensued between "liberals" and "fundamentalists" [1] over

---

[1] "Fundamentalism," "fundamentalist" derives from a movement to preserve fundamentals of the Christian faith threatened by liberal doctrine. In 1895 the Niagara Bible Conference named six essentials to be defended at all costs: the

the nature of the Bible and its scholarly investigation displayed error on both sides. In making sweeping condemnations of biblical criticism, fundamentalists bypassed the necessity in scholarly study of investigating the background of biblical writings. Liberal scholars, on the other hand, assumed Julius Wellhausen's reconstruction of Israel's religious history to be true, forcing and trimming historical and theological detail to fit this Procrustean bed accordingly. Literary analysis alone was thought sufficient to demonstrate the evolution of Israel's religion and no even incongruous theological detail was allowed to challenge the validity of this demonstration. As a result, the last decades of the nineteenth and the first decades of the twentieth century witnessed a decline in biblical and systematic theology. In addressing the American Theological Library Association, Connolly C. Gamble gives the following reasons for the decline in biblical theology:

1. "Detached study of Scripture, rigidly neutral, with no presuppositions or theological bias. . . ."

2. "The new interpretation of history within an evolutionary framework. A very large proportion of biblical interpreters believed that the biblical movement could best be understood in a progressive development from lower, simpler, 'primitive' concepts to higher, more complex, later ideas. With the imposition of this evolutionary pattern upon Scripture, a comprehensive theology derived from the Bible as a whole became impossible to achieve."

3. "The new emphasis on the variety in Scripture, rather than its unity." In other words, says Gamble, there is no biblical theology, but rather, there are theologies with their differences and contradictions.

4. A philosophy of religion after Schleiermacher which emphasized the common elements in all religion and minimized biblical distinctiveness.

5. "The new interest in related studies, resulting in a secularized biblical study." Instead of in theology or religion, which were often controversial subjects, interest now centered in the manifold ramifications of philology and history.

(Seventh Annual Conference, American Theological Library Association, Evanston, Illinois, June 11-12, 1960.)

---

inerrancy of Scripture, the deity of Christ, the virgin birth, substitutionary atonement, the physical resurrection, and the visible, physical second advent of Christ. In 1910-1912, a series of twelve booklets, *The Fundamentals,* appeared containing essays defending Christian doctrine. In 1919 the World Conference on Christian Fundamentals was convened in Philadelphia requiring its members to subscribe to a nine-point doctrinal statement. Its quarterly was named *The Christian Fundamentalist.* See Norman F. Furniss, *The Fundamentalist Controversy,* New Haven, Yale University Press, 1954.

With amazing self-confidence, engendered in part by the conviction that it had science and progress on its side, and in part by the ability and productivity of its proponents, liberal theology took the initiative wherever a beachhead was established. Because of its freshness, vigor, and flexibility, liberalism experienced numerous successful skirmishes in seminaries, congregations, church courts and boards. Although opposed on every hand, it succeeded in convincing many that such opposition was motivated by narrow-mindedness or an obscurantist scholarship whose fundamentalism could never withstand the pressures of time. In a perceptive comment, Andrew K. Rule remarks that men "were invited to make their choice between only three possibilities—Roman Catholicism, fundamentalism, and liberalism. Thus, by powerful implication the possibility of an irenic, scholarly, broad-minded Protestantism that was in harmony with historic Christian thought was denied" (*op. cit.,* p. 663). One who by self-designation has been known as a "chastened" liberal and is a recognized authority on the subject affirms that "the prevailing trend in theology continued to get more and more liberal until shortly after the close of the First World War. Conservative theologians felt themselves to be in a state of siege, with insurgent bands of liberals rising up and marching against them from every quarter" (Walter M. Horton, *op. cit.,* p. 105). The extent and success of the liberal attack have been chronicled by both friend and foe (see, for example, Wilbur M. Smith, *Therefore Stand,* Boston, W. A. Wilde Company, 1945, chapters I and II); many believed that in the older churches and theological schools the cause of historic Christianity had been lost.

II. THE REDISCOVERY OF THEOLOGY

The tide toward theological recovery in America began a decade after that in Europe. Julius Wellhausen's death in 1918 and the appearance of Karl Barth's commentary on the Epistle to the Romans the same year seemed to mark the beginning of a new movement in Europe. Tillich notes the rapidity of its growth by remarking that in 1923 when Harnack (just three years before his death) spoke at Troeltsch's funeral, "the first earthquake of the world to which both men belonged had already happened. They died in an atmosphere strange to that in which they had lived for the most part of their lives. And it seems that in Europe neo-Protestantism died with them" (Paul Tillich, "The Present Theological Situation in the Light of the Continental European Development," in *Theology Today,* Vol. VI, 1949, p. 301).

The effects of the theological renascence in Europe were not felt in America until after 1930. Walter Lowrie's *Our Concern with the Theology of Crisis* (Boston, Meador Publishing Co., 1932) and Edwin Lewis' *A Christian Manifesto* (New York, Abingdon Press, 1934) presaged the day when beleaguered fundamentalists, even though they might fail to recognize them, would find new allies in their battle to preserve historic Christianity. American theologians had heard of Barth and Brunner by the mid-thirties; when political pressures brought Piper and Hromadka to Princeton and Tillich to Union (New York), the new European theology came to be known personally. Brunner's year of residence in America and the coming of other European scholars furthered the new movement in this country. Even more significant for recovering theology from the ravages of liberalism, however, was the work of two American-born theologians, Reinhold and H. Richard Niebuhr. The former's *Moral Man and Immoral Society* (New York, Charles Scribner's Sons, 1932) and his brother's *The Kingdom of God in America* (Chicago, Willetts, Clark & Co., 1937) were the first of a series of pungent publications that sharpened American theology's criticism of the older liberalism and spurred its search for something better. In this and later publications, Reinhold Niebuhr revealed the optimistic view of man's essential goodness and perfectibility to be little better than ridiculous. Utopian, sentimentalized views of human nature became increasingly untenable. A realistic view of man that includes a forthright doctrine of sin is, after all, the first prerequisite of a Christian theology. Without it, man shows himself either duped by his own idolatrous pretensions or hopelessly naive in his understanding of himself and of his fellow men.

Reinhold Niebuhr, who has probably influenced larger numbers of persons than his brother, has always been the analytical critic, sometimes cynical, even caustic. His area of concern has been largely, as he himself averred, anthropology and social ethics. And, even though the fact is certainly not obvious, "Christology has been and is the principal passion and purpose of his theological work . . . the leitmotiv of [his] theology" (Paul Lehmann, "The Christology of Reinhold Niebuhr," in *Reinhold Niebuhr: His Religious, Social, and Political Thought,* ed. by Charles W. Kegley and Robert W. Bretall, New York, The Macmillan Company, 1956, p. 253). From the perspective of historic Christianity, Reinhold Niebuhr's work has had largely a negative impact (cf. E. A. Burtt, "Some Questions About Niebuhr's Theology," in Kegley and Bretall, *ibid.,* p. 356).

H. Richard Niebuhr's contribution has been of a different nature. Author of only one-third the number of books of his better known brother, he nonetheless has been more constructive and positively helpful to theological understanding than Reinhold. In fact, in H. Richard Niebuhr, American theology of the post-liberal era achieved its outstanding theologian. Similarly interested in anthropology and social ethics as Reinhold, H. Richard also labored over questions of theological method and concerned himself with problems in numerous loci of the entire field of theology. His work invariably manifests thoroughness and a masterly handling of detail, but its sophisticated scholarship and style, although a delight to the initiated, undoubtedly limits his readership.

According to H. Richard Niebuhr's own admission, his teachers were Ernst Troeltsch and Karl Barth (H. Richard Niebuhr, *The Meaning of Revelation*, New York, The Macmillan Company, 1941, p. x). The final product of nineteenth-century historical consciousness and method, Troeltsch was the painstaking, analytical historian who clearly saw the central problem of theology but chose the wrong answer. He was an acknowledged master, however, in understanding the problems of sociology and culture, of historical method, of philosophy and theology. In this area of excellence, Niebuhr learned from Troeltsch, but for fundamental theological content, he looked to Barth. In keeping with his historical principles, Troeltsch rejected the uniqueness of the Christian revelation and every attempt to inject into history a trans-historical absolute that becomes determinative for all categories of thought. To this giant from Heidelberg, Barth's affirmation that God has spoken would have sounded unreal and naive. Yet this affirmation is exactly what Christianity claims; one either believes it or rejects it.

At this point of theology H. Richard Niebuhr stands with Barth. Fully aware of the issues involved and of the liberal tradition as well, H. Richard deliberately accepted the fact of a revelation through Israel and Jesus Christ that is final and authoritative for the Christian. Hans Frei is certainly correct in observing that "in regard to theological principles and systematic or dogmatic theology [Troeltsch's] influence on Niebuhr is secondary when compared to the basic tension over theological method that Niebuhr confronted through his interest in the debate between the nineteenth-century tradition and dialectical theology" (Hans W. Frei, "The Theology of H. Richard Niebuhr," in *Faith and Ethics,* ed. by Paul Ramsey, New York, Harper & Brothers, 1957, p. 93). The revelation spoken once for all and recorded in Scripture must be both the starting-point and the norm of Christian experience. In the "revolutionary" activity which revelation initiates and continues within him, the Christian comes to a knowledge of God and finds life's meaning. Leaving the gods which would claim his allegiance—neutrality is the great delusion (*The Meaning of Revelation,* pp. 37 f.)—he commits himself to the God and Father of Jesus Christ who makes Himself known through Christ.

The influence of H. Richard Niebuhr in rediscovering theology has been mediated not only through his books, but also through countless students who have gone from his classes as ambassadors and living embodiments of the Gospel expounded by their teacher. After all, daily contact in the classroom is usually more determinative in creating opinion than is the impersonal reading of books. What was true of H. Richard Niebuhr has been true also of his brother Reinhold, of William F.

Albright, of Otto A. Piper, and of others actively engaged in theological education. Trained by such master theologians, students have gone out to assume positions of responsibility and influence in churches, colleges, seminaries and administrative posts, and have augmented the theological revival.

Not everyone has been favorably impressed by the new emphasis, however. Resistance against the Gospel within the Church is nothing new and the present day of grace is no exception. I personally remember an illustration of this fact that involved one of my own teachers. In a series of articles on "What the Bible Means to Me" (*The Christian Century,* Vol. LXIII, 1946, pp. 266 ff., 299 ff., 334 ff., 362 ff.), Otto A. Piper tried to interpret the Bible "from within the mind" of its authors. His acceptance of biblical teachings and categories as normative and true, Professor Morton S. Enslin called "not only wrong but wrongheaded and utterly out of place in the modern world. . . . If he were living in the first century, his views would be entirely understandable. But the difficulty is that he is living—at least 'according to the flesh,' as Paul might have phrased it—in the twentieth century, and he does not seem to realize that fact" ("Dr. Piper's Bible," *ibid.,* p. 460 f.). Piper's belief in guidance by the Holy Spirit Enslin deemed "meaningless." Moreover, Piper's position that Jesus' ideas are determinative today is impossible, indicated Enslin, for Jesus shared the views of the men of his day. Enslin "can see but one solid foundation and hope, namely, man's brave and undaunted effort through the ages to save himself from ills and to turn them into blessings" (*ibid.,* p. 462).

Further evidence that liberalism has not disappeared from American theology is the presence and great influence of Paul Tillich. Called "the ablest Protestant theologian of the present day," and "also by far the most persuasive exponent of the philosophy of existentialism" (John Herman Randall, Jr., "The Ontology of Paul Tillich," in *The Theology of Paul Tillich,* ed. by Charles W. Kegley and Robert W. Bretall, New York, The Macmillan Company, 1952, p. 161), Tillich must be considered a follower of the liberal tradition. In contrasting Tillich with Barth, Walter M. Horton aptly remarks that "what demands explanation is why so liberal a mind ever was led to approve the 'dialectical theology' movement in the first place, and to participate in its sharp attack on liberal Protestantism" (Walter Horton, "Tillich's Role in Contemporary Theology," *ibid.,* p. 28). Throughout his writings, and particularly in his *Systematic Theology* (Chicago, University of Chicago Press, 1951), Tillich is completely out of sympathy with the broad stream of what can be called classical Christian theology. In such fundamentals as the doctrine of God, of revelation, creation, incarnation, and resurrection, Tillich resolutely sets himself against the biblical position and maintains a sophisticated religious philosophy reminiscent of the Gnosticism that threatened the early Church. Both his popular writings and his more technical works reveal this fact. In his *Dynamics of Faith,* for example, he states that all the qualities which we attribute to God are taken from our own experience and applied symbolically to "that which is beyond finitude and infinity. If faith calls God 'almighty,' it uses the human experience of power in order to symbolize the content of its infinite concern, but it does not describe a highest being who can do as he pleases. So it is with all the other qualities and with all the actions, past, present and future, which men attribute to God. They are symbols taken from our daily experience, and not information about what God did once upon a time or will do sometime in the future. Faith is not belief in such stories, but it is the acceptance of symbols that express our ultimate concern in terms of divine actions" (Paul Tillich, *Dynamics of Faith,* New York, Harper and Brothers, 1957, pp. 47; cf. Nels F. S. Ferré's criticism of Tillich's theology, particularly the latter's use of myth and symbol: *Searchlights on Contemporary Theology,* New York, Harper and Brothers, 1961, pp. 4 ff.; 106 ff.; 120 ff.). On the other hand, Tillich's work is commendable for its amazingly broad sweep of interest and its attempt to relate theology to all areas of life. This approach explains much of his appeal for students and also his stature among great thinkers in every tradition (see also the comments of the American Jesuit, Gustave Weigel, *Theological Studies,* XI, June, 1950).

Besides leaders like Tillich and Enslin, there are many others in the liberal tradition for whom conservatives are biblicists, literalists, obscurantists, or fundamentalists. They are far fewer today than a generation ago, however, and no longer claim the exclusive right to speak for Protestantism inasmuch as they are outnumbered by old-line evangelicals and their now "reconstructed" liberal brethren. Of these latter we have already spoken, but the former also merit consideration. Often forgotten or overlooked in discussions on theological trends, it is nevertheless these evangelicals who are the faithful Christians found in every church where the Gospel has been proclaimed. Unknown and unsung, they form the greater part of the people of God. It is largely because of them and their children that the Church exists as a continuing body from generation to generation. This solid core of Protestantism includes the Reformed and Presbyterian churches, most of whose members are Bible-believing Christians; the large Lutheran tradition which more than any other has succeeded in resisting the corroding influences of modernity; millions of Baptists and other free groups like the Methodists, Episcopalians, and so on, who compose the largest single block of evangelical believers in America. All have had their ministers of the Word of God and their professors of theology whose work was significant but whose names may not have been widely known outside their particular ecclesiastical circles.

But conservatives have also had, and still have, scholars of wide reputa·

tion as well as of great erudition. In the heyday of liberalism Benjamin Breckinridge Warfield was such a one. Unsurpassed in scholarly attainments, intellectual power, and literary style, he championed Reformed orthodoxy at Princeton with a brilliant rationalism that marks certain of his writings as well (for example, "Apologetics," in *The New Schaff-Herzog Encyclopedia of Religious Knowledge*, ed. by S. M. Jackson, Grand Rapids, Baker Book House, 1950, I, 232-238).

Outstanding among Warfield's colleagues are J. Gresham Machen, apologist for orthodoxy in the twenties and Geerhardus Vos, America's leading biblical theologian, whose writings anticipated concepts and motifs found in the finest biblical theology of our day. While *The Origin of Paul's Religion* (New York, The Macmillan Company, 1921) is Machen's best contribution to theological scholarship, *The Virgin Birth of Christ* (New York, Harper & Brothers, 1930) is highly representative of the author's careful investigation, and his *Christianity and Liberalism* (New York, The Macmillan Company, 1923) more clearly than any other volume indicates the theological issues involved in the controversy with liberalism.

Speaking for old-line evangelicals, "those that tarried by the stuff," to use David's words (I Sam. 30:24), one of Warfield's successors, John E. Kuizenga, flouted neo-orthodoxy's claim to have given the Church something new. It reminded him, he said, of the boy who brought the little fish he had caught to the fish market and exclaimed, "Look what I've got!" Surely the Gospel had not been lost from the Church. If there were those within the Church who for a time had forgotten it, they should not presume that their rediscovery of the Gospel would bring something new to those who had never deserted or lost it.

Others likewise represented theological conservatism and spoke for their respective traditions. To mention just two there were E. Y. Mullins, the Baptist, and Francis Pieper, Missouri Lutheran; they symbolized the sturdy evangelical scholarship that built the Christian Church in America and helped formulate its thinking. Continuing the conservative tradition, and encouraged by the wave of theological refreshing in our time, their successors today have demonstrated that orthodoxy has far greater vitality than many had thought and good reasons for an optimistic future. The fortnightly *Christianity Today* and Billy Graham's ministry give evidence of orthodox Christianity's relevance and power.

III. THE PRESENT SITUATION

In discussing the state of New Testament theology at mid-century, A. M. Hunter introduces the subject in an interesting way. Were some unseen scholar who had died at the turn of the century to be revived, says Hunter, and given current New Testament literature to read, he would rub his eyes uncomprehendingly, not at the opinions of this or that literary question, but at the "something of a revolution" that characterizes the tone and temper of the whole approach to New Testament theology (A. M. Hunter, *Interpreting the New Testament*, 1900-1950, London, SCM Press, 1951, p. 124). Hunter's words are as relevant today as they were a decade ago. The somber world of a generation ago which caused many to reconsider their estimate of man has not brightened. The power of sin and the demonic are as much in evidence now as then. The pressure on liberalism from the humanist left has not lessened (as noted, for example, by Carl F. H. Henry in *Fifty Years of Protestant Theology*, Boston, W. A. Wilde Company, 1950, p. 64 ff.). Moreover, philosophical existentialism, including its theological stepchildren, Rudolf Bultmann, Ernst Käsemann and their disciples, still challenges theology. Existentialism's protests against traditional thought and its eccentric view of man have driven not only Barth but many others as well further to the theological right. The impact of the archaeological, historical, and philological work of Albright and his disciples, a number of whom, like George Ernest Wright, are now in positions of influence, has been a boon to conservative Christian thought. Finally, the phenomenon of the ecumenical movement has helped American theology in a twofold way: first, it has brought about closer contact with a more robust European theology, and secondly, it has forced American theologians to reconsider biblical foundations for purposes of ecumenical discussion. Exchange in the latter has pointed up the centrality in Christian theology of the doctrine of the Church as the body of Christ, that divine-human organism created through the Word by the Holy Spirit. Compared with what obtained at the turn of the present century, therefore, the present theological panorama offers much reason for gratitude and encouragement. It is generally agreed that subsequent to the rediscovery of the "strange new world within the Bible" there has been a trend toward a more biblical orientation of life and history.

In surveying theological activity over the last years one notes marked achievements in certain areas of investigation but relatively little in others. Outstanding work has been done in hermeneutics, for example, an important branch of exegetical theology. An interesting project here has been the cooperative application by a group of scholars, including some Americans, and representing the different traditions in the World Council of Churches, on "Guiding Principles for the Interpretation of the Bible" (*Biblical Authority for Today*, ed. by Alan Richardson and W. Schweitzer, Philadelphia, The Westminster Press, 1951, pp. 240 ff.). This undertaking recognizes the need for understanding both the presuppositions basic to valid exegesis and the rules for interpreting the text itself. It insists that the Bible, where God meets man, must be the starting-point; that the Bible has a unified message; that this message is centered in

Jesus Christ; that the interpreter of Scripture must be within the Christian community; and that any teaching which is contrary to Scripture cannot be accepted as Christian. Such assertion is far different from the prevailing spirit at the beginning of the century. At that time scientific objectivity was a fetish for many. Biblical scholars, moreover, tried to imitate certain philosophers by discarding all presuppositions. It was a time, too, when biblical teaching was as commonly rejected as accepted by the exegete.

In both exegesis and biblical theology American scholars have shown considerable work in recent years, much of it of high quality. Beyond question the most notable achievement in exegetical theology is *The Interpreter's Bible* (Nashville, Abingdon-Cokesbury Press, 1952), which manifests a wide range of theological opinion. Some of the essays represent the finest scholarship in contemporary American theology and, along with much of the exegesis and exposition, are faithful to the revelation which they profess. Other contributions are disappointedly reminiscent of unreconstructed liberalism with its prejudices and shortcomings.

With their keen interest in applied Christianity it is little wonder that Americans have been especially productive in the field of ethics. Publications in this area have been numerous in the last few years and many of them have been excellent. The same cannot be said of systematic theology, however. To some people this statement may come as a shock, for it is commonly said that in dogmatic or systematic theology, theology comes into its own. Systematic theology, after all, is called queen of the sciences. Despite these proud claims, the fact is that systematic theology has been having a difficult time in the last few decades. Hemmed in by biblical theology and by history and philosophy, the rights of systematic theology as a distinct discipline have been challenged. Biblical theologians who seek to enhance the prestige of their own discipline at the expense of another actually do violence to the cause of theology as a whole. And when systematic theology is made to appear static, abstract, propositional, rationalistic—to use the adjectives employed in one discussion—and when it is asked whether possibly "there may be another kind of theology than the abstract, the coherent and the propositional" (G. Ernest Wright, *God Who Acts*, London, SCM Press, 1952, p. 32), one becomes uneasy and fearful over apparent prejudice against a good and necessary discipline. Or, when a volume which otherwise has many excellent features declares theology to be only a recital of the great deeds of God (*ibid.*, pp. 11, 33 ff.; cf. Roger Hazelton's criticism of this position in *New Accents in Contemporary Theology*, New York, Harper and Brothers, 1960, p. 69), one quite understandably feels that the theological task is being falsified by oversimplification.

Roger Hazelton remarks in an autobiographical note, "Many of us who studied in seminaries here during the thirties were taught the Old and New Testaments in a way which introduced us to all kinds of fascinating

archaeological data, highly critical reservations, and intriguing hypothetical reconstructions of original documents. But with what we then
understood to be theology, all this had very little to do" (*ibid.*, p. 60).
Fortunately, those days are past and theological interest in the study of
Scripture and in *biblical* theology has forged ahead. Unfortunately, however, systematic theology has not made the same progress. Perhaps the
reasons for this fact lie in an unwarranted use in the past of speculative
reason, in the unbiblical character of some conclusions in systematic
studies, or in the hyper-sensitivity of some theologians because of previous
criticism. Whatever the reasons, they cannot stop systematic theology
from performing its important task. Hazelton observes that "most of
what goes under the name of biblical theology today consists of declarative or imperative statements. It abounds in flat assertions, take-it-or-
leave-it propositions, emphatic repetitions. One soon wearies of the very
style of such writing. Even more, one misses the inquiring, exploring
temper which belongs to genuine theological thought in our own or
any age" (*ibid.*, p. 69; cf. Gustav Weigel, *Catholic Theology in Dialogue,*
New York, Harper and Brothers, 1960, p. 39, for similar sentiment by a
Roman Catholic theologian). True theology, of course, is far more than
this. And it is not merely a "recital." Theology uses all the gifts which
God has entrusted to the theologian for interpreting revelation. Just
as every science must employ the powers of perception, imagination, and
reason to the full, so theology must be a daring enterprise that penetrates
new areas of experience and interprets and judges the whole of life in
the light of God's person and truth. This activity includes and must include what the Church calls systematic theology; those called to labor
in this field need offer no apologies for the existence or nature of their
special task. Convinced, rather, of its legitimacy and necessity, even
among other branches of theological science that also employ reason and
inference, consistency and schematic arrangement, systematic theologians
should prosecute their work with vigor in order to set forth meaningful
and revelant statements of the Christian faith. Who is better equipped
for this task than those who build on the achievements of exegetical,
biblical, and historical theology and, with this firm foundation, then
seek to understand comprehensively the faith of the Church?

Even as late as 1948 one observer felt that American theology was still
in its adolescence (David Wesley Soper, *Major Voices in American Theology*, Philadelphia, The Westminster Press, 1953, p. 11). Compared with
the maturity of some European theology that judgment would seem quite
proper. But there are hopeful signs of improvement. For one thing, there
is genuine and profound theological discussion; evidence thereof in
American religious and theological journals substantiates this fact, not
to mention the solid volumes on theological subjects that appear an-
nually. A high level of intra- and inter-confessional discussion among

several branches of the one body of Christ in the last few years has increased both understanding and fellowship. The fellowship program of the American Association of Theological Schools, in fact, is bound to give harried American professors of theology the needed relaxation for reflection and creative work. *The Study of Theological Education in the United States and Canada,* as well as other assistance given by the A.A.T.S. to theological education, has proved highly beneficial (see, for example, its first report, *The Purpose of the Church and Its Ministry,* by H. Richard Niebuhr in collaboration with Daniel Day Williams and James M. Gustafson, New York, Harper and Brothers, 1956). Leaders in the fundamentalist wing of American Christianity show a wholesome departure from preoccupation with isolated themes like the millennium, verbal inerrancy, and dispensationalism to concern with revelation in its fullness and its application to life. These are among the hopeful signs of an increasing and increased maturity in American theology.

Yet both Carl F. H. Henry at mid-century (*op. cit.,* p. 85) and currently Charles S. McCoy (*The Christian Century,* Vol. LXXIX, 28, July 11, 1962, pp. 859 ff.) charge America with "paucity of vital theology." Interpreting the acclaim given Karl Barth on his recent visit to America as a "self-indictment of our domestic theological endeavors," McCoy calls for a new program of honest theological reflection and action. After getting off to a good start in New England, American theology fell victim to rationalism, then revivalism, and finally to transcendentalism in the nineteenth century. During this same period Germany rose to intellectual and theological dominance, to which American theology has docilely succumbed ever since. Most American theological pursuit is either a popularized approach for preachers and thoughtful laymen, or a proliferation of Continental theological discussion. There is little creativity, little "wrestling in fresh ways with ultimate problems." In 1939-40 it seemed the two Niebuhrs would lead the way to an American theological renaissance, but developments since World War II have not supported this hope. The massive reception granted to Barth and the close attention given even to his casual comments "served to underscore in a painful way the deplorable condition of American theology."

James Daane likewise has pleaded repeatedly for fresh, courageous theological scholarship. Necessary are a frank acknowledgment of the present aridity, a new theological perceptiveness, and the "tolerance which comes with the recognition that the person who engages in theological pursuits into regions little known or as yet untrod has ... the right (not before God, but before man) to be wrong, to make mistakes." Writing from within a tightly orthodox tradition, he goes on to say, "If we continue to so judge each other as to give the impression that those engaged in theological studies cannot speak unless and until they have the whole truth and nothing but the truth, the lean years will return and with them silence and sterility" (*The Reformed Journal,* Vol. XI, 3, March, 1961, p. 10).

Are these spokesmen correct in their indictment of American theology? Are Henry and Daane justified in their censures of conservatism? Henry claims that "a half generation has passed by, and evangelicalism has not bought up the opportunity provided by the bankruptcy of liberalism. Another half generation of evangelical default might well result in evangelicalism's temporary reduction to a cult status" (*op. cit.,* p. 90). Daane charges that orthodox theology is sterile, only half-alive. Could McCoy possibly be misinterpreting America's adulation of Barth? Was Barth's acclaim really an open declaration of our theological inadequacy?

Even allowing for some measure of overstatement, these charges seem justified. American theology, in fact, has not been producing a signifi-cant number of high calibre theological works. Too much of what American students read in theology is translated from foreign, principally German, scholars. Too much American theological activity consists merely of reading and evaluating Continental theological discussion; too little time and effort are given to significant creative application. How-ever valid the post World War II prediction of W. F. Albright ("The War in Europe and the Future of Biblical Studies," in *The Study of the Bible Today and Tomorrow,* ed. by Harold R. Willoughby, Chicago, The Uni-versity of Chicago Press, 1947, pp. 162 f.) and others may prove to be, that Germany will lose its intellectual leadership, American theology in any case must demonstrate its vitality in literary output of greater quan-tity and better quality. Recognizing the different academic setting in Europe, where students work quite independently of their professors and where professors know little of such burdens as grading papers or spon-soring organizations, American theology must nevertheless increase its productivity. Not just some but all seminaries must acquit themselves as institutions of higher learning in the best terms of research and advanced study.

So far we have dealt only with Protestant theology. This is our area of major interest and training. Moreover, the limitations of this essay preclude any extensive analysis of the present situation in Roman Catholic theology. Even a cursory check of Roman Catholic theological and biblical journals and publication lists will indicate the vast demands of time and study required for such an undertaking. A few remarks must suffice to pinpoint the prodigious activity of scholars in this communion.

First of all we should note the intensity and variety of theological work in current Roman Catholicism. Much is astir in Rome itself and that not necessarily in Vatican City and its environs. And the Roman Catholic theological community in America is also heavily engaged in theological endeavors. The word *theological* should be underscored. For Roman Catholics in America have produced a great abundance of theo-

logical essays and reviews; of exegetical, historical, liturgical and philological studies; and of theological treatises on ethical and other questions.
Judging from such journals as *Theological Studies* (1940-   ) published
by the Theological Faculties of the Society of Jesus in the United States,
and *The Catholic Biblical Quarterly* (1939-   ), published by the
Catholic Biblical Association of America, both the quality and amount
of American Roman Catholic theological writing are noteworthy and
respectable.

Secondly, an important feature of contemporary Roman Catholic theological activity is its high degree of biblical emphasis. In his encyclical
Providentissimus Deus of 1893, Pope Leo XIII urged Roman Catholic
theologians to study the Scriptures. In 1915 appeared the *Revue Biblique,*
representing the best Roman Catholic scholarship of France, and *Biblica*
was published in 1920 by the Pontifical Biblical Institute in Rome. Both
journals have earned world renown. In 1943 Pius XII encouraged and
accelerated the gathering interest in biblical studies by issuing the encyclical *Divino afflante Spiritu.* Of its significance Gustave Weigel says,
"It has been called in Catholic circles the Magna Carta of scientific
exegesis within Catholicism. Not only is the explanation of Scripture
according to the rules of modern philosophy blessed, but an important key to the solution of the conflict between theological and philological exegesis is offered. It is the recognition of the existence of literary
genres in the Scriptures" (Gustave Weigel, *op. cit.,* p. 35). The development of biblical studies in Roman Catholic circles has multiplied rapidly since 1943 so that it represents one of the striking theological
phenomena of our times. Unlike those of an earlier period, present
Roman Catholic biblical studies parallel Protestant efforts in many
respects. Weigel, who with fellow-Jesuit John Courtney Murray represents the best theological leadership in American Romanism, states that
whether from his communion or from Protestantism, scholars today
follow the same procedures in their study of the Bible. Remembering
the history of liberal Protestantism and the shortcomings of his own
religious group with respect to biblical study, he notes, however, that
"this meeting of minds meant that both groups had to travel in different
directions in order to come to their present positions. The Protestants
moved from a leftist extreme, the Catholics from a rightist extreme, until
they are now close to each other in the middle" (*ibid.,* p. 31). To illustrate this mutuality Weigel indicates the following characteristics of
present-day Roman Catholic biblical study: (1) complete trust in scientific
philosophy; (2) interest in the Bible's unifying message; and (3) theological interpretation. Since historicism has been "overcome completely"
in Roman Catholic theological studies, it is still necessary, as in Protestantism, to guard against an exclusively philological exegesis. "If someone tells me," says Weigel, "that scientific exegesis—a question-begging

label—is the only instrument capable of giving me scriptural meaning, then I can only compare him to a scientist who tells me that anatomy and physiology are the only tools which lead to the understanding of man. There is an exegesis beyond philological science which is also needed. You can call it theological, mystical, allegorical, or spiritual. I prefer to call it simply ecclesiastical" (*ibid.,* p. 47 f.)

It is interesting that at a meeting of the Catholic Biblical Association of America in 1959 the proposal was made that Roman Catholics and Protestant biblical scholars collaborate in producing a modern version of the Bible to be used by everyone as the one Bible.

A third feature of special interest in Roman Catholic theology in America is the development of Mariolatry, a doctrine in keeping with the wider context of Roman Catholicism. The encyclicals of Pius IX and Pius XII on the immaculate conception of Mary and the assumption of her body and soul to heaven have encouraged a flood of further Mario-logical speculation. A recent congress discussed such topics as Mary's "Spiritual Maternity," her "Universal Mediation," her "Mediation in Acquisition of Graces: Objective Coredemption," and her "Mediation in the Distribution of Graces: Subjective Coredemption" (Cyril O. Vollert, S.J., S.T.D., Ph.D., "The Mariology of St. Lawrence of Brindisi," in *Saint Lawrence of Brindisi: Doctor of the Universal Church,* Washington, The Capuchin Press, 1961, pp. 62 ff.). Further dogmatic pronouncements con-cerning Mary are not unlikely. Pope John XXIII's eulogy of the *Mariale* of St. Lawrence of Brindisi, who in 1959 was declared to be the 31st doctor of the Universal Church ("Apostolic Letter of his Holiness Pope John XXIII by which St. Lawrence of Brindisi is Declared a Doctor of the Universal Church," *ibid.,* p. 23), and designation of the present period of the Church as the Marian age are but two more signs of the current force of Mariolatry. The Minister General of the Friars Minor of St. Francis, Capuchin, gives several reasons for calling the present age the Marian age: first, "because of the overwhelming trend toward Marian studies and the progress made therein, and the resultant growth in devo-tion to the Blessed Mother Mary; then, too, because of the definition of the dogma of her Assumption into heaven and the recent introduction of the feast of Mary, the Queen; then, too, because of her frequent apparitions in different parts of the world; then, too, because of the extraordinarily solemn observances of the 100th anniversary of the definition of the dogma of the Immaculate Conception (1954) and of the apparitions of Lourdes (1958)" (*ibid.,* p. 31). This increasing devia-tion from Scripture alongside the hopeful biblical movement in the Church of Rome points up the ambiguous character of this ecclesiastical fellowship and raises speculation about the nature of any possible theo-logical developments in the future.

A final characteristic of contemporary American Roman Catholic theology which we shall mention is its openness to conversation. What would have been declared impossible a generation ago is actually happening. There is dialogue and discussion between representatives of the two communions both here and in Europe in verbal conferences as well as through lectures, monographs, and symposia. Gustave Weigel's lectures at Yale (*op. cit.*) are but one of many instances of rapport and fraternal discussion. George H. Tavard's *The Catholic Approach to Protestantism* (New York, Harper & Brothers, 1955), written by a Frenchman but widely read in this country, and *An American Dialogue* (New York, Doubleday & Company, 1960) by Robert McAfee Brown and Gustave Weigel, are two other attempts to provide understanding. It is interesting that at the very time the Pope has been encouraging fraternal contact with Christian brethren outside the Roman fold, his Church in America has come of age, as it were. No longer considering itself a minority and an immigrant Church, the American hierarchy is willing to engage in theological conversation. The outcome of this interaction between Protestant and Roman Catholic theology should provide interesting material for future study.

IV. UNRESOLVED PROBLEMS

Among the problems to be met in American theology we mention only the two most basic ones. The first concerns the validity and legitimacy of theological reasoning. Ever since Kant, philosophy and theology have been aware of the limitations of the intellect. Kant had argued that the human mind is unable to penetrate beyond the phenomenal world. Since he did not accept the category of revelation as a part of his thought system, the end result of his work with respect to theology was skepticism. In order to save itself, theology must become philosophy, specifically, moral philosophy or ethics. Moreover, this ethics must be humanistic.

It was this negative kind of reasoning that dominated theological thought until the new emphasis on revelation in our time. The work of Kant was important, however, because theology and philosophy before him had engaged in an unwarranted use of speculative reason and had made unjustified claims concerning the powers of the mind. Kant's demonstration of the error of these claims proved that the foundation of theology could not be laid in natural reason; rather, theology must rest on a message miraculously given by God in history.

A major question today is the place of reason in understanding this message. What is reason's function in the theological enterprise? How valid is its work? How legitimate are its endeavors? Granted that no system of theology is infallible but that all are human constructs, how seriously are we to take the theological task, and how highly shall we esteem it? A prominent Anglican divine has said that " 'systematic theology' represents what is, perhaps, the most daring effort which the human mind has ever made, namely, the attempt to arrive at as near an approximation to absolute truth concerning ultimate reality as the human mind is capable of attaining" (N. P. Williams, "What Is Theology?" in *The Study of Theology,* ed. by Kenneth E. Kirk, London, Hodder and Stoughton, 1939, pp. 13 f.). Some thinkers would discount this comment as something quasi-Thomistic. Dare we dispose of the matter so easily? Here we have not only systematic theology but the entire theological enterprise as well; meaningful statement about God and divine things is at stake. That there is embarrassment and confusion at this point is apparent in both philosophy and theology. In the former, for example, the school of linguistic analysis or logical empiricism (now one of the leading schools of thought) eschews all metaphysics, and claims that propositions are meaningful only when they are tautologies, that is, *a priori* true, or where they can be verified by sense experience (Vide Alfred Jules Ayer, *Language, Truth and Logic,* London, Victor Gollancz, 1958; and Antony Flew and Alasdair Macintyre, eds., *New Essays in Philosophical Theology,* London, SCM Press, 1955). The work of Tillich in America and Bultmann in Europe, although differing widely in detail, appears to many to be prejudicial to theology inasmuch as it seems to them to deny the reality of theological knowledge and of propositional truth. Hermann Diem tries to show Bultmann's virtual destruction of theology (Hermann Diem, *Dogmatics,* trans. by Harold Knight, Philadelphia, The Westminster Press, 1959, pp. 63-81), and indicates the theological problem of our day to be the validity and legitimacy of theological reasoning. Diem is so wary of the use of reason, however, that he leaves almost no room for systematic theology (*ibid.,* pp. 303 ff., p. 310). This example of an outstanding Continental theologian who sells theology short has its parallel in American biblical theologians and others who relegate theology to mere recital of the great deeds of God. If theology is no more than this, its significance among the sciences will diminish and systematic theology will disappear altogether except as a kind of object for study among church historians.

Roman Catholic theology does not face the same problem at this point. Its Thomistic philosophical background allows natural reason, inasmuch as it has not been depraved by sin, to develop a system of metaphysics and to stand in the service of theology. Because evangelical theology believes in man's total depravity including that of his mind, it has no such confidence in the capabilities or alleged attainments of reason. Evangelical thought finds its only source and criterion of truth in the revelation spoken through prophets and apostles, and in the Word Himself. But if theologizing is to begin, reason must do its work. This occurs as reason, enlightened by the Holy Spirit, apprehends the truth of God and sets it down in meaningful patterns of thought. These patterns are fallible, however, and relative to the word. This is the problem. There was a time when thinkers gave serious study to the place, function, and limits of reason in theological endeavor. More needs to be done today in this present "post-liberal, post-idealist, atomic age in theology" (Flew and Macintyre, *op. cit.*, p. v.).

The second basic problem in contemporary theology concerns the nature of the Bible as a revelation from God. Because of its implications this issue will always prompt considerable discussion. The question is: does revelation consist of event only to which Scripture adds human interpretation as the response of faith, or does revelation include both the event *and* its interpretation? Elaboration on this "popular" item of discussion is hardly necessary. The fact is that revelation consists of both event and interpretation. The cliché that revelation consists not of statements about God but of God's self-giving in His saving deeds sounds new and exciting to a first-year seminarian, especially if he comes from an orthodox background. Being only a half-truth, however, the statement falsifies the right position. Revelation is both word and deed, both event and interpretation. Propositional truth is not all but certainly a part of God's revelation. Commenting on the current tendency to limit revelation to event, Hazelton remarks that "this whole way of speaking about revelation has indeed become so much a part of theological discussion that it is hard for us to see what a foreshortened and truncated view of God's Word it often presupposes. Yet already this is growing clearer, and one may safely predict that in the near theological future some conceptions which are so dominant will seem peculiarly dated and unfruitful. . . . Revelation is not a bare act, and Christ is not a sheer event. In God's Word there is meaningful pattern and structure to be detected and pondered by the mind of man, which is made by God for saving knowledge of himself" (Hazelton, *op. cit.*, pp. 74 ff.)

Neo-orthodoxy, whatever its good features may be, needs to come to a better position on Scripture. Its emphasis on human sinfulness, on the shallowness of man's pretensions, on his inability to achieve the good life in his own strength, is commendable. Its insistence that only by revelation shall man ever come to know God; its witness to the sovereignty of God and His saving grace; its demand that all human thought be submitted to the judgment of the Word of God, and its interest in biblical theology, are wholesome features of this movement. Noteworthy, too, are its realistic approach to social betterment and its appreciation as well for the fact of the kingdom of God and its fulfillment beyond history. Every tradition has its weaknesses, however, neo-orthodoxy included. Its particular need in the area of revelation and Scripture must be met if the main stream of contemporary American theology is to progress properly beyond the present dimensions. The doctrine of Scripture is inescapably and uncompromisingly important in this regard.

THE NATURE OF GOD

†

Carl F. H. Henry

Carl F. H. Henry is Editor of the Protestant fortnightly "Christianity Today." He has held the chair of Philosophy of Religion at Northern Baptist Theological Seminary and of Theology and Christian Philosophy at Fuller Theological Seminary. Author of many books, including Remaking the Modern Mind, The Drift of Western Thought, *and* Christian Personal Ethics, *he is also editor of the Contemporary Evangelical Thought series in which this volume is the fourth. He holds the Th.D. degree from Northern Baptist Seminary and the Ph.D. from Boston University.*

4. *Carl F. H. Henry*

THE NATURE OF GOD

To CONSIDER our own time as simply another addition to a long chronology of theological debate is an inadequate evaluation. The present age is not just another extension to the ranchhouse of ideas that spreads and sprawls from early and later Scholasticism to the Renaissance to the Reformation to early modern philosophy to post-Hegelian irrationalism and onward—to whatever peculiar perspective defines the problem of God in our own decade.

Two factors disqualify any such appraisal as an oversimplification. For one thing, our space-time world has become one vast amphitheater where all divergent views of God confront each other in debate more directly and insistently than ever before. Today the God of the Bible is ranged in fresh battle against the ancient gods of resurgent Oriental religions, against the modern gods of Occidental cults, against the speculative gods of liberal theologians, against the rational constructs of contemporary philosophers, and even against contenders supplied by some who claim to revive an authentic theology of divine encounter. Moreover, all theological conflicts now move in to strike the bedrock of discussion concerning the essence and existence of the Living God, even asking whether the emerging future has room for any God at all as a central philosophical theme. Consequently the main extant concepts of God inevitably resurrect many theological and philosophical discussions of the past and reconstruct them to current consideration. Not least among these restored options are some which subjective bias hurriedly and prejudicially disparaged or ignored as mere driftwood on the moving stream of contemporary thought. This widespread theological controversy demands some measure of familiarity with man's many years of theologizing and philosophizing about God, for all previous traditions now seem to be converging for one mighty, final struggle-to-the-death.

To "wall in" and to isolate for limited scrutiny some of the special problems of our period remains nonetheless a proper and necessary task. In these days the problem of God revolves mainly around the dispute over divine transcendence and immanence, a dispute, in fact, which touches on almost every crucial concern of traditional theology. This essay assesses the problem of God in recent religious thought by bringing the debate over divine transcendence into sharp focus.

I. DIVINE TRANSCENDENCE IN BIBLICAL THEOLOGY

Scriptural revelation is remarkably explicit and insistent about the transcendence of God. From its very first pages in Genesis the Bible affirms God's cosmic transcendence (Gen. 1:1), God's moral transcendence (Gen. 2:16 f., 3:11 f., 6:5 f.), and God's noetic transcendence (Gen. 2:17, 3:22). In the context of biblical theology as a whole, the transcendent God is distinguished from the world and from man as the Sovereign Creator of all things; as the Righteous Giver of the Moral Law and Redeemer of fallen and sinful men; as the Truth and Revealer of Himself and of His purposes. In summary: in His essential nature, God is prior to the universe and is exalted above it in His ontological, ethical, and epistemological perfections. He has His real being apart from man and the world, and is the ultimate source and ground of all finite existence, morality and truth.

It is noteworthy that the Bible insists on the fact that the transcendent God reveals Himself in divine truths and precepts disclosed to finite and fallen man. Despite man's spiritual and moral revolt, therefore, the scriptural view of God is "metaphysically affirmative." While man's spiritual estrangement complicates his predicament as a finite knower, yet through divine disclosure in nature and in conscience, and particularly through the remedial revelation which the Bible addresses to him as sinner, man is qualified to define God's nature. The Scriptures contain divinely revealed propositions or truths concerning the character and will of the Living God. The Bible's teaching is not reducible to affirmations about or inferences from man's experience or encounter with God; it asserts something specific about the very being of God.

The liberal theology of the nineteenth and early twentieth centuries revolted increasingly against this scriptural comprehension of God, which Protestantism had championed since the Reformation on the basis of the Bible's unique authority. Affirmed by influential evangelical expositors even into the forepart of our century, the biblical view had remained for most churchgoers the formative framework of their religious thought and life. But more and more the warnings of evangelicals against liberal inroads were ignored and then demeaned, so that denial of the historic Christian view of divine transcendence was already in full force at the turn of the twentieth century.

Critical of the liberal Protestant compromise of transcendence in those early decades were such Continental scholars as August F. C. Vilmar and Wilhelm Loehe, confessional Lutherans; Friedrich August Tholuck, Johann Tobias Beck, Hermann Cremer, Martin Kaehler and Adolf Schlatter. In the Netherlands, Abraham Kuyper and Herman Bavink strongly criticized immanentism, in Scotland, James Orr, and in England, P. T. Forsyth. In America men like William G. T. Shedd, Charles Hodge, F. L. Patton and J. Gresham Machen among Presbyterians; F. Pieper among Lutherans; E. Y. Mullins and with some qualifications Augustus H. Strong among Baptists deplored the liberal rescension. In more recent decades the cause of biblical transcendence is supported by such writers as G. C. Berkouwer, Gordon H. Clark, Cornelius Van Til, Carl F. H. Henry, Edward John Carnell and Bernard Ramm. In opposing the exaggerated immanental tendencies of the times, evangelical scholars have insisted in a variety of ways that God is the unique and irreducible Other, the unconditional Ought, the transcendent Self. For the most part, however, they used biblical rather than secular concepts and language to expound divine transcendence.

But so rapidly was the historic evangelical view erased in the formative intellectual centers of the Western world that the early part of the twentieth century came to be characterized as "the age of immanence." Within a few swift decades the theological atmosphere was pervaded by emphasis on God as the immanent "ground" of all being, as the unity and totality of finite things, and as a universal essence which all existence shares. Defeat and destruction in World War I deflated Europe's optimism, and formally ended the philosophical reign of radical divine immanence on the Continent. America's favorable outcome in the war, however, merely accelerated confidence in evolutionary progress. So while the German perspective experienced a post-war reaction against immanence, the American religious temperament yielded in the twenties and thirties to an emerging humanism that finally dared to identify God with human values. Through Edward Scribner Ames and other religious philosophers of the University of Chicago Divinity School this view gained widening influence in Protestant circles.

II. INTENSIFIED IMMANENCE IN MODERN PHILOSOPHY

Behind this recent theological exaggeration of divine immanence and suppression of transcendence lay a long chain of speculative influences. The medieval scholastics had already set in motion the tendency now carried forward by modern philosophy. Thomas Aquinas' derivation of the existence of God, and the existence and immortality of the soul from the contingency of being and thus from natural theology inaugurated an ever-growing reliance on the competence of empirical investigation of God. Man's need of divine disclosure, and particularly of an authoritative prophetic-apostolic revelation in view of his finiteness and sinfulness, lost its philosophical significance. A Roman Catholic like Aquinas, Descartes gave direction to the modern era of philosophy by resting the case for theism wholly on speculative grounds. Thus was nullified the necessity and propriety of transcendent divine revelation.

Although the early rationalists—Descartes and Spinoza—are "metaphysically affirmative," their speculative exposition of God's essence deviated more and more from the biblical-revelational concept of God. The transition from Descartes' theism to Spinoza's pantheism involved the loss of God's transcendence and uncertainty about God's attributes. (Spinoza identifies only divine thought and extension.)

Alongside these rationalistic delineations of ultimate reality appeared the empirical expositions of Locke, Berkeley and Hume. Locke's speculative theism led on not to pantheism, but to agnosticism concerning the divine attributes and even the divine being. God's transcendence is no longer defined by specific perfections that distinguish him from nature and man.

The great modern philosophers of synthesis sought to correlate these rival traditions of rationalism and empiricism. The way Kant and Hegel relate human reason to the supernatural now becomes decisive for the problem of divine transcendence. Kant's critical philosophy preserves a Transcendent though denying that man is rationally competent to make universally valid metaphysical judgments and reducing God to a regulative ideal. Hegel's dialectical philosophy, on the other hand, preserves the metaphysical competence of reason by denying the Absolute's transcendence and by viewing human reason as an aspect of divine consciousness. Through an emphasis on divine immanence merged into the gradual development of Hegelian pantheism and Darwinian evolutionism, divine transcendence soon wastes away to a mere vestigial remnant of theological thought. Hegel's philosophy reduces the ontological, epistemological and moral transcendence of the Absolute simply to the all-inclusiveness of the whole in contrast to its parts.

Liberal Protestant adaptations of Kant and Hegel spurred the theological revolt against the biblical view of divine transcendence. While their philosophies of religion influenced separate traditions of nineteenth-century thought, the net result in each case was a deviation from scriptural theology. Post-Kantians sought to vindicate knowledge merely of God-in-relation-to-us, and disowned knowledge of God-in-Himself. They deplored biblically-revealed knowledge of the transcendent God as incompatible with the natural limitations of human reason. Post-Hegelians

promoted rational knowledge of God's essence, but assailed any divine
independence of man and the world. On the premise of radical divine
immanence they excluded any biblically-revealed or special knowledge of
God as superfluous, if not indeed as impossible. By espousing the evolutionary theory of reality both groups progressively nullified divine cosmic
transcendence; moral transcendence they explained by man's finiteness
and (fast fading) animal inheritance; epistemological transcendence, by
his (swiftly vanishing) ignorance.

Personalists like Hermann Lotze and Borden P. Bowne championed
God's ontic transcendence by insisting that finite selves are creations
other than God; nevertheless, they viewed nature as part of God, and
dissolved the need for special divine revelation of truths and moral
precepts. In the current of modern philosophies of religion shaped by
Lotze as well as by Kant and Hegel, therefore, divine revelation became
synonymous with human insight and discovery.

III. THE MODERNIST THEOLOGY OF IMMANENCE

The basic nature of theological trends in the late nineteenth and early
twentieth centuries results from a tapering of scriptural doctrines to such
projections of intensified divine immanence. Liberal Protestantism tried
to supply new foundations of religious faith by the rejection in varying
degrees of divine transcendence—not only cosmological, epistemological
and ethical but in many instances even ontological transcendence. Not
content simply to protest against deism, nor against abstract transcendental theories that discounted the revelation of God in nature and
history, this emphasis emerged as a theological bias that promoted both
metaphysical and epistemological monism, and countered divine personality as well as divine transcendence.

Continental theology influenced Protestant learning on both sides of
the Atlantic. Particularly through the teaching and writings of the
German scholars—first Friedrich Schleiermacher (1768-1834), then Albrecht Ritschl (1822-1889) and Ernst Troeltsch (1865-1923)—philosophical
immanentism invaded the theological centers of the Continent, of Great
Britain and of the United States. Often called "the father of Protestant
modernism," Schleiermacher denied that "the true essence of religion"
is to be found in "the usual conception of God as a single being outside ...
and behind the world," and located that essence, rather, in "the immediate consciousness of Deity as we find him in ourselves as well as in
the world" (Schleiermacher's *Speeches*, quoted by A. C. McGiffert, "Immanence," Hastings' *Encyclopedia of Religion and Ethics*, Vol. VII).

In *Theology at the Dawn of the Twentieth Century*, J. Vrynwy
Morgan could remark that "belief in an Immanent Divine Will ...
has practically revolutionized the theology of our fathers" (Boston:

Small, Maynard & Co., 1901, p. xiii). Elsewhere we have traced the remarkable momentum of the theology of radical immanence (Carl F. H. Henry, *Fifty Years of Protestant Theology*, Boston, W. A. Wilde Company, 1950), that swept even such evangelical theologians as A. H. Strong into costly compromise (cf. Carl F. H. Henry, *Strong's Theology and Personal Idealism*, Wheaton, Ill., Van Kampen Press, 1951). Despite the growing rivalry between absolute idealism and personalism, immanence remained the dominant temper of Anglo-Saxon theology and philosophy of religion through the first third of the twentieth century. Those scholars asserting cosmological immanence now identified God's being with part or all of nature, and those asserting epistemological immanence now regarded man's thoughts and ideals as identical with God's.

IV. THE RECENT REASSERTION OF TRANSCENDENCE

How a theologian conceives of God's epistemological transcendence actually influences and controls his pronouncements about all other aspects of divine transcendence, namely, ontological, cosmological and moral. This follows, of course, from the fact that the character of religious *knowledge* governs all one's affirmations about the supernatural. Earlier Protestant theology had affirmed that the Creator and Redeemer and Judge of all the earth has disclosed Himself—including the nature of His transcendence and immanence—in rational truths communicated to sacred writers. Treasuring the Scriptures as a revelation of God, historic Protestantism insisted that the prophetic-apostolic teaching recorded in the Bible communicates authoritative information about God's ontological and moral and epistemological transcendence as well. Despite God's epistemological transcendence, He specially fashioned man for reasonable knowledge and service of his Maker. Even before the Fall the Creator already revealed Himself intelligibly to Adam as the transcendent Lord of all things. After the Fall, moreover, He mercifully revealed Himself in deed and in word to be also the transcendent Judge and Redeemer.

This volume elsewhere notes on what speculative biases the theology of the recent past repudiates the actuality and even possibility of such rational divine revelation of the living God. It is important to recognize that by rejecting and excluding divinely revealed truths (about God and His purposes) this anti-intellectual theology forfeits any claim to divine revelation for any propositions concerning divine transcendence or immanence. Yet the forces of liberal discontent and reaction, more than the forces of conservative theology, demanded a reconsideration of divine transcendence. The dominant temper of grass roots Protestantism among both clergy and laity remained theologically conservative and committed in principle to biblical transcendence, but the evangelical movement did not make headway against the modernist dogma of extreme immanence.

Spurred by an uneasy conscience over the cultural unrelatedness of immanentism, and aided by the widening ecumenical dialogue, revolting neo-
liberal champions of transcendence gained the propaganda initiative
and limelight with their criticism of the modernist doctrine. After the
politico-economic stresses of 1929, American liberals expressed more and
more doubts over God's direct continuity with human experience, reason
and values. The cultural irrelevance of the optimistic doctrine of immanence encouraged the rise of various movements that clamored for theological "realism" and disputed the liberal-humanist tendency to dissolve
God's independence of the world. This so-called realistic movement included critics like Walter Marshall Horton, Robert Calhoun, and Reinhold Niebuhr.

Meanwhile America was beginning to learn of the sharp critique of
liberal immanence shaped by the so-called neo-orthodox "theology of
crisis" of Karl Barth and Emil Brunner on the Continent. Behind their
vigorous demand for the reassertion of God's transcendence stood Søren
Kierkegaard's existentialist reaction against Hegelian pantheism. Simultaneous with the growing Continental revolt against metaphysical
immanence was a waning confidence in the ontological significance of
reason. The importance of this development cannot be minimized. Now
the anti-Hegelian assertion of the metaphysical and epistemological
transcendence of God came to mean not simply that God is *other* than
man, but that He is so *wholly other* that He is unknowable through
the categories of human reason.

Many writers besides Kierkegaard whittled the role of reason in religious experience. The *Unvordenkliche* of Schelling's last period, marked
by a refusal to identify God and existence in rational systems and verbal
statements, lies in the background of Tillich's *Das Unbedingte* (the Unconditioned). Metaphysical philosophers like Henri Bergson wrote of an
élan vital more fundamental than life's rational structures; scientists
suspected that arbitrariness, perhaps ultimate chance, lurked behind their
neat schematizations of the laws of nature. Expressionist artists revolted
against a precisely ordered world and reflected a realm of ultimate un-
pattern. Theologians sought the Transcendent with a new awareness of
the irrationalities of human history, and religious philosophers like
Rudolf Otto stressed the place of awe in religious experience.

The importance, therefore, should not be missed of Brunner's observation that Crisis theology is more concerned with epistemological than
with cosmological transcendence. Its critique of modernist immanence
was aimed particularly at the Hegelian dogma that man's consciousness
is directly continuous with God's consciousness. It strikes with fullest
force against the emphasis on epistemological immanence which characterizes rationalistic philosophies that assert man's self-sufficient capacity
to know God. But Crisis theology does not stop there. Kierkegaard's

demand for a "leap of faith," together with the assertion that God is experienced in existential decision rather than grasped by ideas or comprehended in a rational system, became a primary tenet of neo-orthodox theologians. They altered Luther's emphasis on "the hidden and revealed God" to mean not simply that man knows God only when and as God gives Himself to us, but that He spiritually encounters and confronts man in non-intellectual experiences of revelation.

The existential emphasis on the priority of existence over essence, moreover, ruled out any attempts to probe *behind* the Transcendent's revealing activity (behind its existence *for us*) back to the Transcendent's inherent essence (its existence in itself). While the theology of the recent past expounded a rational view of God in the context of the revelatory event, it insisted that divine disclosure is non-intellectual. Contemporary religious thought frequently defines "revelation" as non-propositional, and discounts the rational exposition of God's essential being as speculative or philosophical. In his volume on *The Transcendence of God* (Philadelphia, The Westminster Press, 1958), Edward Farley surveys the efforts of Paul Tillich, Reinhold Niebuhr, and Karl Heim to relate God as "the transcendent one who is given in the Word made flesh, and the metaphysical *Ens realissimum*," or, as Pascal put it, to relate the God of Abraham, Isaac, and Jacob and the God of the philosophers (p 41). Farley contrasts the "kerygmatic transcendence" of the *dialectical* theologians—attested primarily in terms of the biblical *kerygma* and known presumably in response to the Word—with the metaphysical transcendence of the philosophers. Seldom do recent dialectical discussions acknowledge the fact that historic Christianity never thus drew the line between kerygmatic and metaphysical transcendence. Instead, in contrast to speculative expositions based on philosophical postulation, it expounded metaphysical transcendence on the basis of rational inscripturated revelation. It identified kerygma with what the Bible teaches. But the present contrasting of kerygmatic and metaphysical transcendence presupposes an anti-intellectualistic theory of divine revelation peculiar to the theology of the recent past.

The strictures against metaphysical formulations are commendable insofar as they insist that man has no natural access to God on the basis of finite reason apart from divine revelation, and insofar as they emphasize that secular philosophy (metaphysics as a speculative discipline) does not really expound the nature of the God of biblical disclosure. But many neo-orthodox writers not only deny that man arrives at the content of revelation by speculative methods but also deplore as objectionably "metaphysical" any affirmation about God's inherent nature (even when made on the basis of divine revelation) if this implies a cognitive relationship between God and man. The argument is pressed that if the theologian at any point makes a statement about God identical with what God knows about Himself, such predication implies an identity of man's mind with God's mind and hence subverts the Christian doctrines of man's creatureliness and sinfulness. But such a protest rests actually on non-biblical formulations of man's predicament as a knower, and its logical outcome is skepticism. Although neo-orthodox theologians assert the fact of knowledge of God's being, they usually insist that rational, propositional or verbal formulation is but a fallible human inference from a content of divine revelation defined to be nonpropositional, and deny that divine revelation occurs in the mode of rational propositions. They contend that God's free transcendence precludes rational revelation of His transcendence. But rational revelation offers the only solid alternative to speculative metaphysics, while the attack on metaphysical transcendence launched from the side of non-rational revelation actually dissolves as well the intelligibility of kerygmatic transcendence. No claim to infallibility of evangelical theologians is required to score the important difference between their acceptance of the divinely inspired biblical propositions as expounding the nature of God, and the contrary emphasis that man's sinfulness so affects his will to knowledge that no theological formulations whatever of God's being may be honored as authoritatively definitive.

Among those who hold irregular views of divine disclosure, some theologians—seeking to vindicate valid knowledge of the transcendent God—now appeal to metaphysical considerations ("general revelation") as well as to special "revelational" (dialectical-existential) data. Once this step is taken, several problems rise in regard to divine transcendence: (1) What is the relation of "revelational" transcendence to "philosophical" transcendence? (2) If the latter is to be formulated not in symbolical but in rational terms, does it therefore involve a claim to universally valid truth about God? (3) If rational apprehension of God is possible through speculation, can rational content really be excluded from divine revelation and its human comprehension?

In a word, to exclude rational categories from the kind of "epistemological" transcendence the dialectical theologians insist upon leaves them no real basis for speaking about the transcendent nature of God. In *God Transcendent* (London, James Nisbet and Co., Ltd, 1935), Karl Heim rightly stresses that this controversy over transcendence incorporates all the main features of today's cultural and metaphysical crises. Farley concedes that the inability of contemporary theology to connect epistemological (kerygmatic) and metaphysical expositions has created "more or less of an impasse" in respect to divine transcendence. While a fuller exposition of details of the views of influential contemporary religious writers will be found in Farley's treatise, the following salient emphases summarized from his *The Transcendence of God* and supplemented by additional observations pointedly attest the dilemma that besets recent representations of the nature of God.

Niebuhr on Divine Transcendence

In his approach to divine transcendence, Reinhold Niebuhr first of all describes the transcendent aspect of human nature. Man's transcendence, he says, consists negatively in his freedom from external determining necessities and over internal determinate structures. Man's transcendence is demonstrated positively by his consciousness of external structures and of his own self (in the activity of self-transcendence). Niebuhr then declares the self's uniqueness and mysteriousness to be beyond scientific comprehension and beyond conceptual grasp. Man's transcendence resides in aspects of existence that, assertedly, can be comprehended only in mythic and symbolic (rather than conceptual) terms.

God's transcendence likewise is that of a self whose freedom, says Niebuhr, cannot be reduced to structure. While the human self is free in relation to the structures of nature, God is a free personal self in relation not only to these, but also to all created structures. He transcends the structures of all other selves as well as of nature and of history. Since the biblical prophets depict God as transcendent will, Niebuhr insists on the analogy of personality. This representation "connotes precisely that freedom on the one hand and that relation to organic process on the other which prophetic and Christian faith assumes in understanding God's transcendence over, and His immanent relation to the world" (*The Nature and Destiny of Man,* Vol. II, p. 66, New York, Charles Scribner's Sons, 1943). God's freedom differs profoundly from man's, however. God's is infinite, man's finite; man's is corrupted, God's uncorrupt. Niebuhr develops God's transcendence in such a way that no aspect of His being or consciousness rests on more elemental forms of existence, as required by evolutionary theories. For Niebuhr, God has an element of mystery precisely because He is a Self; in God's own Selfhood exist mysterious hidden depths that are only partially communicable. As a consequence, reality cannot be fully comprehended by reason. God therefore stands in dialogic relation to man. In passing we may note that—whether Niebuhr's premises are true or false—his "therefore" does not hold, and that "dialogic" lacks intelligible significance.

Because God's freedom combines perfect power and perfect goodness, God confronts man as Judge and Redeemer. His free judgment and redemptive mercy are central manifestations of His moral transcendence. For Niebuhr, God's mercy discloses His transcendence more tellingly than do His deeds of creation or judgment. It is the Cross that exhibits God's freedom to forgive; redemptive suffering is what most profoundly symbolizes God's transcendent freedom in relation to other selves.

Niebuhr's verdict on metaphysical transcendence is ambiguous. He rejects creation *ex nihilo* in the usual chronological understanding. At times his emphasis on an intrinsic and organic relation between God and the universe approaches that of A. N. Whitehead and Charles Hartshorne. Despite Niebuhr's stress on the contingency of the world, his critics remain unsure whether Niebuhr considers the Divine Self to be ontologically independent of the creation (cf. Theodore Minnema, *The Social Ethics of Reinhold Niebuhr: A Structural Analysis,* Grand Rapids, William B. Eerdmans Publishing Company, 1958, pp. 107, 113).

Niebuhr's attitude toward ontology is equally ambiguous. On the one hand he deplores all ontology as blunting the kerygma. The Greek philosophers distort God's nature as impassable Being, a misconception which later speculative philosophers and theologians also repeat if in other ways. Yet Niebuhr argues that without ontology biblical faith and the kerygma lean toward obscurantism. He concedes that ontological presuppositions are implicit in the biblical drama. Theology must show, he says, "how what is implied about the nature of God, man, and history is related to what may be known about man, history, and reality through all the disciplines of culture" (C. W. Kegley and R. W. Bretall, eds., *The Theology of Paul Tillich,* New York, The Macmillan Company, 1952, p. 217). Niebuhr feels impelled to bring revelation into conformity with "the truth which may be known by analyzing the structures and essences of reality at all levels" (*The Self and the Dramas of History,* New York, Charles Scribner's Sons, 1955, p. 94).

Edward Farley is right in discerning that Niebuhr "unfortunately . . . never elaborates exactly" what it is that relates kerygmatic transcendence and the truth of ontology, nor how their unity is to be maintained. Sometimes Niebuhr appeals to respect for order and meaning; other times he stresses the mystery and meaning that lie beyond coherence. Since the biblical drama assertedly in mythic, philosophical ontology supposedly provides coherence in those logical affirmations that are ventured apart from the kerygma. Niebuhr therefore pursues the ontological analysis of four "fields of being": individuality (man), meaning, history and nature. These levels are hierarchically arranged with nature at the bottom and individuality at the top. The problem posed by each of these fields may be solved by the Christian faith in a transcendent God. The unique individual, states Niebuhr, "finds the contingent and arbitrary aspect of his existence tolerable because it is related to, judged, and redeemed by the eternal God, who transcends both the rational structure and the arbitrary facts of the universe" (*Nature and Destiny,* Vol. I, p. 86). When man is threatened by the finite order, the transcendent God supplies personal security. It is His self-disclosure culminating in the decisive event of the Cross of Jesus Christ that provides a clue to the meaning of nature-history as a whole. The transcendent God has established a norm in history ("original righteousness"); in Christ He discloses that the content of that norm is sacrificial love. As transcendent source God explains the derivedness and goodness of the universe, and as transcendent ground and goal God nourishes man's hope that all threats to destroy him (including death) will fail.

Different levels of transcendence, therefore, constitute Niebuhr's resultant world-picture. In this respect, notes Farley, it is not unlike that of some contemporary naturalistic scholars (*op. cit.*, p. 65). But from the absence of an immanent self-explanation of these levels Niebuhr deduces the fact of an ultimate source and ground of nature and existence. In contrast to ontological constructions, Niebuhr professes to derive the special content of this ultimate from the biblical representations of a personal Creator God. In Niebuhr's exposition of the kerygma, God is a free self who in the present confronts all natural structures, processes and finite selves. In Niebuhr's ontological reflections, however, God is their transcendent source and ground. Niebuhr joins the two by emphasizing that God as personal Creator is the content of this transcendent ground.

Yet Niebuhr regards the biblical view of creation as mythical and not as a revealed rational explanation of the universe's absolute temporal beginning by efficient divine causation. He refuses to say there was or was not a time when God did not create. But he prizes the mythic affirmation of God's freedom and self-sufficiency, and of the world's dependency and insufficiency.

Niebuhr's world-picture, then, correlates biblical representations (taken as mythical affirmations and not literal rational truths) and compatible ontological speculations. In keeping with the recent modern approach, his exposition of divine transcendence is not intended to imply a coherent, rational world view. Transcendence is considered a Hebrew myth, whose translation into rational categories is said to falsify the actualities. Mythically apprehended, or symbolically expressed, transcendence is said to find its basic meaning in selfhood, whether human or divine.

Tillich on Divine Transcendence

Paul Tillich's formulation of transcendence primarily concerns the decisions and depths of human experience. Farley notes that even Tillich's early writings do not set "the transcendent element ... explicitly in the context of the metaphysical problem of the relation between God and the world. Immanence does not mean a doctrine of God-in-the-world, nor does transcendence refer to God-out-of-the-world" (*The Transcendence of God,* p. 80).

Over against the immanentist movements Tillich gives new prominence to the irrational transcendent vitalities he ascribes to the creative depth of things. To reduce the divine to transparent rational clarity is but to lose "inexhaustible, self-manifesting, unconditional, and transcendent" divine depth (*The Interpretation of History*, New York, Charles Scribner's Sons, 1936, p. 108). Even the attempt of supernaturalism to comprehend God's relation to the world literally, in the categories of human reason, is disparaged as actually dissolving divine transcendence. To apply language non-symbolically to God is said to yield not the transcendent Unconditioned but "a God who *exists* as *a* being, *above* the world" (cf. Farley, *op. cit.*, p. 77). The Unconditioned is not only the support and underlying ground of finitude but also its judge. The Unconditioned precedes and grounds all temporal categories and polarities, but cannot itself be absorbed into them. We cannot apply our predications to the Unconditioned, since it is the universal, all-pervading prius of thought and life.

Tillich develops his transcendental symbols into a philosophical "systematic theology" whose ontological outlines require a radical revision of historic Christian doctrine. Farley thinks the term "hypertheism," used by John Laird of any deity "beyond" the God of ordinary theism, best fits the Tillichian exposition of the Unconditioned.

For Tillich ontology is the systematic embellishment of man's native curiosity and existential involvement and is based in human nature. Ontology arises whenever man tries to answer the question: "What does it mean to *be?*" The self's interaction with the world is Tillich's starting-point, and he considers the subject-object polarity the basic structure of existence. The meaning of "to be is found only within this subject-object polarity," a structure which assertedly conditions all life and language. No language, not even symbols, can directly denote anything outside of this structure, the supernatural realm included. Hence God cannot literally be said to "exist" or to be "personal" since for Tillich existence and personality refer only to entities or processes involved in this subject-object polarity. Finitude is ascribed to all being and knowledge.

Man's "ontological anxiety" is provoked by the prospect of death. Man is driven to ask: "Why is there something; why not nothing?" Anyone who asks this question, Tillich says, "has experienced the shock of non-being and has in thought transcended everything given in nature and mankind" (*Biblical Religion and the Search for Ultimate Reality*, Chicago, University of Chicago Press, 1955, p. 49). Ontology, therefore, is more than simply a search for the texture or structures of reality; it includes the unifying search for the characteristics of "being-itself." This question *why* (whereby ontology parallels the religious quest) reaches for something above the subjective-objective polarity. Hence its content "cannot be expressed literally in terms taken from the subjective or objective side. Ontology speaks analogously" (*The Courage to Be*, New Haven, Yale

University Press, 1952, p. 25). The Ultimate then cannot be delineated in direct or literal terms.

The answer to "why not nothing?" lies in "being-itself," which is the ground of the polarities and also the source of finitude. Non-being threatens all finite being; no particular truth is absolute. According to Tillich, even the biblical affirmation of the transcendent God must bow to "being-itself" as the only nonsymbolic, literal representation of the Ultimate. The only nonsymbolic element in our image of God is the characterization of God as "ultimate reality, being itself, ground of being, power of being" ("Religious Symbols and Our Knowledge of God," in *The Christian Scholar*, Sept., 1955, p. 93). Only "being-itself," unsubject to the world of polarities and finitude, is unmythologized, since symbol and myth are concrete pictures drawn from the subject-object world.

Tillich seeks to relate his Unconditioned to the God of traditional Christian religion. The transcendence of the Ultimate is the eternal dynamic power which perpetually overcomes the threat of nonbeing. The Unconditioned is not only abysmal but, we are told, as dynamic (the power of being) it is also creative and self-manifesting as the ground of being through encounter with ecstatic reason. The Eternal or Unconditioned is not a static substratum of reality, but instead "invades" our history at decisive points *(Kairoi)*. This revelation is mediated only through symbolic ideas. The traditional notion of "God," then, is a symbolic religious expression for the nonsymbolic Unconditioned. In Tillich's view God is only symbolically personal; God continually "becomes a person" in His relatedness to us, that is, in our symbolic representations of Him. God simply cannot be grasped by our categories of thought. When Tillich asserts that "being-itself" is transcendent, is love, mercy, judgment, and so forth, he is symbolically showing how the structures of existence are related to their ground. In his treatment of transcendence, Tillich's main emphasis is on the creative freedom of the Unconditioned. But, as Farley notes, Tillich thrusts aside "every literal attempt to pin down that which transcends" *(op. cit., p. 96).*

Tillich takes as literal the concept of divine transcendence derived from philosophical ontology (the Unconditioned is the metaphysical prius from which all reality comes and in relation to which all structures have their meaning). These he combines with what he interprets symbolically, namely, the religious assertions of divine transcendence (God as personal transcendent will, love, mercy, judgment). But in the final analysis, the Unconditioned "transcends" the God of religious experience; however much religious symbols may be stressed, Tillich does not apply them literally to the ultimate nature of the Unconditioned. In this "correlation" of philosophical analysis with "theological answers," the historic Christian revelational truths about love, mercy and judgment are dissolved in existential speculation about God.

Heim on Divine Transcendence

In Karl Barth's theology of transcendence Karl Heim recognized a challenge to the regnant cultural idolatries of our time. An immanental world view involves one either in relativism or in an arbitrary absolute or idol. But Heim insisted that the modern picture of reality must be directly and meaningfully confronted by the Christian proclamation of the transcendent God. He knew that to dethrone the metaphysical or cosmological immanentism lurking beneath cultural immanentism requires nothing less than the formulation of a Christian metaphysic. The only alternative to arbitrary absolutism or to relativism, to fanaticism or nihilism (the ultimate forms of secularism) is faith that is both grounded in a transcendent God and vindicated by an adequate world view.

Heim's starting-point against monistic immanence is like Niebuhr's and Tillich's. It centers in interpersonal relations and emphasizes non-objectification. The relations of selves to each other and to the world occur in a dimension of transcendence. For this reason Heim vindicates a type of transcendence which is removed from the quasi-spatialism of the pre-Copernican outlook, and therefore is not reducible to objective, three-dimensional relations. Since Heim ascribes a psychic substratum to all nature, neither man nor nature can be reduced to completely objective experience.

Heim expounds divine transcendence via the traditional concepts of God as Creator and Lord (*God Transcendent,* Ch. VII). He invokes the doctrine of creation to attest that a Power other than the universe made it, and at every successive moment is making anew all laws of nature and all causal relations both as a whole and in every part (*ibid.,* p. 16). Since God as Creator is no prime mover (first in a series of causes), but ordains the universe anew moment by moment, Heim argues that this God cannot be apprehended in the categories of our experience. He maintains, however, that God is a personal Reality before Whom we must acknowledge our own personal existence as a divine gift of creation. Moreover, just as God confronts us as Creator, just so by His transcendent command He confronts us also as Lord.

Yet Heim disallows any intermundane cosmic transcendence for God. Dimensional boundaries, he says, cannot be ascribed to Him: "When we distinguish between Creator and creature, between transcendent and immanent, between God and the world, we are not marking out a boundary line between two worlds or two departments of life, which lie adjacent to each other. Nor is this a boundary of dimension such as may be drawn between two 'spaces' " (*ibid.,* p. 217; cf. also pp. 77 and 211).

Once Heim denies that a study of intramundane relations can shed light on God's transcendence, he must face Dorothy Emmett's observation that, in that event, only "some revelation *ab extra* which is entirely unrelated to any ordinary modes of apprehension" can truly define the content of transcendence. Heim's extended discussion of a three-dimensional world of experience she therefore considers extraneous (*The Nature of Metaphysical Thinking*, London, The Macmillan Company, 1953, p. 211). Farley stresses that Heim intends nothing more than to establish the conceivability or intelligibility of God's transcendence, a possibility which modern thinkers automatically deny. In *The Transformation of the Scientific World View,* however, Heim ventures to speak of God as *Urraum,* an all-embracing archetypal space "able to span the differences of the spaces in which we are enclosed" (London, S.C.M. Press, Ltd., 1953, p. 107). This does not mean, for Heim, that God's reality is spatial, even transcendent space. Suprapolar space, as Heim designates supramundane transcendence, is not God's substance or reality, but an aspect or form by which He reveals Himself. In referring to God's transcendence, in fact, Heim no longer uses the term as a rational concept that makes sense in the light of our experience, but employs it, rather, as an existential affirmation. Even the affirmation of God's personality, on which Heim insists, is not to be misunderstood in terms of our knowledge of other persons. While God confronts us as a Thou, He does so in a different sense than do others inasmuch as He is not walled out from us as are finite selves from each other. But a Cosmic Ego is necessary both to metaphysics (persons demand a Person as their originator) and to the practical life (prayer). Yet Heim considers this awareness of God's transcendence neither a matter of calculated observation nor of deductive inference, but of existential decision (Farley, *op. cit.,* pp. 128 f.). Man apprehends transcendence not by being a spectator, but by participating in an event in which he "comes to himself." In short, Heim's view, according to Farley, is simply this: although the *doctrine* of divine transcendence can be theoretically affirmed, "*God's transcendence* is grasped only in personal existence." So long as we merely discuss transcendence in the rational categories of our theoretical experience, we do not and cannot really grasp divine transcendence at all.

Hartshorne on Divine Transcendence

Both Tillich and Heim consider God's transcendence beyond rational definition in terms of our experiential categories. Charles Hartshorne in his pan-psychism, however, assimilates all our experiences into that of God. For Hartshorne, God's transcendence lies in His perfect and unrivaled exhibition of all those categories and polarities which the parts of the whole of experience display in lesser degree. Deeply influenced by the religious philosophy of Alfred North Whitehead, Hartshorne defines God as that all-inclusive reality, which is at once both absolute yet affected by His self-inclusion of all change. God's transcendence is that of an all-embracing organism that endures through all process but is in no way dependent upon process.

Hartshorne invokes the orthodox Christian emphasis that God wills certain purposes, loves the world, and enters into religious relationship with man. He does so, however, in order to reject the biblical affirmation that God so transcends the world as to be completely immutable. The pan-psychist mood of Hartshorne's philosophy makes it impossible for his exposition of divine transcendence to conform with that of biblical revelation. Hartshorne's view of transcendence is centered not in cosmology but in the realm of value.

As Farley indicates, transcendence for Hartshorne means superiority but not otherness nor independence (*ibid.*, p. 154). Since God is the all-embracing, there is nothing outside of God. God is more than the sum of the world and man, however, since the universe is considered merely as God's *body.* But it is not of God's essence to transcend the world, since it is of God's essence to have a world. Hartshorne denies that the world has not always existed. He believes, rather, that God as primordial creator has been creating from eternity. God alone is *necessary* being. His transcendence, therefore, consists in the fact that He is the condition of all creativity and process. God is independent of the various changes in His "total being." The world is extrinsic to Him, therefore, in the sense that neither the world-whole nor its parts share God's necessity of being.

V. THE DILEMMA OF CONTEMPORARY THEOLOGY

If the most recent theological expositions of divine transcendence leave upon thoughtful students any one single impression it is their obscurity and consequent powerlessness to confront the modern secular world and its life views.

Neo-orthodoxy has gained support as a "theology of transcendence," and so it is, broadly speaking. Over against liberal immanence—particularly against equating the supernatural with human reason, human values, or with nature as a whole—neo-orthodoxy vigorously champions the *otherness* of God. But if rational exposition of God's transcendence is impossible; if the relationship between the supernatural and the natural cannot be stated intellectually (but only symbolically or analogically); if the otherness of God is such that no predications can be made of God-in-Himself and we are limited to inference from and reflection on religious experience for our knowledge, have we really answered the question: what is meant by the transcendence of God?

From experience, of course, theologians may infer, however invalidly, certain theories about divine transcendence. An alleged sense of creatureliness, for example, may be held to imply God's non-creatureliness, that is, an object of my dependence. Similarly the sense of guilt may imply God's judgment, and the sense of forgiveness imply God's redemptive activity. Like some neo-orthodox writers, one may even contend that on the basis not simply of my religious feelings, but of how God confronts or encounters me, He should be proclaimed as essentially Lord, as Holy and as Love. No description of divine transcendence on the basis of confrontation or encounter, however, which occurs above or below the threshold of rational cognition, and which derives its epistemic content from personal decision, is able to penetrate beyond the affirmation about God-in-relation-to-me, to an affirmation about God-as-He-is-in-Himself. Moreover, those who rule out rational divine revelation as a way of knowing God must concede that their postulation about God-in-relation-to-us finds no support in the experience of many people, nor is it impervious to the possibility of emotive delusion.

Dialectical theology which insists that divine revelation confronts human reason not in the form of rational truths but in paradoxes incapable of being translated into human concepts has been forced to concede that its affirmations about divine transcendence cannot be taken as literally true representations about God-in-Himself.

This symbolic and non-literal formulation of divine transcendence is especially apparent when dialectical theologians discuss God's cosmic transcendence in relation to the creation of the world. Theologians who permit modern evolutionary theory to dictate their view of cosmic origins are now prone to assign a "symbolic" significance to the Genesis creation account. The "eternal ground" of things, we are told, can only be described symbolically, and to understand the creation "myth" in rational categories or in terms of a coherent world view is to falsify the facts. Renunciation of a rational exposition of God's essential transcendence inevitably follows the rejection of rational revelation and of rational apprehension of God. Some dialectical-existential scholars more thoroughly than others enforce the cleavage between symbolical and literal categories. Reinhold Niebuhr, for example, comprehends God's transcendence mythically and claims that symbols are necessary to grasp the ultimate ground because selfhood and freedom are its basic categories. On the other hand, Paul Tillich invokes symbols as indispensable for understanding the ultimate ground because that ground is assertedly an abyss that underlies every human category (including personality and freedom).

If the nature of God is rationally disclosed and rationally apprehended, the assertion of universally valid knowledge of God's nature (including His transcendent and immanent relations to the world of man) can be vindicated—as by historic Christian theology through its appeal to intelligible divine disclosure and to the inspired Scriptures. But if man's ideas and concepts of the divine are simply products of his own creative consciousness, and imply no claim to literal truth about the objective nature of God, is there any compelling reason to regard the moral transcendence of God any less than His metaphysical (or indeed His epistemological) transcendence as anything other or more than symbol or myth? The renunciation of rational divine revelation can only lead to moral as well as theoretical agnosticism about God-in-Himself.

Has the Christian theologian then no rational knowledge of God? Is there no such norm whereby to evaluate the concept and content of transcendence asserted on speculative metaphysical grounds (whether God be designated the Prime Mover, non-Being, the One, the Absolute, *Urgrund*, or by more recent conceptions)? Has the secular philosopher any basis to affirm and define divine transcendence apart from the biblical revelation? If so, what if any is the role of the biblical data in additionally informing its content? As Farley puts it, "What can be said about the Transcendent on the basis of human capabilities? . . . Does human experience in and of itself arrive at a Transcendent? . . . What can be said about the Transcendent on the basis of the Transcendent's revelation of itself?" (*ibid.*, p. 193). Another question (which Farley neglects to ask) is, do the theologians of divine confrontation or encounter actually incorporate the biblical view of divine transcendence, even while they claim to give a confessional kerygmatic exposition of God's transcendence? Is the biblical kerygma really non-metaphysical?

According to Farley the four philosophical concepts of transcendence depend on (1) a *temporal* imagery—for example, the Transcendent as the Beginning (First Mover) and the Transcendent as the End; (2) a *spatial* image—for example, the Transcendent as Depth (the nature of the real world: Plato's Eternal Ideas, Whitehead's Primordial Element, Heidegger's Being of Being) and the Transcendent as Height (a mystery: Rudolf Otto's Wholly Other) (*ibid.*, pp. 194 ff.). The former concepts respond to man's "whence?" the latter to his question, "what?" These four modes of transcendence are not unrelated, however, for man's station as a creature is "between the Beginning and the End, between the Depth and the Height" (*ibid.*, p. 201). The "Something" which "finitizes" man's existence as "transient in time and as a particularity in space," remarks Farley, is "the limit, the Transcendent" (p. 201). But this "Transcendent," he adds, is not demanded as a postulate of a coherent world-view, but stands outside metaphysics as the outer edge of everyman's experience. Thus propounded, the Transcendent is undefined and God is not necessarily its referent. Although this approach sometimes identifies the Transcendent with God in the generic sense (*theos*), it is not that God who reveals Himself.

With this Farley contrasts what he calls the Christian view, in which the transcendence of the self-disclosing God whose name is *Charis* (grace) is known in the act of redemption. From God's gracious deed in Christ we become aware of "the facticity and radicality of human sin" (*ibid.*, p. 203), of judgment, of redemption, and of our existence from Him (p. 204). Farley equates this foregoing exposition with the "kerygmatic transcendence" elaborated by the theologians of revelation. He goes on to ask: Is the Transcendent as God "in any sense absolute? . . . in any sense the Beginning, the End, the Depth, and the Height?" (p. 204). Farley's reply treats the biblical concepts as existentially significant rather than as propositionally true. That the Transcendent is Creator is "not a cosmological but a revelational assertion," he says (p. 205); it dispels "none of . . . the mysteries connected with the transition from nonbeing to being" (p. 206). Rather the Transcendent as Creator is the subjective assurance that God's power which redeems us is the same power from whom we also have our existence as from the one who freely gives. Since God freely invades history, as decisively demonstrated in the Incarnation, all history is subject to the possibility either of divine judgment or redemption. God, in fact, is the End of history, not in the sense of disclosing special events which uncover the mystery of the future, but in the sense that our transient beings are moving toward acknowledging Christ as the lord of history (p. 206). Moreover, God's gracious work of preservation holds apart the Beginning and the End; hence our Depth is the God whose grace keeps nonbeing from engulfing being (p. 208). As revealed, therefore, God is "creator, fulfiller and preserver." Yet in this revelation God remains hidden; the Transcendent as God is also "the *alienum*"—God is the other, the strange, the God of inscrutable grace, the holy (p. 209). God is the Holy, not merely the Height, whose highness consists in descending from the Height and suffering and dying for us (p. 210).

Because the kerygma presumably thus postulates God's nature, Farley opposes traditional theology which asserts both God's unchanging absoluteness and His relatedness. He complains that while the orthodox Protestant approach identifies the Transcendent as God, it "probably" relies on a particular (secular) metaphysical tradition and "apparently" views the Transcendent as Limit rather than allowing the kerygma to define the nature of God's absoluteness (p. 211). But Farley maintains that we know only the God *related* to us in grace; beyond that there is only "depth of grace." "There is no 'unrelated' God or aspect of God," he says (p. 211). All philosophical concepts of being-itself are to be "judged, transformed and interpreted by the God who is grace" (p. 211).

Whatever their conflict and diversity, the so-called kerygmatic theologians all assert not only the indispensability and priority of divine revelation in view of both man's finitude and estrangement, but insist also on the inadequacy of the logical structure of man's mind to grasp the truth about God, and to know God as He is in Himself. Although

historic Protestant theology anchors all truth about God and His purposes to divine self-revelation, neo-orthodox theology deviates from traditional theology in its restriction of the content and nature of divine
disclosure so as to exclude God's communication of information to man
about God's nature outside such relations. Barth may indeed identify all
revelation as Christomonistic; Brunner may demand general as well as
special revelation; Tillich may attribute a special side to revelation universally. Barth may deny any point of contact in man for divine disclosure; Brunner, on the basis of creation, may argue for a preceding
structure which makes reception of revelation possible. Yet all these
scholars agree in denying that the rational concepts of God shaped by
revelation are literally true. Bultmann demands that the concrete media
of biblical revelation be "demythologized" and "existentialized"; Tillich
requires that the scriptural "symbols" be reinterpreted; Barth affirms
that the believer knows God truly, but does so not on the ground that the
concepts of faith apply to Him univocally as universally valid affirmations but on the ground of a subjective miracle of grace and decision.

Contemporary theology's dilemma over the nature of God and the
definition of transcendence is unique to those religious currents set in
motion by Kierkegaard. Neo-orthodox scholars strip propositional intelligibility from the content of revelation so that divine self-disclosure
communicates no universally valid affirmations. Farley brushes aside the
kerygma in the sense of "a clearly discernible, propositional norm" (*ibid.,*
p. 219). He declares that if the Christian theologian believes that revelation arms him with final truths about the being of God he wrongly
"insists on a *gnosis*" (p. 222). On neo-orthodox principles, therefore, it
would seem impossible to define even the kerygma, a dilemma the New
Testament writers surely would have ascribed to theological ignorance
more than to pious humility.

Basic to the modern debate over transcendence lies the Kant-inspired
bias against man's possession (even on the basis of divine creation) of
rational categories capable of receiving transcendent truth. If this be
so, then all affirmations about the supernatural must automatically be
translated into finite space-time categories; divinely revealed doctrines and
precepts are then excluded, and Christian confidence in the divine revelation of truths or propositions about God and His purposes is nullified.
All affirmations about God's transcendent nature must then be regarded
as "true" only figuratively, or symbolically, or as regulative principles,
but not as literally *true*.

The vulnerable point of contemporary theology lies in its theory of
knowledge, a theory which deprives reason of its proper place in religious
experience and re-enforces an anti-intellectualistic view of divine revelation. So radical is the way in which God's epistemological transcendence

is defined, that it excludes the very possibility of God's telling us anything about Himself. As a result, Christian theology loses the capacity to define God's transcendent relationship to the world and to man.

Of the transcendence of the God of the Bible, His epistemological transcendence included, there can be no doubt. But when the revolt against the exaggerated liberal doctrine of divine immanence swings to the opposite extreme of an exaggerated neo-orthodox doctrine of divine transcendence, then the cost of error in Christian theology is equally high.

Reluctance to become explicit about cosmological transcendence reflects the hold which modern evolutionary theory has upon many modern theologians as the literal truth. Tillich may insist, as indeed he does, that being itself is not to be identified with *anything* (word, polarity, entity, value). He urges us to avoid spatial misconceptions in emphasizing that God is "above" and "beyond" man and the world. He attacks a "side by side" theology as well. Nowhere, however, does Tillich speak of transcendence in the sense that the Unconditioned excludes the finite from itself. Rather, he views being itself as the creative ground of everything else precisely because the finite has its ground in being. All being participates in the Unconditioned, which dynamically overcomes the threat of nonbeing in particular beings.

Niebuhr views transcendence as simple separation from the temporal, yet he writes of "the transcendence of God over" the world (*The Nature and Destiny of Man,* Vol. I, 1943, p. 126). Niebuhr supplies no clear definition of God's metaphysical transcendence, however, no guidance concerning the ontological problem of God's relationship to the world. Since Niebuhr insists that God suffers in time, and rejects the Chalcedonian formulation of the two natures as logical nonsense, Farley aptly presses the question whether Niebuhr does not indeed then imply God's "substantial immanence" in the world: "How then does God suffer if not substantially?" (*op. cit.,* p. 72, where Farley adds: "Ambiguity hides Niebuhr's position from his interpreters.")

Amid these currents of contemporary thought evangelical theology will need to define the biblical view of divine transcendence with patience and precision. After writing a volume on *Divine Immanence* in which he noted that "Christianity, with its correlative doctrine of the Trinity and the Incarnation, laid equal stress both on the transcendence and the immanence of God . . . ," J. R. Illingworth twelve years later published an additional work on *Divine Transcendence* (London, Macmillan and Co., Limited, 1911). In it Illingworth declared that "The divine transcendence . . . is the vital truth on which our whole Christian religion depends, and the justification of the tone of authority with which it confronts the world" (p. 74). Remarkably enough, one can find entire volumes on the nature of God without a single index reference to transcendence, among them Lewis Richard Farnell's Gifford Lectures on *The Attributes of God* (Oxford, Clarendon Press, 1925).

Christian theism holds that while the whole fabric of the universe is permeated by divine immanence, nothing of nature nor in man is to be identified as part of God. Furthermore, God's interpenetration is not simply that of the Absolute, or the sum of all things. His relationships to the world reflect the transcendent superiority of infinite being and perfection over all finite existence and knowledge and goodness. As Illingworth put it, "Metaphysically speaking, God is the absolute, transcendent Being, who makes finite and relative existence possible. ..." (*op. cit.,* p. 13). God is "independent of all necessary or compulsory relations ... or in other words completely self-dependent and self-determined" (*ibid.,* pp. 14-15).

The Old and New Testament Scriptures alike confirm that God is Creator and Ruler and Judge of all. Christians differentiate between God on the one hand and man and the world on the other; they distinguish God from the universe. "In the beginning God created the heaven and the earth" (Gen. 1:1). "He spake, and it was done; he commanded, and it stood fast" (Psalm 33:9). "He commanded, and they were created" (Psalm 148:5). "I am the Lord, and there is none else. I form the light and create darkness, I make peace and create evil. I the Lord do these things" (Isa. 45:7). Moreover, Christians refuse to attribute all man's purposes and deeds to God as the sole principle of life and history; they distinguish between evil and good motives and thoughts and actions. "I the Lord your God am holy" (Lev. 19:2). "With righteousness shall he judge the world" (Psalm 98:9). "Behold, the Lord maketh the earth empty, and maketh it waste, and turneth it upside down, and scattereth abroad the inhabitants thereof ... because they have transgressed the laws, changed the ordinance, broken the everlasting covenant" (Isa. 24:1,5). "My thoughts are not your thoughts, neither are your ways my ways, saith the Lord. For as the heavens are higher than the earth, so are my ways higher than your ways, and my thoughts than your thoughts" (Isa. 55:8,9).

The fact that the Hebrew-Christian community of faith derived its special knowledge of the transcendent God—Creator, Redeemer and Judge —not from the ordinary initiative of human thought but rather from the transcendent activity of divine disclosure, enforces the certainty of transcendence in the scriptural view of God.

The biblical writers unmistakably depict an absolute and transcendent Being who is infinite in knowledge and goodness—or, more precisely stated, who is the ultimate source and ground of truth and righteousness. Although their vocabulary lacked the philosophical terminology of the Greeks, nevertheless the Hebrew religious teachers so expounded the fact of God's transcendence that their concepts and words prepared the way for a clear comparison and contrast of the Judeo-Christian and the Greek views. Later when the biblical revelation of God was stated in the vocabulary of the Greeks, the doctrines of the divine trinity and of the divine incarnation presupposed and reinforced the reality of an absolutely transcendent Being whose immanence cannot be accommodated to pantheistic speculations, and whose sovereign authority comprehends the whole universe. Especially in the unique affirmation that Jesus Christ is very God and very man, the Church affirms the transcendence of God. This emphasis on divine transcendence finds practical reinforcement in the life of prayer, for prayer thrives in religious experience only when the petitioner is confident of communion with that Eternal Being who is exalted above all creaturely limitations. The biblical writers would happily have endorsed this passage from the Clementine Homilies: "He who would worship God ought before all else to know what is peculiar to the nature of God alone, which cannot pertain to another, that . . . he may not be seduced into ascribing deity to another" (quoted by G. L. Prestige, *God in Patristic Thought*, London, S.P.C.K., 1952, p. 25).

In his survey of patristic thought, Prestige summarizes a series of quotations in which the early church fathers assert the incomparable supremacy of God. He says: "The gist of such passages . . . does not indeed amount to a fully formulated doctrine of transcendence as presented in modern philosophies, but it means at least as much as the divine transcendence taught by the Hebrew prophets, which is the main trunk of the Christian idea of God. It links moral and metaphysical qualities in the most definite manner, asserts most strongly the 'incomparable' superiority of God over all creatures, and while hinting that their relative excellence is derived from His perfection, interposes an absolute gulf between the Creator and the creation" (*ibid.*, pp. 26 f.).

It may be acknowledged, of course, that in expounding divine *huperochē* the later fathers often tended to proceed simply along the line of simple negation of creaturely limitations. Modern theologians, too, often project their views independently of biblical truth. Seldom has such a dim awareness of divine realities as propounded by recent Western theology and philosophy shaped the intellectual destiny of any generation. Modern man's speculations about God clearly show that the revolution in contemporary life is basically—even if not admittedly—spiritual and theological.

The modern inability to speak literally of God's essential being, the contentment with merely relational reflections, or with only symbolical or analogical predications about God-in-Himself, augur but further religious decline for the Western world. Without a rediscovery of the ontological realities inherent in the biblical revelation of the transcendent God the Christian religion will not confront the secular world of our age in power. A denial of rational divine revelation and a rejection of scriptural doctrines inevitably throws the religious thinkers of our time back upon some form of natural theology, that is, upon a theology derived from experience. Since experience supplies no ground for theology, the theologians who pursue this course cannot confront the secular forces that grip our generation. Only the literal knowledge and service of the Living God will counteract the erosive threat of secular immanentism and the religious confusion of dialectical philosophers who insist on transcendent reality while contenting themselves with ambiguities of myth and symbol.

THE NATURE OF
REVELATION

✝

John H. Gerstner

John H. Gerstner is Professor of Church History at Pittsburgh Theological Seminary (United Presbyterian Church in the U.S.A.) which emerged in 1959 from consolidation of Western Theological Seminary and Pittsburgh-Xenia (with which he was long associated). He is author of numerous books, among them Reasons for Faith *(1960) and* The Theology of the Major Sects *(1960), and is an authority on Jonathan Edwards and Puritanism. He holds the B.A. degree from Westminster College, B.D. and B.Th. from Westminster Theological Seminary, and Ph.D. from Harvard University.*

5. John H. Gerstner

THE NATURE OF
REVELATION

T HERE are two books of God—the book of nature and the book of revelation. This is the historic Christian doctrine taught in the Bible, affirmed in the creeds of the Church, developed in the writings of the classical doctors, and still today very much alive in evangelical Protestant-ism (though with some defection). The first verse of the Bible states the foundation of natural revelation: "In the beginning God created the heaven and the earth." The last verse of the Bible states the climax of special revelation: "Even so, come, Lord Jesus." The "riddle of the universe" finds its solution in the God who is intimated in the cosmos and gloriously revealed in the sacred Scriptures. The nineteenth Psalm refers to both the volumes of nature and revelation: the "day unto day" that "uttereth speech" plus the "law of the Lord" that "is perfect, con-verting the soul." Most wonderful of all, this Word, that is spoken in the two books, comes alive in one Person, the God-man Christ Jesus. "God, who at sundry times and in divers manners spake in time past unto the fathers by the prophets, hath in these last days spoken unto us by his Son. . . ."

Today, however, the book of nature has been slammed shut while the book of revelation is often misread. In this essay we shall attempt to show that while in fact this is so, in truth it ought not to be. This brings us into some conflict with a widely prevailing theology in our time, neo-orthodoxy.

97

I. REJECTION OF NATURAL THEOLOGY

First, all neo-orthodox scholars have a basic agreement concerning natural revelation, or at least natural theology. The agreement is this: nature does *not prove* the existence of God. Everybody knows that the greatest of the neo-orthodox theologians, Karl Barth, rejects natural revelation (cf. "Nein! Antwort an Emil Brunner" in *Theologie Existenz Heute*, V, 14, 1934). But some have supposed that because he and his former colleague, Emil Brunner, had a controversy about this (Heinrich Emil Brunner and Karl Barth, *Natural Theology;* comprising "Nature and Grace," by Professor Dr. Emil Brunner and the reply "No!" by Dr. Karl Barth, London, Bles., 1946) that Brunner believes in it. Without going into the refinements of difference between Barth and Brunner, it is enough to say that Brunner rejects any valid natural theology and does not merit the epithet "Thomistic" which Barth hurled at him. In any case, all neo-orthodox scholars define all revelation (as we shall see) in such a denatured way that this present point becomes relatively secondary. For Rudolf Bultmann, nature is merely a "dark, mysterious power" full of "weird ambiguity" (*"dunkle, Rätselhafte Macht"* *"Unheimlichkeit und Zweideutigkeit"*). Although it is a work of supererogation to show that the neo-orthodox reject natural theology, I shall cite one more instance, Paul Tillich, because he is often thought to assign so much more place to reason that he should not even be considered one of the neo-orthodox theologians. As a matter of fact, Tillich is more radical in his rejection than any, for he makes reason unable to know or express God (the Ultimate). "Symbolical language alone is able to express the ultimate" (*Dynamics of Faith*, New York, Harper and Brothers, 1957, p. 41). To be sure, he is inconsistent at times and does himself desymbolize (cf. "We may surmise the nature of the whole; we may speak of the whole indirectly; but we do not see the whole itself; we do not grasp it face to face. A little light and much darkness...." *The Shaking of The Foundations,* New York, Harper and Brothers, 1948, pp. 110 f.). But he deliberately insists that "Faith, if it takes its symbols literally, becomes idolatrous" (*Dynamics of Faith,* p. 52).

II. REJECTION OF PROOFS OF BIBLE INSPIRATION

Neo-orthodoxy rejects all attempts to prove the inspiration of the Bible. "There is," declares Barth, "only one norm and it is: God who speaks" (*Church Dogmatics,* New York, Charles Scribner's Sons, 1936, Vol. I/1, p. 157). So emphatic is Barth about this implicit authority of the Word that D. M. Baillie remarked that it was so much a theology of the Word that "it hardly is theology of the Word-made-flesh" (*God Was in Christ,* New York, Charles Scribner's Sons, 1948, p. 53), and Cornelius Van Til observed, "For Barth there is no God who exists independently of his revelation" ("Has Karl Barth Become Orthodox?" in *Westminster Theological Journal,* May, 1954). To question God's Word, according to Brunner, is demonic doubt (*Revelation and Reason,* Philadelphia, The Westminster Press, 1946, p. 206). Furthermore, "The hallmark of logical inconsistency clings to all genuine pronouncements of faith" (Brunner, *Philosophy of Religion,* London, T. & T. Clarke, 1958, p. 55), and we cannot even be sure that what God says is true (Brunner, *Wahrheit als Begegnung,* Berlin, Furch-Verlag, 1938, p. 88). Manifestly, the Word must simply be accepted; to apply any tests of credibility would not merely be presumptuous but absurd. Non-rational, non-critical existential "acceptance," according to Bultmann also, is the way the *kerygma* or Gospel of the New Testament is made contemporaneous.

III. SEPARATION VERSUS IDENTITY OF THE BIBLE AND GOD'S WORD

Neo-orthodoxy refuses as a matter of principle exclusively to associate the words of Scripture and the Word of God, or even to identify them directly. While neo-orthodox scholars tend to teach that the Word of God often comes through the words of the Bible, so far are they from identifying the two that they will not even hold this connection to be invariable. Thus the master himself, at the very outset of his definitive *Kirchliche Dogmatik,* gives himself to this principial matter of the Word and the Bible. According to Barth, the Church witnesses to the Bible and the Bible to the Word. Nevertheless, the Bible *"must never be identified with the revelation itself.* The revealed Word of God through his word which he speaks to prophets and apostles in Jesus Christ, and speaks through their instrumentality ever anew to man" may come through the Bible. The sovereign God maintains a "free disposal of the verbal character of Holy Scripture" (*Church Dogmatics,* Vol. I/1, p. 157; cf. also *Word of God and Word of Man,* Boston, Pilgrim Press, 1928, pp. 43, 65). Barth rejects "Verbalinspiriertheit." According to Brunner, "The word of God in the Scriptures is as little to be identified with the words in the Scripture as the Christ according to the flesh is to be identified with the Christ according to the spirit. The words of the Scriptures are human, that is, God makes use of human, and therefore, frail and fallible words of men who are liable to err" (*Theology of Crisis,* New York, Charles Scribner's Sons, 1929, p. 19). Tillich teaches that the Bible is not the only source of our knowledge of God and that it differs only in degree from other media (*Systematic Theology,* Chicago, University of Chicago Press, 1951, Vol. I, pp. 34 ff.). Bultmann, characteristically, is most radical. For him, the revelation is almost totally dissociated from the Bible; it is, rather, the experience of the Christ event (not identical with Jesus) which is saving (for Bultmann's existential approach see his "Is Exegesis Without Presuppositions Possible?" *Existence and Faith, Shorter Writings of Rudolf Bultmann,* Schubert Ogden, ed., New York, Meridian Books, 1960).

Evangelicalism, on the other hand, refuses to allow a Word of God independent of the words of Scripture. Professor Murray in the same chapter which affirmed the self-authenticating character of Scripture also makes it very plain that it is the entire Bible which is to be believed on its own authority (*The Infallible Word,* A Symposium by the Members of the Faculty of Westminster Theological Seminary, Grand Rapids, Wm. B. Eerdmans Publishing Company, 1953, pp. 7, 8). According to B. B. Warfield, the historic Christian doctrine, which he accepted, takes the Bible as the Word of God in the sense that whatever the Bible says, God says (*Revelation and Inspiration,* New York, Oxford University Press, 1927, Chap. III). Dr. Joseph P. Free, of Wheaton College, says that God guided the Scripture writers to the choice of words (*Archeology and Bible History,* Wheaton, Van Kampen Press, 1950, p. 3), while Charles Hodge in his classic *Systematic Theology* taught that "all the books of Scripture are equally inspired ... inspiration extends to all the contents of these several books" (*Systematic Theology,* 3 vols., New York, Scribner, Armstrong and Company, 1872, Vol. I, p. 163).

Here the argument is joined: the neo-orthodox condemn orthodox theology for accepting the words of Scripture as the Word of God and all orthodoxy condemns neo-orthodox theology for not doing so.[1] First, let us evaluate the orthodox critique of neo-orthodoxy at this point and then turn to the neo-orthodox critique of orthodoxy.

The orthodox critique of neo-orthodoxy is, I believe, devastating. It is a *reductio ad absurdum.* Evangelical scholars insist that if the Word of God is dissociated from the words of Scripture it is dissociated from all definable meaning. If this argument can be made to stick, anyone will grant that it is an intellectual work of demolition. It sticks. For example, E. J. Young argues: "If it is only in the dimension of faith, or *Urgeschichte,* or supra-history, that Jesus Christ is the Servant of the Lord, then the conclusion is inescapable that Jesus Christ is not the Servant of the Lord at all" (in the symposium *Contemporary Evangelical Thought,* ed. by Carl F. H. Henry, Great Neck, N.Y., Channel Press, 1957, p. 33). Gordon Clark's criticism is directed to the Tillichian type of symbolism which, while more radical than some neo-orthodoxy, differs only in degree: ". . . if all language or all religious language is symbolical, the statement that

---

[1] It should be mentioned that orthodoxy also grants that a *saving* knowledge of the Word of God, commonly called illumination, is possible only by the special work of the Spirit of God in the Christian soul.

5 6 4 8 3

the cross symbolizes the love of God is itself a symbol" (in the symposium
Revelation and the Bible, ed. by Carl F. H. Henry, Baker Book House,
Grand Rapids, 1958, p. 40). One of the fullest critiques of neo-orthodoxy
by an evangelical is Paul King Jewett's *Emil Brunner's Concept of Revelation* (London, J. Clarke, 1954). Though himself depreciating the evidence
for the existence of God by saying "We cannot discover him at the end
of a syllogism" (in *Revelation and the Bible,* p. 54), Dr. Jewett gives a
devastating critique of Brunner's (and virtually all neo-orthodox) revelational thinking. After a thorough survey of the body of the Swiss theologian's writings. Jewett concludes: "What this all comes down to is this.
God has given us our reason as an organ of revelation. And yet he reveals
himself in such a way that we cannot rationally understand him. . . . In
the last analysis . . . not only is reason no proper criterion of revealed
truth, but there is no criterion whatever" (*Emil Brunner's Concept of
Revelation,* pp. 184 f.).

But now let us turn to the neo-orthodox critique of evangelicalism.
This attack is directed against territory where all evangelicals stand
together. First, neo-orthodoxy claims that the evangelical approach
finitizes the infinite. If the infinite God is confined to the pages of a book
and the words of men, He is not the sovereign God of revelation. Evangelicalism does more than deny this; she justifies her denial. First of all,
it is not God Himself, of course, but merely the record of His speech which
is confined to the Book. If God can create finite human beings without
forfeiting His own infinity He can create finite words without doing so.
If God by His own sovereign decision confines His further speaking to
the words once for all delivered, how does this limit Him? If He were not
able thus to confine His revelation He would really lack sovereignty.

Second, neo-orthodoxy claims that while the evangelical view, on the
one hand, tends to finitize the infinite, on the other hand, it tends to
infinitize the finite. That is, its doctrine of verbal inspiration assertedly
makes the human agents of Scripture infallible, and this attribute of
infallibility belongs only to the infinite God. Bibliolatry and idolatry
are laid at the door of evangelicalism. "In what is given of God," wrote
John Baillie, "there can be no imperfection of any kind, but there is
always imperfection in what we may be allowed to call the 'receiving
apparatus' " (*The Idea of Revelation in Recent Thought,* New York,
Columbia University Press, 1956, p. 34). R. W. Moore regards verbal
inspiration as "almost blasphemous error" (*A Primer of Christianity,*
Part 2: The Furtherance of the Gospel, Oxford, Oxford University Press,
1950, Vol. II, p. 59). George Buttrick seems to have the same thing in
mind when he declares: "avowal of the literal infallibility of Scripture
held to its last logic would risk a trip to the insane asylum" (quoted from
Engelder, *Scripture Cannot Be Broken,* St. Louis, Concordia Publishing

House, 1944, p. 78). "Idolators of the letter of the Bible must be converted to true worshipers of the spirit of the Bible," adds Huberto Rohden (in *The Christian Century*, April 30, 1952, p. 537).

Evangelicals acknowledge that they claim infallibility for the writers of Scripture at the moment of inspired writing but deny any implication that they idolize either them or their words. Is God unable, they ask, to lift men above the effects of their own sins and weakness if He so chooses? Granted that infallibility natively belongs to God alone, is He unable to bestow an acquired infallibility on creatures? The neo-orthodox will admit that only God is good; can He not also bestow goodness on the creature without deifying him? Why not infallibility? As for bibliolatry, the evangelicals have already shown that they regard the Bible not as the eternal Word of God but derivatively as the record of the divine words spoken in time.

Third, the neo-orthodox are not satisfied with charging evangelicalism with infinitizing human agents; they contend also that it does precisely the opposite, namely, brutalizes them. Verbal inspiration, they charge, means mechanical, dictated inspiration, and involves making men into machines, which is even worse than brutalizing them. The casual way in which Paul Fuhrmann writes of "mechanical or literal interpretation" is utterly typical of such criticism ("Calvin, The Expositor of Scripture," in *Interpretation*, Vol. IV, 1952, p. 193). Archbishop William Temple urged the fact that since none of the Bible gives the appearance of dictated material it could not have been verbally inspired, nor can it be a source for propositional revelation (*Nature, Man and God*, London, The Macmillan Company, 1935, p. 353). Brunner's writings include a sustained criticism of verbal inspiration but nowhere is he more severe than when he says, "Christians of the letter, who suppose, when they simply hold, in a slavish way, to the Bible book, that then they are disciples indeed, while actually in so doing they have nothing at all of the spirit of the Master about them . . ." ("Vom Klugen Haushalter," in *Saat und Frucht*, Zurich, 1946, p. 115, quoted from Paul Jewett, "Emil Brunner's Doctrine of Scripture," in *Inspiration and Interpretation*, John F. Walvoord, editor, Grand Rapids, Wm. B. Eerdmans Publishing Company, 1957, p. 232).

Again, the evangelicals will readily admit that reducing man to machines is culpable, but they deny that they do that. They remind the neo-orthodox that if they would but read the works of the verbal inspirationists they would quickly discover that they denied mechanical inspiration just as vigorously as they taught verbal inspiration. If the neo-orthodox should counter that (whether orthodoxy admits it or not) verbal inspiration necessarily involves mechanical inspiration, the evangelicals would ask: What! can the sovereign God not accomplish the tiny miracle of communicating His will without violating the will of chosen creatures when He is able to run an entire universe without violating a single free act of a single free agent?

IV. THE CRUCIAL ISSUE

The fourth objection of neo-orthodoxy is the charge of obscurantism. Verbal inspiration, it says, cannot be scientifically defended. Historical criticism has demolished any vestige of a notion that the Bible is without error. Edwin Lewis speaks of "the incredible fatuity on the part of the literalist, who insists on the 'absolute inerrancy of Scripture' " (*A Philosophy of the Christian Revelation,* New York, Harper & Brothers, 1940, p. 55). A vastly misleading statement will nonetheless highlight the impossibility of avoiding the historical problem: "Critical scholars have found 10,000 diversities in the preserved manuscripts of the Old Testament and 150,000 in the New Testament, a total of 160,000 in the Bible. So the theory of a mechanical, verbal inspiration simply falls to pieces" (H. C. Alleman, *The Lutheran Quarterly,* 1936, p. 247; cf. also Reinhold Niebuhr, *Faith and History; A Comparison of Christian and Modern Views of History,* New York, Charles Scribner's Sons, 1949, p. 24).

An evangelical answer to this is: Christianity must be, and can be, proven to be the truth of God and that without violating or disregarding recognized critical methodology, or begging the question. Let us say a few things about this.

First, *if* this can be done it is a true solution to a vexing problem. That is, there is no question-begging here, no subjectivism, no dogmatism.

Second, generally speaking, there is nothing novel about the "rational" approach. On the contrary, it is traditional, and for that matter, the biblical approach. The Old Testament, while not given to metaphysical analysis, was not indifferent to the intellect as the appeal of Isaiah (1:18) and the reasoning of the Psalmist (19:1 f.), for example. Christ argued from the Scriptures (Luke 4:21), from the evidential power of His works (John 14:11), and from the Christian experience (John 7:17). The Synoptists, not less than John, wrote their narrative that the reader "might believe that Jesus is the Christ the Son of the living God" (John 20:31). Peter advocates a rational defense (I Peter 3:15). The master apologist of the Bible is, of course, Paul, whose sermon on Mars Hill (Acts 17:22 f.) and Epistle to the Romans, chapter one, are classic examples of Christian argumentation. Moreover, the rational approach was that of the Apologists of the second century, who set the apologetic pace for the following centuries of the Church's history. It has been said that the Christians outthought, outlived and outdied the heathen. It was the Apologists, for all their excesses, who outthought them. The rational defense and propagation of Christianity reached its apogee in the high Middle Ages.

Despite a tendency to become preoccupied with minutiae, the age of Thomas Aquinas constituted a magnificent articulation of the Christian faith in relation to culture. Nor did the Reformation reject this heritage. Although the early Luther was inclined to be bitter about scholasticism (because he blamed it for hiding the saving Christ from him), he was not nearly so anti-rational as some neo-orthodox theologians would have us think. We can cite Paul Tillich himself at this point: "Luther seems to be very much disinclined to accept *anything* from reason; in reality, this is not true. . . . There [Diet of Worms] he adds reason to the Holy Scriptures; he was not an irrationalist. . . . He did not forbid that Melanchthon again introduce Aristotle . . ." (*A History of Christian Thought,* ed. by Peter H. John, second ed., Providence, R.I., 1956, p. 228). The Protestant (both Lutheran and Reformed) scholasticism which set in shortly after the Reformation, so far from being a distortion of the "free spirit" of the preceding age, was nothing other than an extremely able and learned carrying out of its implications. The rational defense of Christianity loomed large in this golden age of Protestantism as was also true in the great English evangelical defense against the vicious attack of Deism. Matthew Toland's *Christianity as Old as Creation* (1730), for example, received no fewer than 150 refutations. Each of the great leaders of the eighteenth-century revival was an able apologete: Spener in Germany, Wesley in England, and Edwards in New England. When, therefore, John Dillenberger writes: "The salvation of the Christian enterprise came not from the rear-guard apologetic of Butler, but from the proclamation of the redeeming Word as preached by Wesley and his associates" (*Protestant Thought and Natural Science,* Garden City, N.Y., Doubleday & Company, p. 155), he seems to forget that Wesley and Butler were at one on the rational defense of Christianity. Wesley even wrote: "It is a fundamental principle with us that to renounce reason is to renounce religion, that religion and reason go hand in hand, and so irrational religion is false religion" (*Journal,* June 15, 1741). In 1763 Wesley wrote *A Survey of the Wisdom of God in the Creation,* or *Compendium of Natural Theology,* which grew to five volumes. The eclipse of the apologetic sun began in the days of Immanuel Kant and it is almost complete today. But it is not complete. Furthermore, eclipses are of short duration.

Third, the rational approach constitutes, if it can be established, a true evangelistic basis for our times. Both neo-orthodoxy and neo-evangelicalism are strongly constrained by a desire to win men to Christ as they understand Him. This goes without saying for neo-evangelicalism, but it is true also in a sense of neo-orthodoxy. Finlayson is correct in saying that: "Without doubt, 'scientific respectability' is the raison d'être of neo-orthodoxy" (in *Revelation and the Bible,* p. 233). And Tillich really explains this when he says: "The whole reason for my work is that I want to make Christian faith possible for the people of our time" (a verbal statement of Tillich's that Norman Pittenger relates in "Paul Tillich as a Theologian" in *The Anglican Theological Review,* XLIII, Vol. 3, July 1961, pp. 268 f.).

We feel toward the neo-orthodox as Paul felt toward his fellow Jews: They have zeal for God but not according to knowledge. Gordon Clark is not being uncharitable and certainly not untrue when he says that "paradox is a charley-horse between the ears." This theology, as Cornelius Van Til contends, calls for a leap into the void; 70,000 fathoms deep according to Kierkegaard. What reason is there—on such an approach—to condemn Sartre's refusal, although the alternative be atheism? If there is nothing that we can really know it is more sane and useful to acknowledge the grim fact and with Martin Heidegger, Henry Miller and others to seek salvation in nothing. Sooner or later adherents of paradox theology must choose between the true God of historic Christianity or the abyss of atheistic existentialism.

Here is Norman Langford's testimony to what Karl Barth has meant to him: "He has shown me that theology can never come to repose in a fixed orthodoxy—not even a neo-orthodoxy!—but must ever be moving on with no knowledge of where the journey will lead" (*Theology Today,* October, 1956). This very uncertainty, which we censure, these men sincerely consider a benefit. But modern irrationalism is one of the strongest arguments for the necessity of rational apologetics as an evangelistic medium. How else are persons to be persuaded and won to the Jesus of history, the true, eternal Son of God, the Saviour of the world? How else can they learn whence they came, why they are here, and where they are going?

Fourth, a very great deal of the literature of apologetics has been and is being prepared. The Church has been at this task for many centuries and has a vast reservoir of apologetic wisdom. Though heresies may be ever new, they are seldom very original. So we may correctly anticipate that for the most part they have been answered even before they raise their current questions. Wellhausen only gave a particular form to criticism previously urged by Jamblicus and Porphyry in the fourth century. Augustine in the fifth century was wrestling with the fundamental principle that Darwin popularized. Tillich and Bultmann are moving toward a position at which gnostics had already arrived millenniums ago.

If anything in this world is uncertain it is the so-called "assured results of criticism." That Acts is not authentic history, that John's Gospel could not have been written in the first century, that Paul was not the author of half of his epistles, that Moses could not have known how to write, that the text of the Old Testament needed constant emendation, all these prejudices and a host of others were, in their day, "assured results of criticism." Today, they are recognized as criticism's "assured mistakes."

We are not obscurantist and do not decry criticism. There are formidable problems to be researched. But we need not fear the outcome. We need to emphasize what sober critics gladly admit, the danger of jumping prematurely to conclusions. We would assure the layman that the field of biblical criticism is not nearly so negative and foreboding as sometimes is imagined.

V. COUNTERING THE OBJECTIONS

Finally, let us consider some of the neo-orthodox objections which have been and will be made to the traditional approach.

1. First, this approach, it is said, overlooks the noetic influence of sin, that is, that the fall of man involves corruption so determinative that man cannot be reached through reason. How, then, can he be reached? By the heart? But must you not first know who Christ is before you can *believe* in Him? There is no direct route to the heart except via the mind. The Gospel may never get beyond the mind, to be sure; but, if it is ever to reach the heart it must get there by the mind. Second, sin has not destroyed the mind any more than it has destroyed the head, the arms, the hands, the feet. All of the faculties and parts of men are intact and ever shall be, so long as man remains man. Third, sin does indeed influence all man's faculties, but not by destroying them. Rather, it tends to deploy them into the service of sin, as the instruments of unrighteousness (Romans 3:10 f.). Not only the mind is under this influence, but the whole man. Fourth, all of these elements being intact are capable and deserving of proper care and training. The legs can be trained to do a four-minute mile, the voice to rival the nightingale, the brain to plumb the mystery of existence and of religion. Fifth, because of this sinful nature of man he will run the four-minute mile to his own glory, will sing for his own praise, will master religion for his own comfort. If running the four-minute mile is not the runner's supposed self-interest, sin will slow him down. If a sinner has been bribed and finds it more to his interest to lose than win the race, sin, which is interested only in itself, will lead him, in spite of his ability and training, to lose the race.

Now consider the matter of mastering religion for self-interest. If the religion of the Bible claims that God condemns men who live only for themselves, the sinful nature is not going to like that. What will sin incline the mind to do? It may suggest re-examination of the religion in the hope that it may be found not to teach this uncongenial doctrine. Thus the Word of God will not have free course in this mind; this man will wrest the Scriptures; he will seek to justify himself. Or, with the same purpose, the sinner may take a different tack. Let a religion teach what it will, he may try to prove that it is not true religion. Or the sinful mind may choose simply to disregard the unpleasant facts, and the sinner may do as he pleases. This is more congenial than reflection on unpleasant truths.

Now what does the Christian evangelist do in this situation? That is not an open question, since God has commanded him to preach the Word in season and out of season. So, let sinful men do what they will with the Christian message, the evangelist must nonetheless go on proclaiming it. He must become all things to all men, and as he has opportunity confront all of the above reactions. To the mind which challenges the correctness of his interpretation he must expound the Scripture cogently. To the mind which denies the divinity of Christianity he must press its rightful claims. To the mind which would ignore the call to repentance he must sound the solemn warning that God is not mocked: "Whatever a man sows that he shall reap."

As long as the man to whom the Gospel comes remains under sin's dominion, he will continue to resist everything that is said. He will go on to the end seeking in vain to justify himself. And the evangelist must go on to the end seeking to convince him of the futility of seeking to justify himself.

No more need be said to show that the "noetic influence of sin" is no excuse for not arguing with men. We have not been commanded to be successful but to be faithful. But more remains to be said. God has promised that faith comes by hearing. That is, as we preach He will Himself change hearts and work faith. "And the Lord's servant must not be quarrelsome but kindly to everyone, an apt teacher, forbearing, correcting his opponents with gentleness. God may perhaps grant that they will repent and come to know the truth . . ." (II Tim. 2:24, 25). There is a "perhaps" here. "Perhaps" God will convert the sinful heart and "perhaps" He will not. "I will have mercy on whom I will have mercy." Meanwhile the witness continues, knowing that God's Word will not return to Him void but will accomplish what He pleases. Accordingly, the evangelist will be "a savor of death to death to some and of life to life to others." He is up against a stone wall when addressing the sinful mind but there works through him a divine power that is able to smash that wall whenever He pleases. Or to change the metaphor, the Bible is a sword (Eph. 6:17). The apologist is the sword-bearer and the Holy Spirit is the sword-wielder. We must keep the sword sharp and ready for God to use whenever He pleases. He will not slay the wicked except by that sword which He is pleased to let us carry for Him.

In summary, here is how we settle the query about apologetics and the noetic influence of sin. Sin has not destroyed the mind, which remains the only door to the heart of the person. While the sinner will strive to keep that door closed to the entrance of gospel light, God has commanded us to keep knocking—witnessing—in His name. Furthermore, He has assured us that He may Himself constrain the sinner to open the door of his heart, in conjunction with our faithful and reasonable presentation.

2. A second objection must now be faced. If the Bible's inspiration is to be proven by critical methods this is an unending task and at most we could have a probability argument. The work of criticism is likely to continue as long as sinful man can utter an objection. But it does not follow that the case for Christianity rests merely upon probabilities (though, if so, that would still be preferable to a purely subjectivistic leap into the unknown). Historical evidence guarantees that there was a Jesus Christ and He Himself proves that He was divine and further certified the Bible as the infallible Word. If this is true, as I have attempted to show in *Reasons for Faith* (New York, Harper & Brothers, 1960, chapter 9), then our faith in the inspiredness of Scripture does not rest on a probability argument but on the testimony of the infallible Son of God. But what, you ask, is the purpose of biblical criticism if the Bible is certified by the Son of God? Biblical criticism is for the purpose of dealing with the objections of the person who does not believe that the Son of God has certified the Bible. He approaches the matter from the opposing side, arguing that if the Bible is corrupt it cannot be the Word of God, while we are saying that if the Bible is the Word of God it cannot be corrupt. If we can convince the critic that Christ was the Son of God and did certify the Bible as His Word, the critic will find the answer to his own criticism. But if we cannot, then we go with him to the texts which he thinks prove the fallibility of the Bible. If the Bible is what Christ said it is, it should not be too difficult to prove that the critic, and not the Son of God, has made an error.

Let me give one specific example. In a single paragraph no one can adequately discuss the great problem posed by "Form-Criticism," but its essence can be stated. Form-Criticism seeks to ascertain what part of a story—say in the Gospels—is original and what (if anything) was added later. Some radical form-critics, like Bultmann, argue that most of the Gospel stories are later churchly additions and it is impossible to discover the authentic original. Against this it may be replied: first, the writings themselves claim to be authentic and ought to be so accepted unless *proven* unreliable; second, there is no *evidence* that there were later churchly additions; third, there is admitted evidence that the "oral gospel" was the early and immediate form of proclamation and that this became settled later in the written form so that the written form was a crystallization of the earliest material; fourth, that if there had been an attempt to put later words into the mouth of Christ and the Apostles, there would have been, as Dr. Everett Harrison has shown (in *Contemporary Evangelical Thought,* p. 53), a "serious controversy" which in fact did not develop; and, last, the history of New Testament research has been steadily showing that the high supernaturalism which was once thought to be a later "Johannine" development is inextricable from the earliest narratives.

3. A third objection now comes to view: It is held that if the infallibility of the Bible could be proven, there would be no need to appeal to faith. If you have reasons for faith, it is said, you *must* believe, and there is no alternative. True, if there are compelling reasons you must believe; but only in the sense that belief is logically necessary. But nobody is forced to believe. Men are quite able and often do resist the soundest of reasons. We are quite free to defy rationality and act contrary to sound judgment. Christ presented a perfect apologetic to Judas Iscariot who chose not to believe. Even after reasons for faith are given, the appeal is very much in order for men to exercise the faith which is logically necessary, but practically evadable.

4. The last objection we consider is a psychological one. Modern people are inclined to regard any claim to biblical inerrancy as unworthy of serious consideration. But does this inclination really prove anything? If it does not prove anything then is it not sheer prejudice? And if men are prejudiced does that oblige us to find something to fit their prejudices, or rather, to attempt to correct them?

Quite unprejudiced persons may have a hostile attitude because of misinformation. They may be hostile to a Christianity which is not Christianity at all. If you patiently and intelligently set forth an adequate explanation rather than assume a condemnatory stance, you may find a man who, instead of being hostile to Christ, will believe in Him almost as soon as he learns His true name.

In conclusion, one more important consensus must not be overlooked in the heat of battle, in spite of the important differences in the area of revelational theology. Orthodox and neo-orthodox both pay tribute to the Word of God which comes through the Bible. However differently they may think of the way it comes through, or even of what comes through—the Word of God does come through. We must not deny that any man believes in the Word of God because he is unable to state his conviction in a consistent manner. The manner of stating this conviction may be opposed, but not at the price of ignoring conviction itself. When men crucify their intellects and do violence even to the written Word of God, let us object and let us oppose, but when in their agonizing way they affirm the revealed Word of God, let our hearts go out to them and our arms go about them.

THE NATURE
OF THE BIBLE

✝

Robert D. Preus

Robert D. Preus is Assistant Professor of Systematic Theology in Concordia Theological Seminary (Missouri Synod), St. Louis. He is a descendant of six generations of Lutheran clergymen; his father, J. A. O. Preus, was governor of Minnesota from 1920 to 1924. He is author of The Inspiration of Scripture, A Study of the Theology of the 17th Century Lutheran Dogmaticians *(1957). He received his B.D. degree from Bethany Seminary, Mankato, Minnesota, and his Ph.D. from University of Edinburgh.*

THE NATURE
OF THE BIBLE

WHAT IS the Bible? Very obviously it is a human book, or series of books, written by a number of human penmen in human language over a period of about fifteen hundred years. It was written *by* human beings *for* human beings. It reflects human thoughts, aspirations, ideas; human love, humility, pain, joy, grief and peace of mind. It portrays with arresting clarity the noblest love, the darkest hate, the firmest faithfulness and the deepest despair of men. No book searches the chambers of the human heart so thoroughly and relentlessly as the Bible. No book reveals the fears, the animosities, the joys and passions of its writers so clearly and movingly. If you would learn to know man as he really is, as he thinks and feels and desires, and stripped of all pretense, read the Bible. Read Psalm 51 and you learn of the sorrow and yearnings of a truly penitent sinner. Read the book of Jeremiah and you gain immediate insight into how a man of God feels when he sees God and His Word rejected on every hand. And what writings have ever been more thoroughly human and personal, what writings have ever more completely laid bare the soul of their author than the letters of Paul who prays, exhorts, comforts, confesses, boasts, and sings in his heart in all of his writings? The Scriptures have been written, and through the years copied, circulated, read and finally collected into a definite canon (normative volume) by *human beings.* The Bible did not fall down from heaven, but originated and grew in the Church of God. Books of the Bible were written according to the demands and exigencies of the times. There is nothing mechanical or artificial or unhuman about the Bible.

Yet we call this book God's Word: in this we say it differs from all

other books. And this is not our own extravagant and capricious judg-
ment; it is also the claim of Christ and the Scriptures themselves, as
we shall presently see. What do we mean when we call Scripture God's
Word? Can these thoroughly human writings be the Word of God?
This is one of the most vexing and pressing questions confronting the
Church today.

I. THE BIBLE IS THE WORD OF GOD

Two approaches commend themselves to the Christian in answering
the question, What is the nature of the Bible? First, we may enquire,
What was our Lord's attitude toward the Bible? How did He use it and
regard it? Second, we may examine what the Bible says about itself:
what are its claims concerning its nature, its authority, its divine origin?
Approaching the question in this twofold manner, we find an answer,
a positive and comforting answer.

It should be of utmost importance to every Christian to know what
Christ thought about the Scriptures and how He dealt with them; for
what He thinks and does will be normative for us, His disciples. A
prominent Norwegian theologian today has said, "If Jesus Christ the
God-Man is in the history of the human race, then He and He alone
knows all things correctly and truly also in respect to the Scriptures.
Therefore a truly Christian theology of Scripture will be known by this,
that it dares to take this position as its basis, that it does not desire to have
any other view of Scripture than that which Jesus had and no other
view of Jesus Christ than that which Scripture presents. This basic
attitude is no argument in a circle but is the very nerve center of the
Christian's life of faith" (Olav Valen-Sendstad, *Ordet Som Aldri Kan Dø*,
Bergen, A. Lunde & Co. Forlag, 1949, p. 78).

We see at the outset that Jesus knew the Scriptures of the Old Testament, He held always a most submissive attitude toward them, He used
them, loved them and lived in them. In all His utterances and applica-
tions it is clear that He held to the divine origin of Scripture: Scripture
was truly the Word of God. When the Pharisees place their traditions
in opposition to Scripture, Christ insists that they have made the Word
of God of none effect.

It is in His temptation that the Son of Man makes most articulate His
position in this matter. He withstands the first thrust of the tempter by
quoting Deuteronomy 8:3 (cf. Matt. 4:4): "Man doth not live by bread
alone, but by every word that proceedeth out of the mouth of the Lord
doth man live." What are these words of the Lord by which man lives?
They are the words of Scripture, as the context in Deuteronomy shows:
they are the words which God communicated to Moses and Moses in turn
to the people. Jesus too is thinking of Scripture when He cites this passage;

for, as He continues his battle with the evil one, two more Scripture passages become His weapon in warding off the attack. There is something remarkable about all this: Jesus too, true man, lives by the Words of God, that is, by Scripture. In conclusion we might remark that no phrase in the Bible emphasizes the divine origin of a word so definitely as this, that the mouth of the Lord speaks it (cf. Isa. 1:20; Num. 23:19; Isa. 34:16, 17; 58:14; Ez. 3:17; Jer. 9:12; Lam. 3:38). How could I describe a message more clearly as God's Word than to say it issues from His mouth? With this phrase Jesus would have us know that Scripture is God's Word in the same sense as a word proceeding from my mouth is my word.

Jesus' utter submission to the authority of Scripture in His life and ministry reveals that He held to its divine origin and nature. As true man He submitted in every way to Scripture. Scripture was the basis of all His teaching and preaching. In struggles with adversaries sacred Scripture is to Him the final authority for faith and life. Even He, the Son, is bound by Scripture, for He says, "Think not that I am come to destroy the law or the prophets (that is, Scripture); I am not come to destroy but to fulfill. For verily I say unto you, Till heaven and earth pass, one jot or one tittle shall in no wise pass from the law till all be fulfilled" (Matt. 5:17, 18). Not the smallest letter or part of a letter can be set aside, He says. The entire life of Christ was directed according to a course set for Him by the Scriptures. For this reason He so often says that He *must* do the things He does (John 20:9; Luke 18:31-33; 22:37; John 5:30). Listen to His words: "The Son of man goeth *as it is written* of Him" (Matt. 26:24). Again: "These are the words which I spake unto you while I was yet with you, that all things must be fulfilled which were in the Law of Moses and in the Prophets and in the Psalms concerning me" (Luke 24:46). Finally, we find Jesus supporting and proving all His doctrine from Scripture. When He speaks of God or of man or of His Messiahship or of salvation, He appeals to Scripture as His basis. And why is the Son of God bound by Scripture? Because Scripture is the Word of very God, and our Lord cannot deny Himself. Today Christians will not wish to break with Christ's attitude toward the Scriptures nor improve upon His method of using them. Rather, learning to appreciate Christ's high view of the Scriptures, that to Him they have proceeded from the mouth of God, we will embrace these sacred writings with the same ready mind, and with avidity we will run to draw water from these wells of salvation.

From our Lord's bearing and attitude toward the Scriptures we perceive that He has simply taken them at their word. The written words of Moses are called the words of the Lord (Exod. 24), and these become the foundation of God's covenant with His people (Exod. 34:37). For this reason God's people are to read this Word, that they might know God's will and His great acts (Deut. 31:7 ff.); and they are to obey this Word of the Lord and live in it (Josh. 1:7,8). It was the claim of the Old Testament prophets too that they declare the Word of God. Hence, the frequent refrains: "Thus saith the Lord," "Hear the word of the Lord," "The mouth of the Lord hath spoken," "The word of the Lord came." They considered themselves penmen of God, moved by the Spirit of God when they spoke and wrote (II Sam. 23:1). And their books were therefore called the "book of the Lord" (Isa. 34:16). All this Jesus takes for granted as He teaches and preaches the Scriptures.

And our Lord's apostles as they write the New Testament are in accord with this conviction. They quote the Old Testament as the Word of God. In citing the Scriptures their common practice is to refer to God speaking *through* the prophets (Matt. 2:15; Rom. 1:1, 2; 9:25; Heb. 1:1; Acts 1:16; 28:25). These flesh and blood prophets, speaking, writing, thinking, reflecting, feeling, are *God's instruments* in speaking to men. So closely do the New Testament writers identify Scripture as God's Word that they sometimes hypostatize these Old Testament writings, as though the writings were a thinking, rational subject, an omniscient Person. The Scriptures are said to speak (Rom. 4:3; 10:11; Jas. 2:23); the Scriptures foresee (Gal. 3:8; the Scriptures raise up King Pharaoh (Rom. 9:17). Thus, we see that the apostles do not shrink from using the subject "Scripture" and the subject "God" interchangeably. And there is really nothing strange about this when we consider that Scripture is God's Word, God's utterances (Rom. 3:2), God speaking. What can be more closely identified with me than my word? Can my word be separated from me? It is not without reason that the old Lutheran theologians refused to call Scripture a creation of God, but suggested that it might better be called a sort of effluence of God.

Two New Testament passages loom large as we consider the nature of Scripture as God's Word. The first speaks with simplicity and unmistakable clarity of the divine origin of Scripture; the second speaks of the relation between the human writers and the divine author. The first passage (I Tim. 3:16) has given rise to the term "inspiration." The passage follows upon a context in which Paul has been warning his younger co-worker to beware of men like Jannes and Jambres who resist the truth and whose rebellion against sound doctrine will wax worse and worse, men deceiving and being deceived. But there is a sure way in which Timothy can avoid the pitfall laid by these evil workers: he is to continue in those things which he has learned from Paul. And the blessed doctrine which he received of Paul is the same which in childhood he learned from his mother Eunice and his grandmother Lois when they taught him the holy Scriptures. These Scriptures are so powerful that they make wise unto salvation through faith in Christ who is their heart and center. If Timothy will abide in these he will be safe from all danger.

But Paul has more to say of the Scriptures than simply this reference to their power. They are given by inspiration. What does this mean? The Greek word *theopneustos* which Paul uses here means "God-breathed." It is a verbal adjective from the word "to breathe," or "to blow." Paul is not speaking of a physical breathing, but says that Scripture is the breath of the living God, the speech from the blowing of the Spirit of God. The adjective here is passive not active: Paul is not saying that Scripture breathes out something, that it is inspiring (although this is true), but that it is breathed forth from God's mouth, it is the product of His breath. All this means that God, strictly speaking, is the author of Scripture. Paul is saying precisely what Christ and the apostles infer when they quote the Scriptures as God's Word.

It should go without saying that Paul is teaching a verbal inspiration. He does not say, "Everything in Scripture is God-breathed." This would imply the inspiration of the content, but not of the words of the Bible, if such a thing were possible. Nor does Paul say, "Scripture as a whole is God-breathed." This would imply that certain passages of Scripture in their contexts may not be God's Word. But Paul uses the distributive term, "All Scripture." Actually there is no other kind of inspiration: since Scripture consists of words, it is these words that are inspired. Scripture inspiration is in the nature of the case verbal inspiration. Words are the means by which a person shares his thoughts and reveals his heart to others. And God has condescended to use this manner of human communication. Through the words of Scripture God brings men to know His thoughts, thereby bringing human speech into His service. Thus he has willed to reveal in a relevant and final form His holy will and eternal plan of salvation, and this to all men, great and small, good and bad, learned and simple.

A final word about this passage. The term "given by inspiration of God" (*theopneustos*) merely expresses a fact, not the how of the fact. Inspiration, like conversion, is a great and incomprehensible miracle of God's grace. We only know that it has happened, and we adore God for that. For here is a Word which is not only divine in its origin, and thus infallible in all its utterances, but a Word which even today speaks to us (note how the New Testament employs the present tense "it says" when citing the Old Testament) and is powerful to work in us a spiritual life which comes to fruition in an eternal life.

But what about the human writers of Scripture? Certainly their thoughts and concerns and passions, their several styles of writing, are reflected in the Bible. What is their part in the writing of Scripture? In answering this question (so far as it can be answered at all) a second passage (II Pet. 1:21) is helpful: "The prophecy came not in old time by the will of man: but holy men of God spake as they were moved by the Holy Ghost." That the apostle here refers to the *speaking* of the prophets does not imply that he has no reference to *their writings*. In the previous verse he has spoken of the prophecy *of Scripture*. Moreover, it is not uncommon in the New Testament to find the word "speak" (*laleō*) used when the writing of a prophet or apostle is definitely referred to (John 12:41; I Cor. 2:6, 7; Heb. 7:14; II Pet. 3:16). Assuming then that Peter has the Old Testament in mind, his meaning is simply that Scripture did not come into being according to human initiative or spirit or will, but by the Holy Spirit. A parallel to the picture Peter is drawing may be found in John 1:13 where we are told that we are born again not of the will of men, but of God. Thus, the theory that Scripture was brought about by any independent activity of men is simply denied here. But the prophets spoke and wrote, being moved (*pheromenol*), carried, borne by the Spirit of God. As the ship upon which Paul journeyed to Rome was carried along by the wind (Acts 27:15 ff.), so the holy writers of Scripture were borne by the heavenly wind, the Holy Spirit.

B. B. Warfield says, "The men who spoke from God are here declared, therefore, to have been taken up by the Holy Ghost and brought by His power to the goal of His choosing. The things which they spoke under this operation of the Spirit were therefore His things, not theirs. And that is the reason which is assigned why the 'prophetic word' is so sure" (*The Inspiration and Authority of the Bible*, Philadelphia, Presbyterian & Reformed Publishing Co., 1948, p. 137). Actually Peter is here asserting explicitly what the other New Testament writers infer when in citing the Scriptures they say the Holy Spirit spoke *through* the prophets (Acts 1:16; 28:25; Heb. 3:7, 8).

Christ's apostles in the New Testament express the same claims for their preaching and writing as they avow for the Old Testament Scriptures. They have been commissioned to speak and write the same message and their message is no different in nature or quality from that of the Old Testament prophets (Rom. 1:1, 2). They are proclaiming nothing but the fulfillment of what was foretold by the prophets; the same things which were before written the apostles now preach and commit to writing (I Pet. 1:10-12). The words of prophets and apostles are made equal in authority (II Pet. 3:2), and New Testament letters are called Scripture along with the Old Testament (II Pet. 3:16). The Gospel message proclaimed in the New Testament was received in no other way than by the revelation of Jesus Christ (Gal. 1:12). Therefore an apostle dares explicitly to call his inspired words the word of God (I Thess. 2:13). The apostles were called to preach and write, set apart by the will of God (Rom. 1:1). Therefore they can speak in the name of the Lord (I Cor. 1:10). They speak the wisdom of God in a mystery (I Cor. 2:7), they speak things which God has revealed by His Spirit (v. 10), they know those things which are given freely by God (v. 12), they speak in words which the Holy Ghost teaches (v. 11). And finally the bold and apostolic boast is made,

"We have the mind of Christ" (v. 16). Thus, it is quite certain that Christ's apostles consider themselves like the prophets of old, instruments of God, instruments who speak and write what God has revealed to them (1 John 1:1-5) and who write with God's authority (I Cor. 14:37; II Thess. 2:15), instruments through whom Christ speaks (II Cor. 13:3). And what is the basis for such confident claims? Christ's commission: "I have sent them into the world" (John 17:18-20). Christ's promise: "Ye shall receive power, after that the Holy Ghost is come upon you: and ye shall be witnesses unto me . . ." (Acts 1:8; cf. John 14:26; 15:26, 27; 16:13). Here was the *a priori* guarantee that the Spirit of truth would be speaking through them, that they would be inspired witnesses of saving truth, that they would be qualified fully and objectively to communicate to the Church every saving truth which it was required to know.

Now what conclusions can we draw from all the evidence displayed above? What significance is there in the fact that all the Bible is truly and in itself the Word of God? We derive this comforting certainty that the holy Scriptures, which are God's Word, carry with them God's authority, God's truth (reliability), God's power. That the Scriptures possess the authority of very God has been amply demonstrated above when we observed the attitude of Christ and His apostles toward them.

The truthfulness and reliability of Scripture are also shown by our Lord's approach to these sacred writings. Throughout His ministry Jesus met people with the Scriptures, and there is no hesitancy, no embarrassment on His part, no evasion or qualification. He simply says, "It is written"; or He quotes a prophet; or He says, "Scripture says"; and what follows is unconditionally true. Jesus simply accepts the historicity and truthfulness of what is recorded in Scripture: He takes for granted the creation and existence of our first parents (Matt. 19:4), the existence of Satan who deceived man in the garden (John 8:44), the historicity of the murder of Abel (Luke 11:51), of Noah and the flood (Matt. 24:37 ff.), of the destruction of Sodom (Luke 17:28 ff.), of the events in David's life (Mark 2:25, 26) and Solomon's life (Matt. 6:29), of Jonah being swallowed by the whale (Matt. 12:39, 40), of Elijah being fed by the widow of Zarephath (Luke 4:25 f.), of Elisha and Naaman (Luke 4:27). Jesus commits Himself to the truths of these accounts, and places His stamp of approval on all the recorded history of the Old Testament. It is significant that He has accepted many accounts which seem incredible to many expositors today, or which at one time or another have seemed so. To Jesus a person is a fool for not believing the Scriptures (Luke 24:25). For the Scripture cannot be broken, cannot be withstood, cannot err (John 10:35). To the Sadducees He says, "Do ye not therefore err, because ye know not the scriptures?" (Mark 12:24). The implication is that they might not err when they know the Scriptures, and that because Scripture does not err. One simply cannot understand Christ's use of Scripture apart from His conviction that they were inerrant.

Finally, what can we say of the power of Scripture? It has the intrinsic power, Paul tells us, to make us wise unto salvation, to work the faith of Christ in our hearts (2 Tim. 3:15), and this because of its message which is Christ. Christ is the soul and center of the Scriptures. Scripture teaches us, it makes us wise, by placarding Christ crucified before our eyes. And for every penitent sinner this is a message of sweetest comfort. It can fill the most despondent heart with peace and joy and hope. For it tells every poor sinner of a Saviour crucified and risen, a Saviour God who has thrust Himself into our misery and taken our place, and who offers us His righteousness, God's forgiveness, reconciliation, salvation. When we embrace this message *we become wise*. Not merely because we have acquired a little more factual knowledge. Paul tells us that this message of Scripture comes to us "not in word only, but also in power, and in the Holy Ghost and in much assurance" (I Thess. 1:5). It is God's power unto salvation. It not only informs us, but seizes us and changes us and makes us a new creation, children of God. Scripture is not merely like a billboard which speaks *about* Christ and eternal life. It *brings* Christ to me, and in turn brings me, a poor, lost sinner to Christ. What the living word of Scripture has done in us is no less than what the living word of Christ accomplished in dead Lazarus: it has given us life.

Authority, power, perfection, truthfulness: all this we mean when we call Scripture the Word of God. Scripture is God's living voice today, a *revelation* of His glory, His mighty acts of redemption, His grace in Christ.[1]

------

[1] Since the evidence for the power of the Word which is Scripture, and the Word which is drawn from Scripture is so vast, we can offer here only a short series of paradigms which we commend to the reader to study at his leisure. We might also urge the reader to consider from Scripture the amazing effect the Word has had upon those who have been touched and uplifted by it.

1) The Word is powerful:
   it builds us up spiritually: Acts 20:32
   it is living and powerful, etc.: Heb. 4:11
   it is power of God: 1 Cor. 1:18
   unto salvation: Rom. 1:16 (cf. 2 Cor. 10:4; Eph. 3:7)

2) Its power is shown in that it does certain things:
   it *grows, increases* and multiplies:
       Acts 6:7; 12:24; 19:20
   it *runs:* 2 Thess. 3:1
   it is not bound: 2 Tim. 2:9
   it opens doors: Col. 4:3

3) It is likened to an instrument of power:
   An inanimate and passive instrument:
       hammer: Jer. 23:29
       shepherd's staff: Ps. 23:4
       sceptre: Ps. 45:6

II. THE MODERN REVOLT AGAINST THE BIBLE

The scriptural position which had been outlined above was generally held in the Christian Church until the periods of the Enlightenment and of classical liberalism. Already in the seventeenth and eighteenth centuries Cartesian and Wolffian philosophies, predicated upon the theory of a closed universe, were denying or undermining the significance of miracles. Such philosophies tended also to undermine the divine origin of Scripture. At the same time Spinoza, Lessing and others were questioning traditional opinions concerning the nature and origin of many books in the Bible; they were applying the methods of historical criticism to Scripture. One of the first theologians to adopt the prevailing philosophy and break with orthodox doctrine concerning the nature of the Bible was Sigmund Baumgarten (1706-57). He failed to understand the orthodox teaching that Scripture was only one mode of revelation, and represented the older view as identifying revelation and inspiration. To him the Bible was only the record, or original source, of revelation.

Baumgarten was followed by Johann Semler (1725-91), who is usually called the father of modern biblical criticism. Semler severed the Word of God from Scripture. Scripture *became* the Word of God, he said, only when and insofar as it speaks to the subjective needs of man; only then could one speak of inspiration. Semler was a thorough rationalist: he denied miracles and predictive prophecy and contended that all theologies were mere human attempts to find truth. Such tenets were, according to Semler, a necessary preunderstanding for the correct approach to the Scriptures: the interpreter must be liberated from the old theory that Scripture's authority is God's authority before he can study it critically like other books. Semler was followed by Vatke (a Hegelian), Baur, Kuenen, Eichhorn, De Wette, Strauss, Graf and others. All were heavily

---

An animate instrument with intrinsic power:
  lamp and light: Prov. 6:23; Ps. 119:105
  a living and incorruptible seed: 1 Pet. 1:23
  rain and dew: Deut. 32:2
  honey: Ps. 119:103
  fire: Jer. 23:29

4) The Word works great spiritual effects:
  it regenerates: 1 Pet. 1:23; Jas. 1:18; 1 Cor. 4:15 (gospel word)
  it works repentance and converts: Ps. 197:7 ff; 2 Tim. 2:25
  it purifies: John 15:3
  it saves: Jas. 1:21; *Jn. 5:24, 39; 6:69;* Acts 11:14; *1 Cor. 1:21*
  it makes holy: 2 Tim. 4:5
  it gives life: 2 Cor. 3:6; Phil. 2:16; *Jn. 6:63* (this is
    related to the 4th classification above)
  it bestows faith: John 1:7; *17:20; Rom. 10:17;* 1 Cor. 3:25
    (people believed by Paul['s] or Apollo's ['preaching'])
  Col. 1:5, 6 (hope which we have with faith)

influenced by the new historical criticism and convinced that Scripture, like all other books, must be studied according to its canons. All entertained theories toward the Bible which made of it something less than God's Word and revelation. All ended in the same theological blind alley, skepticism.

Meanwhile other movements were astir: Kantian and Hegelian idealism, evolutionism. Kant's insistence that there could be no factual knowledge of transcendental reality drove the already harried theologians into disorganized retreat. Following Kant's lead, Ritschl reduced all theology to value judgments to which there was no corresponding reality and the only basis of which was the enlightened reason of the believer. Thus there was no place for a Word of God, a revelation. Intimidated and unable to answer Kant, Schleiermacher retreated into subjectivism, making Christianity not a matter of cognitive knowledge at all, but a matter of feeling, a feeling of dependence upon God. To him the Bible did not communicate God's thoughts toward man, but expressed man's thoughts toward God, man's religious experience. And so it went through the nineteenth century, Luthardt drawing his theology from the "Christian consciousness," von Hoffman from the Spirit-filled "Ego," Kahnis from the "consciousness of the Church," these theologians all the while turning their faces persistently in the wrong direction, away from that revealed Word, that fount of theology which is the Scriptures of God, either ignoring the concept of revelation and God's Word altogether, or centering revelation exclusively in God's past acts of which there was no reliable witness.

From such an oppressive, enervating climate have emerged two great contemporary movements, neo-orthodoxy and the modern biblical theology movement, reminding us again that God has spoken. In fact, modern theology has discussed with so much emphasis and vigor the formerly neglected subjects of special revelation, Scripture and the Word of God, that its spokesmen appear almost as new prophets and even champions of the Bible and of conservative theology. For this recent stress on many vital themes we can indeed be grateful. A closer look at what modern theology teaches concerning the nature of the Bible, however, will reveal that neo-orthodoxy and modern biblical theology agree rather closely with their liberal precursors on a number of fundamental issues: to them the Bible in itself, strictly speaking, is *not* the Word of God; the Bible is authority and power of God speaking. Let us examine the tenets of modern theology on these matters.

Does modern theology teach that Scripture is, properly speaking, God's Word? Karl Barth, perhaps the most conservative leader of that movement called neo-orthodoxy, does indeed *call* the Bible God's Word. But by this he means only that the Bible *becomes* the Word of God when God makes it speak to me (*Church Dogmatics,* Edinburgh, T. & T. Clark,

1936, Vol. I/2, p. 512; also I/1, p. 124). He says, "The Bible is God's Word so far as God lets it be His Word, so far as God speaks through it" (*ibid.,* I/1, p. 123). The verbal inspiredness of Scripture Barth rejects as something mechanical, something docetic, which divests the Scriptures of their human side and curtails the "freedom" of the biblical writers (*ibid.,* I/2, p. 518). It would seem that to Barth the Bible is divine only in the sense that it testifies to the divine Christ (cf. also Emil Brunner, *Revelation and Reason,* Philadelphia, The Westminster Press, 1946, p. 135); its nature is not divine.

If Barth and his followers are somewhat equivocal when they call Scripture God's Word, modern biblical theologians are more forthright. C. H. Dodd, for instance, is frank to tell us that "in the literal sense the Bible consists of the 'words' of men—or rather of their visible symbols in writing. It is not the utterance of God in the same sense in which it is the utterance of men. . . . God is the Author not of the Bible, but of the life in which the authors of the Bible partake, and of which they tell us in such imperfect human words as they could command" (*The Authority of the Bible,* London, James Nisbet & Co., 1928, pp. 16, 17). Inspiration to Dodd pertains not to the Bible but to the human writers of Scripture, to the fact that they are men of religious genius, of deep spiritual insight. He reduces inspiration to divine guidance, a common practice today.

Why do Barth and Dodd and so many other modern theologians refuse to face up to the biblical evidence that Scripture is divine, the product of God's breath? It is no doubt because they are committed to the higher criticism of the Bible, they are convinced that there are errors in the Bible. Dodd says that the words of the Epistle to the Romans carry no more weight than we can allow Paul as a religious teacher: when Paul speaks in his letter, this is not an infallible Word, this is not God speaking. This is precisely Barth's view also: we can criticize the books of the Bible philosophically, historically, ethically, even theologically, he avers; all the Bible is capable of error even in respect to religion and theology; we may argue with James or Paul (*op. cit.,* Vol. I/2, pp. 507, 510).

The divine origin and the veracity of Scripture hang together. When one of these facts is denied the other will usually be questioned. So it is also in regard to the authority and power of God's Scriptures: these properties of Scripture are predicated upon its nature as God's Word. Thus it is not surprising to hear neo-orthodox theologians saying that Scripture is not God's power which makes wise unto salvation, but is only the possibility of becoming that power, where and when God pleases to make it so. Just as the Bible becomes the Word of God in an event of God's choosing, so, say they, it becomes power in an event: intrinsically there is no power in Scripture or in the Church's Gospel proclamation (cf. Barth, *op. cit.,* I/1, 123 ff. Cf. also J. K. S. Reid, *The Authority of*

Scripture, New York, Harper & Brothers, 1957, p. 201 ff.). We might expect just such a view to obtain among those who no longer identify Scripture as God's Word.

Similarly Scripture's authority is threatened or even vitiated when the Bible is no longer considered to be the Word of God. We have already observed how Dodd designates the authority of Scripture as merely that authority which we would accord the human writers, influenced as they were by God. And we can only accept this authority when our own experience compels us to do so. A rather popular view among the neo-orthodoxists sees the authority of the Bible in the fact that it is the earliest and most authentic witness to Christ. J. K. S. Reid says, "The authority of the Bible reposes in the fact that, in statements some right and some wrong, and in practical application some of which is disputable and some even more dubious, a unified witness is borne to Him who is at the center of the Gospel" *(ibid.,* p. 267). John Baillie, too, declares only that in Scripture which pertains to Christ to be authoritative, and that we must distinguish this essential message from Scripture's numerous imperfections such as historical inaccuracies, inaccurate or conflicting reports, misquotations, and so on. Following Dodd, he believes that many assertive statements in Scripture are relative to their age and simply false and wrong *(The Idea of Revelation in Recent Thought,* London, Oxford University Press, 1956, p. 120). Thus we see these theologians substituting the material principle of theology (Jesus Christ) which is the source of our Christianity for the formal principle of theology (Scripture) which is the source of our doctrine. According to this theory Scripture's authority is above that of some evangelical witness to Christ only by virtue of its chronological priority or by virtue of the deep spiritual insight of its writers. However, on this theory we today are able to criticize these writers of Scripture on numerous points, even theological. We clearly perceive that whatever authority Scripture possesses for modern biblical theology and neo-orthodoxy it is no longer the authority of God speaking.

Emil Brunner and others who are existentially orientated have accused orthodoxy of constructing a doctrine of verbal inspiration and authority of Scripture out of a rationalistic concern for guaranteed certainty, a concern to avoid all risk in theology *(op. cit.,* p. 168). Such a charge is utterly false. The orthodox Church has held that Scripture is inspired and inerrant because this was the persuasion of our Lord Himself and because this is the claim of Scripture. Of course, we derive certainty from this fact, a certainty that our doctrine and preachment is true and authoritative and divinely approved. When we preach or teach from Scripture we do not need to wonder or doubt about our message, we do not need to wait for the Holy Spirit to come and add His power to that

Word. Together with Paul we can say, "My speech and my preaching was not with enticing words of man's wisdom, but in demonstration of the Spirit and of power" (I Cor. 2:4). Our certainty is not something of our own contrivance, but a Spirit-wrought certainty.

Again it has been charged that our high position concerning Scripture is no longer tenable, no longer a live option in our scientific age (R. Prenter, *Skabelse og Genløsning,* Kobenhavn, 1955, p. 88 ff. Brunner, *op. cit.,* p. 145. This charge was already leveled a century ago by Luthardt, *Compendium der Dogmatik,* Leipzig, 1866, p. 237). Modern science and the historico-critical method of interpreting Scripture have proved, it is said, that there are errors in Scripture. We can only reply that this charge is advanced by those who already begin with the assumption that there are errors and contradictions in the Bible. And what do they employ to prove their assumptions? Certainly they have at their disposal no absolute and infallible standard or criteria to prove errors in Scripture. No, it is their own human discoveries, human ingenuity, human wisdom by which they judge the Scriptures. Man's science, man's historical method, which are God's gifts, are turned against the Word of Him who bestowed these gifts to us. It is a rather common allegation of the neo-orthodox that in spite of all the errors in Scripture, God somehow thereby gets His truth across to us. (Barth, *op. cit.,* Vol. I/2, p. 530; Dodd, *op. cit.,* p. 17). We can only say that if the historic doctrine of inerrancy seems obscurant and obtuse and blind to certain "facts" of history and science, the view of neo-orthodoxism is simply nonsense.

Finally the orthodox doctrine on the nature of the Bible has been caricatured as deifying the Scriptures, as ignoring their obvious human side (cf. Reid, *op. cit.,* p. 167; Baillie, *op. cit.,* p. 110; W. Elert. *Der Christliche Glaube,* Hamburg, 1956. p. 171). We reply that it is impossible to deify that which is already divine. But we must also repeat that we have no wish whatever to deny or minimize the importance of the so-called human side of Scripture, no more than we would make light of our Lord's human nature. God has condescended to come into our world in human form and to reveal Himself to us in human language. But just as the man Jesus of Nazareth was true God, the human world and language of Scripture is truly God's Word and language and expresses His thoughts toward us. Valen-Sendstad writes, "Therefore faith cannot accommodate itself to speak about 'errors and contradictions' in Scripture, but it does not deny that Scripture has a 'form of lowliness' which offers many possibilities of offence for unbelief. Also in this respect Scripture's appearance is similar to the humiliated appearance of the Son of God: men will take offence until they are convinced by the Spirit and begin to love Jesus Christ and the Scripture" (*op. cit.,* p. 76). Orthodox theology earnestly desires to avail itself of every tool—

archeology, linguistics, text criticism, history—for a better understanding and appreciation of the message of Scripture, a message vouchsafed to us entirely in human garb.

In keeping with its opinion on the origin and nature of the Bible, modern theology rejects the doctrine that Scripture is a divine revelation. There are two popular views today concerning the relation between revelation and the Bible. The position of modern systematic theology (neo-orthodoxy but also Bultmann) makes revelation a confrontation of God with man, a *personal encounter* (Emil Brunner, *The Divine-Human Encounter,* Philadelphia, The Westminster Press, 1943, pp. 94 ff.). Bultmann calls it "personal address" (*Existence and Faith,* New York, Living Age, 1960, p. 64). Thus, revelation does not offer us information about God, but God Himself in communion (Baillie, *op. cit.,* p. 47). This view which leans heavily on Existentialism makes revelation always contemporary. It emphasizes the dynamic nature of revelation almost to the exclusion of the informative and noetic nature and purpose of revelation. It virtually identifies revelation with conversion. On this view the Bible is considered a "possibility," or occasion, of revelation (Reid, *op. cit.,* p. 196). To varying degrees, this position cuts off revelation from history, from God's great acts of redemption which are in our history. Bultmann, for instance, goes so far as to say that there is no factuality behind any of the redemptive "myths" connected with Christ's activity recounted in the New Testament. The only historical and real referent he has for revelation is the so-called kerygma which is merely the theology of the early Church.

The second popular view concerning revelation and the Bible is advanced primarily by those concerning themselves with biblical theology (but not Bultmann). The advocates of this view seek to do justice to the historical aspect of revelation and to avoid the subjectivity of the neo-orthodox position. They center revelation in God's past mighty acts (cf. G. E. Wright and R. Fuller, *The Book of the Acts of God.* New York, Doubleday & Company, 1960). Sometimes they add that man's appreciation of these acts is a part of this revelation (Baillie, *op. cit.,* pp. 62 ff.). To them the Bible is only a record of revelation, and an errant record at that. Many of those events recorded in Scripture, even such important events as the Exodus and the Resurrection, did not happen as the Bible depicts them. For the Bible gives witness only to what the Israelites *believed* concerning God's words and acts. Thus, we cannot know whether any of these events happened in our space and time.

It is ironic how, years before these modern notions came upon the scene, the orthodox doctrine of revelation had incorporated the good and biblical aspects of both views. The older doctrine spoke of revelation as something objective, something always there and available; revelation was centered in God's concrete and historical acts of judgment and redemption; it was centered also in the sacred Scriptures which interpreted these acts and went beyond these acts in revealing the living God. At the same time the orthodox doctrine spoke of the continuity of revelation, of a God who discloses Himself and speaks to us *now* through Scripture and the proclamation of the Church. This position was tied to the doctrine that Scripture was truly God's Word, that is, God's power and revelation.

It has been said that we have gone beyond the facts when we call Scripture a revelation; nowhere does the Bible explicitly claim to be a revelation from God. We might reply that nowhere does the Bible explicitly claim to be a record of revelation or a possibility of revelation, as modern theology conjectures. But our principle and positive reply to neo-orthodoxy must be this. We must all return to the basic conviction of historic Christianity concerning the form of the Bible, that the sacred Scriptures are not merely metonymically or hyperbolically, but, as our theologians have said, truly and in the proper sense, God's Word, the product of His breath (II Tim. 3:16), the very utterances of God (Rom. 3:2).

What does this mean? It has the profoundest meaning for the Church, for her theology and her very life and activity. We *live* by the Word of God. Christ's words are spirit and life (John 6:63). The Scriptures are able to make us wise unto salvation through faith in Christ Jesus (II Tim. 3:15). Whatever we say about Scripture, its authority, its truthfulness, its power, its sufficiency to lead us through all the exigencies of life and death, is predicated by virtue of its divine origin, its inner nature as God's Word.

Now what does a word do? What is its usual function? It is to communicate, to move, to evoke, to delight, *to reveal*. My words are a revelation of my heart. Christ, the hypostatic Word, which is "with God" (John 1:1), who is "in the bosom of the Father," He reveals God (John 1:18). And the prophetic and apostolic Word which on its own testimony proceeds from the mouth of God *reveals* God. This is what we mean when we call Scripture a revelation. And whoever believes that Scripture is God's Word will surely concur with our conviction.

From the foregoing it should be clear that modern theology's doctrine of Scripture is both one-sided and dangerous. Where the divine origin of Scripture is denied, where Scripture is not treated as God's Word, the Bible loses its high position in the Church. The Christian view of revelation is either reduced to some sort of ineffable encounter with God, not unlike two strangers colliding on the street, or it gives way to a fruitless search for God's revelatory acts which lie under countless incrustations of errant records. More than this, revealed theology (language about God) is denied when the revealed nature of the language of Scripture is denied. True theology in the Church becomes an impossible and endless quest, since there is no inerrant basis for theology. Theology becomes mere human opinion, insight, conjecture; or (as the positivists say) mere emotive language which does not inform us or tell us anything about God and His will and activity, but merely moves us like a symphony or piece of abstract art—or at best tells us what theologians *believe* and *think* about God.

From such impoverished opinions we are delivered when we recognize the Bible as *God's* Word. What a joy and comfort to know that whenever you take up this book and read it, whenever you hear it preached in its purity, whenever you meditate upon it, God Himself is present, speaking to you and mediating to you His Son, His Holy Spirit, His forgiveness and all the riches of His grace. And should not this be a joy and comfort to us? You and I, living in this fallen, cursed, confused world can have the confidence, even though we never see God, that He nevertheless speaks to us in the Bible, speaks to us as personally and with the same truth and power as He spoke to Adam in the garden of Eden or to Abraham on the fields of Mamre. What all this means is that the Bible is the most useful and practical book in the world, as Paul says (II Tim. 3:16-17). It not only teaches me how to be a good father, a good citizen, a good neighbor; it not only tells me what are good morals and good principles of living. It gives me a new outlook on life, a heavenly viewpoint, which no other book in the world can give; and it sets me on that way toward eternal life, the way of faith in Christ. The Bible brings God to me, it brings heaven to earth, it brings hope to my confusion and grace into my life of sin and sorrow. It tells me the thoughts of God, His thoughts of peace, and not of evil, toward me. It is the Lord's staff which comforts me in every trouble and distress. It is my spiritual meat and drink which nourishes and strengthens me every day of my life. And greatest of all, it is the Spirit's means to unite me with my Saviour.

THE NATURE OF THE PHYSICAL UNIVERSE

✝

Gordon H. Clark

Gordon H. Clark is Professor of Philosophy at Butler University, In-dianapolis. He is author of A Christian View of Men and Things *(1952),* Thales to Dewey *(1957),* Karl Barth's Theological Method *(1963) and other works. He holds the B.A. and Ph.D. degrees from University of Pennsylvania, where he served as Instructor in Philosophy from 1924-37. From 1937-43 he was Professor of Philosophy in Wheaton College, Illi-nois. A Reformed Presbyterian clergyman, he has taught at Butler since 1945.*

7. *Gordon H. Clark*

THE NATURE OF THE PHYSICAL UNIVERSE

SINCE THE BIBLE not only contains incidental remarks concerning natural phenomena, but incorporates events, dates, and places in its essential message, comparisons between theology and scientific theory have inevitably been drawn. Such comparisons, indeed such a conflict, occurred in pagan antiquity also, for Lucretius wrote out a system of science based on the first principle that "nothing is ever begotten of nothing by divine power" (*De rerum natura*, I, 150).

I. SCIENTISTS AND THEOLOGIANS

In 1896 Andrew Dickson White published *A History of the Warfare of Science with Theology*, in which, often with acrimonious phraseology, he inveighed against the stupidities of religious spokesmen.

Undoubtedly many theologians have made stupid scientific blunders. For example, White describes the theological opposition to inoculation. By White's own account, however, the opposition was at least as much medical as theological. "Foremost among the opponents was Dr. Douglas, a Scotch physician, supported by the medical profession and the newspapers" (Vol. II, p. 56). The author also generously praises Cotton Mather for favoring inoculation, but rather strangely attributes this favor to a decline of theology in Mather.

Other examples of theological blundering are the several theories invented to explain fossils. Yet the author again admits that Voltaire, hardly an orthodox theologian, explained the existence of marine fossils at high elevations as the remains of fish and shells dropped by the crusaders returning from the Holy Land (Vol. I, p. 229).

With respect to the physical sciences White also acknowledges that Cotton Mather accepted the heliocentric theory, but he seems to distort the historical situation when he attributes to theology Leibniz' rejection of the theory (Vol. I, p. 149).

And once more, White derides "the theologic [sic] phrase 'nature abhors a vacuum,' " though he fails to note that this idea was derived from the science of Aristotle.

First, then, one may acknowledge that theologians have made many scientific blunders; but possibly these are due more to what they learned from previous scientists who initiated the blunders than from what they learned in theology.

In the second place, it is most important to see how White conceives of science. If we are to compare science with the Bible, we certainly require a clear notion of what science actually is. Now, White rather obviously considers science to be, as many theologians consider theology to be, a system of propositions absolutely and immutably true. For example, he says that Galileo's "discoveries had clearly taken the Copernican theory out of the list of hypotheses, and had placed it before the world as truth" (Vol. I, p. 130). In the same vein he speaks of "the victory of astronomical science over dogmatic theology" (Vol. I, p. 158). Again, he says, "From ... physical science we have the establishment of the great laws of the indestructibility of matter.... Thereby is ended ... the theological theory of a visible universe created out of nothing" (Vol. I, p. 407).

Poor Dr. White! Physics has long ago discarded matter; and one may now question whether anything is indestructible.

And, finally, on an early page, even though the author does not say so in so many words, the tenor of his argument requires the acceptance of the nebular hypothesis as absolute truth (Vol. I, pp. 17-18).

Now, perhaps White is justified in deprecating the motives of John Henry Newman, if indeed Newman was motivated simply by a desire to defend Ptolemaic astronomy; but in contrast to White's unshakeable faith in Newtonian science it might be wise to consider Newman's more skeptical words on alternate astronomical theories: "Neither proposition is true and both are true; neither true philosophically, both true for certain practical purposes." White scorns this as "hopelessly skeptical" (Vol. I, p. 166); here we seriously propose it for further consideration.

At the same time let us set aside another famous nineteenth-century view of the relation between science and theology. The Ritschlian theory was that religion was confined to the sphere of values, while science occupied the field of truth. Therefore they could not possibly conflict. But such a sharp division, putting all value and no truth on one side and all truth and no value on the other, is an impossible bifurcation of life.

A variation of this nineteenth-century theme occurs in a recent article by Dr. Richard H. Bube ("God's Revelations in True Science and in the Scriptures," in *The Collegiate Challenge,* Dec. 1961, p. 9). The resolution of the conflict is here made to depend on the assumption that "science answers *how* and *when;* Christianity answers *who* and *why.*" Such divisions, Ritschlian or otherwise, cannot be accepted because in reality truth and value are intertwined, scientist and worshiper are the same man, and the Bible talks also of *how* and *when.*

II. THEOLOGY AND CONTEMPORARY SCIENCE

To bring the problem up to date, the views of two important contemporary theologians will now be briefly described.

Karl Barth in his first volume of *Church Dogmatics* has discussed the relation of science to theology. Of vital importance for the present purpose is his description of science. Barth virtually defines science in terms of six norms. Norms three and four, the possibility of verification by any attentive student, and regard to what is physically or biologically impossible, are the points at which the warfare between science and theology is most frequently thought to take place. Scientism rules out theology in general because revelation does not permit of laboratory experimentation and verification by all attentive students. Scientism also rules out miracles in particular on the ground that they are physically or biologically impossible.

Barth's solution of the problem is not, is emphatically not, an effort to propose other norms for science, or to alter them so that the positivistic principle of sensory verification be limited; nor does he propose to reexamine the limits of possibility and to replace the currently dominant scientism with a different philosophy of science. He is satisfied simply to say that theology is another study and is not subject to these norms (*Church Dogmatics,* Vol. I/1, Edinburgh, T. & T. Clark, 1936, pp. 315, 316).

In a Festschrift for Heinrich Barth, his brother, he wrote that philosophers and theologians seek the same thing, the one whole truth, but they seek it in different ways. Neither method excludes the other. Neither is superior to the other. The one starts with God and descends; the other starts with this world, with the concept of causality, and ascends from experience to an overarching structure.

All this sounds very much like the medieval theory of twofold truth: as theologians we believe Jesus was born of a virgin, while as philosophers we know that miracles are impossible.

It is interesting to note that in addition to the six norms Barth also mentions the concept of causality as characteristic of science. Rudolf Bultmann does the same thing. And since he competes with Barth for worldwide recognition, his view of science in its relation to theology equally deserves consideration.

For Bultmann the message of the New Testament, true in itself and highly relevant to twentieth-century civilization, is expressed in the mythological language of an ancient world-view. Modern science makes that world-view incredible, so that to preserve the message its New Testament form must be reinterpreted and demythologized. With Bultmann's existentialistic reinterpretation of Christianity we are not here concerned; the present interest lies in his view of science and of the world by which he judges to be incredible the Incarnation, the Virgin Birth, the miracles, the vicarious atonement, the Resurrection, as well as the existence of demons, angels, the Holy Spirit (and one wonders why not also God?).

Bultmann's reason for denying that God can intervene in the world is the inviolable "causal nexus" which modern science is supposed to have discovered connecting all phenomena. Not to extend documentation to weary lengths, a fair idea of Bultmann's view of science may be given by stringing together a series of phrases from the easily available *Kerygma and Myth* (H. W. Bartsch, ed., New York, Harper & Brothers, 1953). After the long dark ages of superstition, "Now [!] the forces and the laws of nature have [really] been discovered . . . ; the discoveries of Copernicus and the atomic theory" are "facts so compelling as to make [man's] previous view of the world untenable . . . ; the stars are physical bodies whose motions are controlled by the laws of the universe; we can no longer believe in spirits. . . . Sickness and the cure of disease are likewise attributable to natural causation . . . ; we are still assigning them [psychological phenomena] to causes and thus far trying to make them scientifically intelligible . . . ; all our thinking today is shaped irrevocably by modern science" (*ibid.*, pp. 3-5).

Bultmann echoes and adapts Feuerbach (cf. my *Thales to Dewey*, Boston, Houghton Mifflin Co., 1957, p. 476) when he writes, "It is impossible to use electric light and the wireless and to avail ourselves of modern medical and surgical discoveries, and at the same time to believe in the New Testament world of spirits and miracles" (*op. cit.*, p. 5).

This particular point, as distinguished from the previous items, is no more convincing now than it was when Feuerbach cited the amazing new inventions of railroads and steamships. For all his belief in spirits and miracles, the apostle Paul used ships and a physician. Improvements in the two would hardly have caused him to abandon his theology.

The crux of the matter is of course the alleged incompatibility between miracles and natural causation. To quote once more, "A miracle—i.e., an act of God—is not visible or ascertainable like worldly events. The only way to preserve the unworldly, transcendental character of the divine activity is to regard it not as an interference in worldly happenings, but something accomplished *in* them in such a way that the closed weft of history as it presents itself to objective observation is left undisturbed" (*ibid.,* p. 197).

Quotations from other works of Bultmann are unnecessary, for he has little more to say on the nature of science. The firmness of his view, however, might be indicated by a passage in *Jesus Christ and Mythology* (New York, Charles Scribner's Sons, 1958, pp. 36-38) where, borrowing from Auguste Comte, he asserts that although science may change in some details, the method of thinking will never change again; and he seems to suggest that the laws of motion are permanent whereas geocentric and heliocentric astronomy may not be.

Now, to all appearances Barth and Bultmann agree with White that science is infallible and obtains fixed and absolute truth. Unless, therefore, one is satisfied with the irrational theory of a twofold truth, one must, when the findings of science disagree with the statements of the Bible, reject the latter and accept science. Religion must be demythologized. But, we ask, is this the view of science that must be taken; or is there something to be said for Newman's more skeptical outlook?

To be a little blunt, the most noticeable characteristic in these theologians' views of science is their extensive ignorance. They simply do not have the remotest idea of what science actually is. If now we are willing to consider a few specific points, and not be satisfied with vague, popular generalities, the warfare of science with theology, though perhaps not eliminated, will appear in a very different light. First, something will be said about classical Newtonian physics, for example, the laws of motion which Bultmann said were permanent; second, some developments of the early twentieth century will be noted; and finally the implications of the most recent philosophy of science will be studied.

Before this, however, it may be well to give a little evidence that theologians are not the only ones to handle science carelessly. Sometimes scientists themselves make doubtful claims. During the centennial celebrations for Charles Darwin a certain college arranged for a lecture by a zoologist. A discussion session was to follow, which I, perhaps as devil's advocate, was asked to conduct. In his lecture the professor of zoology waxed eloquent. He described an evolutionary process starting with inanimate particles and proceeding without a break through plant life, animals, and mankind. This, he assured the audience, was incontrovertible fact. Not a hint of hesitation marred his superb dogmatism.

When it came my turn, I pointed out that there existed not one only, but several quite different theories of evolution. These differ both with respect to method and with respect to extent. Then I related a conversation with a professor of botany. The botanist told me that he had been raised academically on the theory of evolution. When fossil gaps in the geological evidence were noted, the answer had been that further geological discoveries would close the gaps. But, my botanist professor continued, during the last fifty years advancing geology has not closed these gaps, and the examination of strata is now so extensive that it seems unlikely that future discoveries can radically alter the picture. Therefore, he concluded, I cannot accept a continuous evolution of plant life.

After hearing my story, the zoologist lecturer made a most amazing remark. Yes, he said, the botanical evidence for evolution is virtually nil. And this, after his flawless dogmatism!

III.   CHRISTIANITY AND THE CLAIMS OF PHYSICS

Interesting though evolution may be, the warfare of science with theology, or, better, the relation between science and Christianity will be determined on the field of physics, for physics is the purest and most developed form of science. We shall begin with Newton's *Principia* of 1687. By his general theory of gravitation Newton unified Galileo's laws of freely falling bodies with Kepler's laws of planetary motion, laid the basis of all the particularities of the science of mechanics, and did it so well that his construction stood uncontested until the opening of the twentieth century. A man whose thought can dominate science for a full three centuries must have been a genius. No wonder the rhymester Pope exclaimed,

> Nature and Nature's laws lay hid in night;
> God said, Let Newton be! And all was light.

Because the following argument aims to lay bare certain fatal flaws in the Newtonian system, it is not only polite but even necessary to stress the genius of the man. If the materialists of the nineteenth century used his mechanics as an argument against miracles and God, such at least was not Newton's intention. Newton was a more cautious scientist than the later materialists; he was also a devout believer in God, and his sentiments are rather those of Addison's hymn:

> The spacious firmament on high
> With all the blue ethereal sky
> And spangled heavens a shining frame
> Their great Original proclaim.
> . . . . .
> What though in solemn silence all
> Move round this dark terrestrial ball?
> What though no real voice nor sound
> Amidst their radiant orbs be found?

> In reason's ear they all rejoice
> And utter forth a glorious voice;
> Forever singing as they shine,
> "The Hand that made us is divine."

Nevertheless, despite Newton's personal beliefs and intentions, it was the general law of gravitation, that is, the inviolability of the mathematical laws of mechanics, that was used to undermine Christianity. Gravitation and miracles, mechanism and prayer, mathematics and morality, are incompatible. To this, does a Christian have any reply? He has indeed a very lengthy reply, a sample of which the following purports to be.

Less than a century after Newton's *Principia,* Bishop Berkeley and David Hume exscinded the concept of cause from science so well that Kant never succeeded in restoring it. From that time to the present causality has not been a scientific concept. In 1893 C. S. Peirce wrote, "We still talk about 'cause and effect,' although, in the mechanical world, the opinion that phrase was meant to express has been shelved long ago" (*Philosophical Writings,* p. 17). On this point Bultmann himself must be demythologized: his seventeenth-century world-view is incredible today. Unfortunately, and contrary to Bishop Berkeley's hopes, the excision of cause was of no particular help to Christianity. The inviolability of mathematical law remained. Of course, it remained only on the assumption that the laws discovered now have always operated in the past. Logically and philosophically this assumption is exceedingly difficult to prove; but it is so in accord with common sense that materialism and mechanism easily survived.

A more forceful objection to this type of anti-theological science is suggested in a question that was asked later. For two centuries it had been supposed that science really discovered the laws of nature, and that these laws really described how nature goes on. But eventually the possibility of scientific discovery and scientific description were both questioned. If now it can be shown that the laws of physics do not describe the workings of nature, the question of miracles will be placed in a new light. Obviously there is no point in denying the occurrence of miracles on the ground that miracles violate the processes of nature, if these processes are unknown.

To show that scientific law, specifically the laws of Newtonian mechanism, do not describe how phenomena occur, the example of the pendulum will be used. The law of the pendulum, roughly expressed, states that the period of the swing is directly proportional to the square root of the length. But the scientific methods by which the equation is obtained are based on three remarkable assumptions. First, the mass of the bob is assumed to be concentrated at a point; that is, the body is homogeneous.

This condition is never met in actuality. Second, the string must be tensionless. There is no such string. And third, the pendulum is supposed to swing on an axis without friction. This is impossible. The necessary conclusion therefore is that the scientific law describes only non-existent pendulums, and that real pendulums do not move in accordance with the laws of physics. Accordingly, when it is argued that miracles can never have happened because they violate the laws of nature, the reply is that no laws of nature are known and that even ordinary pendulums violate the laws of physics.

In the next place, science as little discovers as it describes. For one thing, there is a considerable amount of *a priori* mathematical construction, such as the simple use of arithmetic means, the theory of least squares, the constant extrapolation of values both beyond the limits of experiment and between the individual readings. But aside from the effect of particular mathematical choices on the form of the laws of physics, there is a more easily understood consideration that quite clearly shows the impossibility of discovery by science.

In keeping with the general theory of mechanism, Lord Kelvin claimed that if he could construct a mechanical model of a natural phenomenon, he had explained it. The success which the nineteenth century had in constructing mechanical models was stupendous. Such models were therefore assumed to explain. Then Poincaré pointed out that it was always possible to construct many mechanical models of any natural phenomenon. Theoretically it is possible to construct an infinite number. But if this is so, why should a scientist select one particular model and assert that this one explains the phenomenon?

A crude example may enforce the point. Suppose we see an auto moving down the street. Let this be a new phenomenon which we want to explain. We must therefore construct a mechanical model; that is, we must contrive some machinery that could duplicate the car's motion. After some thought you with your brilliance dream up an internal combustion engine, whether of two, six, or eight cylinders is immaterial. But I with less or maybe more imagination suggest a trained squirrel in a revolving cage.

How could we tell which of these mechanical models explained the auto? Of course, the easy answer is to open the hood and look in. If we then see a squirrel, I win.

But unfortunately we cannot open the hood of nature and look in. We see, as it were, just the outside of nature. To be sure, we use microscopes and see within grosser bodies the motions of smaller particles. But no one has ever seen an atom move, much less looked inside an atom. Galileo simply assumed that the motion of an atom was similar to that of the marbles he rolled down his inclined plane. The marble was in fact a mechanical model. There are today other and more complex models of "atoms." But with all our nuclear science, we can never lift the hood and see whether our model is the one true picture of nature. Science cannot discover the workings of nature. To be sure, it can discover or invent jet planes and destructive bombs. And it succeeds in formulating the laws of physics. But it cannot discover the laws of nature.

To this point the discussion has been carried on within Newtonian limits. These limits were broken at the beginning of the twentieth century, and how thoroughly they were broken can be seen in the case of Newton's first law of motion. The law states that a body in motion continues to move in a straight line until acted upon by an external force. Thus a single atom in an infinite non-gravitational space would continue in the same direction forever. With this law as a basis the elliptic deviation of the planets from a straight line is explained by the gravitational pull of the sun.

But this law, the law of inertia, on which for three centuries all physics was based, turns out to be scientifically meaningless. There is no experimental method of determining rectilinear motion. Newton had assumed that the stars are fixed in space, and that therefore a particle moving constantly toward a star is moving in a straight line. But now that stars are seen to move, rectilinear motion loses all meaning.

The first law of motion underlies the entire Newtonian system, and naturally a flaw here will automatically vitiate all that follows. There are ramifications that go beyond the simple difficulties of rectilinear motion. Newton's formulations presuppose the possibility of determining the position and velocity of a particle apart from its relation to any other particle. At the same time the law of gravitation asserts the continuous interaction of all particles. The incompatibility of these two presuppositions was for many years dismissed by scientists as the ethereal speculations of mere philosophers. But when in the more recent past the phenomena of light became more frequent factors in experimentation, the latent contradiction soon resulted in the complete overthrow of Newtonian science.

The amazing scientific ingenuity by which this overthrow was accomplished in detail is a long and interesting story. Part of it has to do with the breakdown of the atomic theory. Instead of the atom's being indestructible and fixed in quality, uranium broken down into lead and nitrogen can be turned into carbon. Interest now came to center in electrons. But electrons are so small that even the light necessary for experimentation affects them. If light of low energy is used, their velocity is hardly changed, but the picture is so fuzzy that the position cannot be determined. On the other hand, if light of shorter wave length is used, the position becomes clear, but the motion is unpredictable.

The literature on the history and the philosophy of science, more and less technical, is extensive and abounds in most interesting details. But for the present purpose two conclusions must be drawn. First, science does not discover the laws of nature. Above it was shown that science cannot discover nature because of *a priori* mathematical construction and because there is no way to "lift the hood" and look in. Now we see that science has not discovered nature because science is constantly changing. If it had ever *discovered* a law of nature, the law ought never to be discarded. But two thousand years of history, or four hundred years if you like, give us no confidence in any hope of a law that will not be changed.

In the second place, we may conclude from the recent developments in physics that the present state of science is one of utter confusion. No one understands this better than the scientists themselves. One of the most frequently mentioned illustrations of this confusion is the simultaneous acceptance of two mutually incompatible theories of light. For certain purposes scientists use the long accepted wave theory. Light is supposed to travel through the ether like waves through the sea. Of course, there is no longer any ether to wave, but light is still regarded as a wave motion. At the same time light is not a wave motion, but is composed of very tiny corpuscles. These illuminating bodies shoot through space like buckshot and so produce the phenomena under investigation.

Other examples of the chaotic implications of the quantum theory, relativity, nuclear physics—that is, twentieth-century science as a whole—can be found in profusion in the voluminous literature. Much, and in a sense all, of this chaos stems from the absence of unambiguous definitions. The older concepts of mass, energy, and inertia have lost their old Newtonian meanings and have not acquired fixed new meanings. Socratic dialogue with the best scientists soon reduces the more confident to inextricable contradictions and the more competent to honest confession of ignorance.

Newton himself, it must be insisted, was not altogether free from this difficulty. On a very early page of the *Principia* Newton wrote, "I do not define time, space, place, and motion, as being well known to all." Only a very great genius could afford to make such a stupendous blunder. Of all unknowns, space, time, and especially motion are the most obscure and enigmatic. No doubt Einstein and other twentieth-century giants have made determined assaults on the defenses of space and time—only to find that they still remain impenetrable. And as for motion! Achilles and the tortoise still show that it is safer to ignore Zeno than to answer him.

Now, in view of the absence of basic definitions, in view of the chaos of our time, and in view of the constant replacement of one scientific theory by another, it should be quite evident that science can provide no firm ground for denying the possibility of miracles or for making any confident declaration regarding spiritual realities. If science cannot answer the question, What is light? it surely cannot answer the question, What is God?

IV. THE DESCRIPTION OF NATURE

The question, What is light? introduces us to the third and final section of this discussion on science. Newton tried to answer the question, What is light? and in general aimed to describe nature. By and large this was also the conscious aim of the early twentieth-century scientists. They agreed that Newton had not succeeded in describing the innermost workings of the universe; they may have modestly admitted their own limitations; but they thought they could at least do better, and at any rate they aimed to describe.

However, Percy Bridgman, more philosophic than most, in *The Logic of Modern Physics* (New York, The Macmillan Company, 1927), came to the conclusion that the purpose of science is not the description of nature. He notes that in the infinitesimal world of electrons direct experience is impossible. And further, "The experimental facts are so utterly different from those of our ordinary experience that not only do we apparently have to give up generalizations from past experience as broad as the field equations of electrodynamics, for instance, but it is even being questioned whether our ordinary forms of thought are applicable in the new domain; it is often suggested, for example, that the concepts of space and time break down" (Preface, p. ix).

One of his earliest and easiest illustrations of the effect of operations on concepts is that of length.

"What do we mean by the *length* of an object? We evidently know what we mean by length if we can tell what the length of any and every object is, and for the physicist nothing more is required. To find the length of an object, we have to perform certain physical operations. The concept of length is therefore fixed when the operations by which length is measured are fixed: that is, the concept of length involves as much as and nothing more than the set of operations by which length is determined. In general, we mean by any concept nothing more than a set of operations; *the concept is synonymous with the corresponding set of operations*" (ital. his; *ibid.,* p. 5).

And further on: "What is the possible meaning of the statement that the diameter of an electron is 10^{-13} cm.? Again, the only answer is found by examining the operations by which the number 10^{-13} was obtained. This number came by solving certain equations derived from the field equations of electrodynamics, into which certain numerical data obtained by experiment had been substituted. The concept of length has therefore now been so modified as to include that theory of electricity embodied in the field equations, and, most important, assumes the correctness of extending these equations from the dimensions in which they may be verified experimentally into a region in which their correctness is one of the most important and problematical of present-day questions in physics. . . . As a matter of fact, the concept of length disappears as an independent thing and fuses in a complicated way with other concepts, all of which are themselves altered thereby . . ." (*ibid.*, p. 21).

In the past the argument against miracles depended on the assumption that nature has always worked as it does now. To deny this uniformity was unthinkable in the Newtonian age. But, surprising as it may be, yet not so surprising on the operational view, Bridgman has harsh words for uniformitarianism. "It is difficult to conceive anything more scientifically bigoted than to postulate that all possible experience conforms to the same type as that with which we are already familiar" (*ibid.*, p. 46).

Of course, it must not be supposed that Bridgman is an apologete for miracles. Nor are operationalists generally motivated by a desire to advance Christianity. But the implications of their theory are ruinous for the old-fashioned "scientific" warfare against theology. Operationalism asserts philosophically what scientific experimentation has been enforcing practically; to wit, that science provides no knowledge of nature itself. It is not the case merely that science has not yet found the truth but may later discover some. Scientific skepticism goes far deeper than this. What twentieth-century science has come to is the view that science will never, can never describe how nature works. Science does not aim at truth; it aims at invention.

John Dewey, neither a scientist nor a Christian, has popularized the idea that the purpose of science is to control nature for practical, i.e. non-cognitive experience. Scientific concepts are not pieces of information about independent antecedent being; they are plans of action. Mass is not a quantity of matter, but a set of operations. Now, it is always possible, at least theoretically, to invent some gadget in two ways—indeed in an indefinite number of ways. Such is the extended significance of the previous remarks on mechanical models. The two models, i.e. the two scientific theories, may be, must be, mutually incompatible. But both are "true" insofar as they work; that is, they are true in the pragmatic or instrumentalistic sense of true. This is not to say that the instrumentalistic theory of truth is a good epistemology. In fact, it is a very bad one (cf. my monograph, *Dewey*, Philadelphia, Presbyterian and Reformed Publishing Co., 1960). The point is simply that two incompatible theories can easily produce the same result. Refrigerators and telephones can be manufactured in many different ways. Two incompatible theories, however, cannot both be true, if they are taken as descriptions of nature. But science now has nothing to do with describing or explaining nature.

Its aim is invention, that is, control of nature. And in this setting the phenomena of light, for example, can be utilized by formally contrary equations.

As Christians we are not called upon to give creedal subscription to the philosophy of operationalism. As science itself has been constantly changing throughout its history, so too the philosophy of science has changed and will change. Operationalism is very popular today. It is also very plausible. Indeed, it seems to be the best explanation of science yet given. But, who knows? In another fifty years some great thinker may invent a different philosophy of science. And so the change of opinion will continue.

What a Christian should say in reply to a future philosophy cannot in any detailed way be predicted now. But now the present chaos in science itself, and the operational philosophy, enforcing the double lesson that science is not stable and is not a transcript of nature, form a propitious situation in which to show the futility of scientific objections to Christianity. If science has not discovered any law of nature, and if it is bigotry to postulate that past events must conform to present experience, and if we are well assured that the future laws of science (not laws of nature) will differ from those now in use, there is no knowledge in science that can oppose the history of the Virgin Birth or the Resurrection of Christ. Many scientists will of course continue to reject these miracles and Christianity with them; but their rejection will not be based on any scientific grounds; it will be entirely religious. And in matters of religion, where a knowledge of God is desired, experimentation cannot hold a dim candle to the sunburst of special revelation.

THE NATURE OF MAN

✝

Fred H. Klooster

Fred H. Klooster is Associate Professor of Systematic Theology at Calvin Theological Seminary (Christian Reformed), Grand Rapids. He is author of The Incomprehensibility of God in the Orthodox Presbyterian Conflict *(1951) and of* The Significance of Barth's Theology *(1961). He has translated some of the writings of the Dutch theologian G. C. Berkouwer. He holds the A.B. degree from Calvin College, B.D. from Calvin Theological Seminary, Th.M. from Westminster Theological Seminary, and Th.D. from Free University of Amsterdam.*

8. *Fred H. Klooster*

THE NATURE OF MAN

WHAT IS MAN? "Who am I?" Answers to these questions are still
among the most sought-after and urgent. "Know thyself!" remains as
challenging an imperative today as it was in Socrates' time. But contemporary man is far more perplexed than any earlier generation by the
quest for self-knowledge, and many thinkers are beginning to wonder
if self-knowledge is actually possible. Elusive though the answer seems
to be, modern man is pursuing the question of his identity with increased
vigor. During the last two decades both theological and philosophical
inquiry has centered increasingly on the doctrine of man.

That twentieth-century man is a vexing problem to himself is no mere
theoretical subject raised for contemplative study; it is a very real and
practical problem raised in anguish and despair. The easy optimism of
the nineteenth century has been replaced by a deeply felt pessimism.
When in despotic apostasy man regarded himself as the measure of all
things, he attempted to banish God from the universe. Man imagined
himself able to rule the world according to his own rational standards
and in his own autonomous strength. Having shrugged off the living
God, modern man now discovers he is in danger of losing himself as
well. In the previous century there were those who thought it impossible
for man to be man in the presence of a sovereign God; today there are
those who are beginning to wonder if man can be man without God.

Modern man's ignorance of himself seems a striking contrast to his
fantastic knowledge of other things. Almost before our eyes an astonishing advance has come in understanding the physical universe. Brilliant
success in science was recently climaxed by man's amazing entry into
space. Such increased knowledge of nature, however, has not been accompanied by a better knowledge of human nature. True, man has come
to a more realistic awareness of himself, but this experience merely

shattered his old myths and left him in skepticism or despair. Stupendous manifestations of evil in industrial society and bestial violence in world wars have shattered the liberal myth of man's innate goodness and essential deity. The name of Eichmann has become a symbol of man's evil, and clinical reports of countless psychologists indicate how widespread such evil is. Confidence in man's rational powers has likewise been undermined by practical as well as theoretical considerations.

Several recent sociologists have given striking depictions of our modern plight. Titles of their works are among the descriptive phrases now a part of our vocabulary. Nowhere, however, is the crisis in contemporary man's view of himself more expertly depicted than in the works of some of our recent novelists, poets and playwrights. Movingly they display the anxiety and despair of "the lost generation" which searches for some meaning in the meaninglessness of life.[1]

The Christian philosopher, Herman Dooyeweerd, aptly summarizes the current situation: "The crisis of Western civilization is depicted as a complete decline of human personality, as the rise of the mass-man. This is imputed, by different leading thinkers, to the increasing supremacy of technology, and to the over-organization of modern society. The result, supposedly, is a process of depersonalizing of contemporary life. The modern mass-man has lost all personal traits. His pattern of behavior is prescribed by what is done in general. He shifts the responsibility for his behavior upon an impersonal society. And this society, in turn, seems to be ruled by the robot, the electronic brain, by bureaucracy, fashion, organization and other impersonal powers. As a result, our contemporary society has no room for human personality, and for a real spiritual communion of person with person" (In The Twilight of Western Thought, Studies in The Pretended Autonomy of Human Thought. Philadelphia, Presbyterian and Reformed Publishing Co., 1960, p. 174). This crisis shows itself in all of life's dimensions. Even the family and the church, where personal relationships are usually the strongest, have not escaped. The real nature of this crisis, as Dooyeweerd continues, is spiritual, for "the average secularized man nowadays has lost any and all true interest in religion. He has fallen prey to a state

---

[1] A helpful survey can be found in the articles of Donald L. Deffner, "The Paperback in the Pew: Portraits of Man in Modern Literature," *Concordia Theological Monthly*, XXXII, 3 (August, 1961), pp. 453-465; and of W. Paul Jones, "Self-Identity and Contemporary Literature," *Theology Today*, XIX, 2 (July, 1962) pp. 224-234 & 255-258. Cf. also the three recent symposia: *What, Then, Is Man?* A symposium of Theology, Psychology, and Psychiatry, Saint Louis, Mo.; Concordia Publishing House, 1958; *The Nature of Man in Theological and Psychological Perspective,* ed. Simon Doniger, New York, Harper & Bros., 1962; *What Is the Nature of Man?* Images of Man in Our American Culture, Philadelphia, Christian Education Press, 1959.

of spiritual nihilism, i.e., he negates all spiritual values. He has lost all his faith, and denies any higher ideals than the satisfaction of his appetites. Even the Humanistic faith in *mankind,* and in the power of human reason to rule the world and to elevate man to a higher level of freedom and morality, has no longer any appeal to the mind of the present day mass-man. To him God is dead, and the two world wars have destroyed the Humanistic ideal of man. This modern man has lost *himself,* and considers himself cast into a world that is meaningless, that offers no hope for a better future" (*ibid.,* p. 174 f.).

This description alerts us to the depth of the current crisis. While F. Nietzsche asserted that God died in the nineteenth century, some now add that man died in the twentieth. Since the relationship between God and man is so close, when faith in God fades, then man's knowledge of himself is also impossible. Scripture reveals that man is the image-bearer of God, and hence knowledge of self is involved in knowledge of God. Calvin correctly grasped this biblical truth when he began his *Institutes of the Christian Religion* by acknowledging that "it is certain that man never achieves a clear knowledge of himself unless he has first looked upon God's face, and then descends from contemplating Him to scrutinize himself" (*Institutes of the Christian Religion,* J. T. McNeill, tr. by Ford L. Battles, Philadelphia, The Westminster Press, 1960, I, i, 2). The crisis in anthropology is thus but part of the predicament of modern man. He is adrift at sea, and although he senses his plight, he is not even aware of its deepest dimension and its far-reaching implications. Modern man's predicament is that he does not know who he is or what his life signifies. This is but part of the deeper crisis, however, the fact that he does not know God.

I. THE BIBLICAL DOCTRINE OF MAN

God reveals *Himself* in Holy Scripture. But He also reveals *man's* nature and destiny in Scripture. Man's unique nature is expressed in the pregnant phrase "image of God." The term itself expresses the fact that knowledge of God and knowledge of man are interrelated. In setting forth his nature Scripture distinguishes between man's states as a created being, as fallen and as redeemed through Jesus Christ. To understand the nature of man, one must see him in terms of his original creation in God's image, his rebellious fall into sin, and his renewal and redemption through Jesus Christ by the Holy Spirit. Such knowledge is possible only through the redemptive work of Jesus Christ by the Holy Spirit. In this survey of the biblical doctrine of man, we have made no attempt to express a natural theology of man. On the contrary, we have tried to reproduce only the scriptural doctrine of man.

Man as Created

The Word of God nowhere depicts man as the product of evolutionary process. Man is not simply a tool-making animal, nor a political or rational animal. He is not descended from the animals at all. Rather, according to Scripture, he is a unique and special creation of God, made in the very image and likeness of God Himself.

Although the entire creative work of God is performed in accordance with His eternal counsel (Eph. 1:11), reference to the decree is made in Genesis with respect to man only. There we read God's solemn divine counsel: "Let us make man in our image (*zelem*), after our likeness (*demuth*): and let them have dominion over the fish of the sea, and over the birds of the heavens, and over the cattle, and over all the earth, and over every creeping thing that creepeth upon the earth" (Gen. 1:26).

Man's special character lies in the fact that he is created in the *imago Dei*. While the other living creatures are created "after their kind," we are told that "God created man in his own image, in the image of God created he him; male and female created he them" (Gen. 1:27; cf. Gen. 5:1 and Ps. 8). The direct agency of God brings forth man in a way that differs from the creation of the animals. We perceive a dual creative activity when "Jehovah God formed man of the dust of the ground, and breathed into his nostrils the breath of life; and man became a living soul" (Gen. 2:7).

The term "image of God" is not elaborated or defined further in the Genesis account. Unique and exalted though he be, man, like the entire cosmos, is still dependent upon God. However, nothing warrants regarding this distinction between man and God, between the finite and the infinite, as an unbridgeable gulf. No estrangement exists between God and Adam despite the distinction between Creator and creature. In fact, there is immediate fellowship and communion between God and man. God addresses Adam, and prior to the Fall, Adam responds in covenantal obedience. The Garden of Eden as Adam's home emphasizes that this fellowship is experienced in the very presence of God. This fellowship and communion are at once religious and covenantal in nature, and are neither dependent upon nor rooted in the Incarnation. Not creation but sin constitutes the gulf between God and man.

The original fellowship and communion between the Creator and his image-bearer also include commands which indicate God's sovereignty over man. Adam is a person addressed by God who is required consciously to fulfill his Lord's mandate. He is blessed by God and commanded to "be fruitful, and multiply, and replenish the earth, and subdue it; and have dominion ..." (Gen. 1:28). In exercising this dominion as God's vice-regent, Adam must also dress and keep the Garden of Eden (Gen. 2:15). But even in the exercise of his dominion, Adam is reminded at once that as a creature he is dependent upon God even for his food. Not only the animals but also God's image-bearer receives permission to use the herbs of the field and the fruit of the trees for sustenance (Gen. 1:29; cf. Gen. 9:3 ff.).

The covenantal relation between God and Adam as well as the un-qualified requirement of whole-hearted obedience comes to clearest expression when God confronts Adam with the probationary command:

> And Jehovah God commanded the man, saying, Of every tree of the garden thou mayest freely eat; but of the tree of the knowledge of good and evil, thou shalt not eat of it; for in the day that thou eatest thereof thou shalt surely die (Gen. 2:16-17).

The test of Adam's obedience is clear, but God the Creator obligates Himself also in these words, not only to invoke the penalty of death for disobedience, but also in the event of obedience to award the promise implied in the tree of life. The unique religious nature of Adam is presupposed in this significant transaction.

This description of man as created gives us the all-important starting point for a true understanding of man. Man is created by the direct agency of God and, moreover, he is made in the very image and likeness of God. He is made "but little lower than God" (Elohim): he is crowned "with glory and honor" and made "to have dominion over the works of [God's] hands" (Ps. 8:5 f.). His God-entrusted task is to subdue the earth in obedience to his Maker. Along with the whole creation, man, the image-bearer of God, is pronounced "very good" by God Himself (Gen. 1:31). Sin inheres neither in man's finiteness nor in his creatureliness. Adam possesses his character by virtue of God's creative endowment. Endowed with true knowledge of God, Adam believingly responds to the revelation of God in the creation all about him as well as to the revelation God verbally addressed to him. His response is one of worship and praise from the heart, for out of it "are the issues of life" (Prov. 4:23). He possesses true knowledge which is nonetheless capable of development and enrichment; he is also righteous and holy (cf. Eph. 4:24 and Col. 3:10). In his entire being—body and soul—and from the depths of his heart, Adam responds in obedient religious worship of God. This is the nature of the God-created man.

Fallen Man

Man is no longer what he was when first created. Scripture teaches that when Adam disobeyed God's commandment and heeded Satan's temptation to eat the forbidden fruit, he fell from his original state of perfection. He thus incurred the penalty of death for his disobedience.

The enigma of Adam's disobedient action is not analyzed or described in great detail. Presented briefly and realistically in Genesis 3, this Fall of Adam is presupposed throughout the rest of Scripture.

By his rebellious act Adam became guilty before God and was punished for his lawlessness by the penalty of death. This penalty shows itself first of all in its deep spiritual dimension as alienation and estrangement from God. He who dwelt in covenantal fellowship with God in Paradise now shrinks from God's presence and foolishly attempts to hide from the omnipresent and omniscient God. God is still able to address Adam even in his fallen state. But Adam is now spiritually dead. He is polluted in every area of his being. Sin takes possession of his heart and makes it exceedingly corrupt (Jer. 17:9). Like a cancer sin permeates the whole person, body and soul. Adam hides from the presence of God. Denying his guilt, he shirks his own responsibility by blaming Eve and Satan. The presence of God is now fearful to him; anxiety and dread fill his soul. He is at enmity even with himself. His knowledge becomes darkened. His will is no longer free but bound as the slave of sin. Thus God's image in man is corrupted and polluted.

Physical death is another result of Adam's sin. Adam was not mortal by nature, nor was only his soul originally immortal. But as the result of sin Adam now dies a physical death, a death that passes on to all men (Rom. 5:12 ff; 1 Cor. 15:22). In connection with this abnormality of death as a punishment for sin, Scripture distinguishes between the body and soul. The "dust returneth to the earth as it was, and the spirit returneth unto God who gave it" (Ecc. 12:7; cf. Matt. 10:28). Sin and death disrupt man's original integral unity. But even the body which returns to dust awaits the resurrection from the dead, and the whole person, body and soul, someday will experience either the eternal bliss of heaven or the eternal punishment of hell. This separation takes place not because the body is inherently evil or the soul inherently divine. Scripture nowhere pictures the body as the prison-house of the soul, nor does it ever present death as the happy release of the soul from the encumbrance of the body. According to Scripture this abnormal separation of body and soul at death is the penalty for sin.

Adam's guilt is passed on to his posterity by imputation for he is the federal head of the covenant as Christ, the second Adam, is the head of the *new* covenant (Rom. 5:12 ff.; I Cor. 15:22). As the physical head of the entire human race, Adam also passes on a polluted or depraved human nature to his children. Consequences of that sinful depravity are seen in Cain's murder of Abel and in the apostasy of Lamech. It reaches the dreadful proportions described in Genesis 6:5 ff. as the occasion for God's judgment in the flood. This apostasy of the sinful heart continues even in Noah's posterity, however, and again reaches the awful dimensions expressed in the building of the tower of Babel (Gen. 11). Such is the continuous history of guilty sinners who ever find new ways to worship and serve the creature rather than the Creator (Rom. 1).

Fallen man, however, is still referred to in some contexts as the image-bearer of God (cf. Gen. 5:1; 9:6; I Cor. 11:7; Jas. 3:9). But it is clear that man, the image of God, is corrupt and defiled. While man remains man, the whole direction of his heart is turned in apostasy against God. This is the biblical picture of man who through Adam's transgression fell into sin. It is this fallen man who, unenlightened by the regenerating grace of the Holy Spirit, faces the enigma and problem of self-knowledge.

Redeemed Man

The biblical doctrine of man involves, finally, the revelation that only by redemption through Jesus Christ can fallen man be restored to a true knowledge of God and of himself. Fallen man thinks of himself as normal and is really unaware of his true nature. He suppresses God's revelation and in all his guilt and depravity continues to rebel against God. True self-knowledge is possible and actual only in acknowledging oneself created in the image of God, fallen into sin through Adam's transgression and redeemed through Jesus Christ by the Holy Spirit.

In Jesus Christ God publishes the Gospel of salvation to sinful man. God in His love provided a remedy for man's sin through the incarnation of His own Son who by His ministry, death, resurrection and ascension provided the way of salvation for God's elect. Administered by the Holy Spirit this redeeming grace of Jesus Christ restores and brings once again true knowledge of the self. The redeemed recognize their fallen, sinful state in all its guilt and pollution. With eyes opened by the Holy Spirit, the redeemed can believe and understand the Word of God which reveals man's original nature by creation and his destiny through Jesus Christ.

The entire redemptive process of sanctification is referred to as a renewal in the image of God. The Christian is commanded to "put away, as concerning your former manner of life, the old man, that waxeth corrupt after the lusts of deceit" and he is exhorted to "be renewed in the spirit of your mind, and put on the new man, that after God hath been created in righteousness and holiness of truth" (Eph. 4:17 ff.), and "that is being renewed unto knowledge after the image of him that created him" (Col. 3:10). This renewal in the image of God is regarded as a comprehensive demand for sanctification of the whole man and for a life-long process whereby we are "to be conformed to the image of his Son" (Rom. 8:29). It is a renewing process. And it includes the entire body of believers who are to grow into unity with Christ and with one another "unto a fullgrown man, unto the measure of the stature of the fullness of Christ" (Eph. 4:13). This is the biblical view of man's nature and destiny.

II. HISTORY OF THE DOCTRINE OF MAN

Issues in Debate

Almost all facets of the doctrine of man are being debated today. Present discussions among liberal and neo-orthodox theologians show one important difference, however, from those of previous days. Prior to the rise of liberalism most theologians accepted the authority of Scripture and acknowledged the historicity of the Genesis account of Adam's creation and fall. With the widespread acceptance of the evolutionary hypothesis, however, and of the neo-orthodox interpretation of the Genesis account as a myth, symbol or saga, a significant change is evident in the total approach to the doctrine of man.

In the early Church discussion centered on the constitutional nature of man. The strong impact of Greek philosophy hindered a clear representation of the biblical doctrine in the theological discussions of that time. Too greatly influenced by the Greek dualism of matter and spirit, theologians debated whether man's nature was composed of two diverse substances, body and soul (dichotomy), or whether three divisions were to be identified, namely, body, soul and spirit (trichotomy). Although dichotomy was more generally accepted, both dichotomists and trichotomists held similar presuppositions as is evident also from their consideration of the question of the origin of the soul.

Three positions were defended with respect to this problem. Least common was that of Origen who held that the soul exists prior to the body (Pre-existentianism) and becomes corrupted when joined to the body after conception or at birth. The position of Tertullian and later of many Lutherans had wider endorsement. Tertullian maintained that the soul as well as the body originates through the parents by procreation (Traducianism). The most commonly accepted view, however, has been Creationism. This view teaches that each soul is a new creation of God. Each view, it was usually admitted, had inherent difficulties and complete satisfaction was rarely present. Today it is acknowledged more and more that the dilemma arises in part because of the presuppositions of the question itself; it reveals more influence of Greek dualism than of the biblical stress upon the unity of man (Dooyeweerd, *op. cit.*; cf. also G. C. Berkouwer, *Man: The Image of God*, Grand Rapids, Wm. B. Eerdmans Publishing Co., 1962).

Strangely enough, attention was not centered as much as one might expect upon the nature of God's image in man. Irenaeus distinguished between the terms *image* and *likeness*, and the scholastics in the Middle Ages debated what part of the image was lost in the Fall and what part remained. But prior to the Reformation this question never seems to have gained as much attention as those mentioned above. Reformed and Lutheran differences on the character of the image led to further discussion, the Lutherans contending that the image was entirely lost in the Fall. Reformed theologians usually distinguished image in the narrow sense which was lost by sin from image in the broader sense which, although corrupted, was not lost. Current discussions are turning anew to these issues. Among the moderns Karl Barth has supported the novel idea that the image is defined in Genesis 1:26 as the male-female relationship.

Throughout the centuries the most widely debated aspects of anthropology, however, have been the questions of sin and grace as related to the nature and extent of Adam's fall and its effect upon man's will. The Augustinian-Pelagian controversy of the fifth century expressed the basic alternatives in this debate. Augustine maintained that man became totally depraved by the Fall, and that the will therefore, was also corrupt and hence unable to initiate or cooperate in the work of grace. Pelagius rejected this view as too pessimistic, and maintained that man had the ability to perform whatever the Gospel required of him. Augustine noted, and correctly, that if Pelagius were right the Gospel would not really be necessary. Seeking a middle road between Augustine and Pelagius, a semi-Pelagian position acknowledged a will weakened by sin but still able to cooperate in the work of redemption. While there have been many variations, these three positions have reappeared throughout history. Pelagianism came to the fore in Socinianism during the Renaissance and again in Liberalism. Semi-Pelagianism became the prevailing Roman Catholic position and reappeared within the Reformation churches in the Arminianism of the seventeenth century (Synod of Dort, 1618-19). Augustine's basic position has continued to prevail among orthodox, evangelical Christians. Contemporary neo-orthodox theologians claim to follow Augustine in their realistic view of sin. The complexity of neo-orthodoxy, however, and especially its unwillingness to acknowledge the genuine historicity of Adam and the Fall, involve a reinterpretation that associates sin closely with man's finiteness. In this regard, neo-orthodoxy shows more affinity with neo-Platonism, a philosophy which Augustine unfortunately never completely overcame, than with the genuine biblical motif of creation, fall and redemption.

History Prior to the Reformation

During the long periods of ancient and medieval history, Scripture was acknowledged generally as the inspired and authoritative Word of God and as the norm for theology and doctrine. The historicity of Genesis was accepted and the doctrine of man was framed against the background of Adam's original creation and subsequent fall. The classical or Greek view of man, however, influenced the leading formulations of the doctrine. Consciously or unconsciously, various Greek elements were woven into the doctrine of man.

The classical view of man was composed primarily of elements from Plato, Aristotle and the Stoics. Man is viewed chiefly in terms of reason and this reason or spirit identifies him with the supernatural. Furthermore, man's body was conceived of as that material substance in which evil inheres. The body, therefore, is mortal as contrasted with the soul or spirit which is immortal. The influence of this classical view of man appears in various ways in the doctrine of man. Although acknowledging the biblical doctrine of creation, many theologians of the Church inconsistently regarded the body as something lower than the soul and essentially evil. Monasticism cannot be understood apart from these considerations. Although Scripture speaks of body and soul as separated temporarily at death, any overtones of the Greek dualism of matter and spirit are wholly foreign to Scripture. Gnosticism and Manicheanism were heretical developments of this unbiblical motif.

In the Scholasticism of the Middle Ages, synthesis with Aristotelian philosophy was openly pursued. Today the Roman Catholic position represents the ecclesiastical endorsement of scholastic theology, especially that of Thomas Aquinas. This theology makes a sharp dualism of nature and grace, the natural and the supernatural, reason and faith. Applied to the doctrine of man, this two-level approach leads to a differentiation between the image and the likeness of God. The image is regarded as the natural endowment which man possesses by virtue of his creation. The likeness, however, is the supernatural gift (donum superadditum) which man receives after his creation but before his fall. The prevailing Roman Catholic view is that this natural image in which man was created consists basically of his rational-ethical nature. Within this natural image a tension (concupiscence) already exists between the higher and the lower elements. This is not regarded as sin, however, until it breaks forth into overt action. To keep this tension or concupiscence in check, God added the supernatural gift of the divine likeness to man's created nature. Not his created nature alone but this created nature together with the donum superadditum constituted man's original righteousness. When Adam fell, the divine likeness was lost but the image remained essentially what it was. Thus fallen man today is held to be basically the same as Adam was when created. He simply lacks the supernatural gift which can now be received through the supernatural means of grace entrusted to the Church. According to the Scholastic theology of Rome, human nature today is not radically corrupted. It is wounded or weakened, but not totally depraved. Man's reason and will are essentially like Adam's at the time of creation. Thus the two-level arrangement is basic to the entire Roman Catholic anthropology. Reason has access to the entire area of nature. But faith is needed to know the divine mysteries of the supernatural area.

A common form of this Scholastic view involved the use of Aristotle's distinction between memory, intellect and will. The natural image of God in man was then said to consist in the qualities which all men possess of memory, intellect and will. But man's likeness or similitude to God concerns the supernatural gifts of grace which are added to this natural image. Memory thus becomes adorned with hope and constancy; the intellect is illuminated by faith; and the will is adorned with love. Luther is correct when he says concerning the various Scholastic distinctions that "although these not unattractive speculations point conclusively to keen and leisurely minds, they contribute very little toward the correct explanation of the image of God" (Luther's Works, Vol. I, *Lectures on Genesis,* ed. by Jaroslav Pelikan, St. Louis, Concordia, 1958, p. 60). He adds: "Memory, will, and mind we have indeed; but they are most depraved and most seriously weakened, yes, to put it more clearly, they are utterly leprous and unclean" (*ibid.,* p. 61). If these powers constitute the image of God in man, Luther contends, "it will also follow that Satan was created according to the image of God, since he surely has these natural endowments, such as memory and a very superior intellect and a most determined will, to a far higher degree than we have them" (*loc. cit.*).

The far-reaching implications of Scholastic dualism are increasingly recognized today as fundamentally opposed to the Word of God. Dooyeweerd contends that this dualism is a contributing factor in the crisis of Western civilization. "This false division of human life into a natural and a supra-natural sphere became the starting-point of the process of secularization, which resulted in the crisis of Western culture, in its spiritual uprooting. In fact, it abandoned the so-called natural sphere to the rule of the apostate religious basic motive, initially to that of Greek thought, later on to that of modern Humanism" (*op. cit.,* p. 194).

Views of the Reformers

The Reformers made a radical break with the Roman Catholic dichotomy of nature and grace and attempted a consistent return to the biblical pattern of creation, sin, and redemption by grace. They saw that the Scholastic doctrine of body and soul was similar to the Greek dualism of matter and spirit. They also recognized that the scriptural terms *image* and *likeness* were parallel and synonymous. Although Luther and Calvin differed in some phases of the doctrine of the image of God in man, they were in agreement with the biblical thought of Augustine over against the semi-Pelagianism which had become dominant in Roman Catholicism. The main features of the views of Luther and Calvin must be sketched, therefore.

Luther insists that we must distinguish between man as created and man in his present fallen condition, and he also admits that it is very difficult to know just what the image really was since sin has wiped it out. From the Genesis account he nevertheless sets forth what he understands to be the scriptural doctrine of the image. "Therefore my understanding of the image of God is this: that Adam had it in his being and that he not only knew God and believed that He was good, but that he also lived a life that was wholly godly; that is, he was without the fear of death or of any other danger, and was content with God's favor.... In Adam there was an enlightened reason, a true knowledge of God, and a most sincere desire to love God and his neighbor, so that Adam embraced Eve and at once acknowledged her to be his own flesh. Added to these were other lesser but exceedingly important gifts—if you draw a comparison with our weakness—namely, a perfect knowledge of the nature of the animals, the herbs, the fruits, the trees, and the remaining creatures" (Luther, *op. cit.*, p. 62 f.).

Luther sees the image of God in the whole man, body and soul. When the leprosy of sin was still absent "both his inner and outer sensations were all of the purest kind. His intellect was the clearest, his memory was the best, and his will was the most straightforward—all in the most beautiful tranquillity of mind, without any fear of death and without any anxiety. To these inner qualities came also those most beautiful and superb qualities of body and of all the limbs, qualities in which he surpassed all the remaining living creatures." In other words, Luther held that Adam's eyes were sharper and clearer than those of the lynx and eagle, that he was stronger than the lion or the bear which he handled and commanded like a trained dog.

"But after the Fall death crept like leprosy into all our perceptive powers, so that with our intellect we cannot even understand that image." The image of God is completely lost in fallen man. "Therefore when we speak about that image, we are speaking about something unknown. Not only have we had no experience of it, but we continually experience the opposite; and so we hear nothing except bare words" (*ibid.*, p. 63). Man is wholly corrupted and miserably weakened. He is utterly leprous and unclean. Both reason and will are fallen and corrupt. Even the physical senses are more brutish than human. The wild boar's sense of hearing, the eagle's sense of sight and the lion's strength surpass those of man. "Therefore no one can picture in his thoughts how much better nature was then than it is now" (p. 67). In contrast to the happiness and godly bliss of Adam, "we are never secure in God; apprehension and terror cause us concern even in sleep. These and similar evils are the image of the devil, who stamped them on us" (p. 63). The effect of original sin is not limited to Adam, therefore; "everything we use in this life has become corrupt" (p. 64).

Although Luther believes that the image of God is completely lost in fallen man, he recognizes that its restoration comes through the Gospel. "But now the Gospel has brought about the restoration of that image. Intellect and will indeed have remained, but both are very much impaired. And so the Gospel brings it about that we are formed once more according to that familiar and indeed better image, because we are born again into eternal life or rather into the hope of eternal life by faith, that we may live in God and with God and be one with Him, as Christ says (John 17:21)." This redemptive process, says Luther, continues throughout life and reaches completion only in heaven. "But when it is finished in the kingdom of the Father, then the will will be truly free and good, the mind truly enlightened, and the memory persistent. Then it will also happen that all the other creatures will be under our rule to a greater degree than they were in Adam's Paradise. Until this is accomplished in us, we can not have an adequate knowledge of what that image of God was which was lost through sin in Paradise. But what we are stating faith and the Word of God teach, which, as if from a distance, point out the glory of the divine image" (p. 65).

John Calvin has probably expressed the interrelation of the knowledge of God and the knowledge of man more emphatically than any theologian has done. He contends that "nearly all the wisdom we possess, that is to say, true and sound wisdom, consists of two parts: the knowledge of God and of ourselves" (*Institutes of the Christian Religion,* I, i, 1). These are so closely related that it is not easy to say which "precedes and brings forth the other" for "in the first place, no one can look upon himself without immediately turning his thoughts to the contemplation of God, in whom he 'lives and moves.' " To put it even more sharply "we cannot have a clear and complete knowledge of God unless it is accompanied by a corresponding knowledge of ourselves" (I, xv, 1). But the converse is also true: "Again, it is certain that man never achieves a clear knowledge of himself unless he has first looked upon God's face, and then descends from contemplating him to scrutinize himself" (I, i, 2). However, such true knowledge of self is not possible today unless we "know what we were like when we were first created and what our condition became after the fall of Adam" (I, xv, i). Calvin contends that the philosophers have gone astray because they failed to reckon with man's fall. Confusing the two states of man, these philosophers are like men "seeking in a ruin for a building, and in scattered fragments for a well-knit structure" (I, xv, 8). In contemplating the speculations of the philosophers regarding intellect and will, Calvin replies: "Well reasoned so far—if there had been no change in man. But since this was hidden from them, it is no wonder they mix up heaven and earth!" (I, xv, 8).

Although Calvin unfortunately uses such phrases as "immortal spirit" and "prison house of the body" (I, xv, 1-2), the context of his thought is quite different from that of the Scholastics. Furthermore, Calvin does not recognize the image of God with respect to the body as clearly as Luther does. "The proper seat of his image is in the soul," says Calvin, and yet he is willing to admit that man's "outward form" and upward stance may be included in the image "provided it be regarded as a settled principle that the image of God, which is seen or glows in these outward marks, is spiritual" (I, xv, 3). While his polemic with Andreas Osiander may have led him to underemphasize the significance of the body in the image of God, it is not correct to say that Calvin completely excluded the body from the image. Calvin summarizes his view of the image by saying "the likeness of God extends to the whole excellence by which man's nature towers over all the kinds of living creatures" and then elaborates this principle as follows: "Accordingly, the integrity with which Adam was endowed is expressed by this word, when he had full possession of right understanding, when he had his affections kept within the bounds of reason, all his senses tempered in right order, and he truly referred his excellence to exceptional gifts bestowed upon him by his Maker. And although the primary seat of the divine image was in the mind and heart, or in the soul and its powers, yet there was no part of man, not even the body itself, in which some sparks did not glow" (I, xv, 3).

According to Calvin the image was not entirely lost as a result of Adam's fall. Here he differs from Luther, although there is greater similarity in thought than might be expected. While Calvin states that "God's image was not totally annihilated and destroyed" by Adam's fall, he immediately adds, "yet it was so corrupted that whatever remains is frightful deformity" (I, xv, 4). Thus "the perfect excellence of human nature which shone in Adam before his defection" was "subsequently so vitiated and almost blotted out that nothing remains after the ruin except what is confused, mutilated and disease-ridden" (I, xv, 4).[2]

Like Luther, Calvin believes that the redemptive work through Jesus Christ involves restoration of man in the image of God. According to Colossians 3:10 and Ephesians 4:24 the redeemed are renewed in true knowledge, righteousness and holiness. Recognizing these terms as synecdoches, Calvin contends that "what was primary in the renewing of God's image also held the highest place in the creation itself" so that "God's image was visible in the light of the mind, in the uprightness of the heart and in the soundness of all the parts" (I, xv, 4). The renewal

---

[2] Cf. II, ii, 12, where Calvin expresses his agreement with the commonly used expression of Augustine "that the natural gifts were corrupted in man through sin, but that his supernatural gifts were stripped from him." The context indicates how different this usage was from the Scholastic distinction, however. Cf. also II, ii, 14.

in the image of God in some part is "now manifest in the elect, in so far as they have been reborn in the spirit; but it will attain its full splendor in heaven" (I, xv, 4).

A remarkable similarity is evident in the views of Luther and Calvin, although there are also striking differences in the formulation of their positions. Both Reformers have largely overcome the influence of Greek dualism so prevalent in the Scholastic views. The biblical motif of an original creation in the very image and likeness of God is recaptured. The radical effects of Adam's fall upon the image is acknowledged. Restoration or renewal in the image of God through the redemptive work of Jesus Christ is emphasized by both theologians, and this renewal is recognized as the life-long task involving the sanctification of the redeemed sinner.

The differences here between Luther and Calvin appear in a certain reluctance on Calvin's part to regard the body as significantly involved in the image. Although Calvin does not deny the relation, Luther was far less embarrassed by this inclusion; in fact, he engages in a somewhat romantic extremism. Although Calvin has largely overcome the Scholastic position, he gives undue prominence to the soul as the seat of the image. He also expresses a certain primacy of the intellect. Another difference between Luther and Calvin concerns the extent of loss of the image through Adam's fall. Although Luther thought the entire image was lost by the Fall, Calvin held that fallen man was still image bearer in a certain sense even though what was retained was also thoroughly corrupt, vitiated and defiled. In another context Calvin speaks of the natural gifts which were corrupted and the supernatural gifts which were lost. Later Reformed theologians express this distinction in terms of a broader and narrower sense of the image. The image in the narrow sense, namely, true knowledge, righteousness and holiness, they contend, was lost by the Fall. But the image in the broader sense was not lost. However, not all who made this distinction have sufficiently indicated, as Calvin did, that though man remained image bearer of God, the whole man is corrupted, deformed, vitiated and ruined.

Liberal Theology

In the post-Reformation period all the above views continued to find adherents. A synthesis with current philosophy, however, led in some theologians to a Protestant Scholasticism with disastrous results. Influenced by Kant's philosophy and stimulated by the development of modern science, a new type of theology called liberalism or modernism made its appearance with Friedrich Schleiermacher (1768-1834). This liberal Protestant theology dominated the nineteenth century and made significant inroads into Roman Catholicism as well. Liberalism reached its zenith in Albrecht Ritschl and in the science of religion school of Adolph Harnack, Wilhelm Herrmann and Ernst Troeltsch.

Emil Brunner, an influential contemporary neo-orthodox theologian, describes the liberalism to which he formerly adhered as "essentially nothing more nor less than a repristination of later Platonism either taking form from the more ethically oriented Stoicism or from the Neoplatonic mysticism. In its choice between a religious philosophical idealism and the Christian faith, modern theology, whether it is Schleiermacher's, Otto's, Ritschl's, Herrmann's, or Harnack's, has cast its lot with idealism against faith." (Emil Brunner, *The Theology of Crisis*, New York, Charles Scribner's Sons, 1929, p. 12). As a return to the Renaissance and to elements of Greek thought, liberalism stressed the continuity between God and man. In idealistic fashion man was regarded as essentially divine and innately good. Man's reason was considered autonomous and accordingly any need of divine revelation was rejected. A Pelagian view of man's goodness joined forces with an optimistic view of evolutionary progress. Liberalism as a whole was anthropocentric rather than theocentric.

Sometimes regarded merely as "the liberal spirit of toleration" or a "laissez-faire economics," liberalism nonetheless involves a creed. That creed, as American neo-orthodox theologian Reinhold Niebuhr puts it, is "primarily faith in man." Himself once a liberal, Niebuhr describes this theology as "primarily faith in man; faith in his capacity to subdue nature, and faith that the subjection of nature achieves life's final good; faith in man's essential goodness, to be realized either when man ceases to be spiritual and returns to nature (romanticism), or when he ceases to be natural and becomes rational; and finally, faith in human history which is conceived as a movement upward by a force immanent within it. Whether this faith rests upon Darwin or upon Hegel, that is, whether nature is believed to guarantee progress or whether progress is conceived of as man's gradual spiritualization, and his emancipation from natural impulses, prejudices and parochial attachments, the optimistic conclusion is the same" ("Ten Years That Shook My World," *The Christian Century*, April 26, 1939, p. 543).

A wide gulf separates this modern theology from that of the Reformers and Augustine. In his trenchant critique, *Christianity and Liberalism* (New York, The Macmillan Company, 1923), J. Gresham Machen was certainly correct in showing that liberalism no longer deserved the designation "Christian."

Man's optimistic view of man was shattered by World War I. The experiences of men in a world at war increasingly revealed the internal anarchy of Western civilization and the sinfulness of the human heart. A whole generation of liberals heard the bombshell of Karl Barth's *The Epistle to the Romans* (London, Oxford University Press, 1933), and recognized that it reflected their own experiences too. They recognized that liberalism's faith in man was unrealistic and meaningless in a world at war. In industrial Detroit, Niebuhr had similar experiences. He came to realize that the Ritschlian moral homilies he preached to assembly-line workers were "irrelevant to the brutal facts of life in a great industrial center . . . [and] futile" (*op. cit.,* p. 545). The revolt against liberalism was worldwide. In place of an immanent "God" came an emphasis upon transcendence and the "Wholly Other." Man was viewed more realistically and seen to be evil and sinful. Confidence in man's rational power was shattered and the need for revelation was admitted. Existentialistic philosophy, closely allied to the new theological movement, stressed irrationalism and the meaninglessness of life.

The new theology was called by various names, but because it stressed the sinfulness of man and the need of revelation, it has most frequently been loosely designated "neo-orthodoxy." In addition to Barth and Niebuhr, Emil Brunner and Paul Tillich are usually classified as "neo-orthodox." Despite the term, neo-orthodox theologians retain what they consider to be the permanent fruits of liberalism. Among these is the higher-critical view of Scripture. While realistically acknowledging the universal sinfulness of man, neo-orthodox theologians refuse to accept the historicity of Genesis as the account of Adam, the first man, and of his actual fall into sin from a state of integrity. Thus, while the old liberalism continues to find adherents, it has been replaced largely by neo-orthodoxy. In this new theology, however, biblical orthodoxy has not found genuine expression. Its view of man illustrates this point.

Neo-orthodoxy: Niebuhr and Barth

Reinhold Niebuhr's *The Nature and Destiny of Man* is the classic expression of neo-orthodox theology in the United States. Here he contends that the paradoxes of human self-knowledge have usually resulted from the failure to recognize the two aspects of man's nature as a finite creature and a free spirit. Niebuhr contends that naturalistic views saw only man's continuity with nature as a finite creature while idealistic theories emphasized only his discontinuity from his environment as a free spirit. And even Romanticism, which attempted a compromise, lost the individuality of self-hood as did idealism and naturalism. "Without the presuppositions of the Christian faith," says Niebuhr, "the individual is either nothing or becomes nothing" (*The Nature and Destiny of Man,* A Christian Interpretation. Vol. I, *Human Nature,* New York, Charles Scribner's Sons, 1941, p. 92). Christianity regards man as both a finite creature and a free spirit, and it also recognizes man's sinfulness.

What does Niebuhr mean by the paradoxical nature of man as a finite creature and a free spirit? He uses dialectical correlations to express this double environment, such as: nature and freedom, nature and spirit, body and mind (or spirit), finitude and freedom, necessity and freedom, time and eternity, creature and image of God. The first aspect of man as a finite creature continuous with his environment is obvious. It means "that man is a child of nature, subject to its vicissitudes, compelled by its necessities, driven by its impulses, and confined within the brevity of the years which nature permits its varied organic form" (*Human Nature*, p. 3). This organic nature or essential structure of man includes "all his natural endowments and determinations, his physical and social impulses, his sexual and racial differentiations, in short his character as a creature imbedded in the natural order" (*ibid.*, p. 270).

But there is also a less obvious fact of man's nature, Niebuhr contends. Besides this organic tie to nature, man is also a free spirit capable of transcending nature and even himself. He is the image of God which means "that man is a spirit who stands outside of nature, life, himself, his reason and the world" (*ibid.*, p. 3). At its acme this is man's self-consciousness or self-transcendence, and it was Heidegger who in recent times gave the ablest non-theological analysis of this aspect of human nature. "His essential nature also includes the freedom of his spirit, his transcendence over natural process and finally his self-transcendence" (*ibid.*, p. 270; cf. p. 162). Thus Niebuhr expresses his understanding of "the paradoxical approach of Christian faith" in the paradox of "human freedom and finiteness" by setting "the doctrine of man as creature in juxtaposition to the doctrine of man as *imago Dei*" (*ibid.*, p. 166).

Niebuhr's nature-spirit duality reminds one of certain Greek and Scholastic motifs. There is the freedom of man as spirit or image of God. And this combined with the finiteness of man's creatureliness and continuity with nature gives to him a dialectical contradictory existence, but not a necessarily sinful one.

Niebuhr insists that finiteness must not be associated with evil or sin. Evil in man is rather "a consequence of his inevitable though not necessary unwillingness to acknowledge his dependence, and to accept his finiteness and to admit his insecurity, an unwillingness which involves him in the vicious circle of accentuating the insecurity from which he seeks escape" (*ibid.*, p. 150). In contrast to Ritschl who believed that the problem of finiteness and freedom underlies all religion, Niebuhr contends that the Bible subordinates the problem of finiteness to that of sin. Niebuhr insists that even though the relationship is very close, finiteness does not constitute man's sin. Because man is nature and spirit, he is necessarily "both free and bound, both limited and limitless" and this causes anxiety (*ibid.*, p. 182; cf. p. 178). "Anxiety is the inevitable concomitant of the paradox of freedom and finiteness and it is the internal precondition of sin." Anxiety is the "precondition and not the actuality" of sin, Niebuhr contends; it is morally neutral. Anxiety is "the internal description of the state of temptation," but it "must not be identified with sin because there is always the ideal possibility that faith would purge anxiety of the tendency toward sinful self-assertion."

This concept of anxiety as necessarily stemming from the paradox of man's finiteness and freedom reminds one of the Roman Catholic view that concupiscence rises from the natural tension of the material body and the spiritual soul. Niebuhr, like Rome, refuses to designate anxiety sin: it is only the precondition of sin.

Intimately related to this view of man's paradoxical nature as finite creature and free, transcendent spirit, is Niebuhr's unwillingness to accept the Genesis account of Adam's state of integrity prior to his actual, historical fall into sin. This view he rejects as "the historical-literalistic illusion" (*ibid.*, p. 276; cf. pp. 267 ff.), and asserts that "the relation of man's essential nature to his sinful state cannot be solved within terms of the chronological version of the perfection before the Fall. It is, as it were, a vertical rather than a horizontal relation. When the Fall is made an event in history rather than a symbol of an aspect of every historical moment in the life of man, the relation of evil to goodness in that moment is obscured" (*ibid.*, p. 269).

It is in this connection that Niebuhr also speaks of original righteousness (*justitia originalis*). He attempts here what he calls a corrective between the Roman Catholic and Protestant views. Corresponding to the two elements of man's essential nature, namely, (1) his finite, physical nature and (2) his transcendent, free spirit (*imago Dei*), are two parallel elements involving the perfection of the essential nature of man. The perfection of nature (1) he calls the natural law "which defines the proper performance of his functions, the normal harmony of his impulses and the normal social relation between himself and his fellows within the limitations of the natural order" (*ibid.*, p. 270). And corresponding to the freedom of man's spirit as the image of God (2) is original righteousness called faith, hope and love which are analogous to the "theological virtues" of Catholic thought (p. 271).

Since Niebuhr does not acknowledge the historicity of Genesis and rejects Adam's state of integrity before his historical fall, he does not regard these elements of God's image in man as characteristics possessed by Adam by virtue of God's creation. Hence Niebuhr can seek a middle road between the Roman Catholic and Protestant views of the effect of sin upon the image. In opposition to Protestantism, Niebuhr believes that the image of God is not lost but is preserved in spite of sin. And over against Catholicism which held that sin did not corrupt man's nature but involved the loss only of the *donum superadditum* of original righteousness, Niebuhr contends that both the natural and spiritual elements which constitute man's essential nature are retained in the sinful creature although both are affected by sin. "Both are corrupted by sin; but both are still with man, not indeed as realizations but requirements" (*ibid.*, p. 276). Understanding the myth of Genesis to mean that "perfection before the Fall is ... perfection before the act" (p. 278) Niebuhr speaks of a similar "perfection" in every man today. The consciousness of "original righteousness" is seen "in a moment of the self which transcends history, though not outside of the self which is in history" (p. 279). That consciousness is the locus of original righteousness. When the myth of the Fall is thus interpreted symbolically, it is a symbol of all human history (pp. 279 f.).

Thus Niebuhr contends that man's sin does not mean losing the image of God nor even its corresponding original righteousness, but "original righteousness or perfection is present with sinful man as 'law,' " and just as the "natural law" is required of man as creature, so the virtues of faith, hope and love, "are the requirements of his freedom and represent the *justitia originalis*. This righteousness ... is not completely lost in the Fall, but remains with sinful man as the knowledge of what he ought to be, as the law of his freedom" (*ibid.*, p. 280).

The contrast between Niebuhr's view of man and the scriptural doctrine of the Reformers is immediately evident. Although Niebuhr's realistic awareness of sin can be appreciated in contrast to the blind optimism of liberalism, Niebuhr has also failed to grasp the biblical sense of the radical character of sin and its effect upon man the image of God. Unlike the Reformers, Niebuhr has refused to acknowledge the biblical distinction between man as created, and man fallen into sin by Adam's transgression. And Niebuhr's insistence upon the preservation of the image of God in spite of man's sin over against both Protestantism and Roman Catholicism indicates an unwillingness to take seriously the scriptural references to a renewal in the image of God as is expressed in Colossians 3 and Ephesians 4. In Niebuhr's view of man, one notes a similarity to certain Scholastic overtones of nature and grace now cast upon a new dialectical canvas of man as finite creature and free spirit.

The father of neo-orthodoxy, Karl Barth, also rejects the historicity of the Genesis account in its traditional orthodox sense. Acknowledging the higher critical approach to the Bible, Barth regards the Genesis account of Adam and the Fall as a saga. His view of man, however, and especially of the *imago Dei,* he elucidates with minute reference to the text of Genesis, and in an entirely novel way. Barth's approach must be seen in the broader context of his anthropology.

Barth asserts that the proper point of departure must be "the founding of anthropology on Christology" (*Church Dogmatics,* New York, Charles Scribner's Sons, III/2, p. 44). "As the man Jesus is Himself the revealing Word of God, He is the source of our knowledge of the nature of man as created by God" (*ibid.*, p. 3). Founding anthropology upon Christology is not a matter of "a simple deduction of anthropology from Christology" since "there can be no question of a direct equation of human nature as we know it in ourselves with the human nature of Jesus" (p. 47). Barth does not mean that one is enabled by the Spirit of God in union with Jesus Christ to understand what Adam was before the Fall and thus grasp the original nature of man. He means, rather, that true human nature is first present in Jesus Christ. "Jesus is man as God willed and created him" (p. 50). Thus one's real beginning should be John 1 rather than Genesis 1. Nevertheless, in the saga of Genesis God has given us a prefiguration of Jesus Christ, the true man as God willed him. We share human nature with Him by virtue of the fact that Jesus Christ first expressed it. In this way anthropology is based upon Christology.

Barth regards the *imago Dei* as basic to man who exists as the covenant partner of God. With respect to the constitutional nature of man, Barth emphasizes the unity of man and avoids the old dualism of the Greek views. "Through the Spirit of God," he says, "man is the subject, form and life of a substantial organism, the soul of his body—wholly and simultaneously both, in ineffaceable difference, inseparable unity, and indestructible order" (*ibid.,* p. 325). He rejects the Scholastic view of an analogy of being (*analogia entis*) between God and man. There is only an analogy of relationship (*analogia relationis*) for man's being is a "being in covenant with God and in encounter with fellow men.... Man's being exists, and is therefore soul; and it exists in a certain form, and is therefore body" (p. 325; cf. p. 220). Body and soul thus express the "existence and nature" of the being of man in covenant with God and in encounter with fellow men. "We find our bearings and our instruction as we look to the constitution of the humanity of Jesus.... He is one whole man, embodied soul and besouled body" (p. 327). Furthermore, spirit is the basis of soul and body. "Man exists because he has spirit. That he has spirit means that he is grounded, constituted and maintained by God as the soul of his body. In the briefest formula, that is the basic anthropological insight with which we have to start" (p. 344).

In summary, Barth's view of the constitution of man is "that man is the soul of his body as established by God, namely, by the Spirit of God. He is 'soul and body totally and simultaneously, in indissoluble differentiation, inseparable unity and indestructible order'" (*ibid.,* p. 437). That Barth's view differs from classic views of man's constitutional nature is evident at once. Since his view of the image of God is basic to a grasp of this difference, we shall examine it in some detail.

We shall begin with Barth's comprehensive definition of man: "That real man is determined by God for life with God has its inviolable correspondence in the fact that his creaturely being is a being in encounter —between I and Thou, man and woman. It is human in this encounter, and in this humanity it is a likeness of the being of its Creator and a being in hope in him" (III/2, p. 203). The detailed analysis upon which this definition rests is found in an earlier volume of the *Church Dogmatics* where he analyzes the Genesis account of creation. Barth is amazed that expositors have so long debated the question of the image of God and have again and again "ignored the definitive explanation given by the text itself" (III/1, p. 195). He believes this definition of the image is given in the words "male and female created he them" of Genesis 1:27 and their repetition in Genesis 5:1-2. "Could anything be more obvious," Barth asks, "than to conclude from this clear indication that the image and likeness of the being created by God signifies existence in confrontation, i.e., in this confrontation, in the juxtaposition and conjunction of man and man which is that of male and female? . . . But the text itself says that it consists in a differentiation and relationship between man and man, and they ought to have kept to this point" (*ibid.*, p. 195).

Barth believes, therefore, that he has grasped the definition of the text of the Genesis saga by seeing the image of God in the male-female relationship. "Thus the *tertium comparationis*, the analogy between God and man, is simply the existence of the I and the Thou in confrontation. This is first constitutive for God, and then for man created by God. To remove it is tantamount to removing the divine from God as well as the human from man" (*ibid.*, p. 185). From the male-female relationship Barth derives the man-fellow-man relationship and basically the I-Thou relationship between God and man. In this way God "wills and creates man as a partner who is capable of entering into covenant-relationship with Himself—for all the disparity in and therefore the differentiation between man as a creature and his Creator. The grace of man's creation—in which all creation is now revealed as an act of God's creation—consists not only in the fact that He sets man in fellowship with Himself as a being existing in free differentiation and relationship, but in the fact that He has actually created him in fellowship with Himself in order that in this natural fellowship He may further speak and act with him" (p. 185).

Thus, according to Barth, God's image does not reside in any "peculiar intellectual and moral talents and possibilities of man," not in man's reason, nor in something which distinguishes him from the beasts, nor even in his dominion over the animal kingdom and the entire earth (III/1, p. 185). Actually, says Barth, man has the differentiation of sex in common with the beasts, something which indicates man's creature-liness. But in distinction from the beasts man is not said to be "created or to exist in groups and species, in races and peoples, etc. The only real differentiation and relationship is that of man to man, and its original and most concrete form of man to woman and woman to man. Man is no more solitary than God. But as God is One, and He alone is God, so man as man is one and alone, and the two only in the duality of his kind, i.e., in the duality of man and woman. In this way he is a copy and imitation of God. In this way he repeats in his confrontation of God and himself the confrontation in God. In this way he is the special creature of God's special grace. It is obviously the incomprehensible grace of God that His singularity finds correspondence in a created singularity" (p. 186). Thus this sex relationship between male and female, while creaturely and common to man and beast, is in man "the only real principle of differentiation and relationship, as the original form not only of man's confrontation of God but also of all intercourse between man and man, it is the true *humanum* and therefore the true creaturely image of God" (p. 186).

According to Barth, then, God's image in man is a relationship expressed in the terms I-Thou. The original or the prototype by which man was created is "the relationship between the I and the Thou in God Himself. Man is created by God in correspondence with this relationship and differentiation in God Himself; created as a Thou that can be addressed by God but also as an I responsible to God; in the relationship of man and woman in which man is a Thou to his fellow and therefore himself an I in responsibility to this claim" (*ibid.* p. 198). Apart from the supposed definition of Genesis 1:28, Barth claims support for this interpretation in the plurals of "Let us make man," "our image," and "our likeness" in verse 26 (pp. 182 ff.; cf. also the translation of the terms *zelem* and *demuth* as well as the interpretation of the prepositions on pp. 183 f. and 197 f.).

Since Barth interprets the *imago Dei* as a relationship, it is not surprising that he should also deny that this image has been lost by sin. Rejection of Adam's state of integrity in which he possessed a divinely created character involving conformity to God is also involved in such a denial, of course, and this Barth admits. "The Reformation thesis concerning the loss of the *imago Dei* through the fall is understandable and necessary," says Barth, "against the background of the Reformation understanding of the *imago* as a *rectitudo animae,* or *status integritatis,* which man had originally possessed but immediately forfeited by reason of his guilt and as its consequence and punishment. But there is no basis for this conception of the *imago* in Gen. 1. The biblical saga knows nothing of an original ideal man either in Gen. 1, Gen. 2 or elsewhere" (III/1, p. 200). Hence Barth contends that the image has not been lost, neither "partially or completely, formally or materially... What man does not possess he can neither bequeath nor forfeit." The intention and promise of God, on the other hand, "cannot be lost or subjected to partial or complete destruction. This is proved by the fact that the history of God's fellowship and intercourse with man is not abrogated with the fall as the actualisation of man's rejection of this relationship. On the contrary, it really begins with the fall."

In conceiving of the image as the male-female relationship of man and woman, Barth has charted a new course in the *imago* doctrine. A full analysis of it is not possible within the space limitations of this chapter. However, to say that sin has not affected the image, but that the I-Thou relationship really begins with the Fall, immediately indicates the un-biblical character of Barth's concept. In this context he is unable to do real justice to the New Testament emphasis upon the renewal and res-toration of the image, as presented in Ephesians 4:24 and Colossians 3:10. Furthermore, Scripture speaks of Jesus Christ as made like us in all things, but without sin. And it is in the light of His redemptive work, that we are to be conformed to His image. Barth has reversed these biblical assertions. His attempt to found anthropology upon Christology involves a most interesting theological activity, but it does not result in genuinely biblical teaching.

III. CONCLUDING OBSERVATIONS

Our historical survey has shown how many diverse attempts have been made to answer the perplexing question, What is man? In essence, how-ever, there are but two answers and various syntheses of the two. The classic non-Christian answer is that of the Greeks. And we have seen how the Roman Catholic view, especially through Thomas Aquinas, attempted a synthesis of Aristotle and Christianity in a position known as Scholas-ticism. We have also seen how the Reformers, especially Luther and Calvin, tried to return to the full-orbed position of Scripture. The Renais-sance, on the other hand, simply attempted to revert to the classic Greek view of antiquity. Liberalism was a new effort to assimilate Christianity with idealism, but resulted merely in a humanistic confidence.

No wonder, then, that the contemporary man is confused. His liberal, idealistic, humanistic faith has been shattered. And the current crisis in-volves far more than simply trying to understand oneself. Novelists again and again depict the breadth of man's estrangement not only from himself, but also from God and his fellow man. True self-knowledge, of course, is possible only as man has a correct knowledge of God. The deepest, most serious dimension of the current crisis is man's unwilling-ness to know God, i.e., the living God of Scripture, the God of Abraham, Isaac and Jacob. The corollary of this apostate ignorance is his inability, therefore, to come to self-knowledge. The *Angst*, despair and declared meaninglessness of life on the part of existentialist philosophy illustrates how unwilling contemporary man is to heed God and to subject himself to His authoritative Word.

Man in and of himself cannot answer the question of his nature. Through sin he has lost true knowledge of God and therefore self-knowledge. Hence, however great may be his scientific endeavors, man cannot provide an answer for his search. His scientific and philosophical endeavor must itself be enlightened by the revelation of God concerning the nature of man. Whatever helpful information each of the sciences may uncover in studying reality, it will be unable to bring about true self-knowledge. God alone can tell man what he really is. And when man listens to the revelation of God he learns of his grandeur as the image and likeness of God Himself. This revealed knowledge must itself permeate the pursuit of each particular science in order to bring about a fuller knowledge of the created cosmos in the light of God's revelation.

Alongside the current crisis in man's attempt at self-knowledge are several significant trends. The new interest in Scripture is certainly important, for it is from an obedient listening to Scripture that self-knowledge must come. One cannot overlook the widespread unwillingness, however, to accept the scriptural account of man's origin and of his rebellious fall into sin by the historical transgression of God's probationary command through Adam, the first man. The tendency of neo-orthodox theologians to regard Genesis as saga, myth or symbol is such an obstacle that the whole view of man is cast into an unbiblical framework from the very outset. Calvin saw the need of recognizing man as created, fallen into sin through Adam's transgression, and as redeemed through Jesus Christ in the communion of the Holy Spirit. How right he was in unmasking the error of regarding man's present estate as normal. The striking thing is that such an erroneous evaluation of normalcy is being made today even when the fact of man's sinfulness is recognized. The entire locus and nature of sin is being cast into new molds because of the rejection of the historicity of the Genesis account.

On the other hand there is widespread recognition today that man is an organic unity. Even where the Bible is not seriously heard, sharp division between body and soul in the sense of dichotomy with the overtones of the Greek dualism of matter and spirit is widely rejected. What will come of this is impossible to predict. At least it provides a possibility for recognizing that Scripture stresses the unity of man as heart, and that a different emphasis so often heard in theology reflected more of Greek thought than of biblical.

Contemporary experience has demonstrated that loss of the knowledge of God has brought with it the loss of genuine self-knowledge. This situation itself has not resulted, however, in an attempt to recover knowledge of God. Surely this fact should challenge Christians to an evangelistic witness. The pressing question of man's nature is answered in Scripture; here man is revealed as the image and likeness of God. This is his grandeur. This also explains his misery when he becomes estranged from God, from his fellow man and even from himself. Current theories as to the nature of this image of God have not faithfully presented the biblical record as indicated by the views of Niebuhr and Barth.

Once again orthodox Christians face the danger of trying to correlate currently popular views and biblical motifs. That danger is present not only in neo-orthodoxy which reflects tenets from Kantian and existential philosophies; the danger is also real that in viewing God's image in man, orthodox believers will tacitly assume the validity of the static-dynamic dilemma. In both Barth and Niebuhr we have seen such a dynamic motif in operation. This was particularly clear in Barth who defines the image of God as the I-Thou relationship between God and man. Surely a personal relationship exists between God and man. But because Barth rejects the historicity of Genesis, he refuses to allow a state of integrity for Adam in which he possessed the image of God in the sense of conformity to God. Although the terms true knowledge, righteousness and holiness do not express the full content of the original image of God in man, they indicate something of that full image when regarded as synecdoches.

One cannot reproduce the biblical doctrine of the image of God as something only statically possessed by Adam, nor can one express it only in terms of a dynamic relationship. Both aspects are involved, and the current neo-orthodox emphasis upon a dynamic aspect always involves the rejection of the important so-called "static" aspects of that image. While it may be necessary to give the dynamic aspect of man's task in being renewed in the image of God more emphasis than some Reformed theologians have done, this must never occur at the cost of denying the image which Adam truly possessed prior to his fall into sin.

On the other hand, one must also avoid the danger sometimes present in Reformed theologians who distinguish between the image in the broader and the narrower sense. Such a distinction is meaningful since fallen man is still in some sense referred to in Scripture as the image of God. But one must avoid the Scholastic error of thinking of the broader sense of the image as unaffected by the Fall. The whole man, body and soul, was created in the image of God and in conformity with God in true knowledge, righteousness and holiness. But the whole man in body and soul was also corrupted by the Fall, even though he remains the fallen image bearer. The choice is not between a static or a dynamic conception of the image. Rather, Scripture presents Adam as having the image which he was dynamically to employ in the service and glorification of God. And redeemed man in whom the image of God is restored in principle must also dynamically grow and develop through the guidance of the Holy Spirit into complete conformity with God through a life-long process of sanctification.

What, then, is man? He is created in the very image and likeness of God Himself. When he falls into sin, he corrupts that image in his total person, body and soul. Only by the grace of Jesus Christ can fallen man be renewed and restored in the image of God. Thus true knowledge of self comes only through a true knowledge of God; for fallen man this knowledge is possible only through the grace of Jesus Christ in the fellowship of the Holy Spirit. True knowledge of self is possible only where there is true knowledge of God. Is it strange, then, that man is ever restless till he rests in the living God!

THE NATURE OF SIN

✝

J. Oliver Buswell Jr.

James Oliver Buswell, Jr. is Dean of the Graduate Faculty at Covenant College and Seminary (Evangelical Presbyterian), St. Louis. He served Wheaton College, Illinois, as third president, from 1926-40, when he went to Faith Theological Seminary as Professor of Systematic Theology. In 1941 he became President of the National Bible Institute, later Shelton College, in New York City. The first of his two volumes titled A Systematic Theology of the Christian Religion *appeared in 1962.*

9. J. Oliver Buswell, Jr.

THE NATURE OF SIN

Basic to the Christian view of sin are the truths of God's absolute holiness, and of His plan of redemption through Christ as revealed in the Scriptures of the Old and New Testaments. Lacking these two considerations, non-biblical thought, despite its extensive literature in the field of ethics, finds the Christian doctrine of sin quite puzzling.

In answer to the question "What is sin?" the Westminster Shorter Catechism teaches our children to say, "Sin is any want of conformity unto, or transgression of the law of God."

This definition is specifically based on I John 3:4. Literally translated, the passage reads, "Everyone who does that which misses the mark, also does that which violates the law; and missing the mark is violating the law." "Want of conformity," is just another way of saying, "missing the mark," and "violating the law" is another way of saying "transgression of the law of God."

I. THE DENIAL OF SIN

Sometimes the denial of sin stems from naive ignorance. How well I remember a little completely extrovert barber with a foreign accent, who, after much obscenity and much boasting of dishonesty and so on, asked me abruptly, "What's yo business?"

"I preach the Gospel," I replied. "Jesus Christ will save you from your sin if you accept Him."

The word "sin" seemed to lodge in his mind, and he asked quite naively, "What is sin?"

I thought of the scriptural and catechetical definition, remembered the man's limited horizon, and made the best explanation I could, giving him the substance of the definition, "any want of conformity unto, or transgression of the law of God."

"Oh," he mused, "Sin. I don't do no sin."

And he seemed quite simply sincere and well pleased with himself!

I did what I could to present the holiness of God and the Cross of Jesus Christ but the poor man seemed completely "dead in sin." His sensibilities to the problem of sin seemed wholly atrophied, and I never saw him again.

Christian ethics has always had to contend with contradictory non-Christian views. This was no less true in respect to ancient systems of philosophy such as those of the Epicureans and Stoics whom Paul confronted in Athens, than in the case of contemporary thought. In the recent past evolutionary liberalism weakened the doctrine of sin and spread a kind of escalator optimism. It was often said, "If man ever fell, he fell upward." Even after the First World War, M. Coué struck a popular note with his

> *Tous les jours en tous les lieux*
> *Je deviens de mieux en mieux.*

But two world wars, interspersed with periods of extreme economic inflation and depression, dimmed this evolutionary optimism. The notion that "Every day in every way the world gets better and better" has lost its popular appeal.

More frank than evolutionary ethics was naturalistic ethics whose manifesto was *Naturalism and the Human Spirit,* published in 1944 (Y. H. Krikorian, ed., New York, Columbia University Press). The fifteen contributors, prominent American teachers of philosophy, agreed "There is no 'supernatural.' God and immortality are myths" (p. 295, cf. p. 358). Further, according to Herbert Schneider's chapter, the terms *good* and *evil, right* and *wrong* have no cosmic significance.

In our day the "analysis" philosophies, chiefly logical positivism, have asserted that ethical statements are meaningless nonsense. Ethical questions, they have argued, are not only unanswerable, they are unaskable. This extreme position was not long maintained, however. In his *Ethics and Language* (New Haven, Conn., Yale University Press, 1944), Charles L. Stevenson endeavored to give ethics a meaning. His later writings make further concessions. To his bold assertions in the first edition of *Language, Truth and Logic* (New York, Oxford University Press, 1936) A. J. Ayer, probably the best known of the logical positivists, made some modifications in the second edition (1946). The symposium *Logical Positivism* edited by Ayer in 1959 (Chicago, Free Press) shows considerable mellowing. One finds Fredrick Waismann conceding "To say that metaphysics is nonsense *is* nonsense" (p. 380). The book contains not one but three chapters on ethics: Moritz Schlick's "What is the Aim of

Ethics?"; C. L. Stevenson's "The Emotive Meaning of Ethical Terms"; and Otto Neuwrath's "Sociology and Physicalism."

Although in his inaugural address entitled "Can a Christian be a Logical Positive?" (September, 1960), Professor W. F. Zuurdeeg of McCormick Theological Seminary answers the question in the affirmative, I can as yet discover in the logical positivist movement no theism and no approximation to the biblical doctrine of sin.

II. THE MODERN REVOLT IN THEOLOGY

In modern theology it is more difficult to pinpoint the opposition to the biblical doctrine of sin than the opposition to other basic Christian doctrines. This difficulty arises because many non-biblical contemporary theological movements borrow one aspect or another from the biblical doctrine of sin. Such borrowings in the writings of Reinhold Niebuhr and other neo-orthodox scholars Carl F. H. Henry discerningly appraises in his chapter, "Man's Dilemma: Sin," in *The Word for This Century* (Merrill C. Tenney, ed., New York, Oxford University Press, 1960), the Wheaton College Centennial volume.

In his main section on sin (*Theology of the New Testament*, Vol. I, tr. by Kendrick Grobel, New York, Charles Scribner's Sons, 1951, pp. 227-269), Rudolf Bultmann makes many statements to which a Bible-believing theologian may heartily assent: "[Since for Paul it is] taken for granted that evil is in any case 'sin'—rebellion against God, guilt toward God—[Paul's] idea of God . . . must first be presented. . . . God, for Paul, is not the mythological designation for an ontological state of affairs but the personal God, man's Creator who demands obedience of him" (p. 228).

But what Paul teaches is not what Bultmann believes about God and sin. For Bultmann the ultimate nature of sin is self-assertion of any kind, "failure to acknowledge one's own creatureliness" (p. 232). Paul's idea of sin does not stop here at the Creator-creature relationship. The Tenth Commandment which Paul quoted (Rom. 7:7, 8) convicted him not merely of creaturely "desire," but of all kinds of *sinful* desire. This larger view of sin is the only one consistent with the Tenth Commandment in its entirety (Ex. 20:17; Deut. 5:21; cf. James 1:14, 15). Butlmann completely forgets the context of the Tenth Commandment and describes sin as creaturely desire of any kind, that is, *desire as such* (p. 248).

In Paul's delineation God is more than simply the Creator; He is also the Self-Revealer in the literal historical sense. He has revealed His holy law in the Ten Commandments; yes; but even before that, from the very beginning of human history, God has revealed His absolutely holy nature and His character as the Redeemer of His people. Moreover, for Paul these matters of revelation have been recorded and conveyed in the documents of historiography; these documents Paul regarded as the Word of God. For the Apostle Paul, Jesus Christ is God manifest in the flesh, but as such He is still a part of horizontal history. He is "of the seed of David according to the flesh."

Bultmann is right in saying that sin is "guilt toward God"; Bultmann's God, however, never gave the moral law from Mount Sinai in a historical event, nor did He smite Ananias and Sapphira with sudden death because they lied to the Holy Ghost. According to Bultmann all such scripturally recorded acts of God are "myth," and should be eliminated. There is in Bultmann's view no intelligible, definable content to the law of God, nor even to His own moral character. The *kerygma* brings us a message "from" (*von*) God, but we know nothing "about" (*über*) God. We have nothing to say "about" Him, not even that He has given us the Decalogue.

Paul Tillich is another existentialist scholar whose statements often sound very much like the biblical view. "Sin expresses most sharply the personal character of estrangement over against its tragic side. . . . The word 'sin' can and must be saved . . . because the word has a sharpness which accusingly points to the element of personal responsibility in one's estrangement" (*Systematic Theology*, Chicago, University of Chicago Press, 1951, Vol. II, p. 46). In a meeting of the American Philosophical Association at New Haven, however, Tillich did not hesitate to say, "When I use the word 'sin' I do not mean anything like the violation of the ten commandments."

It his *Systematic Theology*, Tillich says, "The very heart of what classical Christianity has called 'sin' is the unreconciled duality of ultimate and preliminary concerns, of the finite and that which transcends finitude, of the secular and the holy" (Vol. I, p. 218). He had just said, "All finite relations are in themselves secular. None of them is holy." In Volume II the thought is expanded but not essentially changed. While Tillich is emotionally stirring when he writes of "concern" (*Angst und Sorge*) trembling on the brink of "non-being" (*me on*, which he distinguishes from literally "being nothing," *ouk on*), his doctrine of sin is not biblical. For Tillich the fall of man was not a literal act of sin. "The notion of a moment *in* time in which man and nature were changed from good to evil is absurd, and has no foundation in experience or revelation (*ibid.*, Vol. II, p. 41).

We must remember, of course, that if the fall of man did not take place at a particular "moment in time," then the biblical doctrine of sin and the correlative doctrine of the atonement (see Rom. 5:12-21) are both destroyed.

Karl Barth excels Tillich in emotive powers. Barth's realm of "non-being" (*das Nichtige*) is not identical with Tillich's "non-being" (*me on*). See, for example, Barth's statement, "Chaos is what God did not will. It is, therefore, that which is not (*das Nichtige*)" (*Church Dogmatics*, Edinburgh, T. &

T. Clark, 1958, Vol. IV/2, p. 469. Barth's view involves a more radical paradox of contradictory orders of time. In his *Dogmatics in Outline* (New
York, Philosophical Library, 1947) he states that "Man ... as a sinner ...
puts himself where God cannot see him" (p. 117). God's time is "another
time than the one we know. ... Death is timeless. Nothing is timeless.
So we men are timeless when we are without God and without Christ.
Then we have no time" (p. 130). When I called on Barth near Zurich in
1950, I asked him, "If, as you say in your *Dogmatics in Outline,* the sinner
does not exist in God's time, how can the Word of God reach me, the
sinner?" His answer was a laugh and a shrug.

The notion of contradictory orders of time is the warp and woof of
Barth's theology. See, for example, his discussion of "the differentiation of the time" in *Church Dogmatics,* Vol. IV/1, p. 322 f. (*op. cit.,*
1956). In Part 2 of the same volume, p. 110, he says we must regard Christ's
"humiliation" and "exaltation" as taking place "at the same time," and
not as successive "states," as orthodox theology holds.

Fred H. Klooster says, "... there is ... a significant difference between
Barth and evangelical theologians ... he denies that humiliation and
exaltation are states that follow each other in time. ... Barth speaks of
the resurrection as the revelation of Christ's exaltation, but ... this exaltation is already present in the Incarnation ..." (*Christianity Today,* July
3, 1961, p. 16 f.).

Christ's "time" for Barth is at the boundary or end of our time. "As
the Crucified, He lives at the very point where our frontier is reached and
our time runs out. ... All evil begins with the fact that we will not ...
accept the limitation of our existence ... and be certain ... of the fulfil-
ment of our life in the expectation of its end. The root of all evil is
simply, and powerfully, our human care" (Barth, *op. cit.,* p. 468).

For Barth, in other words, the source and root of sin is our unwillingness to agree that in our human, historical time order there is nothing
but "that which is not" (*das Nichtige*), and that salvation in Christ is in
a radically different time order. (In addressing a meeting of the N.Y.U.
Philosophy Circle, Tillich expressed himself very similarly: "There is no
hope in human history. It is blasphemy to say that there is. Hope must
be sought in some non-historical dimension." The quotation is not word
for word, but accurate in substance.)

On the other hand, the biblical view places *both* sin and redemption
in Christ in the same time order. The sinner is not, as Barth alleges,
"behind the back of God's grace" (*Dogmatics in Outline,* p. 117). The
sinner does indeed exist in God's time, and that in dreadful reality. He
is the object of the offer of grace. The missionary program of the Church,
in obedience to the Great Commission, is not something which goes on
behind God's back, nor something which God contemplates paradoxically
and obliquely out of the corner of His eye, as it were. From the biblical

viewpoint the reality of the sinner, and the missionary program of reaching that sinner constitute the central theme of God's time.

III. GENERALIZATIONS

Modern theology shows a deplorable tendency to deny or to weaken the idea of the horizontal, historical transmission of the Gospel. ". . . we may say that the theology of Kierkegaard, Barth, Brunner, Bultmann, Tillich, and Niebuhr is largely the existentialist reaction to the liberalism of Schleiermacher, Ritschl, and Harnack" (Robert Paul Roth, *Christianity Today*, March 27, 1961, p. 3). The existentialist label is not the important point in Roth's statement, however. Barth has repudiated existentialism, and so has Heidegger. Despite their common concern over man's predicament, these theologians do not believe that the predicament can be met on a horizontal dimension by redemptive history and a divine message conveyed by a Book, or by what one may simply and factually say to one's neighbor.

Certainly we would not minimize the vertical dimension, for the Holy Spirit convicts even while we are preaching (John 16:8). But if the horizontal dimension is excluded we have no "good news" to preach. The vertical experience, the leap of faith (Kierkegaard), the *kerygma* (Bultmann), or *Krisis, unter das Urteil* (Barth), or existential concern (Tillich), or whatever it may be called, is not the Christian experience at all if it is coupled with a denial of the historical, biblical message.

If no definite, revealed content can be attached to the idea of God or to the idea of God's moral law, then sin becomes a merely subjective matter. Herman Ridderbos states the question: "Is sin really described in the biblical sense when it is qualified in Bultmann's terms . . . ? Does not sin become in this way a purely anthropological concept, that is, merely sin against man's own destination?" (*Christianity Today*, May 22, 1961, p. 8.)

IV. A PHILOSOPHICAL PROBLEM

To clarify one's doctrine means also to clarify one's ontology and epistemology. Generally speaking, active Gospel-spreading Christianity has been characterized by ontological and epistemological realism. God is; God has created the world; God has revealed Himself in world history; God has made my mind capable of receiving His Word, and of knowing something about His world (cf. Heb. 11:6). Reality (God and His creation) is somehow communicated to man and man therefore has some measure of genuine knowledge of this reality.

The biblical view of sin, I feel, *must* be conceived in the following simple, realistic terms: in the real world I have sinned against the real God, and in that same real world He offers me salvation through Christ.

At the opposite extreme from realism as here defined we have egocentric solipsism, to which, interestingly enough, no one admits adhering. The "egocentric predicament" is a philosophical term; it means that all that I know immediately is what *I* know immediately. By focusing on the ego, objective reality tends to fade. Just short of egocentric solipsism begin the various grades and degrees of metaphysical idealism, phenomenalism, process philosophy (Whitehead), positivism and neo-Kantianism, which more or less approach the realistic position. In my opinion, however, all these systems depart from biblical realism and in greater or less degree capitulate to the egocentric predicament.

The observation is rather common in philosophical circles that for two hundred years idealism has dominated the philosophy departments in religious schools. I believe this condition has been generally true since Leibnitz (1646-1716) and Berkeley (1685-1753). Hegel (1770-1831), of course, gave tremendous impetus to the idealistic drift of theology and philosophy. Even among evangelical philosophy teachers today it is difficult to find those who adhere to simple biblical realism, or those who do not make some concessions to subjectivism and egocentricity. In my opinion where subjectivism and egocentricity crowd out biblical realism the awful reality of sin soon fades away.

To those who sense the relationship between metaphysics and theology I suggest that the general weakening of the biblical doctrine of sin in modern theology is in large part due to the drift from realism toward egocentricity.

Likewise, I believe, biblical criticism has hastened the drift from realism. Machen and Warfield were biblical realists who met criticism with facts. Many others, however, chose the easier course of retreat into the subjectivity of existential experience instead of the laborious task of meeting one kind of critical scholarship with a better critical scholarship, as did Machen and Warfield.

V. HISTORICAL REALISM NECESSARY

As a young man I knew my father to be a great-hearted and godly personality who communicated with me both personally and by letter. When I was a child he had carried me on his shoulders. During my youth he had chastened, admonished, and comforted me. Later he participated in the beginning of my ministry. I both knew him, and knew much about (*über*) him. I had scarcely any greater sorrow than when I had grieved my father.

As a Christian my sense of sin is just like this experience of grief. "I have sinned against my Heavenly Father." "Against Thee, and Thee only have I sinned." With this confession goes the act of faith by which the sinner casts himself wholly upon the grace of God in Christ. "Purge me with hyssop and I shall be clean."

It was when Isaiah saw the Lord "high and lifted up" (Isa. 6:1-8) that he was made conscious of his sin and cried out, "I am a man of unclean lips, and I dwell in the midst of a people of unclean lips, for mine eyes have seen the King, the Lord of Hosts." It was after Saul of Tarsus had become intensely aware of the holy law of God that he came under conviction. "I know that in me, that is my fallen nature, the good does not dwell.... Wretched man that I am, who will deliver me ..." (Rom. 7:18, 24).

But Isaiah's vision would have been meaningless apart from his mission to his people as a step in the historical unfolding of God's redemptive program. Similarly Paul's vision on the road to Damascus would be regarded as mere hallucination, had he not received the historical nexus in the words "I am Jesus, whom thou persecutest." He had been "kicking against the goads," that is, resisting the implications of factual evidence. The entire experience is intimately interlaced with the continuity of historical events, a fact which illustrates the principle I have been affirming. I do not believe that Isaiah or Paul or anyone else is ever convicted of sin in the biblical sense without some realistic consciousness of horizontal historical revelation.

VI. THE BIBLICAL PICTURE OF SIN

In the following section let us turn away from the more controversial questions and focus our attention more constructively upon biblical doctrine as such. A detailed examination of the biblical picture of sin makes its simple realism perfectly apparent. Man has corrupted himself in God's created temporal order, and has thus brought corruption into God's creation. Moreover, everything is done in God's holy presence. "Nor is there any creature out of sight before him, but all is naked and laid open to the eyes of him with whom we have our account" (Heb. 4:13).

Paul describes sin in two vivid passages, Romans 1:18-2:13 and Romans 3:10-18. In the former passage he begins by describing the original status of man, to whom the knowledge of God was revealed. Paul then associates this state with the fact that nature itself gives sufficient evidence of God's "eternal power and divine character," thus leaving men "without excuse."

Paul's argument is not that every individual human being is guilty of every particular sin enumerated, but rather that these acts of crime and depravity characterize fallen humanity as a whole. Three times we read that "God gave them up." Man, says Paul, preferred to worship and adore the creature rather than the Creator, "wherefore *God gave them up* in the evil desire of their hearts unto uncleanness, so that they mutually dishonor their own bodies" (v. 24). "*God gave them up* to the penalties of dishonor" (v. 26). After specifying horrible crimes of corruption and perversion, Paul summarizes by saying, "and just as they did not see fit to retain God in their knowledge, *God gave them up* to an unfit mentality, to do things which are shameful" (v. 28).

The word which I have translated "shameful," *me kathekonta,* is a Greek philosophical term which Paul appropriately adopts to describe the moral corruption of humanity. This word in itself is proof that both pagan and Christian ethical thought observe evidences in human conduct of the fact that man is not what he ought to be.

Paul then proceeds (vv. 29 ff.) to a generalized description of human depravity in two highly eloquent prose poems. These passages in the original Greek show a balanced structure and an awesome use of resounding onomatopoeia whose impact on the emotions to produce a sense of horror is difficult to convey in translation. While the following presents the cognitive meaning, it quite fails to convey the emotional, and thus the full ethical impact of Paul's words.

"[They are] filled with every injustice, malignity, rapacity, spite; diseased with envy, murder, strife, deceit, evil mindedness. They are whisperers, slanderers, hateful to God, impudent, arrogant, boastful, plotters of evil, unfaithful to parents, unintelligent, treacherous, devoid of affection, pitiless."

After taking up related questions, especially that of the Jews to the moral law, Paul summarizes once again (Rom. 3:9-18). This time he fashions a mosaic of Old Testament passages to pronounce a terrifying indictment against man.

"We have previously charged that all, both Jews and Greeks, are under sin, just as it is written,—
There is not a righteous man,
Not even one,
    There is no man who understands,
    There is no man who seeks for God.
All have turned aside.
Together they have been made worthless.
    There is not one who does good things.
    There is not even one.
Their throat is an open tomb.
With their tongues they have deceived.
    The poison of cobras is under their lips
    Their mouth is full of cursing and bitterness.
Swift are their feet to shed blood.
Destruction and wretchedness are in their ways.
    The way of peace they have not known.
    The fear of God is not before their eyes."

A reader of these words might say, "But that is entirely too severe! Not all human beings are like this!" True, not every person is characterized by each of these attributes of corruption. Nor is that what Paul is arguing. But humanity as a whole demonstrates all these attributes of corruption, and all too often. In a fallen temple not every block is broken or marred in exactly the same way; similarly not all individual persons are guilty of all or of the same forms of corruption. But because every block in a fallen temple is a part of the ruin, the whole structure is characterized thereby.

Countless thoughtful men have had the experience, when they are confronted with what Scripture teaches about fallen humanity, although they are not guilty of many of the individual crimes mentioned, of having to confess, "That is the race to which I belong; I am of that kind. I belong to that ruin."

VII. THE OLD TESTAMENT RECORD OF THE FALL

The original sin which involved the whole human race is presented in the third chapter of Genesis. Concerning this account, H. N. Gardiner in a conversation years ago spoke rather contemptuously. He called it "the myth of the snake in the garden of Eden."

"Every philosophy has to meet the problem of evil in some form," I said, "and I have never found a better presentation of the problem of moral evil than I find in the third chapter of Genesis."

"But you make it an allegory, do you not?" said he. "You don't believe there ever was such an incident, do you?"

"As an allegory," said I, "the story would mean very little to me, since I am never tempted to sin in the abstract. But as a record of an historical incident, an incident which has affected the entire human race, yet a particular temptation and a particular act of self-corruption, the record is supremely important for me."

VIII. THE NEW TESTAMENT PICTURE OF MAN'S FALL

The most extensive commentary in the entire Bible on the sin of Adam is Romans 5:12-21. Here we read that through the representative act of the progenitor of the human race, all his descendants are constituted sinners and are consequently liable to death.

That Adam's sin is regarded in the Scriptures as a representative act, one that involves all natural descendants is attested to by plain and direct statements to that effect: "It is for the following reason that, just as through one man sin came into the world and death through sin, thus also death came in unto all men,—it is for the reason that all sinned [that this is so]" (Rom. 5:12). The words "all sinned" in this verse do not mean merely that all men have sinned at some time or other, but that all sinned representatively when Adam sinned. The context makes this perfectly clear; it makes the sin of Adam just as truly a representative act, and just as historically valid, as the atonement of Christ in which we through Him our representative have died for our sins. Compare Paul's comment given earlier, namely, "One died for all, therefore all died. He died for all in order that those who live no longer should live to themselves, but to him who died for them and rose again" (II Cor. 5:14, 15). Nothing could be clearer than Paul's statement (Rom. 5:12 ff.) that sin came into the world through the sin of Adam, and that death thus came into the world because sin thus came into the world.

The implications of Adam's sin Paul summarizes in this triumphant manner: "Law then came along, in order that the trespass might increase; but where sin increased, grace was super-abundant. The result is that just as sin reigned as king in death, so also grace reigns as king through justification unto eternal life through Jesus Christ our Lord" (vv. 20, 21). This climax introduces his fervent appeal for holy living in chapters 6, 7, and 8 of the Epistle to the Romans. We who have accepted the atonement of Christ must continuously appropriate His cleansing and sanctifying power through the Holy Spirit.

The climax of Paul's discussion concerning the implications of Adam's sin leads also to an appropriate evangelistic appeal. The doctrine of original sin indicates that the Holy Spirit convicts and makes every human being conscious of sin. Since this is the diagnosis of man's condition, the lost may be persuaded by this very fact to accept the remedy offered in Christ.

IX. DOCTRINAL IMPLICATIONS OF THE ANALOGY

It is of the very essence of Christianity that we accept Christ's atonement as accomplishing that which is necessary to pardon all our sins. According to Scripture, especially as presented in the fifth chapter of Romans, we must acknowledge our involvement in the original sin of man, if we are to participate, or at least if we are to understand our participation in the redemption purchased by Christ. Scripture makes an analogy between the original sin of Adam and the atonement of Christ. Once accepted, this analogy carries with it certain doctrinal implications.

To accept the analogy between original sin and the atonement provided by Christ necessarily excludes certain doctrinal theories which are more or less prevalent among students of theology. In answer to this kind of theology we must indicate that such an attitude toward the doctrine of original sin undermines the doctrine of the atonement as an historic, literal fact, a transaction accomplished once for all on the Cross of Calvary.

X. MODIFICATION OF THE DOCTRINE OF CREATION

Independent of the neo-orthodox and existential theologies, or any other explicit theological system, for that matter, I find among our contemporaries a tendency to reject the historicity of Genesis without any awareness whatever that such rejection involves the doctrine of the atonement. When we study the creation of man and his antiquity on the earth, we encounter this very problem. I would merely point out here that any theory of pre-Adamic man, any theory of the gradual evolution of man from a non-human form, any theory which in any way sets aside or weakens the individuality of Adam and the particular historicity of the event recorded in the third chapter of Genesis, very definitely undermines and, if consistently carried out, completely destroys the Christian doctrine of the atonement. If Adam is not to be regarded as the progenitor of the human race, and the representative of us all in the original act of human sin, then it follows scripturally, Christ cannot be regarded as the One Who has made atonement sufficient for all, as the One Who is the "Only Redeemer of God's elect."

XI. THE REPRESENTATIVE PRINCIPLE

Scripture teaches that Christ as our substitute bore our penalty in our place. On the cross He became our *representative*. He died in my place as my representative and substitute when it was I who should have died. His death therefore is to be considered as my death for my sins. It follows from the analogy developed in Romans 5:12-21 that when Adam sinned he sinned as my representative. I became a wicked, guilty sinner in the Garden of Eden. While I was not personally present, my representative was there; on the representative principle what he did I therefore did. This, it has been shown, is the meaning of the words "all sinned" in Romans 5:12. Indeed, this principle of representation runs through the entire range of human life. Representative action is a sociological fact everywhere, and is recognized in all orderly legal systems.

I became a wicked guilty sinner in the Garden of Eden. I turned my back upon fellowship with my holy God. I deliberately corrupted the character of godly holiness which God imparted to His creation. I willfully began to spread corruption through the creation over which God had intended my kind to rule. I was not there. No, but my representative was there, and he acted as such in my place. I was driven out from the garden, and excluded from the tree of life.

Such procedure is not fair or equitable, it is objected. In human affairs I can repudiate the actions of my representatives. Exactly. While I cannot protest the act of my representative in the Garden of Eden, and although I know I might have done just as he did, yet, through the Holy Spirit, I have repudiated the first Adam by going to the One Who died for me "without the camp." That day outside the walls of Jerusalem I died for my sins. I was not there, but my representative was there. Because He died in my place, I died.

If the doctrine of original sin seems hard and unreasonable, and the unconvicted heart of the natural man may reject it, yet the fact that I am offered the privilege of choosing another representative, and thereby repudiating the former, makes it less difficult for me to accept the plain teaching of Romans 5:12-21.

What took place at the Cross of Calvary is to me the most vivid and clearest illustration of the representative principle than any other presentation of the doctrine. As I contemplate that scene I can only acknowledge in my inmost being that I was one of those who despised the Son of God. What happened there, just as truly as what happened in Eden, and perhaps more vividly, represented the human race to which I belong. I mocked and buffeted Him. I made the crown of thorns and pressed it upon His head. I spat in His face. I drove the spikes into His hands and feet. I derided and challenged Him, "If thou be the Son of God come down from the cross!"

The crucifixion of Jesus Christ, "God manifest in the flesh," was a representative act which implicates the entire human race. Not only are the Jews guilty. It was a Gentile judge who sought to wash his hands of personal responsibility. It was Gentile soldiers who put on Him the purple robe and the crown of thorns. Gentile soldiers drove the nails into His hands and feet. A Gentile spear pierced His side. Gentiles cast lots over His garments. Jew and Gentile together, the entire human race is guilty.

The crucifixion of the Son of God is the most obvious, comprehensive, representative act of human sin. Even if he should find it difficult to accept his own involvement in the sin of Adam, no thinking person convicted in the least by the Holy Spirit can honestly fail to acknowledge, "It was my sin, representatively, that put Jesus on the Cross."

THE NATURE
OF REDEMPTION

✝

Roger Nicole

*Roger Nicole is Professor of Theology at Gordon Divinity School,
Beverly Farms, Massachusetts. He holds the Licence D'enseignement ès
Lettres Classiques (M.A.) from the Sorbonne, a Th.D. from Gordon
Divinity School, and is a candidate for the Ph.D. at Harvard Divinity
School. He served as president of Evangelical Theological Society in
1956. He is preparing a volume on the doctrine of the atonement, on
which theme he has delivered lectures at several seminaries.*

10. *Roger Nicole*

THE NATURE
OF REDEMPTION

CHRISTIANITY is essentially and pre-eminently a redemptive religion. In fact, it claims to be *the* redemptive religion, the only faith which truly provides salvation for man (Acts 4:12; Rom. 10:13-15; I John 5:12; etc.). Since the concept of redemption is manifestly of the highest significance for the Christian, the importance of carefully analyzing its precise nature and implications should not be overlooked.[1]

Definition

In a theological context, the word redemption may vary considerably in its scope. We distinguish among the following related levels of meaning:

1. On the broadest plane, redemption embraces not only the actual divine plan for restoring the sinner, but also all the presuppositions and implications of this plan, such as the nature of God who made it, the nature of creation which benefits by it, the nature of sin which necessitates it, etc. In this wider sense, redemption is practically synonymous with the total scope of the Christian faith, which, as already noted, emphasizes the redemptive nature of Christianity.

2. In a somewhat more restricted use, the word redemption denotes specifically God's saving purpose and activity. This meaning includes both the accomplishment and the application of salvation and combines the concepts listed below under 3 and 5.

---

[1] Portions of the material in this essay were presented in lecture form at the Mid-year Lectures of the Western Conservative Baptist Theological Seminary, Portland, Oregon (1953), and at the Payton Lectures of Fuller Theological Seminary, Pasadena, California (1959).

3. Redemption may refer to the objective basis for the sinner's restoration as found in the person and work of Jesus Christ the Redeemer. In this context, alternative terms for redemption are Christology, the study of Christ, and soteriology, the study of the Saviour.

4. Redemption may refer more specifically to Christ's work as distinct from the study of His person. In that case, attention focuses on the atoning or reconciling aspect of His priestly office. This meaning of redemption is among the most common, and is the one that underlies the scope of our present study. Frequently used synonyms at this level are "atonement" and "reconciliation."

5. The word redemption may also refer to the application of salvation, that is, to the Holy Spirit's subjective impartation to the sinner of the saving benefits secured by Christ. In this sense, redemption is the study of salvation, or soteriology.

6. Finally, redemption may also mean the ultimate consummation of the plan of grace, namely, the believer's entrance in resurrection splendor into the heavenly glory. Redemption is then synonymous with glorification. Romans 8:23 is a case in point.

As already indicated, this chapter on redemption is concerned with definition No. 4. This is the most usual approach to the subject. Furthermore, it is the general framework assumed by, and foundational to, the remaining essays of this volume.

Outline

In surveying this vital subject, we will first of all establish our moorings in the whole body of biblical revelation. Then we shall examine the views of a contemporary, Dr. Vincent Taylor, who has written extensively on this theme. We shall conclude our essay on redemption by emphasizing the importance of penal substitution for a wholesome understanding of the work of Jesus Christ.

I. BIBLICAL MOORINGS

Perhaps the importance of redemption is reflected by the extraordinarily variegated terminology used in Scripture in reference thereto. The atoning work of Christ and its effects are often presented in metaphorical language that stems from numerous life situations intended to illustrate what the saving process involves. Any view of salvation that is consonant with the Bible, therefore, must so fit the whole range of expressions that each term and each metaphor can be readily accounted for. We will list some of the more important groups of these expressions and provide brief comments on each category.

A. Reconciliation

"If, while we were enemies we were reconciled to God through the death of his Son, much more, being reconciled, shall we be saved by his life" (Rom. 5:10).

"... the reconciling of the world ..." (Rom. 11:15).

"... God, who reconciled us to himself through Christ, and gave unto us the ministry of reconciliation, to wit, that God was in Christ reconciling the world unto himself, not reckoning unto them their trespasses and having committed unto us the word of reconciliation. We are ambassadors therefore on behalf of Christ, as though God were entreating by us; we beseech you on behalf of Christ, be ye reconciled to God. Him who knew no sin he made to be sin on our behalf; that we might become the righteousness of God in him" (II Cor. 5:18-21).

Cf. also Ephesians 2:16 and Colossians 1:10.

In addition to these passages, we should note many others where sinful man is described as an enemy (Rom. 5:10; Eph. 2:12; 4:18; Col. 1:21; etc.), or where Christ is said to make peace (Eph. 2:14; Rom. 5:1; etc.). Reconciliation implies the laying aside of opposition and enmity. The question follows, then, "Whose enmity is removed? It is God's enmity against man, or is it man's enmity against God?" In view of the biblical data, the answer in our judgment should be not one or the other, but both and *primarily the former,* that is, God's enmity against man. We especially wish to dispute the frequent allegation that God needs no reconciliation, and that the only enmity to be removed therefore is that of man against God. In this essay, we can summarize the argument very briefly.

1. Where the word reconcile or its cognates occur in a context of relationship between men (I Sam. 29:4; Matt. 5:23-24; I Cor. 7:11; cf. also II Macc. 1:5, 5:20, 7:33, 8:29; Josephus, *passim,* etc.), the biblical language implies that when *A* is reconciled to *B* it means that it is *B* who relinquishes his grievance against *A* and not *vice versa.* This fact is important in properly interpreting the Scripture passages listed under A.

2. Parallel clauses in Romans 5 and in II Corinthians 5 elaborate on the nature of this reconciliation: "justified by his blood," "saved from the wrath of God" (Rom. 5:9), "not reckoning unto them their trespasses" (II Cor. 5:19). These phrases make it particularly plain that the reconciliation envisioned by Scripture is one which offsets God's wrath and His judicial reckoning of man's sin.

3. Reconciliation is represented as something accomplished in the past (Rom. 5:9; II Cor. 5:18), but the benefits of which are still now being proffered to men (II Cor. 5:20) and being received by men (Rom. 5:11). This could hardly be the case if man's enmity to God were in view.

4. The Bible emphasizes Christ's death as the instrumental cause and ground of reconciliation (Rom. 5:10; II Cor. 5:19; Col. 1:20), and His sin-bearing as the basis of our righteousness (II Cor. 5:21). This perspective is in keeping with the Godward aspect of reconciliation, but would be obscure and inappropriate indeed if Paul had in view only a manward aspect.

5. The many passages referring to God's wrath against sin, to man as alienated from Him, to the peace established by Christ, and so on, tend to give further support to the interpretation of reconciliation as having primarily a Godward reference.

It should be emphasized that the biblical and evangelical view of reconciliation is far removed from the grotesque caricature too frequently made of God, the Father: full of vengeful fury against the poor help-less sinner, He desists from His insatiable hatred only because of the interposition and vicarious suffering of a third party, Jesus Christ. Need-less to say, it is easy to resent such a God and to call Him a "dirty bully." The fact is, however, that informed evangelicals have never advocated such a view; it represents, rather, a misinterpretation of the evangelical position by uninformed liberals. Conservatives have always stressed the love of the Triune God as basic to reconciliation: this love is the moving cause rather than the effect or product of Christ's atoning work. This reconciliation, however, is not accomplished in defiance of the eternal perfections of God—His justice, holiness, immutability, sovereignty; rather the fact that these, as well as divine love, are seen in their most challenging expression at the Cross is what constitutes the triumph of the resourcefulness of grace. Furthermore, we must recognize that in Christ we face not a "third party" who has come to effect peace between warring factions, but God Himself, who bears the full burden of man's sin and provides the full cost of the reconciliation He wishes to secure. To intro-duce a disjunction between the Father and the Son in this matter is to do violence to the work of Christ and to undermine the significance of the unity of the Godhead in the Trinity.

The reconciliation effected by Christ is in fact so complete that the re-deemed are represented in Scripture as in "covenant" with God (Heb. 8:6, 13; 12:24; 13:20), as adopted into the household of God (Rom. 8:15; Gal. 4:5; Eph. 1:5), as children of God (Hosea 1:10; John 1:12; Rom. 8:14, 19; Gal. 4:7; Phil. 2:15; I John 3:1, 2), as recipients of a marvelous inherit-ance (Acts 20:32; 26:18; Rom. 8:17; Gal. 3:29; 4:7; Eph. 1:11, 14, 18; 3:6; Titus 3:7; Heb. 9:15; James 2:5; I Pet. 1:4; 3:7, 9), as united to Christ as branches to the vine (John 15:1; Rom. 6:5; 11:24), as body to head (I Cor. 6:15, 19; Eph. 1:22, 23; 4:15, 16), and as the bride to her husband (Hosea; II Cor. 11:2; Eph. 5:23, 25, 31, 32; Rev. 19:7; 21:2, 9).

B. Propitiation

"... Christ Jesus whom God set forth to be a propitiation through faith in his blood, to show his righteousness ..." (Rom. 3:25).

"...a merciful and faithful high priest in things pertaining to God, to make propitiation for the sins of the people" (Heb. 2:17).

"He is the propitiation for our sins: and not for ours only, but also for the whole world" (I John 2:2).

"He sent his Son to be the propitiation for our sins" (I John 4:10).

These (together with Luke 18:13, Hebrews 9:5, where cognates are used in marginal alternates) are the only instances of this word in the *ASV*. In all these cases, this term is a very accurate and appropriate rendering of the original Greek term, found not only in the passages listed, but furthermore in more than 150 Old Testament texts in the LXX.

This word, both in Greek and in English, connotes appeasement, averting of wrath by means of an appropriate transaction or sacrifice. The presence of this terminology bears additional witness of a very clear nature to the fact that the reconciliation envisioned in Scripture is primarily that of God to man. (Cf. above under A.)

It has been urged, however, especially by C. H. Dodd (cf. *The Bible and the Greeks*, London, Hodder & Stoughton, 1935, reprint 1954, pp. 82-95), that the biblical use of these terms does not connote the averting of divine wrath. This, in his opinion, would rest in a crude and heathenish concept of God and imply a process of celestial bribery repulsive to the Christian conscience. He therefore translates "expiation" or related terms. This view appears to have prevailed in the RSV and in the so-called New English Bible.

It would not be appropriate in this brief presentation to go into a detailed discussion of Dodd's position. This has been done very ably by Leon Morris (*The Apostolic Preaching of the Cross*, London, Tyndale Press, 1955, p. 125-185), and at great length by the present writer (*Westminster Theological Journal*, xvii [1955], 117-157). These studies appear to have conclusively established that C. H. Dodd's argumentation is vitiated by an amazingly incomplete presentation of relevant evidence and by a repeated failure to take into account possible alternative interpretations of that part of the evidence which he actually adduces. Dodd himself acknowledges that these Greek terms do connote appeasement of wrath, and that they are sometimes found with that meaning in the LXX. Under these circumstances, it appears highly unlikely that the LXX translators and the New Testament authors would use such terms without meaning propitiation: just as unlikely in fact as the surmise that in our day Dodd would use propitiation without meaning appeasement of wrath!

The importance of this aspect of the work of Christ is made more apparent by the great stress placed in Scripture upon the concept of the wrath of God. Leon Morris, who has written excellent pages on this topic (*op. cit.*, pp. 129-136, 156-166), estimates that more than 630 passages of the Old and New Testament are concerned with this subject. This is a formidable body of evidence which simply cannot be ignored. It is Dodd, not the biblical writers or translators, who finds the idea of propitiation objectionable.

Meanwhile, it is important to remember that in the Bible the thought of propitiation is related to a most lofty conception of God, and therefore free of any and all of the superstitious, crude, or revolting features that commonly burdened pagan concepts. Propitiation is the gracious provision made by God Himself, whereby the effects of His righteous anger against sin may be averted and the sinner may receive the blessings of His paternal love without infringement on His holiness and moral government.

C. *Sacrificial and Ritual Language*

> ". . . our passover also hath been sacrificed, even Christ" (I Cor. 5:7).
> ". . . Christ . . . gave himself up for us, an offering and a sacrifice to God, for an odor of a sweet smell" (Eph. 5:2).
> ". . . ye were redeemed . . . with precious blood, as of a lamb without blemish and without spot, even the blood of Christ" (I Pet. 1:18, 19).
> ". . . he offered up himself" (Heb. 7:27).
> ". . . the blood of Christ who through the eternal spirit offered himself without blemish to God" (Heb. 9:14).
> ". . . once at the end of the ages hath he been manifested to put away sin by the sacrifice of himself" (Heb. 9:26; cf. 28).
> ". . . when he had offered one sacrifice for sins forever . . ." (Heb. 10:12).
> ". . . this is my blood of the covenant, which is poured out for many unto remission of sins" (Matt. 26:28; cf. Mark 14:24; Luke 22:20; I Cor. 11:25).
> Cf. also Revelation 1:5, 6; 5:9, 10; 7:14, 15.

To the above texts may well be added a multitude of others where Christ is referred to as a priest (Heb. 2:17, 4:14, 15; 5:1-10; 7; 8; 9; etc.), or as the Lamb (John 1:29; Rev. 5:12, etc.), or again where the emphasis is placed on His blood (Acts 20:28; Eph. 1:7, etc.), or yet where the deliverance from sin is presented as a purification or cleansing (Heb. 1:3; 9:14; I John 1:7, etc.; cf. also the symbolism of Christian baptism). Indeed the sacrificial terminology is a most pervasive feature of the totality of Holy Writ. It is one of the great connecting features between the two Testaments, perhaps most emphatically articulated in the Epistle to the Hebrews.

A great deal of scholarly discussion has been conducted as to the precise meaning and import of sacrificial ideas. In some cases, the conclusions reached have apparently been unduly influenced by considerations derived from sacrificial practices in non-revealed religions, or by a determined prejudice against the whole principle of piacular sacrifices. Whatever devout Christian thinkers may hold as their own view, the position of the Scripture on this point, the unity of the two Testaments among themselves, and specifically the outlook entertained by Christ and the Apostles are scarcely open to question. Those who insist that the concept of substitutionary penal offering is not espoused by biblical writers are burdened with two very serious difficulties.

1. Their exegesis of a vast number of texts of Scripture is so labored and contrived that it bears upon itself the stamp of artificiality. The fact that many whose own views differ *toto caelo* (some indeed not professing to be Christians at all) concur as to the meaning of these texts with the evangelical interpretation and with the overwhelming preponderance of the Christian Church through the centuries can hardly be thought to be merely coincidental. This fact bears witness that these texts mean indeed what they have generally been thought to mean, to wit, that the Christian faith, in its original documents, viewed Jesus Christ as the sacrificial Lamb, who of His own will offered Himself on the Cross of Calvary, to bear in the place of sinners the awful penalty and curse which was the inescapable effect of their sin in a world ruled by a holy and righteous God.

2. The views of the meaning of sacrifice which are suggested as alternatives to the evangelical view are usually so complicated that it is difficult to understand how the Gospel which rests upon them could possibly make an appeal to the mind and soul of simple men, neither versed in, nor prone to the minutiae of such theological distinctions. This would be particularly true of a view which has recently found some support (C. H. Dodd, F. N. Hicks, O. C. Quick, V. Taylor, etc.) that the primary meaning of all sacrifices was the offering and release of life rather than the piacular infliction of death upon the victim. Even in our own age of increased knowledge and culture, the evangelistic appeal of this view could not be deemed very impressive, and one must seriously question that it could have had any significant impact upon the simple folk who preponderated in the primitive Church.

Furthermore, if the meaning of sacrifice is such as these scholars aver, it is difficult to see why the acceptance of Christianity has been everywhere accompanied with a cessation of animal sacrifice of all sorts. None other than Adolf Harnack called attention to this fact, as noted by Warfield, who closes a valuable article on "Christ Our Sacrifice" with the following words:

> Christianity "came to proclaim the real sacrifice for sin which God had provided in order to supersede all the poor fumbling efforts which men had made and were making to provide a sacrifice for sin for themselves; and, planting men's feet on this, to bid

them go forward. It was in this sign that Christianity conquered, and it is in this sign alone that it continues to conquer. We may think what we will of such a religion. What cannot be denied is that Christianity is such a religion" (B. B. Warfield, *Biblical Doctrines*, Oxford University Press, 1929, p. 435).

D. *Language of the Court of Law*

". . . my righteous servant shall justify many, and he shall bear their iniquities . . . he bare the sins of many" (Isa. 53:11, 12).

"Christ, having been once offered to bear the sins of many . . ." (Heb. 9:28).

". . . who his own self bare our sins in his body upon the tree" (I Pet. 2:24).

"Him who knew no sin he made to be sin on our behalf" (or rather "instead of us") (II Cor. 5:21).

"Christ redeemed us from the curse of the law, having become a curse for us" (Gal. 3:13).

". . . being justified freely by his grace through the redemption that is in Christ Jesus . . ." (Rom. 3:24).

"There is . . . no condemnation to them that are in Christ Jesus" (Rom. 8:1).

". . . in whom we have redemption through his blood, the forgiveness of our trespasses" (Eph. 1:7; cf. Col. 1:14).

See further many texts which speak of law and judgment and of God as the judge; of condemnation and punishment; and inversely of justification and forgiveness or remission.

The frequency of this type of terminology indicates that here again we are facing one of the basic representations of Scripture, one which goes to the very essence of the relationship between God and man. It is in these terms that the nature of sin as the transgression of the divine law can best be set forth. It is in these terms also that the remedy of sin as a satisfaction of the proper demands of justice can be suitably portrayed. This is the fundamental prerequisite for a due recognition of the nature of *grace*. Those thinkers in the history of Christian dogma who have had a strong theology of grace, whether St. Paul, Augustine, Anselm, Luther or Calvin, are the ones who have sensed deeply the gravity of sin and the plight of sinful man before the judgment seat of God. It is here that the chief weakness of so-called subjective views of the atonement resides: to ignore the judicial factor leads one to reduce the whole work of redemption to an only moderately successful program of rehabilitation of man, in which Christianity is only one of a number of valuable approaches entitled to an equal measure of consideration. This is a far cry from the biblical claim that there is no "other name under heaven, that is given among men, whereby we must be saved" (Acts 4:12). This is a far cry from the deep Reformation insight in the truth of justification by faith. To preserve this priceless heritage, it is imperative that due recognition be given to the forensic element and the judicial language so commonly featured in Scripture.

E. Language of the Market-place

"The Son of man came . . . to give his life as a ransom for many" (Matt. 20:28; Mark 10:45).

". . . who gave himself a ransom for all" (I Tim. 2:6).

". . . being justified freely by his grace through the redemption that is in Christ Jesus" (Rom. 3:24).

"Christ Jesus who was made unto us . . . redemption" (I Cor. 1:30).

". . . in whom we have our redemption through his blood, the forgiveness of our trespasses" (Eph. 1:7; cf. Col. 1:14).

". . . who gave himself for us that he might redeem us from all iniquity . . . " (Tit. 2:14).

". . . having obtained eternal redemption. . . . Death having taken place for the redemption of the transgressions . . ." (Heb. 9:12, 15).

"Ye were redeemed, not with corruptible things, with silver or gold, from your vain manner of life . . . but with the precious blood of Christ . . ." (I Pet. 1:18, 19).

"Ye were bought with a price" (I Cor. 6:20; 7:23).

"Christ redeemed us from the curse of the law" (Gal. 3:13; cf. 4:5).

". . . thou wast slain and didst purchase unto God with thy blood men of every tribe" (Rev. 5:9; cf. 14:3, 4).

". . . the church of the Lord which he purchased with his own blood" (Acts 20:28).

"The redemption of God's own possession . . ." (Eph. 1:14; cf. I Thess. 5:9; Heb. 10:39; I Pet. 2:9).

"Forgive us our debts" (Matt. 6:12; cf. Matt. 18:21-35; Luke 7:41-43, 47).

Cf. also passages in which God is represented as the redeemer of His people in the Old Testament, and additional texts in which the terms "remit," "remission" are used with respect to sin.

The variety both of the constructions and of the terminology (at least three entirely different Greek roots are used, the first of which is resorted to by the LXX for the rendering of four distinct Hebrew roots) bears witness to the fact that the New Testament writers, without having a stereotyped way of expressing themselves, attached great importance to the idea of purchase as a frame of reference illustrating the saving work of Christ.

Some authors (notably C. H. Dodd, H. Oltramare, A. Ritschl, B. F. Westcott, Th. Zahn, to mention but a few) have urged that the word redemption is used in the general sense of "deliverance," without any reference to the payment of a price. This interpretation, which is nowhere

mandatory, is simply incompatible with the express statements of a number of texts quoted here (Matt. 20:28; Mark 10:45; Rom. 3:24; Eph. 1:7;
Col. 1:14; Heb. 9:15; I Pet. 1:18; I Cor. 6:20; 7:23; Rev. 5:9; Acts 20:28),
where the price is specifically mentioned, not to speak of other passages
where the same terms are used with respect to purchases made in everyday
life. Leon Morris is quite right in saying: "Both inside and outside the
New Testament the payment of price is a necessary component of the
redemption idea. When the New Testament speaks of redemption,
then . . . it means that Christ has paid the price of our redemption" (op.
cit., p. 58).

That this language was understood in this sense by the Early Church
is made clear by the rise and relative success of the theory that Christ was
surrendered by God as a ransom to Satan. Such a view could never have
originated, let alone have received wide acceptance, unless the terminology
of redemption had been understood in its specific meaning. Meanwhile,
the grotesque and even repulsive features of this theory (Satan has some
right over the sinners which God has to purchase from him, God enters
into bargain with Satan and stoops to deceive him in the process, etc.) are
not necessary implications of the acceptance of the idea of redemption
in its original sense. If the question be pressed "to whom was the ransom
paid?" the answer should not be: "to Satan," but rather, "to the Triune
God in satisfaction of the full claims of divine justice against the sinner."
It may be wise to state further, before leaving this topic, that the idea
of a ransom paid to Satan did not represent these Church fathers' total
outlook, nor even their main emphasis in relation to the work of Christ.
We readily grant that this aspect of their presentation was objectionable,
but this is no sufficient reason to caricature them, as if this feature were
the sum total of their understanding of the atonement. In fact, it is only a
very minor part of it, and for the remainder we find in them an echo of
the rich variety of the biblical representation.

Assuming then that the biblical terminology does indeed connote rescue
by payment of a price, we ask: from what predicament does the rescue
actually save men?

In common language, the word ransom and its cognates were frequently
used with reference to a payment which insured the liberation of prisoners
(both prisoners of war and those who were incarcerated on legal grounds)
and the emancipation of slaves. It secured a deliverance from the thrall-
dom of servitude or, although more rarely, from the penal consequences
of the violation of law.

There seems to be a close parallelism in the usage of Scripture. Christ
redeemed us from the curse of the law (Gal. 3:13; 4:5), from the guilt of
sin (Rom. 3:24; Eph. 1:7; Col. 1:14; Heb. 9:12, 15), and from the power
of evil manifest in the corruption of man's nature and in his vain manner
of life (Titus 2:14; I Pet. 1:18; cf. passages where man's natural condition

is compared to slavery: John 8:34; Rom. 6:17; 7:14). Sin, original and actual, produces a twofold baneful effect upon man's life and nature: guilt and pollution. To this, in the marvelous purpose of God, corresponds a twofold blessing of redeeming grace: deliverance from guilt or justification; and renewal of nature, or regeneration, carried out in sanctification and glorification. This opens up before us the eschatological vista, in which redemption is envisioned in terms of the final completion of the restorative work of grace accomplished at the end of the age (Rom. 8:23; Eph. 1:14; 4:30).

In closing, it may be wise to advert briefly to the expression "commercial theory," used sometimes to stigmatize those who take seriously the biblical terminology of redemption. This mode of speech is calculated to suggest that such people are lowering the saving work of Christ to the level of a mere business transaction. Nothing could be further from the truth: along such lines one might as well accuse our Lord or the Apostle Paul of promoting an "agricultural theory" because they compared their own relationship of Christ to His own with that of a tree to its branches (John 15:1-6; Rom. 6:5)! The Scripture itself does use the language of purchase, but this does not imply that a correspondence in value or methods is established between business and Jesus Christ. It is only on the basis of an indefensible confusion of thought that the term "commercial" can be used as an argument against the evangelical view. The same remark could be made with respect to the cavalier fashion with which Anselm's splendid treatise *"Cur Deus Homo?"* is sometimes lightly dismissed as advocating a commercial theory of the atonement.

F. *Language of the Battlefield*

"... having despoiled the principalities and powers, he made a show of them openly, triumphing over them in it" (Col. 2:15).

"... that through death he might bring to naught him that had the power of death, that is the devil: and might deliver all them who through fear of death were all their lifetime subject to bondage" (Heb. 2:14, 15).

"... the captain of their salvation" (Heb. 2:10).

"Deliver us from evil" (Matt. 6:13; Luke 11:4).

"... who delivered us out of the power of darkness and translated us into the kingdom of the son of his love" (Col. 1:13; cf. also Rom. 7:14; 11:26; I Thess. 1:10, where the same word for deliver is used).

"... our Lord Jesus Christ who gave himself for our sins that he might deliver us out of this present evil world" (Gal. 1:4).

"Death is swallowed up in victory ... thanks be to God who giveth us the victory through our Lord Jesus Christ" (I Cor. 15:54, 57).

One should also take into consideration numerous passages where Satan is represented as the adversary (this is the meaning of the name *Satan*), where the struggle occurs between the forces of good and evil, where Christ appears as humanity's champion, and where Christians themselves are enlisted in the battle royal against demonic powers. It is probably in this universe of discourse that Genesis 3:15, "He shall bruise thy head, and thou shalt bruise his heel," finds its meaning as the *protevangelion*.

The significance of the work of Christ in this respect has been recently brought to the forefront of attention through the presentations of G. Aulèn, S. Cave, R. Leivestad, J. S. Whale, and others. To be sure, this note was not absent in the evangelical outlook of earlier years. Witness this statement from Eadie:

> "Redemption is a work at once of price and power, of expiation and conquest. On the cross was the purchase made; on the cross was the victory gained. The blood that wipes out the sentence was there shed, and the death which was the death-blow of Satan's kingdom was there endured. . . . That power which Satan had exercised was so prostrated, that everyone believing on Christ is freed from its vassalage. Christ's death was a battle, and in it God achieved an immortal victory." (John Eadie, *Commentary . . . on Colossians*, 2nd ed., Edinburgh, 1884, pp. 169, 170. This text is quoted by T. J. Crawford, *The Scripture Doctrine of the Atonement*, 2d ed., Edinburgh, 1874, p. 27. Reprint, 1954).

Meanwhile, we may well be grateful to the above named scholars for having given renewed emphasis to this note of victory. We must remain careful, however, not to equate this aspect with the totality of the atonement, nor to give such an inordinate amount of attention to this idea that other strains of biblical teaching are allowed to suffer.

G. Other Forms of Expression

Before closing our brief discussion of the New Testament language of redemption, we may advert to additional terms which do not fit readily in the categories thus far considered, either because they are more comprehensive (but also consequently less specific) than any of these subdivisions, or because there is no clear metaphorical background to their usage in soteriological terminology, or yet because they represent in our judgment only peripheral aspects of the work of Christ.

The most important of these is the group *"save, salvation, Saviour."* The name "Jesus" also fits here. These are used very frequently in both the Old and New Testaments, and bespeak rescue from some desperate plight. The words themselves give no clue to the nature of the predicament, nor to the method by which the rescue is effected. The answer to these questions lies in the context and in the more specific terminology studied above.

A similar remark may be made with respect to the terms *"deliver, deliverance, deliverer."* These are found very frequently in the Old Testament. The New Testament group, when the reference is to salvation, represents a variety of Greek words. Some examples of these have been listed under F., because the deliverance envisioned is that gained from oppressive enemies. In other cases the terms more readily apply to deliverance from captivity (a. Heb. 2:15; b. Luke 4:18; Rom. 8:21; c. Rom. 7:6). Here, in contrast to category E., these words do not imply that a ransom is paid, although, of course, the idea of a ransom is in no wise precluded. The terms in question simply do not pronounce how the liberation is effected.

I Peter 2:21-24 provides an interesting case where the sufferings of Christ are presented as an example. This is a valuable insight in a context in which the substitutionary and expiatory value of the death of Christ is magnificently expressed. In the total biblical outlook this remains a peripheral consideration and should not be allowed to occupy a central, let alone an exclusive, position.

One may note with some surprise that certain terms which are very commonly used in theological discussions are absent from this review of the biblical vocabulary.

Atonement is used fairly commonly in connection with Old Testament sacrifices, but the King James Version uses the word only in the New Testament in Romans 5:11 and this was replaced by "reconciliation" in the ASV, probably for the sake of consistency. Theologically, this makes no significant difference, for the two words are practically synonymous.

Satisfaction is used only twice in the King James Version (Num. 35:31, 32), but this also was removed in the ASV. In any case, the reference is not to the work of Christ. In spite of its absence from Scripture, this term does represent scriptural ideas examined in this study under D and E. As Dr. Jewett puts it: "It embraces in its connotation all the major categories used in Scripture to describe the meaning of Christ's atoning work" (*Baker's Dictionary of Theology*, Grand Rapids, Baker Book House, 1960, p. 473). Like the words *trinity* and *deity*, *satisfaction* is not found in the English Bible, but it does nevertheless convey in a compact form strictly biblical concepts.

The words *substitution* and *vicarious* are not found in Scripture, but the idea of substitution is amply and unmistakably taught. The analogy with Old Testament sacrifices, the language examined under D and E, the prepositions (particularly *anti*, "instead of," Matt. 20:20; Mark 10:45), the direct statements of many texts (Isa. 53:4-6, 8, 12; II Cor. 5:21; Gal. 3:13; Heb. 2:9; I Pet. 3:18, etc.), all contribute to establish this great truth, which, as we shall see later, is at the very heart of a proper representation of the atoning work of Christ (cf. F. W. Camfield, "The Idea of Substitution in the Doctrine of the Atonement," *Scottish Journal of Theology*, I [1948], 282-293).

H. Correlations of Biblical Terminology

The reader may have noticed that the various categories which we have passed under review are not segregated in stern isolation, but do often exhibit close kinship to some of the other categories. For instance, propitiation may be termed the Godward aspect of reconciliation. The blood may be the symbol of the accomplished sacrifice, or the price offered in ransom. A debt may be considered from a commercial or from a legal viewpoint. Furthermore, Scripture may bring various forms of expression in close juxtaposition within a brief context. We call attention here to the following correlations:

Reconciliation	God's wrath removed Rom. 5:9, 10	Propitiation
	Reconciled .... by the death Rom. 5:10	Sacrifice
	Peace .... by the blood Col. 1:20	
	Reconciled .. not imputing trespasses II Cor. 5:19	Court of Law
	Unto God .... redeemed Rev. 5:9, 10	Purchase
	Peace with God Rom. 5:1, 9, 10	Battlefield
	The kingdom of his love .. deliverance Col. 1:13	

Propitiation	In relation to reconciliation, cf. above	
	Propitiation .... in his blood Rom. 3:25	Sacrifice
	Propitiation .... by the priest Heb. 2:17	
	Propitiation .. to show righteousness Rom. 3:25	Court of Law
	Saved from wrath .... justified Rom. 5:9	
	Propitiation .... redemption Rom. 3:24, 25	Purchase
	From wrath .... deliverance I Thess. 1:10	Battlefield
	Enmity removed Rom. 5:10	

Purchase	In relation to reconciliation and propitiation, cf. above	
	Redeemed .... by blood Acts 20:28; Eph. 1:7; Col. 1:14; I Pet. 1:18; Rev. 5:9	Sacrifice
	Redeemed .... from the curse Gal. 3:13	Court of Law
	Redemption .... from iniquity Tit. 2:14	
	Redemption .... forgiveness Eph. 1:7; Col. 1:14	
	Through redemption ...... justified Rom. 3:24	
	Redeeming .... captives Heb. 2:14, 15	Battlefield

Court of Law	In relation to reconciliation, propitiation, purchase, cf. above	
	Justified .... by his blood Rom. 5:10	Sacrifice
	Forgiveness .... redemption through blood Eph. 1:7; Col. 1:14	
	Righteousness . propitiation in blood Rom. 3:25	
	Remission of sins .... blood shed Matt. 26:28	
	Forgiveness .... triumph over principalities Col. 2:13-15	Battlefield

Sacrifice	In relation to reconciliation, propitiation, purchase, court of law, cf. above	
	He gave himself ...... and delivered Gal. 1:4	Battlefield

Battlefield	In relation to all the others, cf. above.	

The following diagram is intended to give some idea of the affinities involved.

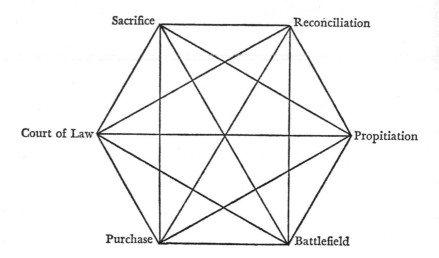

It is no doubt apparent from the above that the scriptural representation is not only rich and varied but remarkably well correlated. It forms a unified whole in which every part should receive its due recognition and attention if the full-orbed biblical Gospel of grace is to be proclaimed.

II. VINCENT TAYLOR ON THE ATONEMENT

Dr. Vincent Taylor, for many years principal of Wesley College in Leeds, and an accomplished New Testament authority, has given very particular attention to the doctrine of the atonement. With the exception of the Roman Catholic scholar Jen Rivière (1878-1946), no one in the twentieth century has written so extensively and over such a long span of years on this topic.

In *Jesus and His Sacrifice* (London, Macmillan, 1937, xiii, 339 pp., hereafter referred to as *JHS*), he conducts a detailed investigation of the teaching contained in the Passion-sayings of Jesus. A study of the Old Testament background precedes a discussion of the sayings, classified according to the sources in which they are found. The form-critical method applied in a rather conservative way is here widely used for the distinction and evaluation of these sources. A constructive synthesis of the results concludes the book.

In *The Atonement in New Testament Teaching* (London, Epworth, 1940, 320 pp. This is the text quoted here as *ANTT*. A second issue, with greatly modified pagination because of the war, appeared in 1945), Dr. Taylor examines the remainder of the New Testament with respect to pronouncements on the atonement. He distinguishes four strata of teaching: 1.) primitive preaching and belief as represented by the Synoptic Gospels, the Acts, I Peter, the Apocalypse, and finally James, Jude, II Peter, and the Pastoral Epistles; 2.) the teaching of Paul; 3.) the teaching of the writer of the Epistle to the Hebrews; 4.) the teaching of John (Fourth Gospel and I John). Here again the volume closes with a synthesis, intended to gather together the various strains of New Testament teaching.

In *Forgiveness and Reconciliation* (London, Macmillan, 1941, xxiv, 288 pp. This is the text quoted here as *FR*. A second issue with different pagination appeared in 1946), he engages in a direct study of the concepts of forgiveness, justification, reconciliation, fellowship, and sanctification in the New Testament and considers their relation to and bearing upon the doctrine of the atonement.

This trilogy, each part of which has been reissued several times, would suffice to secure for its author a place among the leading modern exponents of the atonement. Dr. Taylor has, however, contributed more recently another volume to this topic: *The Cross of Christ* (London, Macmillan, 1956, viii, 108 pp., referred to as *CC*). In this work, he covers the same ground in a summary fashion, giving to his exposition the benefit of additional years of research and thought. He states in his preface:

> "Although I have previously treated the doctrine of the atonement . . . , these lectures are an independent attempt to set forth its meaning. I think that theologians ought not to be in bondage to what they have already written, but should strive repeatedly to express themselves more adequately, seeking, in the words of Solon, to 'grow older learning every day' " (page v).

In addition to these whole volumes devoted to the atonement, Dr. Taylor has written a number of articles on this topic, notably in the *Expository Times*. Several of his other works also contain materials bearing upon this doctrine, e.g. *The Names of Jesus* (London, Macmillan, 1953, ix, 179 pp. Cf. especially: "Soteriological Titles," pp. 107-123); *The Life and Ministry of Jesus* (London, Macmillan, 1954, xi, 236 pp.); *The Person of Christ in New Testament Teaching* (London, Macmillan, 1958, x, 321 pp.); not to speak of his monumental commentary, *The Gospel According to St. Mark* (London, Macmillan, 1952, xx, 696 pp. Cf. especially his "detached note" on the interpretation of 10:45, pp. 445-446).

All of these contributions are marked by general clarity of style, attractiveness of presentation, orderly disposition of the materials, competency in research and documentation, and a clear vision of many of the exegetical, historical and theological problems that demand attention. Dr. Taylor is manifestly motivated by an earnest desire to ascertain and to follow the teaching of the New Testament, as countersigned by the historic witness of the Church and the illumination of the Holy Spirit (cc, p. vi). The methodology of biblical theology, which largely predominates in his work, enables him to maintain a close contact with the sources in their individual distinctiveness, yet not so as to preclude a recognition of a basic unity of teaching in the New Testament.

A careful investigation of the New Testament documents, classified according to the scheme indicated above (p. 208), indicates that there are fourteen distinct ideas represented more or less abundantly in the documents, embodying primitive preaching and belief, all of which are to be found again in St. Paul and St. John, and with two exceptions in Hebrews. St. Paul, St. John and Hebrews exhibit in addition some features peculiar to themselves.

Among the points which have the largest and clearest representation in all four strata, Dr. Taylor enumerates the following, numbered 3 through 6 in his list:

3. vicarious nature
4. representative aspect
5. relation to sin
6. sacrificial significance

Such a combination of terms would lead the reader to expect that Dr. Taylor holds that the New Testament as a whole supports a substitutionary, penal view of the atonement. This is not the case, however, for in the detailed treatment of these various points, certain far-reaching qualifications are set forth which lead to a decidedly different construction of the doctrine. The evangelical will entertain serious reservations on the following point.

A. Dr. Taylor's View of Reconciliation

In his presentation of reconciliation, Dr. Taylor emphasizes primarily the manward aspect of this work and severely curtails the Godward aspect, in some instances to the point of apparent outright denial: "The reconciliation is that of men to God, not that of God to men" (FR, p. 100). He expresses a word of caution, however, in relation to Col. 1:19-22.

> "Reconciliation is here conceived as a complete change from estrangement and hostility on the part of man to loving fellowship with God. Nothing is said in this passage of the divine side of the relationship, but we ought not to assume that it can be ignored because God is not reconciled to man" (FR, pp. 96-97).

Yet he feels it very significant that "never do we read of God being reconciled" (FR, p. 86).

The present writer is unable to see such far-reaching theological implications in this instance of the grammatical usage of the passive. If the matter were to be pressed, the analogy of Matthew 5:24 would lead to a conclusion contrary to Dr. Taylor's, for there he who is to *be reconciled* is the very one *against* whom a grievance is entertained. To emphasize that "we never read of God being reconciled," would in this light suggest that He may well entertain grievances against man, but that man is never represented as animated with hostile feelings against God. This is diametrically opposed to the point that Dr. Taylor wishes to make. It also is contrary to fact, for the Scriptures do say that man is opposed to God in thought and deed (Col. 1:21). This merely proves that no great weight of inference can be allowed to rest upon the mere fact that the precise phrase "God is reconciled" is not found among the three cases of the New Testament use of the passive of this verb in relation to the atonement (Rom. 5:10 twice, II Cor. 5:20. The two secular occurrences of this passive in the New Testament, Matt. 5:24, I Cor. 7:11, afford embarrassment, not support to Dr. Taylor's thesis).

Our earlier discussion of the terminology of reconciliation (cf. above, p. 195–96) has shown, we trust, with sufficient clarity, what are the evangelical position and main lines of argumentation on this subject. No further elaboration is needed here.

B. Dr. Taylor's Opposition to Propitiation

In close keeping with his misgivings on the Godward aspect of reconciliation, Dr. Taylor deems the term *propitiation* wholly inappropriate. This is a point on which he insists repeatedly.

> "It [is] certain that there is no suggestion . . . of propitiation, no thought of appeasing the wrath of an angry God" (*ANTT*, p. 181. Cf. 132, 200, 277).
> ". . . we are far removed from propitiatory ideas which are sub-Christian in their character and implications" (*ANTT*, p. 290).

He expresses enthusiastic approval of C. H. Dodd's "invaluable" (*JHS*, p. 53) study, regarding which we took the liberty of voicing strong objections here (cf. above, p. 197) and elsewhere.

> "We have already accepted the view, so conclusively argued by C. H. Dodd, that the meaning . . . is not 'propitiation' but 'expiation' " (*ANTT*, p. 219. Cf. also pp. 124, 132, 181, 200).

In a brief passage in *The Names of Jesus* (p. 122), Dr. Taylor seems to be somewhat swayed by the argument of Dr. Leon Morris, but even in this context he translates "expiation." In *The Cross of Christ* no trace of hesitation is any more visible; propitiation is called "a misleading rendering" (p. 32); Dodd is referred to approvingly (p. 32); and without further explanation the word "expiation" is substituted for propitiation (pp. 56, 63, 64, 69, 70). Dr. Taylor goes so far as to say: "He [Jesus] never speaks of appeasing the anger of God" (*CC*, p. 21. And yet see Luke 18:13!)

"In speaking of Christ's death as a sacrifice, I do not mean that His death 'propitiates' the Father, so that, in consequence, He becomes gracious to sinners and forgives their sins. This conception is pagan" (*CC*, p. 91).

This representation of the case, be it noted in passing, is a caricature rather than a portrayal of the evangelical view. Perhaps our earlier discussion may have made this clear.

Dr. Taylor favors the substitute rendering "expiation" as being less specific than "propitiation." Yet sooner or later the question must arise: "Who requires expiation and why?" If the answer is "God does, in the exercise of His righteousness," we are back to the traditional view, entirely consonant with the carefully avoided term "propitiation." If the answer is "Man does, for the satisfaction of his moral needs," we are faced with a view of salvation which is so greatly at variance with the biblical view on so many points, that one is surprised to see its proponents attempting to harmonize their position with Scripture or trying to explain away the implications of just one term like "propitiation."

C. Dr. Taylor's Rejection of Substitution

Despite the use of the word "vicarious" and "representative" as together descriptive of the work of Christ in relation to man (*JHS*, pp. 261, 281, *ANTT*, pp. 72, 85-87, *FR*, p. 231, *CC*, p. 90, etc.), Dr. Taylor vehemently repudiates the idea of substitution. Witness the following quotations:

> "The suffering of Jesus ... is neither crudely substitutionary nor automatic in its action" (*JHS*, p. 283. For other examples of the adjective "crude" cf. *JHS*, pp. 104, 282, *FR*, p. 249).
> "There is no sign of substitution in this conception, no thought of a work of Christ the benefits of which are received simply on the grounds that everything necessary has been done in our stead" (*ANTT*, p. 74).
> "He [Paul] avoids the vocabulary of substitution and does not even use the word 'mediator' " (*ANTT*, pp. 125, 126).
> "... in none of the passages we have examined is it [the work of Christ] described as that of a substitute" (*ANTT*, p. 258).
> "... the theory of Penal Substitution, which modern Christianity has no option but to discard" (*ANTT*, p. 10. Cf. *JHS*, pp. 285, 286, *FR*, p. 245).

What then is the meaning of "representative" and of "vicarious"? In reply to such a question Dr. Taylor takes recourse to a form of language reminiscent of J. M. Campbell of Scotland.

> "The truer view of the representative activity of Jesus is one which recognizes that in His suffering and death He has expressed and effected that which no individual man has the power or the spirituality to achieve, but into which, in virtue of an ever-deepening fellowship with Him, men can progressively enter so that it becomes their offering to God" (*JHS*, p. 283).

"This work of Christ is vicarious; it is wrought on behalf of men, doing for them what they are not able to do for themselves" (*FR*, p. 231. Cf. also *JHS*, p. 282, *CC*, p. 90).

If this be the meaning of "vicarious," it would appear proper to say that the cobbler acts vicariously when he repairs my shoes: he does for me what I cannot do myself! The evangelical insists that his vicar is one who takes his place, one who steps in his shoes, so to speak, and that is precisely what he needs in the presence of a Holy God.

In view of his aversion to the concept of substitution, it is interesting to note the following concessions made by Dr. Taylor:

> On Mark 10:45—"Undoubtedly it contains a substitutionary idea" (*JHS*, p. 104). "There is undoubtedly a substitutionary aspect in the offering of Jesus..." (*JHS*, p. 282. Cf. also *CC* p. 90).
>
> Paul's "teaching...has the appearance of substitution" (*ANTT*, p. 124).
>
> "Perhaps the most striking feature of New Testament teaching concerning the representative work of Christ is the fact that it comes so near, without actually crossing, the bounds of substitutionary doctrine. Paulinism, in particular, is within a hair's breadth of substitution.... A theologian who retires to a doctrinal fortress guarded by such ordnance as Mark x. 45, Romans vi. 10*f.*, 2 Corinthians v. 14, 21, Galatians iii. 13, and 1 Timothy ii. 5*f.*, is more difficult to dislodge than many New Testament students imagine" (*ANTT*, pp. 288-289. Cf. also *FR*, p. 229, *CC*, p. 48).

Such statements enable the reader to understand readily Dr. F. W. Camfield's judgment: "It is difficult to escape the impression that Dr. Vincent Taylor's anxiety to eliminate the idea of substitution from Evangelical theology has coloured his interpretation of the New Testament witness" ("The Idea of Substitution in the Doctrine of the Atonement," *Scottish Journal of Theology* I [1948], p. 282).

In view of this eagerness to contend that Scripture does not teach substitution, we are happy to note that Dr. Taylor gives an example of scholarly candor when he openly acknowledges that the Reformers at least did so teach (*JHS*, p. 159, *ANTT*, pp. 276-277). On this point he clearly and openly parts company with them.

D. Dr. Taylor's Rejection of the Penal Character of Christ's Sufferings

In the light of what precedes one would naturally expect Dr. Taylor to object to the idea that Christ's sufferings had a penal character. He dismisses any thought of transference of guilt in Old Testament sacrifices (*JHS*, p. 51), and of transfer of penalty in New Testament teaching, which he calls "patent illegality" (*JHS*, p. 288).

"The idea of one accepting penal suffering instead of another ... is completely mistaken" *(JHS,* p. 289).

"There is no question of transference of punishment from
their shoulders to His own" *(ANTT,* p. 131).

"It has long been agreed that Christ was not punished in man's
stead" *(FR,* pp. 252, 253).

"His obedience is not rendered instead of ours and our punishment is not transferred to Him. Nowhere have we found any
support for such views" *(ANTT,* p. 258).

He views the word "impute" as burdened with unfortunate associations
(FR, p. 55) and calmly asserts that Calvin weakened his statement on
justification "by the introduction of the idea of imputation" *(FR,* p. 70)!

The idea of "vicarious punishment" is emphatically rejected: "nor,
again, is there any trace of the idea of vicarious punishment; primitive
Christian thought knew nothing of the belief that Christ was punished
for us" *(ANTT,* p. 74). Theories of vicarious punishment are flatly
declared "untenable" *(FR.,* p. 245. Cf. *CC,* p. 94). The interpretation of
Gethsemane and of the cry of dereliction (Matt. 27:46) as the bearing of
the curse of sin is summarily set aside.

"We may dismiss at once 'the traditional interpretation,' if
by this is meant the view that the saying implies that Jesus
was abandoned by the Father and, as a substitute for sinners,
endured the pains of the lost" *(JHS,* p. 159).

"The explanation that Jesus was abandoned by the Father and
endured the punishment of the lost no longer merits discussion" *(The Life and Ministry of Jesus,* p. 217).

For this he substitutes the interpretation that Jesus had a feeling of
dereliction which was delusory!!

Despite all this Dr. Taylor retains the word "penal": "It is impossible
to think of the suffering of Jesus Himself as anything else but penal
suffering" *(JHS,* pp. 289-290, cf. pp. 160, 286-290, *ANTT,* p. 131, etc.).
What does he then mean by this? Following J. M. Campbell and the
Moberlys to a considerable extent, Dr. Taylor stresses the fact that Jesus
in His love and sympathy made common cause with men, even as to the
disciplinary and retributive consequences of their sin; "Christ's saving
deed was an act of submission to the judgment of God upon sin" *(CC,* p.
93). In view of this position, it is not surprising that Dr. Taylor says:
"Everyone desires a better word than penal" *(ANTT,* p. 130). This does
not say enough: penal appears wholly unsuitable to represent Dr. Taylor's
view. To use this word with a meaning so radically different from its common acceptance appears to be misleading.

Meanwhile, even with the meaning suggested by Dr. Taylor, the question still remains: How can Christ's death be "an act of submission to the
judgment of God" unless Christ did in fact endure the brunt of this

judgment? And how could He endure the brunt of this judgment, unless He were in some real sense subject to this judgment, that is, charged with the guilt of sin? And how could the Sinless One be charged with the guilt of sin, unless it had been transferred upon Him? This transfer Dr. Taylor rejects as artificial (*FR,* p. 266, "a patent illegality," *JHS,* p. 288) and unethical (*ANTT,* pp. 253, 277), a legal fiction (*FR,* pp. 63, 247; *CC,* p. 38). But how favorably this artificiality compares with the artificiality of making an act of submission to a judgment to which Christ does not have the slightest legal relation! And how ethical was it for God to allow the innocent Christ to succumb in despair and perish in submission to a judgment which could not have any legal relevance for Him? If the terms "artificial" and "unethical" are to be used, the reader will have to judge which view of the atonement they most aptly characterize.

E. Dr. Taylor's View of the Appropriation of Redemption

Again and again Dr. Taylor stresses—and we believe rightly—the importance of man's appropriation of the blessings of Christ's work (*JHS,* pp. 265 ff., 290 ff., *ANTT,* pp. 134 ff., 222 ff., 263 ff., *FR,* pp. 190, 228 f., *CC,* p. 97, etc.). His views on this area of doctrine, however, are naturally affected by his view of the atonement. Thus we are not to be surprised that he rejects the Reformation doctrine of justification (*FR,* pp. 66-70). The doctrine of imputed righteousness he calls a "disastrous interpretation" (*ANTT,* p. 120). To be sure, he rejects perhaps even more emphatically the traditional Roman Catholic construction (*FR,* pp. 65-66), but in his attempt to steer a middle course, he defines the righteousness of justification as "the righteous mind of the man whose trust rests not in himself, but in Christ and His work" (*FR,* pp. 238-239). With all due regard for the vigor with which Dr. Taylor emphasizes that neither this righteous mind, nor the faith-union of man to Christ is meritorious, it remains that in his view the ground of acceptance with God is an attitude infused in man and not the finished work of Christ (Cf. *JHS,* p. 265, *ANTT,* p. 143, *FR,* p. 107, *CC,* p. 38). It is here that, in spite of Dr. Taylor's efforts to ward off this position, faith becomes a work (Cf. *FR,* pp. 63, 66, 239)! Thus the benefit which accrues to the believing sinner from Christ's death is not in the first instance a clearing away of guilt, a restoration to proper standing before God through the imputation of his sins to Christ and of Christ's righteousness to him, but rather primarily a communication of life, the beginning of an ever-deepening fellowship. In this respect Dr. Taylor leans toward a form of the Mystical theory of the atonement.

In keeping with this approach, it is not surprising to find a recurrent tinge of sacramentalism in Dr. Taylor's concept of salvation; this is usually associated with the Lord's Supper (cf. *JHS,* pp. 265, 268, 292, 321, 322, *ANTT,* pp. 136, 140, 141, 187, 224, *FR,* p. 232, *CC,* p. 22), but also borders on baptismal regeneration (*ANTT,* p. 232).

Another consequence of this outlook is that the uniqueness of the work of Christ is at times compromised.

> "It is ... impossible to conclude that He looked upon His suffering as utterly solitary, without parallel or analogue in the experience of men" (*JHS*, p. 269. One should read the whole development, pp. 265-269).
> "The Atonement is consummated when, through faith-union with Christ, men accept and embrace all that He has done on their behalf, when they make His self-offering their own through personal trust in Him, sacramental communion with Him, and sacrificial living in the fellowship of His sufferings" (*FR*, pp. 232-233).

Despite the above strictures and additional objections which the evangelical might have at various points not directly relevant to our present scrutiny (e.g., denial of the inerrancy of Scripture, affirmation of the universal fatherhood of God and consequent weakening of the doctrine of adoption, etc.), these books have several features of considerable delight to the evangelical reader, such as Dr. Taylor's emphatic rejection of any purely subjective view of the atonement (*JHS*, pp. 278, 279, 300-303, *FR.*, pp. 241-242, 249), his recognition of the unity and harmony of the New Testament teaching on the subject of atonement (*ANTT*, pp. 190, 234, *FR*, p. 230, etc.), his vindication of the holy character of God's love (*JHS*, p. 288), and his forthright stand on the trinity (*ANTT*, p. 308). All these the conservative applauds and commends. Dr. Taylor's choice of terms, although sometimes confusing because he appears to alter substantially their traditional meaning, points however to the fact that in attempting to give a careful statement of the New Testament doctrine of atonement, one will be irresistibly impelled to use the traditional terminology, even when one does not hold the traditional view of the atonement. This gives welcome additional proof to the fact that the evangelical view coincides with the biblical presentation.

We conclude this brief survey with Dr. Taylor's own gracious words:

> "We are able to learn much from the mistakes of the past as well as from its achievements, and especially from the writers who do not convince us" (*CC*, p. 12).

III. THE CENTRALITY OF SUBSTITUTION IN REDEMPTION

Just as the atonement is at the heart of the Christian faith, so substitution is at the heart of the atonement. On the Cross of Calvary the Lord Jesus Christ took the sinner's place: bearing the burden of man's sin and guilt, Christ suffered in his stead the punishment which man rightly deserved. This is the truth that underlies any biblical presentation of the atonement. The mystery of this truth and the fact that such substitution is not commonly experienced in daily life make this basic tenet the object of repeated attack. Many thinkers have even attempted to construct some view of the atonement that avoids the stumbling-block of substitution. Usually such efforts begin by stressing a secondary feature or by-product of the atoning work of Christ, often one which has been somewhat neglected by evangelical preachers and writers. Then these efforts try to account for Christ's death and its effects in terms of this one feature, being careful to by-pass any idea of penal substitution. Such schemes seem to forget that, severed from its foundation in vicarious atonement, the secondary truth being emphasized can no longer be maintained logically: by eliminating the substitutionary principle, these theories lose the very support they need for their tenets.

There is, for example, what is known as the Example Theory of the Atonement. According to this view, the purpose of Christ's death was in no way to satisfy divine justice, but solely to provide a model of exemplary death, to show men how to die.

Now it is true that in dying on the Cross of Calvary, the Lord Jesus Christ gave men an unusual example of utter devotion and sacrificial love. This is stated in the Scriptures (I Pet. 2:21-24). But any act is truly exemplary only if it is properly motivated. A wish merely to leave a good example is hardly a sufficient motive, especially if death ensues. A fireman who loses his life in trying to rescue a child from a burning house may be cited as a worthy example. But a man who throws himself into the fire, not to rescue anyone or anything, but simply to demonstrate how to die is hardly to be imitated! Far from being an example, such a death will be viewed, rather, as the final pitiful act of a demented mind. If Christ voluntarily surrendered Himself to death in order to bear the penalty for our sins, then we must bow in grateful adoration before this supreme example; but if His only purpose was to leave a model, we can easily see that His voluntary sacrifice would be a wasteful throwing away of God-given life, and no marvelous display of heroism worthy of our emulation. The Example Theory of the Atonement provides no proper foundation for looking upon Christ's death as exemplary. Only as this death is the necessary culmination of Christ's work on earth as the sinner's substitute can its value as an example be maintained.

According to the Moral Influence Theory Christ's death provides such a moving expression of the grace of God that it melts humanity's wicked enmity against God. Reconciliation in this context means only the setting aside of man's hostility to God; Christ has come to lead man in that direction by touching manifestation of the divine love.

Here, again, we would grant that the death of Christ manifests, and supremely so, the greatness of divine grace: "God so loved the world that he gave his Son" (John 3:16), "God commends His love toward us in that while we were yet sinners Christ died for us" (Rom. 5:8). Many other

Scriptures could be cited here. Further, this display of love is among the most effective grounds on which man may be summoned to turn from sin and back toward God (cf. II Cor. 5:14-15, 20 and other passages). But if moral influence alone is the chief purpose of the death of Christ, then this death would seem to be merely a theatrical display engineered without inherent necessity. Obviously, as soon as this artificiality is recognized, the intended moral influence no longer functions. If a fireman imperils his life to save others, he shows deep concern for those who might perish in the flames, and his act may be said to exert moral influence, both on the spectators and on those whose lives are threatened. If, however, a man were to throw himself into a fire, not to rescue others, but simply to show sympathy toward sufferers and to exert moral influence, then his act would be considered a wanton waste of energy that could have been used otherwise to greater advantage. His sympathy is lost and meaningless, and his influence remains ineffective. This fact was acknowledged by Horace Bushnell himself, a leading American exponent and sponsor of the Moral Influence view. He noted to his own dismay that the atonement, on his own grounds of presentation, somehow failed to move the hearts of people and to exert the influence which the evangelical view of Christ's work had exerted, and continued to exert even during his lifetime. Bushnell therefore rewrote the second half of his famous work, *Vicarious Sacrifice,* and published it under the title, *Forgiveness and Law.* While this latter presentation is still not satisfactory from the evangelical point of view, it nevertheless represented a distinct improvement over what was advocated in the earlier writing, especially in trying to deal more seriously with the concepts of justice, law, and propitiation in structuring the atonement. The atonement is shown to prove the love of God and to exert moral influence only as Christ is viewed as the divine substitute, the one who bears in the place of the sinner the burden of inescapable penalty for sin.

There have been numerous forms of the Mystical view of the atonement. Because we cannot discuss their differences within the limits of this essay, we simply point out their main common feature; that is, the mystical views emphasize that life is communicated to the sinner by personal union with Christ. In his estrangement from God, man needs a new impartation of unsullied life before he can experience fellowship with God. Jesus Christ provides this sinless life.

It is surely true that in assuming human nature and in dying on the Cross of Calvary the Lord Jesus Christ has laid the foundation for His mystical union with the redeemed, a union which provides all the blessings of the Christian life. More particularly, this union for the believer is the origin of a new life which exercises an ever-deepening influence over his nature. But, we must insist, unless there is first a removal of the guilt of sin and a restoration to right standing before God, even the impartation of a new nature does not supply what is needed. Moreover, unless Christ died in union with, yea as a substitute for, the sinner in order to absolve him of the guilt of his sin, it is difficult to see how His death adds anything to a union already implicit in the Incarnation, or perhaps even in creation! If, after a prisoner has been pardoned, I instill in him new courage and help him live a normal life, my action is greatly beneficial. But if I infuse new life in the heart of one sentenced to death, and if I enable him to adapt himself, not to his present condition of condemnation, but to a normal life of freedom, when no provision whatever is made for pardon or release, then my endeavor seems hardly worthwhile. This illustration is imperfect and limited, of course. But it indicates that apart from Christ's substitutionary bearing of man's guilt and apart from the consequent justification accruing to the believer, even the blessing of regeneration, if it were conferred, would be of no value.

The theory of Vicarious Repentance is associated particularly with J. McLeod Campbell, and with R. C. and W. H. Moberly. Although it has had comparatively little following in its original form, this theory has nevertheless exercised considerable influence and deserves some notice. Perhaps the key principle of this view of Vicarious Repentance is that Jesus Christ, in His atoning death on Calvary, has registered man's complete assent to the righteous judgment of God against sin. In other words, Christ accomplishes for man that duty of perfect repentance which man because of his sin is unable to perform for himself. While substitution is in evidence here, it occurs in the area of repentance—an unusual, if not impossible situation.

We recognize, of course, that in Christ's death we have a portrayal of God's righteous judgment upon sin and an expression of the "obedient servant's" complete submission to that judgment. This can be true, of course, only if Christ is viewed as laden with the guilt of sin: we cannot properly speak of judgment unless he who is stricken endures the punishment due to the sin with which he is justly charged. Only by recognizing the principle of penal substitution can any truth inherent in Vicarious Repentance find proper support. The principle of vicariousness in repentance, however, from which the theory draws its name, cannot be endorsed without modification: repentance, after all, is something which God demands of the sinner and which has not been vicariously performed for him by Christ. Campbell and the Moberlys themselves acknowledged this observation.

The so-called Governmental or Rectoral Theory of the Atonement stresses the importance of justice in the divine government of the world. According to this view, two factors prevent God from freely forgiving every man's sins: a) man's obduracy in sin (this may be remedied, however, by repentance and faith); and b) the demands of the moral governance of the world. If God simply forgave all sins, He would seem actually to condone sin and to make unholy alliance with it. In order to remit sin without injury to the moral order, God must once and for all clearly express His true hatred for sin and for everything sinful. This He did in the death of Jesus Christ. According to the governmental view, therefore, our Lord did not die in any particular sinner's stead, and did not bear the penalty consequent to the sins of any one individual; Christ's death was designed, rather, to exhibit for all time God's true attitude toward sin, and to enable repentant sinners to receive free forgiveness without jeopardizing the demands of this world's moral government.

It is true, of course, that the death of our Lord has a direct relationship to God's justice, and that the demands of the law cannot be simply set aside in a great show of benevolence. In this respect, the governmental theory is far superior to those views which allege that the purpose of the atonement was merely to influence man. But unless the Lord Jesus is the sinner's substitute, bearing man's guilt and suffering the penalty of his sin, how can Christ's death possibly be an act of justice and an expression of moral government? To strike an innocent man in no way counteracts the injustice of failing to punish the guilty: far from being a redress, such a course of action, on the contrary, would only level additional injury to the cause of moral government. To exhibit justice one must exercise justice. A great weakness of the governmental view lies at this very point: in avoiding penal substitution, it represents as the supreme display of righteous government an act in which, according to its own interpretation, righteousness is not even in operation. Moreover, if God freely changes the penalties for sin and can be satisfied with merely a token punishment instead of the full penalty, it is difficult to see how such a procedure enhances or even manifests God's justice. If criminals are condemned to pay a fine, and a friend steps forward to pay the full amount in their stead, the demands of the law are upheld and the guilty may be freed. But if someone pays only a token fine for an offender, the judge is in no sense entitled therefore to dismiss all cases and to free all criminals who confess and repent. Only as Christ is the sinner's substitute and bears in His body the full weight of man's guilt and penalty, can His death on the Cross enable God to vindicate His government and to be just while "justifying him who has faith in Jesus."

In recent years the element of victory in the redeeming work of Christ has received renewed emphasis. This, perhaps, is the most prominent feature of the view set forth by Gustav Aulèn. While he calls this theory the "classical" view, the term hardly describes what we normally honor as the "classical" perspective. The adjective *"triumphantorial"* is truer to the case and gives a more modest appraisal. According to Aulèn's theory, the main purpose of our Lord's death and resurrection was to accomplish for man a significant triumph over his age-long enemies: sin, death, disease, Satan, and the Law. Coming as man's champion, Christ brought these foes to naught and secured for man the victory and release which man in his own strength could never have achieved. Aulèn emphasizes that in this process not only is God's victory accomplished and man reconciled to God, but "God is Himself reconciled"; how this comes about is not made clear, however.

We recognize that the death and resurrection of Jesus Christ did in fact constitute a most significant victory over the mortal enemies of man. (How these enemies are selected or identified may be a matter of theological disagreement.) But the significance of this victory and the conditions under which it was achieved can be understood only if our Lord appears on the Cross of Calvary as the sinner's true substitute. If all that is at stake is a divine defeat of the powers of darkness, then it is difficult to see why the Incarnation is at all prerequisite to such a battle. If all that Jesus did was to fight against sin, death, and the Devil, He apparently could have won a more significant victory had he defeated them sooner, without undergoing the agonies of the Passion, and without succumbing temporarily to death and burial. To understand and appreciate fully our Lord's great struggle, it is necessary to assume that additional motives, besides that of defeating the Devil, made imperative the tragic character of His Passion. A strong fighter may allow his activity to be restricted for valid reasons: if, after a deadly struggle, he emerges victorious although greatly bruised, he deserves the greater admiration for his victory. If, without good reason, however, a fighter fails to apply all his powers, and consequently suffers severe injury, one will quickly say he deserved his fate and should perhaps have lost the battle altogether. Only when one perceives that, because divinely appointed as the sinner's substitute, the Lord Jesus was burdened with the awful load of man's guilt, does the dramatic character of His fearful struggle with the powers of darkness come into true focus. Only then is it possible to appraise the momentous significance of His glorious victory.

In a very arresting chapter, following his survey of unsatisfactory views of the atonement, T. J. Crawford formulated four general remarks concerning inadequate theories. These remarks have lost nothing of their appropriateness (although we need to remember that Crawford used the word "Catholic" in a sense which parallels closely that of the word "evangelical" in the present essay).

> "Almost all the theories *contain a portion of truth,* though by no means the whole truth, as set forth in Holy Scripture, with reference to the subject in question" (*op. cit.* p. 395).
> "*The portion of truth which they contain has, to some extent, been unhappily neglected or overlooked by defenders of the Catholic doctrine*" (p. 396).
> "*Whatever truth may be contained in them is not in the least degree inconsistent with the Catholic doctrine, but may be maintained to the fullest extent along with it*" (p. 398).

"Whatever truth there may be in any of the theories ... is incapable of being maintained, either on reasonable or on Scriptural grounds, apart from the Catholic doctrine of the Atonement" (p. 399).

"One should not say: 'Together with many other truths, we find this one in the Gospel'; One should not even say: 'This truth is the most important one in the Gospel'; One should say 'This truth is the Gospel itself,' and all the remainder of the Gospel, if I may use this expression, is either the shape that this doctrine assumes, or its translation, or its application. This truth is everywhere present in the Gospel as the blood is everywhere present in the human body. Everything reminds of it, everything reproduces it in the eyes of whoever has understood this primary truth; even where any other would not even suspect its presence, he sees it, he feels it: wherever he may look, whatever detail he may examine, whatever application he may consider, everywhere he meets and recognizes the cross. . . . . . . Erase from the Gospel, I do not say the cross, but the evangelical meaning of the cross, and you will make these eighteen centuries absurd or impossible" (Alexandre Vinet, *Etudes Et Méditations Evangéliques,* II, Lausanne; Payot, 1952, pp. 248, 255, translation ours).

A part of this quotation from the great Swiss theologian appears in the frontispiece of George Smeaton's fine volume on *The Atonement as Taught by Christ.* Let it stand also at the conclusion of this essay.

THE NATURE
OF HISTORY

†

C. Gregg Singer

*C. Gregg Singer is Chairman of the Department of History at Catawba
College, Salisbury, North Carolina. A Southern Presbyterian minister,
he was formerly Vice President of Belhaven College in Mississippi. He
is completing a volume assessing contemporary philosophies of history.
He holds the A.B. from Haverford College, M.A. and Ph.D. from University of Pennsylvania. He is author of* South Carolina in the Con-
federation, *published by University of Pennsylvania Press.*

11. C. Gregg Singer

THE NATURE
OF HISTORY

T HE LAST few decades have witnessed a renewal of interest in the nature
and ultimate meaning of history which is almost unprecedented in modern
historical scholarship. Not only historians and philosophers, but people
in general, are applying themselves with a dedicated seriousness to the
interpretation of history. Born of an optimistic liberalism, former assumptions have been called into question and found wanting by an impressive
number of scholars, for the cultural pattern has not unfolded as the
prophets of the first decades of the present century authoritatively predicted. The present crisis, which grips not only the West but the whole
world, has played a vital part in pushing many contemporary scholars
and thinkers to re-examine the meaning of the historical process. However,
it would be misleading to suggest that the present crisis alone has brought
this interest into sharp focus. Already in the nineteenth century process
philosophers, under the leadership of Hegel, had revived the philosophical approach to the study of history and had incorporated his views into
their respective systems of thought to varying degrees. Their successors
in the twentieth century have been Spengler, Toynbee, Sorokin and, to a
certain extent, Reinhold Niebuhr and Rudolf Bultmann.

In the attempt to go beyond the factual data of history to seek their
deeper meaning Augustine is actually the forerunner of all such philosophers of history, even though they may have wandered far afield from his
theological perspective. Their neglect of his scriptural frame of reference
has been disastrous for, without a biblical foundation, all attempts along
these lines were doomed to failure. Unfortunately, however, Christian
scholarship has failed to give adequate attention to the pressing problem

of properly interpreting history from its own theological perspective. All too often it has virtually surrendered this important and strategic area of apologetics to secular scholarship. Such surrender is totally unnecessary for not only Augustine in his *De Civitate Dei,* but also Calvin and other Reformation leaders in their great formulations of Christian truth furnished the Church with a world and life view which made possible, and invited, the enunciation of a biblical concept of history. In his *Institutes of the Christian Religion* and other writings, Calvin gave the Church a theology which is unsurpassed for the proper study of history. As the final triumph of the Reformation, Calvinism gave to the Church a theology which provides a Christian frame of reference for a truly biblical view of history.

At the outset we should note the inaccuracy of applying the designation of "a Christian philosophy of history" to any speculative effort that uses only rational means to discover the meaning of history. For such efforts convey the erroneous suggestion that history is to be interpreted by some rationalistic frame of reference alone without any recourse to theism. A purely philosophical conception of history, furthermore, carries with it the idea that it is man and not God who gives significance and meaning to life in all its facets.

For the Christian, history has perspective only in the light of revealed theology. For him there is no man-made philosophy of history; he interprets his entire earthly life *sub specie aeternitatis.* So indelibly has this theological approach impressed itself on the history of thought that even those philosophers who have been most determined to escape its influences have been unable to do so; their humanistic interpretations of history still bear the imprint of Augustine or of Calvin. Secularize history as he would, even Karl Marx could not escape the demands which the Bishop of Hippo laid on anyone who sought to interpret history for future generations. This is likewise the case for Spengler and for Toynbee. The proper understanding of history can come only from a biblical frame of reference.

This biblical frame must rest upon a theology that fully incorporates every aspect of biblical truth perceived by the enlightened mind through the power of the Holy Spirit. Only such a theology provides the necessary ingredients for a view of history which can adequately meet the challenge and dilemmas of history. Only such a view of human events can adequately meet the challenge of cataclysms like the fall of Rome, the rise of modern totalitarianism, or the frightening possibility of annihilative nuclear warfare in the historical process.

I. THE BASIC THEOLOGY

Foundational to the Christian view of history is the doctrine of Scripture itself. If man cannot know God with some degree of assurance, cannot have knowledge of Him, of His actions and of His will for man in the form of propositional truths, then man can know neither himself as an individual nor the meaning of his own experience in its historical form. The *Westminster Confession of Faith* states that the Scriptures principally teach what man is to believe concerning God and what duty God requires of man. This concept of Scripture is no less necessary for a meaningful view of history than it is for the knowledge of redemption. God reveals Himself redemptively to man in the Bible, in the sense that only here does man learn about the person and work of Christ. From the Scriptures man also receives the necessary insights concerning God's own evaluation and interpretation of human life. God, therefore, addresses man in terms of propositional truth which is therefore infallible and binding upon him.

A meaningful view of history, therefore, depends completely on the assurance that the Scriptures are God's trustworthy revelation to man. If he cannot know God with certainty, then man can never really penetrate the mystery of his own existence here on earth; life must, and will remain for him an unfathomable enigma, forever beyond his apprehension. The true meaning both of individual events and of the composite stream of human history is found only in God's interpretation thereof; clues to this meaning are found primarily in the Scriptures.

Man is not free to contradict or to challenge God's interpretation of what has gone before. If he does so, he is guilty of sin. Man's persistent refusal to see in the Bible the clue to the meaning of his own experience is merely another evidence of the total depravity of human nature. But this does not mean that we are to regard the Bible as a kind of textbook which gives some explicit interpretation for every event which comes under its scrutiny. Rather it means that the theistic presuppositions necessary for man's insight into the proper meaning of history are found in the Scriptures alone and not in human reason or experience. Man is no less responsible for thinking God's thoughts after Him in the interpretation of human life than he is in any other area of his activity. Any theology which denies the infallibility of the Scriptures is hard pressed, therefore, to present a meaningful and consistent explanation of the historical process.

Equally necessary for the Christian view of history is the biblical doctrine of the sovereignty of God. The Scriptures insist that God is sovereign over all His creatures and all their actions; they are equally clear in maintaining that God exercises this sovereignty to fulfill His own pur-

poses and to manifest His own glory. This doctrine is not confined to a
few isolated references, but functions as a continuous and coordinating
theme from Genesis through the Revelation. Moreover, no event or
person is exempt from obedience to the divine decrees. God is the Lord
of all, not only of some, history. He does not break into the stream of
events merely at certain moments to accomplish certain limited purposes,
nor is His effective will confined to one major current such as so-called
"holy history" in the swirling tides of secular and seemingly uncontrolled
events. The biblical teaching of God's sovereignty in human affairs is
asserted with unsurpassed clarity in the *Westminster Confession of Faith:*
"God from all eternity did, by the most wise and holy counsel of his own
will, freely and unchangeably ordain whatsoever comes to pass; yet so
as thereby neither is God the author of sin, nor is violence offered to
the will of the creatures, nor is the liberty or contingency of second
(secondary) causes taken away, but rather, established" (Chapter III,
paragraph 1). This great biblical truth is not to be confused with any kind
of philosophical determinism which subjects man to the blind control of
fate as does much Greek and Roman thought, or to the equally blind
direction of Marxian dialectical materialism. The biblical pronouncement
of God's sovereignty in all human affairs and activities stands in sharp
contrast to any form of determinism. Moreover, this sovereign Deity, who
sees the end from the beginning, is a personal God. He is just and righteous in all His ways and doeth all things well; His sovereignty is exercised in accordance with His wisdom, holiness, righteousness, and goodness. Quite obviously this biblical concept of divine sovereignty differs
from philosophical determinism at every conceivable point; those who
insist there is but little difference between the two systems understand
neither of them. Their supposed similarities all disappear in view of the
great differences between the impersonalism of these speculative systems
and the personal God revealed in the Scriptures.

The sovereign God confers meaning and purpose on history, not only
by creating man for His own glory, but also by ordaining that man should
realize and fulfill the purpose of his existence on earth in organized political communities, whatever their geographic extent or temporal duration
might be.

Inextricably linked to the biblical insistence on the total sovereignty
of God is the doctrine of creation. The nature of this intimate relationship between creation and the exercise of divine sovereignty appears in
the statement and answer of question number eight in the *Shorter
Catechism:* "How does God execute His decrees?" And the answer to this
question is: "God executeth His decrees in the works of creation and
providence." God is the author of history only because He is the creator
of man and of the world in which man was to live, and to fulfill His
divinely assigned purposes. In the act of creation, therefore, God brought

both man and history into being. This fact is of tremendous importance
for any view of history which seeks to be truly Christian; the doctrine of
creation is no peripheral adjunct to the scriptural concept of history,
but rather its very center. The God of Christianity does not deal with a
world that evolved by chance nor does He assume sovereignty over
creatures who came into being by some mysterious process over which
He had no control. Without this divine authorship of man in the
stream of events, no truly biblical theology of history is possible. In His
exercise of the decrees of providence the divine Author expresses and
accomplishes the purposes inherent in the act of creation.

The climax of the biblical account of creation is not achieved, however,
until the appearance of man who was created in the image of God. Thus
history is defined and understood properly only when the biblical doctrine of man is kept in focus. Man cannot truly study himself nor find
anything of historical value unless he views himself and his past in the
light of this doctrine. History is primarily concerned with man as man and
the development of those institutions through which he fulfills the God-
given purposes of his existence on earth. The view of man created in the
image of God is, therefore, absolutely essential for a biblical understanding of history. Any other view not only does irreparable harm to
the scriptural position, but also makes human history unintelligible. To
posit man as the product of evolutionary forces may seem, at first glance,
to make him a noble creature and possessed of endless possibilities for
a glorious future. Actually, however, it destroys his true role in the
historical process and reduces him to a passive recipient of the effects of
natural and environmental forces. Over these he has no control although
they themselves are utterly impersonal and blind in their effects on human
life. The outcome of such a view, namely, this evolutionary degradation
of human personality, must inescapably render history meaningless and
hardly worthy of study. If the human past is simply the product of the
influence of blind and impersonal forces at work in humanity, then the
past has little to say to the present. Even this debacle could have meaning
in the sight of God, of course, for it is He who still controls the process of
degradation. Such a perverted view of human personality would mean,
however, that in exalting himself above God, man has lost the key to the riddle of even the purported evolutionary process. It is well known that the
dominant force of the evolutionary philosophy in the political and
social sciences has engendered increasing uncertainty among historians
and the social scientists about the meaning of the human past and the
promise of the future. In fact, some of these men question whether the
study of history can any longer be justified as a meaningful intellectual
activity. The denial of propositional revelation in the Scriptures has
resulted in a growing disposition to doubt the possibility of achieving
truth in secular history. The Marxists frequently appeal to history to

support the contention of their ultimate domination of all peoples. Despite this appeal, the very nature of dialectical materialism undermines belief in that very rational character of the historical process which alone can justify and sustain even their attempts to interpret history. In essence, the determinism of Marxism destroys those foundations of rationality which appeal to history as their witness. History thus becomes a witness without meaning.

The biblical view, on the other hand, affirms the meaningfulness of history. This meaning stems from the fact that man is under an intellectual mandate from God, in the stewardship of his mind, to discover the meaning of his own existence on earth, to whatever extent he can as a sinner, and in the light afforded him in the Scriptures. When Adam sinned and thus involved the whole human race in both the physical and spiritual effects of that first transgression against the revealed will of God, history did not, therefore, lose either its meaning or its divinely assigned purposes. A sinful humanity could in no way thwart the realization of the decrees of a sovereign God who makes even the wrath of man to praise Him and the processes of history to glorify Him. His glory was to be realized both in the redemption of elect sinners and in the righteous judgment and condemnation of those who refuse His gracious offer of salvation in Jesus Christ.

Thus from the fall of Adam to the last great judgment, man's history was to experience an increasing and ever-present cleavage between believers, those who are citizens of the City of God on earth, and unbelievers, those who are citizens of the earthly city. Yet through both of these groups the purposes of God will be fully realized. Common grace became the means whereby the Lord of history governs and sustains His creation and the earthly activities of both the regenerate and the unregenerate. Common grace makes civil life possible in a sinful and rebellious society; this grace by the beneficent bestowal of gifts even enables the unregenerate to make brilliant discoveries in medicine and in the other sciences, to erect and maintain human governments, to produce great masterpieces in the arts and letters, and to enrich culture generally. The blessings of common grace make civilization possible, and it is common grace that sustains the historical process.

By the operations of common grace evil rulers and nations, even in the heat of their own sinful rebellion, actually carry out the will of God in regard to the elect and His visible Church. Empires and kingdoms rise and fall according to God's plan; through them He brings judgment upon nations who have forsaken righteousness and through them He brings judgment to bear even on the Church. History is replete with examples of this truth. The Lord used Babylon to execute judgment upon the Children of Israel; Rome was used to judge those ancient empires which had trampled under foot the law of a sovereign God. Later the Teutonic invaders brought Rome to justice. In our own day, in a very real sense, Hitler was God's instrument of warning to the West as a whole of impending doom, and to a German Church which had cradled modern rationalism and higher criticism. In short, common grace so governs historical events that God's special or redemptive grace may be fulfilled as well. By the very benevolence of God which it bestows upon the unregenerate, common grace may justify the condemnation of the unbeliever; similarly, special grace outworks God's purpose for the elect, that He may be glorified in their redemption. Thus the plan of redemption is of transcendent importance for the proper understanding of human history.

The Scriptures abundantly suggest that Christ's coming into the world was a decisive event in human affairs. His Incarnation was the great demarcation, the great watershed between what we call ancient history and all that has since transpired. This event occurred in the divinely evaluated and interpreted fullness of time and history. No other event compares with it, for it is truly unique. Only in connection with the birth of Christ do the Scriptures use the phrase, "in the fullness of time." So unique is the Incarnation that even unbelievers incorporate it into their chronological reckonings. Thus the Christian view of history places supreme emphasis on the birth of Christ and recognizes it as a focal point to which all other historical dates must be referred for chronological ordering.

All of ancient history, therefore, must be interpreted in the light of the Incarnation. Egypt, Assyria, Babylon, the Alexandrian Empire and Rome are viewed historically as instruments of a sovereign God to bring about the "fullness of time" into which Jesus Christ was born. Unknowingly and unwillingly, and yet freely, they accomplished His purpose both of judgment and of redemption.

Like the birth of Christ, so the Church, that great company of the elect, that institution at the very heart of the historical process in all ages, is the great divide of history to which all other events relate. Scripture also indicates clearly that all events in both ancient and modern history, refer in some way, known to God alone for the most part, to the life and work of the Church. These events are not only related with the birth of Christ, but have a more immediate bearing on the Church in their own day. They all serve God's purposes as regards His will for the elect, for it is through this divinely ordained institution, the Church, that the events of history derive meaning and purpose.

This means that contemporary historical events can be understood only in the light of their divinely assigned role. They are entities in and of themselves. Sometimes their purposes may be clearly discernible to believers; at other times, they may be only dimly perceived, if at all. The Church at all times can and must be alert to warnings of judgment that come in the rise of Hitlers and other totalitarian despots of our day, else these divine warnings would be given in vain. But beyond this awareness the Christian dare not go. It is not given to man to read history as God sees it. By faith therefore we know Him to be the sovereign Lord of history and we know that nothing occurs either by grim fate or capricious chance. In this assurance we must be content.

The assurance that history is meaningful and that its meaning is directly related to God's purposes makes it possible to discuss the whole matter of progress, a concept that has been uppermost in secular interpretations of history since the days of the Enlightenment. The Scriptures say a great deal about progress and affirm a very real progress reveals itself within history. But the biblical conception is far different from that of the evolutionists, and the other secularists, who define progress as an advance toward some kind of humanly achieved millennium where wars, famines, poverty, diseases, crime, illiteracy, ignorance, and fear will be no more. Nor is the biblical view the least like that of the Marxists who anticipate the triumph of the proletariat, and the establishment of a communist regime. These views not only ignore the sovereignty of God and the problem of human sin, but also describe progress in terms of material and physical advancement to the exclusion of the spiritual.

The biblical concept, on the other hand, depicts progress in terms of man's growth in grace, of his increasing conformity to the will of God, and of the renewal of the divine image in the believer. Although the Bible insists that the whole stream of history moves steadily toward a divinely ordained goal, it does not interpret progress merely as a progression of time. The ongoing of time in the Hegelian sense can never be equated with progress. Never is the Christian free to regard either the Hegelian, the Marxist, or the evolutionary concept as those of the Scriptures. Time in itself has no redemptive power, nor does its passage bring moral or spiritual improvement. Moral and spiritual superiority, whether of nations or of men, is not simply a matter of age or maturity.

Scripture emphasizes that true progress comes from growth in grace in this life. Although believers never achieve God's will totally in this life, they pursue it increasingly throughout life, therefore they are being restored into the image of God by the power of the Holy Spirit. In this sense, and in this alone, progress is thus an ever-present factor in human history wherever the elect are found. But this progress takes place within individual lives and is not a phenomenon in society at large, except to the extent that a community may be predominantly Christian and reflect in its corporate life this growth in grace. Progress in its spiritual sense can never be characteristic of a total society, because the mixture of believers and unbelievers is always present. This is true despite the fact that the Church has, at times, among certain groups and nations, had a sufficiently strong witness and impact to penetrate civic life and unregenerate society to an amazing degree.

The Scriptures offer no support for those concepts of society which espouse the working of some process in history similar to that which allegedly functions in the biological history of the race. Ever since the Enlightenment, liberals have insisted that society, in all its aspects, is gradually evolving from a lower to a higher stage of existence. Through this process they expect a day to come when humanity will usher in its own kingdom of righteousness and peace. This hope is the central core of all liberalism, and many liberals, therefore, have appraised the League of Nations, the United Nations Organization, socialism, centralized government, and even communism (without its Russian accretions) as important aids towards their utopian goals. Since they consider man essentially good, education and similar agencies may achieve his perfection; and progress, therefore, is almost inevitable.

Liberals of the later nineteenth century expected to realize their hopes in the twentieth. Although some were willing to make room for the sovereign Lord of history to cooperate in this great democratic experiment, most of them seem to regard Him as something of an alien intruder whose claims must be vigorously resisted by an enlightened humanity.

We also learn from the Scriptures that history is moving toward one final climax, namely the return of Jesus Christ in triumph and judgment. This biblical interpretation alone allows no place for the cyclical views of the Greek historians, nor for the later Hegelian concepts of history as an unending process. When Jesus Christ returns, this span of history will cease. Perhaps at this point the cleavage between the biblical position and the views of Hegel, Marx, Spengler, Toynbee, and other contemporaries, becomes most obvious. The modern mind simply cannot accept the idea that humanity does not control its own destiny. It refuses to believe that the ultimate manifestation of the glory of Jesus Christ is beyond all human manipulation, whether they be statesmen or educators. It denies that the sovereign Ruler of the universe will bring all sinful humanity to judgment in a final accounting for its long history of willful rebellion against His righteousness, goodness, and mercy.

II. THE LIBERAL REVOLT

The biblical view of history which received its classic treatment by Augustinian and Reformed scholars has undergone much attack both from within and without the Church. In the early modern era severe criticism came from the philosophers of the Enlightenment, especially from the French; German and English Deists, and even their American counterparts, also vented their hostility. Their belief in man's inherent goodness and perfectibility led to a philosophy of history which was essentially evolutionary in character. This, in turn, resulted in a secularization of the whole biblical concept of the ultimate triumph of the Kingdom of God. German idealism produced a new outburst of attacks, and Hegel set forth a philosophy of history that consciously repudiated the biblical view at almost every turn. The sovereign God was replaced by a dialectic process; history had neither a real beginning nor ending, its only goal being the progressive (but never fully achieved) realization of spirit as that spirit (*Geist*) found acceptance among particular nations or peoples in successively unfolding eras of history.

Whatever remnants of Christianity some theologians and philosophers professed to see in Hegel's idealistic approach disappeared entirely in the adaptation of Hegelianism to the demands of Marxist materialism. Marx not only banished the sovereign God, but rewrote the whole concept of history far more drastically than Hegel. Because matter is eternal in dialectical materialism, and there is no God and man has no soul, it requires no author for the historical process. Neither is there any progress in terms of man's conformity to the will or image of God. Progress became identified, rather, with the triumph of the proletariat and with the realization of a classless society, at least in theory. In such a system it is quite impossible to salvage anything Christian, and it becomes quite apparent that this Marxist interpretation is the most completely secularized version of the biblical position that has yet appeared. Perhaps this explains communism's tremendous appeal for contemporary scholarship, for it must certainly be recognized that either in its original form, or in its several modifications, Marxist philosophy dominated much of historical writing and the social sciences. This does not mean, or even suggest, that most of the social scientists of our country are convinced, or dedicated, to the Marxist philosophy in the sense that they openly belong to the Communist party or accept its program of action. Rather do we mean that to a greater or lesser degree many of these individuals have accepted numerous axioms of Marxism and have incorporated them into their own personal philosophies of history and society. The penetration of Marxist presuppositions is easily seen, for example, in the Turner thesis concerning the influence of the frontier in American history; it likewise appears in the works of Charles A. Beard which try to interpret the formation of the Federal Constitution and the emergence of the Federalist and Jeffersonian parties almost entirely in terms of economic determinism. Indeed, it is probably not too much to say that the theory of economic determinism is probably the most widely held philosophy of history among American historians today. Many of them have sought to blend this modified Marxian approach with democratic idealism for, in a large measure, American history has been characterized by an optimism concerning America's future. These men have felt the need to weld the democratic philosophy of the Declaration of Independence and economic determinism into such a frame of reference that would fit the demands of their optimistic views. These attempts failed to bring a conviction as to their adequacy, however, and Carl Becker, in his later career, lost the early optimism toward democracy that pervaded his earlier writings. Beard also greatly modified his attitude toward economic determinism. Despite the inadequacy of these more recent interpretations of history, many historians have remained unwilling to turn once again to the Christian view. Instead they have made repeated efforts to examine history itself for fresh clues as to its meaning. Spengler and Toynbee both represent such efforts, but neither writer has successfully escaped the subtleties of economic determinism. Many historians turned to positivism as the only satisfactory approach to the problem of meaning in history. But the only conclusions to which they seem to be driven is that history has no ultimate meaning, because each historian supplies just another interpretation.

The question still remains, if history has no meaning, how can we justify its study and how can we claim that a proper knowledge of the past can help the present age guide its affairs toward a better future? This query constitutes a formidable dilemma for positivism; it is equally embarrassing for Marxism as well, for if blind impersonal matter controls humanity, if human personality is completely dominated by matter dialectically in motion, how can the historical process have any meaning, and how can we speak with authority in the present to shed light on the future?

Such questions present seemingly insoluble dilemmas to much of historical scholarship; some historians are visibly disturbed by the increasing uncertainty and aimlessness of their colleagues. While deeply aware of that intellectual disaster that awaits any discipline which loses faith in the meaning and value of its own area of knowledge, and while equally dissatisfied with contemporary philosophies of history, they have not wished, however, to return to the Augustinian or Calvinist interpretations, although they might regard them with a kind of nostalgic yearning and hope. For historians of this bent, neo-orthodoxy in its various forms appears a ready haven and welcome answer to their dilemmas. Neo-orthodoxy becomes a kind of escape whereby they can return to a biblical view of history without accepting the Augustinian-Calvinistic concept of the Scriptures, a view which they feel that modern critical scholarship has made untenable.

III. NEO-ORTHODOXY AND HISTORICAL INTERPRETATION

To what extent has neo-orthodoxy really solved their problems? Indeed, it should be asked: can neo-orthodoxy provide an interpretation of history which is essentially Christian on the one hand, but which, on the other hand, pays attention to the claims of higher critical scholarship in order to escape the charges of "fundamentalism" or "obscurantism" where the historic view of inspiration is concerned? In short, does neo-orthodoxy offer a true haven for those historians who sincerely seek to find in Christianity the right means of restoring meaning and purpose to their scholarly endeavors? These questions are vital not only to the historians themselves, but to the entire evangelical world. To a great extent, evangelicals are dependent on these same scholars for accurate knowledge and interpretation of the human past and of contemporary events as well. Can neo-orthodoxy rescue the social sciences from the snare of Marxism on the one side and the allurement of existentialism on the other? What does neo-orthodoxy have to offer the disillusioned liberal of our day? To what extent does it support a truly biblical view of history?

We have already indicated that a view of history which is true to the Scriptures must rest upon a doctrine of Scripture that supports its claims of inspiration and infallibility. It is here that the initial weakness of neo-orthodoxy as a movement becomes apparent. While the present chapter cannot deal with this particular problem at great length, it should at least emphasize that neo-orthodoxy's inadequate view of Scripture makes the system unsuitable for sustaining a biblical view of history adequate to the needs of the twentieth century. Although not all neo-orthodox scholars agree on the meaning of biblical inspiration, they seem unanimous in rejecting the historic doctrine of Scripture. The extent to which neo-orthodoxy denies that Scripture contains revealed propositional truth, to that same degree it violates the proper interpretation of all history. Only on the basis of the historical concept of the Scriptures, which stresses the propositional truth associated with God's revelation of Himself to man, can the true meaning of any and all historical events be ascertained. Barth's rejection of the doctrine of common grace seems to follow logically from his basic view of revelation and without this doctrine, history must remain essentially meaningless and an insoluble dilemma. To deny propositional truth in the Scriptures is to deny it in history at large.

Not all neo-orthodox theologians deny common grace as does Barth. It remains true, however, that their inadequate views of Scripture have far-reaching effects on their approach to the problem of the meaning of history. There is much of value in Otto Piper's God in History (New York, The Macmillan Company, 1939), a volume which can be read with genuine profit by discerning evangelicals. But the looseness of his attitude toward the authority of Scripture in general and the historicity of Genesis in particular seriously weakens his entire concept of history. Piper's attempt to distinguish between original history (Urgeschichte) and prehistory has profoundly important implications for his interpretation of history as a whole; it fails to solve those problems which he professes to find in the older orthodox theologians and creates new problems as well. Piper takes the position that Adam's fall occurred in the spiritual realm rather than in the earthly world of time and space; yet he insists that this interpretation in no way undermines the reality of this event (*ibid.,* p. 39). Piper follows this course in order to free Protestant theology from what he considers the baneful influences that nominalism exercised on the Reformers and from their "necessary, but one-sided insistence on justification by faith" (p. 53). But the result of this approach is far from satisfactory and Piper himself ultimately concludes that "it is not possible . . . to establish harmony between the record of Genesis III-XI on the one hand, and prehistorical discoveries on the other, unless it is fully recognized that history, as recorded in the Bible, because of its connection with the spiritual world differs fundamentally from that kind of history related by secular historians" (p. 62).

However much Reinhold Niebuhr may differ from his neo-orthodox colleagues in his own particular view of the authority of the Scriptures, his conclusions in the matter are just as far-reaching in regard to the question of propositional truth. In *Beyond Tragedy* he writes: "The message of the Son of God who dies upon the Cross, of a God who transcends history and is yet in history, who condemns and judges sin and yet suffers with and for the sinner, this message is the truth about life. It cannot be stated without deceptions; but the truths which seek to avoid the deceptions are immeasurably less profound. Compared with the Christ who died for man's sin upon the Cross, Jesus, the good man who tells all men to be good, is more solidly historical. But He is the bearer of no more than a pale truism" (New York, Charles Scribner's Sons, 1937, p. 20-21).

Only one or two comments are pertinent here. In the first place, if it is true that the words of Christ upon the Cross cannot be stated without deception, then no sound judgment of any kind may be made one way or another concerning His ethical teachings. To be "deceivers yet true" on the historicity of the biblical account of redemption is to render any sound conception or interpretation of history impossible. If the scriptural account of the redemptive work of Christ is not propositionally true, then our knowledge of history in general must suffer accordingly. In vain are Reinhold Niebuhr's efforts to escape the destructive tendencies of his own position on Scripture by grappling with the various aspects of the biblical view of history. The devastating effects of this primary denial of the trustworthiness of the Bible frustrate every effort to present a Christian philosophy of history that is free from the liberalism which he opposes. The denial of propositional truth in sacred history brings with it a logical necessity to deny it in the secular realm. But even if this logical necessity is avoided, the historian still has denied himself a necessary key for the interpretation of the secular realm.

As Otto Piper shows in *God in History,* the biblical doctrine of sin fares no better at the hands of neo-orthodoxy than do the other doctrines essential to a consistent Christian view of history. Piper rejects the biblical doctrine of sin in order to restate it in terms of his own position. He places the Fall of Adam in the spiritual order hoping thereby to properly accommodate it to New Testament eschatology (*op. cit.*, p. 58). He insists that this is necessary in order to avoid limiting man's redemption to merely mental or physical change and to insure instead a deliverance of his metaphysical nature (*ibid.*, pp. 58-59). Piper's denial of the historicity of the biblical account of the Fall is obviously related to his desire to revise the doctrine of original sin in keeping with the neo-orthodox concepts of eschatology and of redemption, views which are to be found nowhere in Scripture.

Reinhold Niebuhr's approach to the doctrine of sin is no more satisfactory despite "his preoccupation with sin and grace." He rejects the biblical account of Adam's Fall in the Garden of Eden as myth. "It does not take place in any concrete human act. It is the presupposition of such acts" (*Beyond Tragedy,* p. 11). Nevertheless, in spite of placing its origin in myth, Niebuhr considers sin to be very real and defines it as that capacity of man "to throw the harmonies of nature out of joint." He denies that the act of sin destroyed man's previous state of perfection by creation; at the same time, however, Niebuhr is careful to point out that sin is not the result of an original defect in man by creation. Sin for Niebuhr is man's misuse of his radical freedom, a misuse that takes place in history and brings man to the need for redemption. Niebuhr's failure to see sin in its biblical setting as rebellion against the will of a righteous and holy God has profound implications for his whole view of history.

Even further from the biblical position of sin is Rudolf Bultmann's view. He interprets sin as man's inability and unwillingness to be free from decisions he has made in the past. This radical departure from the historic doctrine of sin undercuts the rest of his theology and leaves very little Christianity. His doctrine of redemption is eschatological in nature, but not in the scriptural meaning. In short, his teaching has no truly biblical system of doctrine sufficient for supporting a theology of history. Although like Niebuhr and other contemporary theologians he delights in using biblical terminology, Bultmann supplies a whole new meaning of his own which is quite foreign to the Scriptures and is so impregnated with existentialist meaning that history ceases to have any real significance.

Departure from biblical form and meaning is quite evident in contemporary treatments of the atonement, and the neo-orthodox defection from this basic doctrine, so pivotal for a truly biblical perspective of history, reveals how far short their interpretation of history falls of the scriptural yardstick. Since redemption from sin is procured only by Christ's atoning death, a doctrine which lies at the very heart of the

Christian life, then this truth must also lie at the very heart of the Christian view of history.

Piper's position here is far from satisfactory. He declares that through Christ the history of His chosen people became an act of divine salvation; by making the misery of the human race His own, Christ became the Lord of history (*op. cit.,* p. 112). If Christ is eternally and truly God, we would ask, how could such an act, as wonderful as it undoubtedly was, make Him what the Scriptures already declare Him to be? Indeed, one must ask how His birth could be in the fullness of time and how the Son of Man could effectively bring salvation, if He were not already the Lord of history and therefore able to bring those events to pass in a manner which transcends human reason. The very idea of the fullness of time must remain inexplicable unless Jesus Christ were already the Lord of history and of His chosen people.

As a consequence of his conception of the death of Christ, Niebuhr has no Church at the heart of history to which all events in history have reference. There is no doctrine of election to bring it into existence or to give it life. For Niebuhr, the Church is composed of God's people only in the sense that its members are those who have seen in Christ the original essence of human nature and who desire to bring an end to their estrangement from God. Thus, in Niebuhr as in Piper, eschatology is shorn of its biblical content. Their views of sin, the atonement, and the nature of the Church make no provision for an eschatology which is biblically oriented; there is neither a final judgment nor a glorious triumph of Jesus Christ in terms of Christian orthodoxy. Progress in history would seem to consist of abolishing in believers that original defection and estrangement which came as a result of the entrance of sin into human life.

In summary, the presuppositions of neo-orthodoxy are clearly incapable of supporting a biblical doctrine of history. Not only does the denial of propositional truth in Scripture destroy the real meaning of salvation, it also undermines the entire Christian position in regard to the meaning of history. Failure to appropriate the biblical view of the Church, a necessary consequence of their denial of the orthodox view of the inspiration and authority of the Scriptures, and of sin and redemption, has deprived neo-orthodoxy of the key which it must have if it is to discover the meaning of the flow of historical events. The forced separation between *Heilgeschichte* and secular history in which some of this school have indulged has had the effect of denying the sovereignty of God over the latter and removes the focal point from which they derive their ultimate meaning.

In view of its doctrinal inadequacies, it should be expected that neo-orthodoxy should be uncertain as to the course of history; it is no accident that Reinhold Niebuhr, despite his great dislike for what he calls an outmoded liberalism, accepted many of its presuppositions and goals in his own political, social, and economic philosophy. These same inadequacies have made it possible for other members of this school to adapt to various factors of totalitarianism. Neo-orthodoxy has been unable to provide them with a theistic frame of reference by which these historical developments may be properly evaluated. Almost inevitably their eschatology is bound to be fuzzy at best, and foreign to the biblical perspective, and their statements are full of paradox. For Niebuhr the resurrection of the body is a myth which must not be pressed too far (*Beyond Tragedy*, p. 304). He says further that at best this doctrine is "a more sophisticated expression of the hope of the ultimate fulfillment of human personality than all of its modern substitutes" (*ibid*; p. 306). This is a far cry from the great Scripture promises given to believers concerning their own bodily resurrection and the end time of history. Bultmann is perhaps farthest from the biblical position for he practically banishes any truly biblical eschatological view of history by confining it to the present. "But now we can say—*the meaning in history lies always in the present*—and when the present is conceived as the eschatological present by Christian faith the meaning of history is realized" (*History and Eschatology*, Edinburgh, University Press, 1957, p. 155). And again he writes: "Always in your present lies the meaning in history, and you cannot see it as a spectator, but only in your responsible decisions. In every moment slumbers the possibility of being the eschatological moment. You must awaken it" (*ibid.*, p. 155). Whatever else this may mean, it is quite obvious that Bultmann removes any eschatological control of history from the hands of the sovereign God and places it in man. Existentialism has replaced Christian orthodoxy and history has lost its last vestige of God-given meaning. At every point in time man interprets history to suit himself.

Neither in Niebuhr nor Bultmann is there any place for the glorious return of Jesus Christ in triumph and judgment, an event which will bring history to a close. For these men, history has no goal in the biblical sense. Nor does Karl Barth in his position offer much relief from this subtle form of humanism.

Our evaluation of neo-orthodoxy's views of history suggests at least two conclusions. In the first place, this view is at no point truly biblical, despite the system's apparently sincere deference to the Bible and frequent appeals to biblical material. Neo-orthodoxy simply fails to do justice to those great doctrines of Scripture which are essential to the Christian view of history.

In the second place, this neo-orthodox revision of the older liberal position is, at many points, not too different from that which it seeks to correct. For this reason, neo-orthodoxy offers no real alternative to the liberalism of the latter nineteenth and early twentieth century on the one hand, nor to the Marxist and democratic philosophies of history on the other. The neo-orthodox approach to the problem of the meaning of history must be adjudged quite as unsatisfactory, therefore, as that of previous liberal versions, and there is no real reason to suppose therefore, that it will have any more than a passing attraction for historians. The only authentic key for understanding history with all its complexities, tortuous paths and vicissitudes, is found in historic Christianity which anchors in the sovereignty of God and in the infallibility of the Scriptures. Any attempted theology of history which casts itself adrift from these two basic tenets must renounce all hope of ever achieving true insight into the nature and meaning of history.

JESUS OF NAZARETH

†

Bastiaan Van Elderen, Jr.

Bastiaan Van Elderen, Jr. is Associate Professor of New Testament at Calvin Theological Seminary (Christian Reformed), Grand Rapids. He recently spent six months in Palestine pursuing archaeological and biblical studies in association with the Near East School of Archaeology in Jerusalem, Jordan. He holds the B.A. from Calvin College, B.D. from Calvin Theological Seminary, A.M. from University of California, and Th.D. from Pacific School of Religion.

12. *Bastiaan Van Elderen, Jr.*

JESUS OF NAZARETH

WHEN Saul of Tarsus was struck down on the way to Damascus, his first reaction was to determine whose voice was saying to him, "Saul, Saul, why do you persecute me?" The simple and forthright identification that follows: "I am Jesus of Nazareth whom you are persecuting," [1] made a radical change in Saul. Promptly surrendering himself, Saul asked, "What shall I do, Lord?" This term, "Jesus of Nazareth," forms the special concern of this chapter.

Since a study of "Jesus of Nazareth" depends upon New Testament materials, we must understand the exact nature of these documents. Varying evaluations of biblical sources during the past century have produced divergent approaches and positions concerning the historical Jesus. It was the modern philosophy of history and its application to biblical literature that motivated the nineteenth century quest for the historical Jesus. Regarding the term "historical Jesus," James M. Robinson writes, " 'Historical' is used in the sense of 'things in the past which have been established by objective scholarship.' Consequently the expression 'historical Jesus' comes to mean: 'What can be known of Jesus of Nazareth by means of the scientific method of the historian' " (*A New Quest of the Historical Jesus*, London, SCM Press, 1959, p. 26).

At the end of the nineteenth century the legitimacy and possibility of this quest of the historical Jesus were questioned first of all by Martin Kähler, who distinguished between "Jesus" and "Christ," *"historisch"* and *"geschichtlich"*; "Jesus," he contended, described the man of Nazareth, "Christ," the Saviour proclaimed by the Church; *"historisch,"* moreover, said Kähler, describes the bare facts of the past while *"ge-*

---

[1] Although the textual evidence is weak for this reading of Acts 9:5 and 26:15, it is the uncontested reading of 22:8.

schichtlich" indicates something of permanent significance (*Der soge-
nannte historische Jesus und der geschichtliche, biblische Christus,* Munich,
Chr. Kaiser Verlag, 1956, reprint, pp. 41-44; the first edition appeared
in 1892, a second in 1896). Albert Schweitzer also participated in this
development with the publication in 1906 of his *Von Reimarus zu
Wrede* (English translation, *The Quest of the Historical Jesus,* New
York, The Macmillan Company, 1910). That the original quest was
impossible and illegitimate was substantiated, too, by Form Criticism
and the emphasis on the *kerygma.* An extreme development of this
skepticism is seen in Rudolf Bultmann's *Jesus,* which appeared in 1929
(English translation, *Jesus and the World,* New York, Charles Scribner's
Sons, 1934).

Currently, however, there is a new quest for the historical Jesus, one
which Robinson considers possible and legitimate (*op. cit.,* pp. 48-92;
Robinson calls this the " 'Post-Bultmannian' Quest of the Historical
Jesus," p. 12). This post-Bultmannian movement is trying to define
some continuity between the "Christ of faith" and the "historical Jesus"
(cf. Ernst Kasemann's formulation of this in "Das Problem des historischen Jesus," published in *Zeitschrift für Theologie und Kirche* 51,
1954, pp. 125-53; see especially p. 152). This new quest involves a novel
definition of history. According to this system, history is the act of intention, the commitment, the meaning behind the external occurrence.
"The nineteenth century saw the reality of the 'historical facts' as consisting largely in names, places, dates, occurrences, sequences, causes,
effects—things which fall far short of being the actuality of history if
one understands by history the distinctively human, creative, unique,
purposeful, which distinguishes man from nature." [2]

These twentieth-century developments, sketched here altogether too
briefly, have contributed significantly to a better understanding of the
New Testament. In some ways Form Criticism's emphasis on *Sitz im
Leben* has been wholesome and valuable. Unfortunately, in many instances Form Criticism has drawn inferences and conclusions that lie
outside its formal discipline. The determination of form can hardly
decide the veracity or historicity of the content. To say that the Gospels
contain selected data which fulfill an author's purpose, rather than
biographical or historical data per se, demonstrates that these documents contain a selection of interpreted historical facts. These three
features—historicity, interpretation, selectivity—characterize the early
Church's attitude to the data about Jesus of Nazareth. To eliminate the
historical aspect makes the interpretative meaningless and vice versa.

---

[2] Robinson, *op. cit.,* p. 28. Robinson suggests that Bultmann apparently has
been influenced by this new movement (pp. 19-21). For a different evaluation
of Bultmann's role in this, see S. Ogden, "Bultmann and the 'New Quest,' "
in *Journal of Bible and Religion* 30 (1962), pp. 209-18.

To deny the historicity of data makes interpretation thereof abstract, without foundation, and irrelevant. Simply because the early Church always emphasized the historical Jesus, however few the historical facts were, its message was concrete, relevant, and challenging. Moreover, to neglect the interpretative aspect ignores the use that the early Church made of the historical Jesus. In this sense the distinction between *Historie* and *Geschichte* is not valid when applied to the New Testament materials. What is designated *Geschichte* has meaning and relevance for the early Church precisely because it is anchored in historical fact (*Historie*). The early Church was not concerned with *Historie* per se, but used it as a basis for interpretation and as a call to repentance and commitment.

The thesis of this present essay is that the historical Jesus (of Nazareth) is a basic constituent in the message of the early Church, both in the Gospels (where historical details are predominant) and in the Acts and the Epistles (where interpretation and challenge predominate). This thesis is borne out by a study of the name, Jesus of Nazareth, by an examination of the historical allusions in the preaching of the early Church as seen in the Acts and the Epistles, and by an evaluation of the use of historical data in the Gospels.

I. EXEGETICAL STUDY: JESUS OF NAZARETH

The word "Nazareth" and its cognates occur thirty-one times in the New Testament. Twenty of these instances are found in the Gospels and the Acts of the Apostles and are used in conjunction with the name of Jesus.

The simplest construction joins the name of Jesus with the prepositional phrase "from Nazareth." This particular combination occurs exclusively in Matthew 21:11, John 1:45, and Acts 10:38. The first of these has its setting in Christ's triumphal entry into Jerusalem; when the people of the city inquired "Who is this?" the crowds responded, "This is the prophet Jesus from Nazareth of Galilee." In the John passage (1:45) Philip describes Jesus to Nathanael by saying "We have found him of whom Moses in the law and also the prophets wrote, Jesus of Nazareth, the son of Joseph." And in Acts 10:38 Peter tells Cornelius "how God anointed Jesus of Nazareth with the Holy Spirit and with power." These designations clearly allude to the historical Jesus, the one who grew up in Nazareth and whose home was in this place. Such designation, as in the first two passages, is to be expected during His earthly life. The third passage applies this identification even after the ascension. In presenting the message of salvation, Peter focuses attention upon the historical Jesus by using this designation and by indicating certain historical facts about Him.

The adjective "Nazarene" occurs four times in Mark, twice in Luke, and each time with the noun "Jesus." It literally means "coming from Nazareth." An unclean spirit identifies Jesus in this way (Mark 1:24, Luke 4:34). The blind Bartimaeus, hearing that "Jesus the Nazarene" was passing by, cried out: "Jesus, son of David" (Mark 10:47). The maid who spoke to Peter in the courtyard of the high priest said, "You also were with the Nazarene, Jesus" (Mark 14:67). The "young man" at the tomb identified Jesus as "Jesus, the Nazarene, who was crucified" (Mark 16:6). And in their conversation with Jesus, the men from Emmaus referred to "Jesus the Nazarene" (Luke 24:19).

The basic meaning of "Nazarene" and "from Nazareth" is very similar. These terms identify the historical Jesus in terms of geographical origin. While the unclean spirit recognized Jesus as the "holy one of God," he at the same time specified His historical origin. Bartimaeus called Him the son of David, but knew Him as "the Nazarene." The message regarding the risen and exalted Lord speaks of "the Nazarene, who was crucified." In every instance these declarations clearly affirm and in no way ignore the historical origin and significance of Jesus.

Another word that identifies Jesus is the Greek expression *Nazōraios*. Found only in the Gospels and Acts, "Jesus the *Nazōraean*" is found once in Matthew (26:71), once in Luke (18:37), three times in John (18:5, 7, 19:19), and six times in Acts (2:22, 3:6, 4:10, 6:14, 22:8, 26:9). The etymological relationship between this word and the noun "Nazareth" is not easy to define. Studies by G. F. Moore (*The Beginnings of Christianity*, Vol. I, London, Macmillan and Co., 1920, pp. 426-432), W. F. Albright ("The Names 'Nazareth' and 'Nazoraean,' " in *Journal of Biblical Literature* 65, 1946, pp. 397-401), and H. H. Schaeder (*Theologisches Wörterbuch zum Neuen Testament*, 1932, IV, pp. 879-884) have shown that the Greek *Nazōraios* is derived from the name "Nazareth," certain phonetic changes having occurred in the transcription from Aramaic to Greek. The RSV has translated every occurrence of this Greek term as "Jesus of Nazareth."

Matthew's reference to *Nazōraios* seems to make some kind of association with Nazareth. In 2:23 the Gospel writer mentions that on returning from Egypt the holy family settled in Nazareth. He interprets this as a fulfillment of the word spoken by the prophets: "He shall be called a Nazoraean (RSV: Nazarene)." The exact location of this prophecy is debated; among those suggested are Judges 13:5, 7 (regarding Samson who was to be a Nazarite) and Isaiah 11:1 and 53:2 (reference to the "root"—Heb.: *nazir*). In any case, Matthew's connection between Nazareth and *Nazōraios* would hardly seem to be merely a popular etymology. This relationship is further substantiated by the fact that Matthew and Luke use this word where the parallel passage in Mark uses the word Nazarene (cf. Luke 18:37, Mark 10:47, Matt. 26:71, Mark 14:67).

In John's Gospel the term is used by the enemies of Jesus. His captors in the Garden of Gethsemane twice answer Jesus' question "Whom do you seek?" with the words "Jesus the Nazoraean" (18:5, 7). Similarly, the superscription on the cross identifies the condemned man by this phrase and intends thereby to indicate His place of origin. By adding the words "the King of the Jews," Pilate's irony came into sharp focus. No wonder the Jews objected—a king from lowly Nazareth (cf. John 1:46, 7:41, 52) was a serious affront to them.

By using the phrase "Jesus the Nazoraean," Peter and Paul identified the subject of their preaching as an historical person. This is how Peter designated Jesus in his Pentecost sermon (Acts 2:22), described Him before the Sanhedrin (4:10), and healed the lame man in His name (3:6). On the Damascus road even Jesus speaks of Himself in this way to Saul of Tarsus (22:8). Years later, in his defense before Agrippa, Paul uses this phrase (26:9). When the accusers of Stephen speak of "this Jesus the Nazoraean" (6:14), one senses even a note of contempt.

In the Gospels and Acts these various designations occur twenty times with the name Jesus in order to indicate His geographical origin and thus to distinguish Him from others bearing the same name. In this way Jesus' historicity would be fixed in the minds of the native Palestinians. On the other hand, this kind of designation would not have the same significance for people outside of Palestine, and therefore is not used in such situations. In other words, whenever and wherever such designation would be meaningful, the early Church identified the Jesus it proclaimed as the historical Jesus of Nazareth. By these additional phrases the early Church at one and the same time identified the risen and exalted Lord as the man from Galilee known to His fellows as the Nazarene.

II. HISTORICAL FACTS STRESSED IN THE EARLY CHURCH ·

What data about the Jesus of Nazareth seemed significant to the early Church? It was concerned about the historical Jesus and never separated His teachings from His life; in fact, the early Church placed almost all its emphasis upon Jesus' work and life. The Acts of the Apostles records significant information about the attitude of the early Church towards the Jesus of Nazareth.[3] Since the early chapters of Acts record events that antedate the writing of the Gospels (possibly the Gospels were written near the end of Paul's life at the very earliest), it is the Book of Acts that must supply this evidence concerning the early Church. However, the exact nature of Acts as a source book for this material must be rec-

---

[3] A helpful study in this area is William M. Ramsay, *The Christ of the Earliest Christians* (Richmond, John Knox Press, 1959).

ognized. For one thing, Luke wrote the Book of Acts at least twenty-five years after these recorded events took place. His purpose was not simply to present a history of the early Church, much less the facts of the life of Jesus, but also to present and interpret the new movement to Theophilus. Therefore, although the historical Jesus was not the primary concern of the author, nevertheless He is clearly seen in Acts as a constituent part of the kerygma of the early Church.

A further observation regarding Acts as a source book concerns the speeches. It is doubtful that Luke recorded them in full as they were originally presented. The exact nature and character of these speeches have been extensively studied. At best they are faithful summaries, perhaps not always verbal reproductions, of the original. Luke apparently reports only those portions that he considers significant for a given situation and relevant for the total impact and purpose of his writing. The authenticity of the Lucan speeches can hardly be denied.[4]

Where the appointment of someone to replace Judas Iscariot is recorded, Peter notes some of the qualifications for an apostle (Acts 1:21 f.) An apostle must be one who was with Jesus during His earthly ministry from the time of His baptism by John to His ascension. This would qualify an apostle as a personal witness. Stress is clearly placed upon direct knowledge of the actions and life of the historical person.

Peter's sermon delivered on Pentecost and recorded in Acts 2 contains some definite allusions to the historical Jesus. Here too it is highly significant that no reference is made to the teaching of Jesus; while none of His sayings are quoted, there are references to Jesus' life and experiences. If these allusions are expurgated from the sermon, the whole argument is invalidated and the case not at all proven.

Because he is addressing Jews and proselytes, Peter makes effective use of the Old Testament to prove the Messiahship of Jesus. Using the phrase "Jesus the Nazoraean" (2:22), he also identifies Jesus, however, in terms of His earthly ministry by appealing to their knowledge of details regarding Jesus' life (2:22). Then he alludes to the mighty works, wonders, and signs which God did through Jesus in their very presence. Peter also refers to the crucifixion (2:23, 36), the resurrection (2:24, 32), and the

---

[4] Compare F. F. Bruce's conclusion: "These considerations . . . give us good ground for believing that the speeches in Ac. are not Luke's invention, but summaries giving at least the gist of what was really said on the various occasions, and therefore valuable and independent sources for the life and thought of the primitive Church" (*The Acts of the Apostles,* Grand Rapids, Wm. B. Eerdmans Publishing Company, 1960, p. 21). Although suggesting that the speeches in Acts are the inventions of Luke, C. K. Barrett nevertheless observes the following: "The speeches in Acts, by whomsoever made, all revert to the story of Jesus. This is never recounted—Luke was too economical an artist for this; but everywhere it is allusively present" (*Luke the Historian in Recent Study,* London, Epworth Press, 1961, p. 60).

ascension and exaltation (2:33). Regarding the resurrection, he calls it the fulfillment of prophecy (2:25-31).[5]

These facts clearly indicate the early Church's desire to present the historical Jesus. The crucifixion and resurrection are clearly emphasized, as well as other activities of Jesus. If these were fabrications, those who are appealed to as witnesses (the local Jews) would certainly have objected. Their reaction does not indicate this, however. Instead, as Luke reports, "Now when they heard this they were cut to the heart, and said to Peter and the rest of the apostles, 'Brethren, what shall we do?'" (2:37). An address based on false evidence and illogical argument would hardly elicit such response.

In healing the lame man at the Beautiful Gate, Peter clearly stressed the historical Jesus by calling upon "the name of Jesus Christ the Nazoraean" (3:6). Following the healing, Peter had occasion to proclaim Jesus to the people assembled in Solomon's Portico. Here he stressed the trial and death of Jesus; he indicated the Jews' choice of Barrabas (3:14), Jesus' innocence implied also in Pilate's desire to release Jesus (3:13)—and although they did so in ignorance (3:17), the Jews' responsibility for putting Jesus to death (3:13-15). Peter also emphasized the resurrection (3:15, 26), ascension (3:21), and exaltation (3:13). The following day before the leaders of the Jews Peter again stressed that the healing of the lame man was "by the name of Jesus Christ the Nazoraean" (4:10), and added a reference to Jesus' crucifixion by the Jews and His resurrection by God. Consequently the leaders placed restrictions on the use of the name of Jesus (4:18), indicating thereby the danger they saw in the spreading of this movement that centered in the historical person, Jesus. In the prayer service following Peter's and John's release, an interesting reference is made to the role which, in the predestined plan of God, both Herod and Pontius Pilate played in the trial of Jesus.

It is evident from the healing of the lame man and subsequent events that the early Church continually stressed the Jesus of Nazareth as an historical person and as an integral part of her message about Him. Later when the Sadducees wanted to curtail the ministry of the apostles, Peter responded by affirming the resurrection and exaltation of Jesus whom the Jews "killed by hanging on a tree" (Acts 5:30 f.). The Sadducees were concerned about the bringing of "this man's blood upon" them (5:28). The whole episode centered about the man Jesus and the spread of

---

[5] In Acts 2:32 Peter mentions that the apostles are witnesses of the resurrected Jesus. This theme of the resurrection recurs often in the preaching of the early Church (3:15, 4:33, 5:32, 10:41, 13:31, I Cor. 15:15; cf. Acts 1:22). This repetition was necessary since the resurrection could not be verified in the same way as other facts regarding the life of Jesus nor was it witnessed by the people of Palestine as were these other facts.

His movement. In this atmosphere the apostles continued to preach Jesus as the Christ (5:42).

The accusation against Stephen mentioned Jesus of Nazareth (6:14) who would destroy the temple and change the customs of Moses. In his defense, Stephen referred to the fact that the Jews had betrayed and murdered Jesus (7:52), the Just One who had come in the historical succession of the prophets. Philip also, in his ministry to the Samaritans and the Ethiopian eunuch, made reference to Jesus (8:12, 35), although no indication is given as to what historical facts he mentioned.

In Saul's conversion, the central and prime importance of the historical Jesus is seen in Jesus' self-disclosure as "Jesus of Nazareth" (cf. the initial footnote of this chapter). While the New Testament nowhere clearly indicates that Paul ever saw or heard Jesus face to face during the Saviour's earthly ministry, there is a real possibility that he did.[6] Prior to his conversion, Paul surely must have known some of the historical facts about Jesus; as a young theologian in Jerusalem he would be aware of new movements and the testimony of those whom Saul persecuted must have included some of these facts. As a faithful Jew and punctilious Pharisee, he refused to identify the Jesus of Nazareth as the promised Messiah (Christ) of the Old Testament, nor would he ascribe to the Jesus of Nazareth any supernatural or divine attributes. Conversely, this is shown clearly by the message Saul immediately proclaimed after his conversion: Jesus is the Christ (Acts 9:22) and Jesus is the Son of God (9:20). His confrontation with the Jesus of Nazareth on the way to Damascus confirmed the reality of the resurrection and ascension; further, it validated the proclamation of the early Church that the historical Jesus is the promised Messiah. These facts were responsible for the revolutionary experience in the life of Saul the persecutor. On the other hand, this narrative also shows that simply a knowledge of the historical facts (which Saul undoubtedly had) is not sufficient to bring about a living relationship with Jesus. Such a living relationship, however, depends upon knowledge and conviction concerning the Jesus of Nazareth, the historical Jesus.

In his message to Cornelius, Peter assumed that the centurion and his household were familiar with the "good news of peace" preached by Jesus Christ (Acts 10:36), and how it had been proclaimed throughout Judea. Peter then referred to Jesus' good works and healing ministry (especially to the demon-possessed), and identified Him as Jesus of

---

[6] II Corinthians 5:16 cannot be cited as evidence for this thesis, since "from a human point of view" qualifies "regarded," not "Christ." Paul is contrasting two different ways of viewing or regarding the Christ, not two different Christs. The reference is to a pre-conversion and post-conversion knowledge of Christ. Interpreted in this way the passage does not negate the significance of the historical or human Jesus.

Nazareth. By implication or direct reference Peter placed considerable stress upon the historical facts in the life of Jesus of Nazareth, including those of the crucifixion and resurrection.

An analysis of the early chapters of Acts shows, therefore, that the early Church considered the ministry of Jesus—from His baptism by John the Baptist to His ascension—a necessary part of the kerygma. It concerned itself with the facts of Jesus' life more than with His teachings, for these facts and details made the call to repentance meaningful and demonstrated what the new life in Christ involved. To remove these historical facts from the kerygma leaves only a residuum of exhortations which are practically meaningless and without validation. One must conclude, therefore, that for the early Christians the proclamation of the good news was inseparably linked with personal demonstration and validation in the life and work of the Jesus of Nazareth.

The question inevitably arises whether the later chapters of Acts which record Paul's ministry show the same concern for historical facts about Jesus. Since few of Paul's sermons are recorded in Acts, information on this question comes principally by implication and inference. As in the preaching of the Palestinian Church, there is little emphasis in Paul's message on the teaching and sayings of Jesus. The fact that Paul preached outside Jesus' homeland would have a bearing upon his references to the historical Jesus. Even apart from these considerations, however, Paul's ministry shows special concern for the historical Jesus.

Luke records the sermon preached by Paul in Antioch of Pisidia (Acts 13:16-41), in which the Apostle presented a brief review of Old Testament history and added to this historical survey the ministries of John the Baptist and Jesus. Regarding Jesus, Paul mentioned His trial (13:28), crucifixion (13:29), death, resurrection (13:30, 33, 34), and post-resurrection appearances (13:31). The life of Jesus is shown to be a continuation of God's revelation in history to His people; there is continuity between the history of the Old Testament people of God and Jesus of Nazareth. To the Jews and proselytes of Antioch this fact gave meaning and validity to Paul's message.

Paul's sermons at Lystra (Acts 14:15-17 and at Athens (17:22-31) present an interesting contrast to that delivered at Antioch where the audience was predominantly Jewish. Both at Lystra and Athens Paul appeals to natural revelation (much as in Romans 1:19-23), and his use of the Old Testament is quite different. While Paul's message does not especially emphasize historical facts about Jesus, it regards the historical Jesus as significant. Paul's address to the inhabitants of Lystra has no reference to the life or ministry of Jesus. Since only one phase of Paul's ministry at Lystra is mentioned, however, and since the opposition to Paul in this place was instigated by Jews from Antioch and Iconium (Acts 14:19), the issue at stake undoubtedly was Paul's presentation of Jesus. From Luke's account of the message at Lystra one cannot really conclude anything concerning Paul's attitude to the historical Jesus.

Paul's audience in Athens was quite different from that in both Antioch and Lystra. Here he was addressing the Greek intellectuals, philosophers among the Stoics and Epicureans. His message as recorded has but a passing reference to Jesus—"by a man . . ." (17:31). More must have been said about "this man" in this or in earlier discussions (cf. 17:18), however, since the reference would otherwise be unintelligible. Such further elucidation must have included details about the earthly life and ministry of Jesus, inasmuch as the recorded material speaks merely of "a man." It was the reference to the resurrection that brought consternation to his hearers.

Paul's farewell address to the Ephesian elders (Acts 20:18-35) touches on Jesus' earthly life by referring to His purchase of the Church with His blood (20:28). In Festus' report to Agrippa regarding the charge of the Jews against Paul, reference is made to the historical Jesus who the Jews contended was dead but Paul asserted to be alive (Acts 25:19). Obviously this fact about the historical Jesus was a major issue in the trial, although Tertullus does not mention it in his presentation (Acts 24:2-8). In his defense before Agrippa, Paul describes how, before his conversion, he opposed the name of Jesus of Nazareth (Acts 26:9). He contends now, however, that his ministry and teachings concerning Jesus are consistent with the Old Testament revelation (Acts 26:22), especially in regard to the suffering and resurrection of Christ (Acts 26:23).

In view of the foregoing study one can safely conclude that the early Church up to and including Paul had a real concern for the historical Jesus. The summaries of the early kerygma as formulated by C. H. Dodd on the basis of the Petrine and Pauline speeches show the same kind of emphasis (*The Apostolic Preaching*, New York, Harper & Brothers, 1944, pp. 21-24). Especially in ministering to the Jews the early Christians stressed again and again that the Church was the continuation of the Old Testament people of God. Jesus, moreover, was the climax of prophetic tradition (Acts 3:22-26), the fulfillment of the promise and hope of the Old Testament. For two reasons the first-century Jew found great difficulty with this affirmation. The claims made by Jesus Himself and by His followers violated the Jews' cherished principle of monotheism. Nevertheless, the witness of the early Church was that the historical Jesus of Nazareth claimed to be God and demonstrated this fact by His life. This dual emphasis on the human Jesus and divine Christ was offensive to the Jew. Moreover, since the idea of a suffering Messiah was totally foreign to the Jew, the suffering of Jesus of Nazareth on a Cross disqualified Him as the expected Messiah. The early Church had to prove that these sufferings were definitely implied in the Old Testament predictions. Thus the historical Jesus and His sufferings were presented or implied in the kerygma. Luke explicitly reports that in the synagogue at Thessalonica Paul argued from the Scriptures, "explaining and proving that it was necessary for the Christ to suffer and to rise from the dead and saying, 'This Jesus, whom I proclaim to you, is the Christ'" (Acts 17:3). It is interesting that Paul's conviction that Jesus is the Son of God (Acts 9:20) and that Jesus is the Christ (Acts 9:22) came as the result of his conversion. These themes characterized his earliest preaching.

Another significant emphasis in the preaching of the early Church, especially to Gentiles, was that the historical Jesus would return some day as judge. This motivation to repentance is found in Peter's message to Cornelius (Acts 10:42), in Paul's address on Mars Hill (Acts 17:31), and in Paul's witness to Felix (Acts 24:25). These emphases in the kerygma derive their meaning and significance from an implied affirmation of the historical Jesus. To remove the historical Jesus from the kerygma makes these emphases meaningless and irrelevant.

A first examination of the Pauline epistles might suggest the presence of but few direct references to the historical Jesus. The catalogue of references and allusions becomes quite impressive, however, when one observes the following qualifications. First of all, one must remember the nature of the Pauline letters. They were occasional rather than regular letters and were addressed to specific problems in a given Church. Secondly, because only those matters are dealt with that were problems in a given Church, these letters do not reflect Paul's over-all thinking on a given issue. It would seem, then, that the historical Jesus was not a disputed issue in the churches to which Paul was writing. On the other hand, this fact would heighten the significance of what references thereto do occur. Failure to mention or emphasize certain points does not indicate a denial or lessening of their significance. Conversely, to suggest that Paul's view on marriage was of prime significance in his preaching because he devotes a long chapter to it (I Corinthians 7) is unwarranted.

Paul makes a definite reference to the birth of Jesus in Galatians 4:4— "born of a woman." Jesus' appearance in the flesh is alluded to several times—Romans 1:3, 4 (including a reference to His descent from David; cf. II Tim. 2:8), 8:3, I Timothy 3:16; cf. Philippians 2:7 ff. Paul's allusions to the life and ministry of Jesus are not very numerous. He refers to the obedience of Jesus in Romans 5:19 and Philippians 2:7 ff., and to His meekness and gentleness in II Corinthians 10:1. Events in Jesus' life mentioned by Paul are from the closing days of His life. In I Corinthians 11:23 Paul describes the meal Jesus shared with His disciples on the night of His betrayal. Jesus' trial before Pilate is mentioned in I Timothy 6:13. More than thirty references to the Cross and death of Jesus appear in the Pauline epistles. His burial is mentioned in I Corinthians 15:4 and implied in passages such as Romans 6:4 and Colossians 2:12.

Paul mentions the resurrection of Jesus more than twenty times and uses language that suggests his interpretation of it. The verb used to express this idea in all cases except one (I Thess. 4:14) is *egeirō*. Twelve times this verb occurs in the active voice with God (or Father) as subject and Jesus as object. By using the aorist tense in each case the writer stresses a simple action or single event, not something repeated or continued. In those cases where the indicative mood is used the idea of past time is also added. In still other cases where the perfect tense is used the stress is placed on the past act with its abiding result or continuing effect (for example, I Cor. 15:4 *passim*). By using these tenses the writer clearly stresses the "once-ness" of the resurrection, and in the case of the perfect tense, the abiding condition of Jesus' being raised. All this suggests that the writer conceived of the resurrection as a definite historical event. Allusions to Jesus' ascension and exaltation are found in Ephesians 1:20, 4:9, Philippians 2:9-11, Romans 8:34, Colossians 3:1.

In summary, then, the Pauline epistles contain the following direct references and allusions to facts about Jesus of Nazareth: His birth and lineage; His life of obedience, meekness, gentleness; His fellowship meal with His followers; His betrayal; His resurrection; His ascension and exaltation. In view of the above observations, this list is impressive and shows that the historical Jesus must have occupied a significant place in Paul's message.

The other New Testament writings reveal much the same emphasis. The Epistle to the Hebrews contains a number of allusions to the life of Jesus: His descent (7:14); His flesh (5:7, 10:20); His body (10:10); His obedience (5:8); His temptation (2:18, 4:15); His suffering (2:9, 13:12 *et al.*); His Cross (12:2); His death (2:9, 13:20). The first Epistle of Peter stresses practically the same items: His body (2:24); His flesh (3:18, 4:1); His blood (1:2, 19); His suffering (2:21, 4:1, 13, 5:1); His Cross (2:24); His death (3:18); His resurrection (1:3, 21, 3:21). These representative surveys, although not exhaustive, nevertheless demonstrate the thesis that the early Church viewed her message as grounded in the life and ministry of Jesus and in what God did and revealed in the historical Jesus of Nazareth.

III. HISTORICAL DATA IN THE GOSPELS

The formulation of this heading may appear redundant, since it is the very nature of the Gospels to be historical. One must remember, however, that these data are used by each individual author to set forth his specific purpose and intention. Any attempt to prepare a rigid and tight harmony of the Gospels is therefore not warranted. Oscar Cullmann's observation is much to the point here: "Four biographies of the same life could not be set alongside one another as of equal value, but would have to be harmonized and reduced to a single biography in some way or other. Four

Gospels, that is, four books dealing with the content of a faith cannot be harmonized, but require by their very nature to be set alongside one another" (*The Early Church*, Philadelphia, The Westminster Press, 1956, p. 54).

History in the Gospels is *Heilsgeschichte*. It is part of God's self-revelation to man. Its aim is to testify to that divine-human fact of God's intervention in human history which brought man salvation in Jesus Christ. This salvation is centered in the advent, ministry, death, and resurrection of Jesus Christ. In this formal aspect the twentieth-century definition of history is certainly more adequate for biblical history than the nineteenth-century definition. The Bible, and more particularly in the present discussion, the Gospels, present historical facts about God's dealings with His people and interpret them in terms of His redemptive plan. Hence, history in the Gospels is interpreted history.

More specifically, each Gospel writer interpreted the life and ministry of Jesus with a specific purpose and intention in mind. Each one did not simply record this "interpreted history" in the same way, but presented certain historical data and sequence with interpretation in order to fulfill a specific purpose and apologetic interest. Since the Gospel writers are not simply recording historical data, but are writing to meet a specific need in the early history of the Church, the *Sitz im Leben* of the writing of the Gospels can contribute greatly to one's understanding of the content and arrangement of a given document. To abstract a document from its historical setting and occasion is just as gross an injustice to Scripture as wrenching a pericope or text from its context. The recording of the event as well as the event itself must be investigated and understood.

Some implications of this view of biblical history for the study of biblical history in general and of the Gospels in particular are:

1. All recorded material must be viewed in terms of the over-all purpose and intention of divine revelation.

2. A given writer has the freedom to rearrange and dislocate certain passages in terms of his specific intention; for example, Matthew's Five Discourses, Luke's Great Insertion (9:51-18:14, also called the Travel Narrative). The exegete must ascertain this intention and perspective of the author and the occasion for writing.

3. All of the recorded sacred history is important and of intrinsic value in setting forth God's revelation. The kerygma cannot be isolated from its historical framework or its historical content.

4. Since the first-century Semitic mind was not interested particularly in the accuracy or scientific precision that marks the twentieth century, the exegete must not impose these contemporary standards and criteria on the Gospels.

The relevance of this approach to the historical data in the Gospels and its interpretation is evident in the following examples. While Luke records a rejection at Nazareth at the beginning of the Galilean ministry (4:16-30), Mark and Matthew place it much later in the same ministry (Matt. 13:54-58, Mark 6:1-6). Some have argued that there were two rejections at Nazareth, one at the beginning of the Galilean ministry (recorded by Luke) and the other later during the same ministry (recorded by Matthew and Mark). But the similarity of certain details and Luke's use of this pericope make this theory unlikely. It seems that Luke located the rejection at this point in order to set forth a pattern regarding the ministry of Jesus. Various elements that Luke stresses in this pericope were characteristic features of Jesus' whole ministry. C. K. Barrett has listed these as "(1) the immediate acceptance of the gracious words of Jesus by all fair-minded hearers; (2) the prediction of the Gentile mission; (3) the wrath of the Jews and their rejection of Jesus; (4) His miraculous deliverance from death" (*Luke the Historian in Recent Study*, London, Epworth Press, 1961, p. 65).

The healing of Peter's mother-in-law is placed early in the Galilean ministry by Luke (4:38, 39) and Mark (1:29-31). Matthew reports it after the Sermon on the Mount (8:14, 15). Prior to each of the major discourses in the first Gospel is a narrative section which sets the stage for the discourse. The narrative material preceding the second discourse describes Jesus' mighty works, especially in healing (including the pericope under discussion). The second discourse deals with the mission of the disciples (9:35—10:42). This approach adequately explains Matthew's location of the pericope concerning the healing of Peter's mother-in-law in contrast to that of Mark and Luke, who perhaps located it chronologically.

These examples show it is possible to recover the Jesus of Nazareth without questioning the historicity of a given event or record. In such a project all four Gospels in their entirety are legitimate sources. The presupposition of the unity and totality of Scripture (discussed elsewhere in this symposium) demands this wholeness. The current post-Bultmannian movement has retained an inadequate view of the sources; it is primarily kerygmatic and only secondarily a custodian of factual details for historians of posterity. Although the movement's new insights are to be appreciated, nevertheless its rejection of certain materials in the Gospels because of certain theological presuppositions is to be deplored. The scholar who accepts all four Gospels as God's revelation must exhaust their contents and may not eliminate or set aside any part thereof. The very contents of the Gospels neither compel him to this dissection nor do they encourage an unhealthy skepticism. The Gospels do indeed present the Jesus of Nazareth, but never simply as a man. He is depicted as one with a mission, a purpose, a goal; He is fully human, but more than human because He stands in a unique relationship to God: He Himself is God.

IV. CONCLUDING OBSERVATIONS

The Christ of faith cannot be divorced from the Jesus of history. The one is meaningless without the other: "Great indeed, we confess, is the mystery of our religion: He was manifested in the flesh, vindicated in the Spirit, seen by angels, preached among the nations, believed on in the world, taken up in glory" (I Tim. 3:16). The Gospel is a message about an historical event—"the Word became flesh and dwelt among us ..." (John 1:14)—and an interpretation of this event—"God was in Christ reconciling the world unto himself" (II Cor. 5:19).

What God did for us in Jesus Christ took place in the first half of the first century of our era. In varying degree the four Gospels describe the life and ministry of Jesus. And the sermons in the first part of Acts show how the early Church proclaimed Jesus of Nazareth.[7] Even though the historical facts in the kerygma are not numerous, to remove them destroys the very message of the Gospel. P. Althaus is correct when he writes: "The revelatory character of the history of Jesus is not known by means of historical reflexion or historical reasoning. But on the other hand, it is not known *without these*. For the gospel deals with facts which, it is claimed, happened in this history of ours; it has 'historical facts' as content, and its foundation in history is a part of its credibility" (*Fact and Faith in the Kerygma of Today*, Philadelphia, Muhlenberg Press, 1959, p. 34). J. Jeremias has similarly stressed the unity of the historical Jesus and the kerygma: "The good news of Jesus and the Early Church's proclamation of faith are inseparable from one another. Neither of these two major issues may be isolated. For the gospel of Jesus remains dead history without the proclamation of faith by the Church, which ever afresh expands, avows, and attests this gospel. Nor can the Kerygma either be isolated. Apart from Jesus and His gospel it is merely the proclamation of an idea or a theory. He who isolates the message of Jesus ends up in Ebionitism. He who isolates the Kerygma of the Early Church ends up in Docetism" (*The Expository Times*, Vol. LXIX, 1958, p. 339.

The saving event in Jesus Christ was once-for-all, as the writer to the Hebrews takes great pains to stress (9:26, 28; 7:27; 9:12; 10:10). Nowhere does the New Testament refer to the death and resurrection of Christ as repeated events. This is shown, for instance, in the use of *egeirō* for the resurrection of Christ: it always appears in the aorist tense (a simple single act) or in the perfect tense (a past act with an abiding result).

---

[7] Inasmuch as these sermons antedate the writing of the Gospels, they show how historical facts, though not numerous, were part of the kerygma from the very beginning. The fact that eye-witnesses could be hearing this kerygma lends greater significance to the factuality and accuracy of the historical facts. Peter alludes to this by the phrase "as you yourselves know" (Acts 2:22) when he describes facts concerning Jesus of Nazareth in his sermon on Pentecost.

How many facts regarding the historical Jesus are essential for the kerygma? On the presupposition of the unity and totality of Scripture, this question is not valid. By definition of such unity and totality we must admit all the facts recorded in the New Testament. No selection or elimination is possible. The message we proclaim must not be limited only to the historical facts already preached by the early Church; it must include also the facts furnished by the Gospels and the later writings of the New Testament. The New Testament revelation in its totality presents the historical Jesus in His full stature; it reveals Him as Saviour and God.

THE RESURRECTION
OF JESUS CHRIST

✝

George E. Ladd

George Eldon Ladd is Professor of Biblical Theology at Fuller Theological Seminary in California. He is author of Crucial Questions About the Kingdom of God *(1952),* The Blessed Hope *(1956) and* The Gospel of the Kingdom *(1959). His projected writings include a volume in New Testament biblical theology. He holds the Th.B. degree from Gordon College, B.D. from Gordon Divinity School, and Ph.D. from Harvard University.*

13. George E. Ladd

THE RESURRECTION
OF JESUS CHRIST

THE SIGNIFICANCE of the resurrection of Jesus Christ for Christian faith and life is sounded by the apostle Paul in the words, "If Christ has not been raised, then our preaching is in vain and your faith is in vain. . . . If Christ has not been raised your faith is futile and you are still in your sins" (I Cor. 15:14, 17). If any element in the Christian faith may be called the central doctrine, it is the resurrection of Christ.

I. THE CENTRALITY OF THE RESURRECTION

Even a superficial survey of the New Testament makes it abundantly clear that the central message of the early Christians to the world was that of the fact and significance of Jesus' resurrection. Our churches have developed the custom of celebrating this event once a year on Easter Sunday, thus making its observance a seasonal matter. Seldom is a sermon on the resurrection heard at other times. This limitation of remembrance is not in the least the New Testament pattern. For the earliest Christians the resurrection was not a comfortable life insurance policy guaranteeing life after death which was reviewed and renewed once a year; rather, it was the very fountainhead of Christian life and faith. In fact, Sunday, the first day of the week, is itself a witness to the centrality of the resurrection. Scholars have been unable to recover the steps whereby Sunday came to replace the Jewish Sabbath as the day of worship. There is no doubt, however, that the first day of the week soon displaced the seventh (I Cor. 16:2; Acts 20:7) because this was the day of Jesus' resurrection (Matt. 28:1): rather than the day of rest at the end of creation; Christian worship celebrated the victory of life over death.

The centrality of the resurrection in early Christianity is evident from the Book of Acts. One of the first recorded incidents after Jesus' ascension is the choice of a disciple to replace Judas in the apostolate. The stated qualifications show that at this early time the main function of the apostolate was not to rule the Church but rather to witness to the resurrection (Acts 1:22). We note from Acts also that the first Christian sermon, that of Peter on the day of Pentecost, focuses on the fact of the resurrection. Almost nothing is said about the life and earthly career of Jesus. Peter made no appeal to Jesus as one whose character and personality made Him worthy of devotion and discipleship. Nowhere in his sermon did Peter recall Jesus' high ethical teachings or try to demonstrate His superiority to the many rabbinic teachers among the Jews. He made only passing reference to the mighty deeds which had marked Jesus' ministry as evidence that God's blessing had rested on Him (Acts 2:22). The all important thing was the fact that this Jesus who had been executed as a criminal had been raised from the dead (Acts 2:24-32). Not on the basis of Jesus' incomparable life, unexcelled teachings, or awe-inspiring works does Peter make his appeal. Peter calls upon Israel to repent, to receive the forgiveness of sins, and to be baptized in the name of Jesus Christ (Acts 2:38) simply because God has raised Jesus from the dead and exalted Him to His own right hand in heaven.

The centrality of Christ's resurrection in the preaching and teaching of the early Church is illustrated even more vividly in the fourth chapter of Acts. Two of the most important Jewish sects were the Pharisees and the Sadducees. The former were the leading party, and accepted the teaching of the Scribes or Jewish theologians. Important in this scribal theology was belief in the resurrection, whose roots are found in the Old Testament. The Sadducees, consisting largely of priestly families active in the temple cult, accepted only the books of Moses, and therefore denied the teaching of resurrection (Acts 23:8). In the earliest days of the Christian Church the Sadducees were annoyed, therefore, because these followers of the dead Jesus were "teaching the people and proclaiming in Jesus the resurrection from the dead" (Acts 4:2).

This is a very striking statement. Wherein lies its significance? As indicated, the Pharisees believed and taught resurrection from the dead. Since it was customary for Jewish rabbis or theologians to sit in the vast courts of the temple in discussion with groups of their disciples, reference to resurrection of the dead would no doubt have been made sooner or later. Why then should the Sadducees be exercised over a similar teaching by the followers of Jesus?

The only answer would seem to be that proclamation of Jesus' resurrection by His disciples gave the doctrine both new proportions and new significance. The rabbis taught resurrection as a matter of theoretical theology, and debated such questions as the subjects and the time of the resurrection. The Christian approach was different. It offered no abstract theory or cold theology. It proclaimed, rather, a contemporary living fact which, if true, challenged all Judaism to acknowledge the occurrence of a new redemptive act of God in their midst which they could neither sidestep nor ignore. Furthermore, the wording of the Sadducees' statement indicates that the disciples were proclaiming more than simply an event which they had witnessed, namely, the resurrection of a crucified teacher; they were proclaiming "in Jesus the resurrection from the dead." The resurrection of Jesus carried implications of incalculable significance. No longer was the resurrection of the dead merely a debated theological hope for the future; rather, it was a present fact which placed resurrection from the dead in a new perspective that demanded recognition and personal decision.

II. THE IMPORTANCE OF THE RESURRECTION

Granting the fact of its centrality in the message of the New Testament Church, we must ask, Why was the resurrection of Christ so central? Is not the Cross of Christ, rather, the main symbol and essential doctrine of the Christian faith? Paul deals with this question in his masterful discussion in I Corinthians 15. He asserts unequivocally that if Christ's resurrection is not a fact, then Christian preaching is emptied of reality, faith is futile, forgiveness is a fancy, and immortality is a mockery (I Cor. 15:14, 17, 18). He links everything to the fact of the resurrection. If Christ is not risen, the Christian preacher has lost his message. Since preaching occupies a central role in our Protestant churches, we might well ask: What is preaching? The word *kerygma* means both the act of preaching and the content of preaching. Paul's use of the term emphasizes especially the latter meaning. When he writes that God was pleased through the "foolishness of preaching" (I Cor. 1:21) to save those who believe, he did not mean the physical act of standing before men and delivering a sermon; he referred, rather, to the Christian proclamation or message as being foolishness in the eyes of men. The entire Christian message rests on the validity and reality of the resurrection. If Christ has not been raised, Christian preachers have nothing to say and should go out of business.

The content of the Christian message can perhaps be most easily subsumed in the love of God. "God so loved the world. . . ." This love is not some vague, general love, however, a nebulous doctrine deviously deduced from the fluctuations of history and from the frustrations of personal experience. God's redeeming love for the world can be known in one central and specific fact: "God so loved . . . that he gave." "God shows his love for us in that while we were yet sinners Christ died for us" (Rom. 5:8). Here is the one irrefragable proof of God's love—the fact of Christ's redeeming death on the Cross.

But what is the Cross without the resurrection? When His disciples beheld Jesus' awful agonizing death, did they throw themselves on their faces at the foot of the Cross and, overcome with awe and amazement, cry out, "We never knew how much God loved us! Behold God's love"? Apart from the resurrection the Cross spelled only tragedy, defeat, despair. For the disciples, Jesus' death meant the end of their world; or, rather, it meant return to the old world and way of life they had known before meeting Jesus. They did not gather to formulate plans for taking the message of God's redeeming love manifested in the Cross to a world of dying men, for their hopes were dead. "We *had* hoped" said one of the Emmaus disciples (Luke 24:21); hope was in the past tense. It died with Jesus. Only as the death of Christ was vindicated and interpreted by His resurrection could it be understood as the supreme evidence of God's love for a lost world. Apart from the reality of the resurrection, then, the Christian message has lost its substance and reality. There is no good news if Jesus is dead.

Apart from the resurrection, faith is futile. This seems like a bold statement, for is it not faith in the living *God* which is fundamental to life? Can faith in the living God be disturbed by the reality or the unreality of a single event? Did not the author of Hebrews make faith in God basic to all else when he wrote, "For whoever would draw near to God must believe that he exists and that he rewards those who seek him" (Heb. 11:6)? Is it not faith in the living God, then, that vindicates our confidence in the resurrection of Christ?

While this approach is persuasive, it is contradicted by the further course of Paul's thought. If Christ is not risen, faith is a futile thing. The reason for this truth is not obscure. The God who is worshiped in the Christian faith is neither the product of that faith nor the creation of theologians or philosophers. This God is not an invention or discovery of men. He is the God, rather, who has spoken to mankind by revealing Himself in a series of redemptive events that reach back to Israel's deliverance from Egypt, and even beyond that. God did not make Himself known through a system of teaching nor a theology nor a book, even though revelation includes both the Bible and theological truth. God made himself known through a series of events which are recorded in the Bible, and to which the Bible, as a part of the totality of revelation, provides the normative interpretation. The climax of this series of redemptive events was the coming of Jesus of Nazareth, and it is His resurrection which validates all that came before. If Christ is not risen from the dead, the long course of God's redemptive acts to save His people ends in a tomb on a dead end street. If the resurrection of Christ is not a reality, then death has the last word and we have no assurance that God is the living God. Without Christ's resurrection, faith becomes futile because the object of that faith has not vindicated Himself as the

Lord of life. If Christ is dead, then Christian faith is incarcerated in the tomb along with the final and highest self-revelation of God in Christ.

If Christ is not risen, forgiveness is a fancy. The forgiveness of sins is grounded in the death of Christ upon the Cross (I Cor. 15:3); but if Christ is dead, there is no forgiving efficacy in His death. We are yet in our sins.

If Christ is not risen, the hope of immortality is a mockery. The Greeks believed in the immortality of the human spirit and could conceive of a blessed after-life in a realm far removed from the present world of earthly existence. The biblical view conceives man as a dynamic unity of body and soul or spirit. It does not describe eternal life or salvation in terms of bare spirit but in terms of the whole man. Oscar Cullmann has made it quite clear in his little book *Immortality of the Soul or Resurrection from the Dead* (London, the Epworth Press, 1958) that the biblical concept of man permits no view of immortality apart from the resurrection of the body. And, according to the biblical witness, hope of resurrection depends upon Christ's resurrection. Therefore if Christ is not risen, we have no message of resurrection, and the hope of immortality is only a dream.

III. THE FACT OF THE RESURRECTION

Up to this point our discussion has been relatively free of problems. It is when we press more closely into questions of the fact of the resurrection and of its nature that problems emerge. *How one understands the resurrection of Christ determines the nature of one's Christian faith and theology.*

Many moderns cannot accept the nature of Christian faith as it is disclosed in the Bible. It cannot be too strongly emphasized that this attitude arises not from the nature of the Christian faith but from the presuppositions the modern man brings with him. Christianity recognizes the existence of a living God who is the creator and sustainer of all life and existence. He cannot be identified with His creation pantheistically, nor can He be detached from His creation deistically. He stands above His creation and yet is continually active in it. As the living God, He is able to act in ways which transcend ordinary human experience and knowledge.

These assertions are a problem for the modern man. He assumes that the world must always and everywhere be subject to inflexible "laws of nature." Even God cannot deviate from His usual ways of acting in His world. A prominent modern theologian accordingly rejects the possibility that Jesus' resurrection means the restoration of life to a dead body, for such an action "is inextricably involved in a nature miracle. Such a notion he [the modern man] finds intolerable, for he can see

God at work only in the life of the spirit (which is for him the only
real life) and in the transformation of his personality. But quite apart
from the incredibility of such a miracle, he cannot see how an event
like this could be the act of God, or how it could affect his own life."
Therefore, "an historical fact which involves a resurrection from the
dead is utterly inconceivable" (Rudolf Bultmann, *Kerygma and Myth*,
ed. by H. W. Bartsch, New York, Harper & Brothers, 1961, pp. 8, 39).

Such an attitude prejudices the case in advance and delivers a decision
before the evidence has been heard. This attitude places God's activity
only in the soul and not in history. It rejects the Bible's witness to God's
self-revealing activity not only in the soul of men but also in objective
events. In other words, modern man's presuppositions yield a Christianity
which differs radically from the Bible's witness to God's redeeming acts.

According to the New Testament, an objective act occurred in a garden
outside of Jerusalem. In this event the crucified and entombed Jesus
emerged from the grave into a new order of life. We do not intend to
prove the fact of the resurrection and thereby compel faith; faith cannot
be compelled by a recital of "historical" or objective facts but results
only by the working of the Holy Spirit upon the human heart. At the
same time, the Holy Spirit used the witness of the disciples to the reality
of the resurrection of Christ, and we likewise bear witness to the facts
of the New Testament record.

The Gospels attest three specific facts. First, Jesus was dead. Few
serious scholars question this. Secondly, the hopes of the disciples were
also dead. Jesus had preached the coming of the Kingdom of God; His
disciples had followed Him in the eager expectation of witnessing its
coming (Luke 19:11) and of seeing the redemption of Israel (Luke 24:21).
Even though Jesus had warned them of His impending death on a number of occasions and had tried to prepare them for it (Mark 8:31), the
disciples never really understood what He was saying. It is important
to realize that the first-century Jews did not identify the Suffering Servant
of Isaiah 53 with the Messiah. By definition Messiah was not to suffer
and die but to reign in His Kingdom. When Jesus surrendered Himself
helplessly into the hands of His enemies, when He suffered execution
as a common criminal, hope in Him as Messiah was broken. The disciples thought the end of Jesus and His preaching had come, as well as
the end of their hopes.

Thirdly, confidence and certainty suddenly and abruptly replaced the
disciples' discouragement and frustration. Suddenly they knew Jesus was
no longer dead. Something happened which convinced them that Jesus
was alive. They were sure they had seen Him again, heard His voice,
recognized His person.

Even Bultmann admits that the resurrection faith is an historical
faith. Scholars who find it impossible to believe in an actual resurrection

of Jesus admit nonetheless that the disciples believed it. They believed that their teacher and master, who was dead and had been buried, was alive again. They were confident they had seen Him once again, had recognized His features, had heard His voice and had listened to His teachings. They believed that His presence was not something "spiritual," that is, nonmaterial or "ghostly," but an objective, bodily reality. *This confidence was the faith that created the Church.* That which brought the Church into being and gave it a message was not the hope of the persistence of life beyond the grave, a confidence in God's supremacy over death, a conviction of the immortality of the human spirit. It was belief in an *event* in time and space: Jesus of Nazareth was risen from the dead. The disciples' belief in the resurrection of Jesus is an incontrovertible, historical fact; without it there would have been no Church.

But this is not the decisive and crucial fact. *Some prior event created the disciples' belief in the resurrection of Jesus.* This is the crucial issue: it was not the disciples' faith which gave birth to the stories of the resurrection; it was an event behind these stories which created their faith. They themselves had lost faith and hope. They were "foolish men, and slow of heart to believe all that the prophets have spoken" (Luke 24:25). The fact of the resurrection and faith in the resurrection are inseparable but are not identical. The fact created the faith.

It is here that the twentieth-century man raises his questions. What is this *fact* of the resurrection? What happened to produce the disciples' faith? These problems arise because of the modern concept of history and historical events. The ancient world faced no such difficulties, for men believed that the gods could descend to earth to converse with men and to produce all sorts of unusual phenomena. Leaving these views behind, the modern world instead interprets history in terms of continuity and analogy. Historical experience, we are told, is an unbroken nexus of cause and event; all historical events must have rational historical causes.

Since the rise of this historical method, criticism has attempted to explain the rise of the resurrection faith and the resurrection narratives on historical grounds. The central problem, therefore, is the "historicity" of the resurrection fact.

That death is the end of personal, historical existence is self-evident fact. When a man dies, he leaves this earthly scene forever and his body returns to dust. But what happens to his spirit or soul is a theological, not an historical question. That the resurrection fact cannot mean the "resuscitation of a corpse," therefore, is an accepted historical fact (Bultmann). Many religions have stories of such restorations to life, but the historian treats them as legendary. And the stories of Jesus' return to life the historian feels must be understood in terms analogous to similar stories in other religions.

For historical criticism the question remains: what *did* happen? What "historical" event created the resurrection faith and produced the stories of the resurrection appearances and of the empty grave?

Historical criticism has offered numerous answers. One of the earliest historical explanations of the resurrection faith was that the disciples stole Jesus' body and concealed it, then began to proclaim that He was not dead but had returned to life. This theory founds the resurrection message on a deliberate fraud, and establishes the Christian Gospel of life and salvation on a lie. Such a view hardly merits refutation.

Another theory suggests that Jesus really was not dead but only swooned because of weakness and loss of blood. Then the coolness of the tomb and the fragrance of the aromatic spices together with the hours of rest revived Him. Returning to consciousness, He emerged from the tomb, appeared to His disciples, and led them to believe that He was risen from the dead.

Another more recent theory attributes the source of the resurrection stories to Mary. She is said to have lost her way in the garden and coming to the wrong tomb, found it empty. Beholding the gardener through tear-filled eyes, she leaped to the conclusion that it was Jesus, risen from the dead.

Such theories refute themselves. The only plausible "historical" explanation is that the disciples had real *experiences;* but, their experiences were subjective and not objective. Imagination is just as *real* as objective reality—it merely belongs to a different order of reality. On the basis of this theory, the disciples experienced *real* visions which they interpreted to mean that Jesus was alive and victorious over death. While the Gospel stories are couched in terms of physical and objective contacts with Jesus, by definition such stories cannot be historical. The reality behind them was a series of real subjective experiences, visions, or hallucinations in which the disciples were sure they experienced the living Jesus.

This theory, while plausible, raises another problem: what caused the subjective experiences? What produced the visions? Visions are psychological facts; they are reality. But visions do not occur arbitrarily. To experience them requires certain preconditions on the part of the subjects concerned, preconditions that were totally lacking in the disciples of Jesus. To picture the disciples nourishing fond memories of Jesus after His death, longing to see Him again, not expecting Him really to die, is contrary to all the evidence we possess. To portray the disciples as so infused with hope because of Jesus' impact on them that their faith easily surmounted the barrier of death and posited Jesus as their living, risen Lord would require a radical rewriting of the Gospel tradition. While it may not be flattering to the disciples to say that their faith could result only from some objectively real experience, this is actually what the Gospels record. Must faith necessarily have some kind of objectivity to sustain it? Or is faith its own support? In the case of the disciples, faith did not produce the visions, and visions did not produce faith. No explanation is adequate for the rise of the resurrection faith except this: Jesus rose bodily from the dead.

Many scholars have been oblivious to the difficulties of the "vision" theory. As a strict historian Bultmann accounts for the resurrection faith only on the ground of the personal intimacy which the disciples had enjoyed with Jesus during His earthly life. This personal impact of Jesus led the disciples to experience subjective visions (*ibid.,* p. 42). Johannes Weiss gives a classic statement of this position by saying that "the appearances were not external phenomena but were merely the goals of an inner struggle in which faith won the victory over doubt.... the appearances were not the basis of their faith, though so it seemed to them, so much as its product and result." A faith which could be awakened only by objective appearances "would not possess very much in the way of moral or religious value" (Johannes Weiss, *Earliest Christianity,* New York, Harper & Brothers, 1959, Vol. I, p. 30). However much it may flatter the disciples' faith, such a view requires a radical rewriting of the New Testament data.

The problem cannot be solved this easily, however, as Günther Bornkamm, one of Bultmann's most able and influential disciples, clearly recognize. He admits that the disciples' despair and discouragement cancel out any likelihood on their part of a subjective explanation of the resurrection event. He also concedes what we contend, namely, that "the appearances of the risen Christ and the word of his witness have in the first place given rise to this faith" (Günther Bornkamm, *Jesus of Nazareth,* New York, Harper & Brothers, 1960, p. 183). This we consider a logical and necessary conclusion.

IV. THE NATURE OF THE RESURRECTION

To admit the priority and objectivity of the resurrection event does not settle all the problems, however. We still face the most important question: what is the nature of the resurrection? In this discussion we will limit ourselves to an analysis of the New Testament witness against the background of the modern approach to history.

Bultmann interprets the resurrection in existential terms. For him the resurrection means that Jesus is risen in the kerygma, that is, in the proclamation of the Gospel, that the kerygma is itself an eschatological event, and that Jesus therefore is actively present to meet the hearer in the kerygma. All speculations over the nature of that resurrection, all accounts of an empty grave and the like he considers irrelevant to the resurrection fact (Rudolf Bultmann, *Das Verhältnis der urchristlichen*

Christusbotschaft zum historischen Jesus, Heidelberg, Carl Winter, Universitätsverlag, 1961, p. 27).

Since Bornkamm admits that the vision theory is inadequate to explain the rise of the resurrection faith, we might expect a more satisfying answer from him concerning the nature of the resurrection. The Easter faith, he says, is "that God himself had intervened with his almighty hand in the wicked and rebellious life of the world, and had wrested this Jesus of Nazareth from the power of sin and death which had risen against him, and set him up as Lord of the world" (G. Bornkamm, *op. cit.,* pp. 183 f.). This language, however, seems to mean something far less than a bodily resurrection, for Bornkamm at once goes on to explain it as "an event *in* this time and this world, and yet at the same time an event which puts an end and a limit to this time and this world" (*loc. cit.*). Here, too, we seem to have an existential interpretation. It must be remembered, however, that for an existentialist theologian the experience of "authentic existence" or, in Christian terminology, of saving faith, involves not mere subjectivity but objectivity as well (R. Bultmann, *Kerygma and Myth,* pp. 199 ff.).

Bultmann considers the resuscitation of a corpse incredible. Even if his objection were valid, it carries no weight, for the New Testament nowhere pictures Jesus' resurrection as the resuscitation of a corpse but as the emergence within time and space of a new order of life.

Certain elements of first-century Judaism believed in the resurrection of the physical body, that is, in the return to life of the same body that died. This is illustrated by the story of the Jewish elder, Razis, who lived in the days of the Seleucid persecution. Rather than fall into the hands of the hated Greeks, Razis took a sword and "standing on a steep rock . . . he tore out his bowels, taking both his hands to them, and flung them at the crowds. So he died, calling on Him who is lord of life and spirit to restore them to him again" (II Maccabees 14:46).

Such a story in no way describes the nature of Jesus' resurrection. Jesus' resurrection is not the restoration to physical life of a dead body; it is the emergence of a new order of life. It is the embodiment of eternal life in time and space. It is the beginning of the eschatological resurrection.

There are two traditions concerning the nature of the resurrection body, that of Paul and that of the Gospels. These two traditions are often said to conflict and to represent two mutually exclusive concepts. Paul is said to conceive of a body of spiritual substance entirely different from that of the earthly body, one consisting perhaps of particles of light, and belonging to a totally different order of existence than does this present earthly order of matter. On the other hand, the Gospels are said to picture the resurrection body as something crassly material which is able to interact with the physical senses of the earthly body.

In brief, the Gospels are purported to picture the revivification of a physical corpse, while Paul is said to describe a new and different level of life belonging to an extra-earthly spiritual realm. Let us examine these two traditions.

In I Corinthians 15, Paul discusses the resurrection of believers in considerable detail. Not only here but throughout his letters he places this eschatological resurrection at the end of the age in close logical connection with the resurrection of Jesus. Verse 20 states this relationship: "But in fact Christ has been raised from the dead, the firstfruits of those who have fallen asleep." As all who stand in physical solidarity with Adam experience Adam's death, so all who stand in spiritual solidarity with Christ will experience the life into which Jesus entered at His resurrection (v. 22). "But each in his own order: Christ the firstfruits, then at his coming those who belong to Christ" (v. 23).

The resurrection of Christ and the resurrection of those who belong to Christ constitute two parts of a single entity, two acts in a single drama, two stages of a single process. The temporal relationship is un-important. It matters not how long an interval of time intervenes be-tween these two stages of the resurrection. This does not affect the logical relationship, or, it would be better to say, the theological relationship. Jesus' resurrection is the "firstfruits" of the eschatological resurrection at the end of the age. Gathering firstfruits—a common experience in Palestinian agriculture—brought in the first grain of the harvest; it indicated that the full harvest itself was ripe and ready to be gathered in. While the firstfruits was not the harvest itself, yet it represented more than simply a pledge and promise of the harvest. It was the actual beginning of the harvest. In the firstfruits the act of reaping had actually begun.

Jesus' resurrection, which gives men the warm confidence and hope of a future resurrection, is not an isolated event; it is the beginning of the eschatological resurrection itself. If we may use crude terms to try to describe sublime realities, we might say that a piece of the eschatologi-cal resurrection has been split off from the end and planted in history. An event belonging to the age to come has taken place in the midst of this age. The first act of the drama of the Last Day has taken place before the Day of the Lord.

The resurrection of Jesus is not simply an event in history. Nor should it be described simply as a supernatural event—a miracle, as though God had interfered with the "laws of nature." The resurrection of Jesus is no less than the appearance upon the historical, temporal scene of something which is eternal. Supernatural? Yes, but not in the usual sense. It is no "disturbance" of the normal course of events; it is the manifestation of something utterly new. Eternal life has appeared in the midst of mortality.

Two objections might be raised at this point. First, such an eschatological order of eternal life is impossible; and second, if there were such an order, *it could have no interaction with present historical existence.* If either of these propositions is true, then Paul's view of Jesus' resurrection is obviously untenable. But who would dare to assert either of these statements? And how could they be sustained? The only way we could be assured of an eschatological order of eternal life would be through God's revelation to us. This indeed is the heart of the biblical message: revelation of a life that men do not know but are invited to share. A man may choose not to believe the biblical revelation, of course; but simply to assert that such an order of life does not exist cannot cancel out the reality of its existence.

To assert that the world of eternal life can have nothing to do with present historical events is likewise to exceed one's rights. This assumes a philosophical presupposition that bifurcates the temporal and historical realm and that of the spiritual and eternal; but this assumption denies the fundamental character of the biblical witness. That the eternal has entered into time, the divine into the historical, the absolute into the relative, is both the glory and the offense of the Gospel. The heart of the biblical revelation is *Heilsgeschichte;* God has redemptively revealed Himself in the events of historical experience recorded in the Bible. The climax of this *Heilsgeschichte* is Jesus Christ; and the culminating event of the revelation in Christ is His resurrection. This event occurring in time and space embodies eternal, absolute significance. In this event death is defeated; in the midst of death and mortality are manifested life and immortality (II Tim. 1:10).

The fact that the resurrection is both an eschatological event and a bodily resurrection supremely attests the interrelatedness between the eschatological and the historical. Paul's insistence upon this fact explains in large measure the reason for his long discussion of the resurrection in I Corinthians. The Greeks had no trouble in accepting an immortality of the soul or a "resurrection" (that is, flight) of the spirit from the material world to a transcendent, spiritual realm. Hermetic and Gnostic literature reveals the Greek love of dualism, of two divergent orders of being, one of physical mortality and the other of spiritual immortality. The Greeks conceived of evil as the entanglement of the soul in the evil, material order; salvation meant disengaging the soul from its ensnarement in the material and returning it to the heavenly realm of immortal, spiritual existence.

If Paul had preached a Gospel simply of spiritual immortality he would not have offended the Greeks. It was his message of the resurrected body that disturbed the Greek mind (Acts 17:32). The problem in Corinth was not over the credibility of immortality and eternal life as

such, but whether this immortality manifests itself in terms of bodily
existence.

Paul sets forth his thought about the resurrection of the body in I
Corinthians 15:35-54. It can be summed up in two words: continuity
and discontinuity between the resurrection and the physical body. (The
relevance of this discussion to the nature of Jesus' resurrection rests on
the fact that Paul views the resurrection of believers to be of the same
order as the resurrection of Christ.) First, the resurrection will be a
bodily resurrection. This was the problem the Corinthians had to face.
They could conceive of an immortal life of the spirit, but they had no
experience of a body that could be immortal. Paul's answer is that there
are different kinds of bodies on earth and in heaven. The sun, moon
and stars are different kinds of bodies, reflecting differing degrees of
splendor. There are different kinds of flesh: of man, animals, birds, and
fish. Therefore there should be no problem in believing that God has
a body which will be adapted to the eschatological order of eternal life.

This resurrection body stands in continuity with the mortal physical
body. This Paul indicates in two passages. He illustrates the relationship
between the two bodies by the metaphor of sowing and reaping. From
a kernel of grain placed in the ground comes a new life. So the new
resurrection life is different, but it is not altogether different from that
of the physical body. A necessary relationship exists between the two,
as brought out in the antitheses of verses 42-43: perishable, imperishable;
dishonor, glory; weakness, power. If the *body* which was buried (sown)
in the grave is not raised, then these contrasts lose their meaning. Moreover, verse 44 shows that these contrasts refer to the *body:* "it is sown
[buried] a physical body, it is raised a spiritual body." It is the body not
the spirit or the soul which is buried and raised again.

But what is raised is not the *same* body that was buried. "What you
sow is not the body that is to be" (v. 37). The difference between the
two bodies is designated by the words "physical" and "spiritual" (v. 44).
Both words refer to bodies; but the spiritual body means the redemption
and transformation of the physical body (Rom. 8:23).

The meaning of "physical" and "spiritual" is crucial. Man's "physical"
(RSV) or "natural" (KJV) body is a *psychikon soma* to use the Greek
words, while *psyche* refers to the life or vitality of man. The English
word "soul" carries connotations not necessarily found in *psyche.* The
psychikon soma, therefore, is that *soma* of flesh and blood (v. 50) adapted
to the existence of this old order with its sin, decay, weakness and death.
Psychikon soma cannot mean a body made of *psyche,* but a body belonging to the *psychikon* order of existence. So by analogy, the *pneumatikon soma* is not a *soma* composed of *pneuma* or spirit. *Pneumatikon*
here refers to the Spirit of God, or rather to the new age in which the

life imparted by the life-giving Spirit will completely swallow up the weakness and decay and mortality of the *psychikon* order (II Cor. 5:4). God's Spirit, in other words, will be the animating power in resurrection. The resurrection of our mortal bodies will occur because the Holy Spirit, who now indwells us, will someday give them life (Rom. 8:11). The *pneumatikon soma* is the *soma* designed for that redeemed existence where God's people, raised from death and decay and weakness, in transformed bodies will enjoy the full meaning of eternal life. But this resurrection body belongs to a new and different order; it is the body of the age to come. The body of this present age may well be described as physical, that is, consisting of corruptible flesh and blood. We know its composition because we can analyze it. The body of the future age cannot be further defined so far as its composition is concerned; we must leave this to God. Paul says only that it is *not* flesh and blood (v. 50); it is not physical (*psychikon*: v. 44). He makes no positive statement as to its composition except to insist that it will be a real body.

This discussion of the nature of the believer's eschatological resurrection body is relevant for understanding the nature of Christ's resurrection body. As we have seen, Jesus' resurrection is the first phase of this eschatological resurrection; therefore His resurrection body must be of the same order as the resurrection bodies of the redeemed at the end of the age. He is the firstborn from the dead (Col. 1:18). But a problem here faces us: Do not the Gospel writers present a concept of Jesus' resurrection body entirely different from Paul's? Was not Jesus' body in fact a *physical* body with all the characteristics of the body which had died?

Actually the Gospels record two series of facts which witness to the same elements of continuity and discontinuity we found in Paul.

At great length the Gospels attest that Jesus' resurrection was indeed a bodily resurrection. The empty tomb finds its significance here. Many biblical critics reject the validity of the empty tomb on the ground that it is a later apologetic story designed to support belief in the resurrection. This objection overlooks the important fact that the Gospels nowhere use the empty tomb as an apologetic to prove the reality of the resurrection. The empty tomb in itself needed explanation. Mark records the first reaction of the women to the empty tomb (as well as to the message of the angels) as one of fear and astonishment. Luke tells of two disciples who knew of the empty tomb but refused to believe the resurrection until they were confronted by the risen Jesus (Luke 24:22 ff.). John relates that on the basis of the empty tomb Mary concluded that Jesus' body had been removed (John 20:2). It was not the empty tomb but the appearance of the grave clothes which aroused belief in John (John 20:6-8). Apart from the appearances of Jesus, the empty tomb was an enigma. The empty tomb, therefore, witnesses not so much to the fact of Jesus' resurrection as to the nature of that resurrection, namely, a bodily resurrection.

The bodily character of Jesus' resurrection is attested also in other ways. His body made an impression on the disciples' physical senses of touch (Matt. 28:9, John 20:17, 27), of sight and of hearing (John 20:16; Mary probably recognized Jesus by the tone of His voice when He spoke her name). Other elements at first seem to suggest that Jesus' body was a physical body. He Himself said, "a spirit has not flesh and bones as you see me have" (Luke 24:39). The context indicates, however, that no "scientific" analysis of the body is intended here; Jesus only meant to prove that He was not a disembodied spirit but possessed a real body. Paul also insists on the bodily nature of the resurrection. We ought therefore not to stress unduly the words "flesh and bones," in Luke 24: 39, assuming that they designate a body exactly like the physical body.

We know, too, that the resurrected Jesus was able to eat. He ate a piece of fish in the presence of His disciples (Luke 24:42, 43). However, the words "before them" (v. 43) would indicate that He did this to manifest the bodily nature of His resurrection. The inference cannot be drawn, therefore, of a physical body.

Several other facts refute such an assumption. If Jesus' body was physical, then it possessed powers never before experienced on earth. It had the amazing power, for example, to appear and disappear at will. On two occasions John records that Jesus suddenly appeared to His disciples, "the doors being shut" (John 20:19, 26); Jesus did not enter through an open door. *Although* the doors were shut, "Jesus came and stood among them" (v. 26). We read, too, that after breaking bread with the two Emmaus disciples, Jesus suddenly vanished out of their sight (Luke 24:31). When they returned to Jerusalem and were relating their experience, Jesus all at once stood among them. He came with such suddenness that they were startled, frightened, and supposed Him to be a spirit (Luke 24:36, 37). The resurrected body of Jesus possessed new and amazing powers; it seemed to belong to a different order of reality.

Furthermore, a close study of the text nowhere suggests that the stone before the tomb was rolled away to let Jesus out. The earthquake and rolling back of the stone are recorded by Matthew (28:2) not as the resurrection event itself but as signs of this wonderful event. Only one conclusion is possible: the body of Jesus was gone before the stone was rolled away. The stone needed not to be removed for Him to escape the tomb, for Jesus had already escaped it. Removal of the stone was intended for the disciples, not for Jesus.

These facts suggest a twofold conclusion: first, the resurrection of Jesus was a bodily resurrection, and second, His resurrection body possessed powers that transcended the usual physical limitations. While it could interact with the natural order, at the same time His resurrection body transcended this order. This witness of the Gospels is indeed essentially the same as Paul's. Jesus' resurrection belongs to a new and higher order of life, that of eternity, of the age to come. The Gospels emphasize one further fact, namely, the possibility of a real measure of interaction between the present physical order and that of the future "spiritual" order. The "spiritual" can manifest itself in terms of the "physical." We cannot know, however, that this was anything more than accommodation by Jesus to demonstrate the bodily reality of the resurrection.

V. THE RESURRECTION AND HISTORY

We come now to the most difficult problem of the resurrection as far as the modern man is concerned, the question of the resurrection and history. Can the resurrection of Jesus be called an "historical" event? The answer depends upon one's definition of history. If "history" designates all the events of the past, then the resurrection of Jesus is an historical event; it is an event which took place in time and place. However, this is not what "history" means to the modern historian. As a matter of fact, we do not have full access to all past events. We have only historical records, records that are fragmentary, fallible, and often self-contradictory. For the modern historian, then, "history" means a critical reconstruction of the events of the past.

No historian, no thoughtful person, for that matter, assumes that something happened simply because an ancient document says so. Ancient records are full of superstition, legend and mythology. Critical procedures are necessary, therefore, to sift out the factual and historical from the non-factual and legendary. "History" is not what is found in the records; it is, rather, the scholar's reconstruction after the historian has sifted and criticized the documents.

When the historian, *qua* historian, sifts the Gospel records by these same critical procedures, he reaches a negative conclusion about the historicity of the resurrection. Entirely apart from the question of possible legendary accretions is the fundamental question of the resurrection fact itself. In analyzing the ancient records and trying to reconstruct the events of the past, the historian makes use of the basic principles of continuity and analogy. By continuity he means that historical experience is an unbroken flow of interacting events; all historical events must be produced by historical causes. Sometimes, of course, the causes are so complex and tangled they cannot be unraveled. To meet this situation, various theories are projected in order to postulate the best solution. Often the sources of information are too inadequate to permit recreating the actual course of events. In such instances, help may be found in studying analogous events; clues from the known may be applied to the unknown.

If our analysis of the nature of Jesus' resurrection is correct, then historical criticism must come to an impasse in its study of this event, for Jesus' resurrection has neither historical causation nor analogy. It is an event which occurred *in* history—in time and space; its cause, however, is not historical, but supra-historical, that is, God. Further, it has no analogy. Lazarus' resurrection is not analogous, for it was really a re-vivification, that is, a return to physical life that must again die. Jesus' resurrection, on the other hand, issued in a never-ending life. Ascended to heaven, Jesus still lives today in His resurrected body; Lazarus, however, died and was buried. Lazarus could never say, as did Jesus, "I am the resurrection and the life . . . because I live you shall live also."

Technically speaking in the sense of modern historical terms, Jesus' resurrection cannot be called an "historical" event, for it does not mean a restoration to earthly life, but the *appearance within history of eternal life, a new mode of existence.* To someone unaccustomed to the method of historical thinking, the above statement may be an offense, for it may appear to deny the *factuality* of the resurrection within history. We would emphasize, then, that the resurrection is an objective event which took place *within history;* but, in the modern definition of the term, it is not an "historical" but a supra-historical event. It is the demonstration within history that the ultimate goal of God's people is "beyond history" in a new and redeemed order in the age to come where the present observable "laws" of life, growth, decay and death are transcended. Christ's resurrection means that God has displayed in this age a glimpse of what the nature of life will be in the age to come.

That there *can* be such a transcendent realm no one can successfully deny. One may profess skepticism, of course. But to deny such a realm involves denying something of which there is no human knowledge. And by definition one can deny only that for which there is a reasonable basis for knowledge. What may be above history or beyond history is a matter of faith, not of historical knowledge.

The "modern man" finds Jesus' resurrection a problem because the New Testament pictures transcendent life emerging within history, something which violates his concept of history. This is Rudolf Bultmann's problem. He labels such ideas mythological. Mythology for Bultmann is "the use of imagery to express the otherworldly in terms of this world and the divine in terms of human life, the other side in terms of this side" (Rudolf Bultmann, *Kerygma and Myth,* p. 10). In other words, mythology is language used to describe the alleged action of God within history. We can take time only to point out the underlying philosophical presupposition of this approach, namely, that the realm of God and the realm of human history are two separate entities which do not and cannot interact. The realm of God's activity is that of individual existence, not history. To speak of God acting in history, then, must be understood as mythological language, something which the modern man no longer accepts. Bultmann accordingly refuses to understand the resurrection of Christ as an event in history which happened on that first Easter Sunday. For Bultmann the resurrection of Jesus takes place in the kerygma, in the preaching of the Gospel. This means that in the kerygma Jesus is actually present. All speculations about the risen one's mode of existence, all stories about the empty tomb, and so on, are simply irrelevant to the reality of the resurrection as it relates to Christian preaching and my response to it (see Rudolf Bultmann, *Das Verhältnis der urchristlichen Christusbotschaft zum historischen Jesus*, p. 27).

Oscar Cullmann has called the modern "offense of the Gospel" the fact that the Bible pictures revelation as occurring in historical events. The fundamental question is not the nature of history but the nature of God. Can God act in historical events? Can God act in "non-historical" or better, in "supra-historical" events within the stream of history? Who is to say God cannot so act? The biblical story of redemptive history makes both revelation and redemption inseparable from such acts. It is in these supra-historical events that the redemptive acts have taken place. If Bultmann prefers the term "mythological" to distinguish the nature of such events from "historical" events which are entirely capable of explanation in terms of causality and analogy, well and good. We will not choke over a word. But to deny that such "mythological" events can actually occur within the stream of history is something else; to this we must object. Such a denial violates the very nature of biblical revelation and redemption. To bifurcate completely the world of history and the realm of God is unnecessary and unbiblical. That God, the Transcendent One, acts in historical events is of the essence of Christian faith.

The question now comes, if Jesus' resurrection is not an "historical" event but is supra-historical, can it be established and known by historical reconstruction and methodology? The answer would seem to be "No." How can one "prove" the supra-historical by historical means even though the supra-historical has appeared within history? Even though they could be established, historical proofs cannot compel faith, for faith comes by hearing, and hearing by the Word of God (Rom. 10:17). If historical proofs were the way to saving faith, the main business of the Church would not be to preach the Gospel in the power of the Holy Spirit but to prove the resurrection as an "historical" event. When this proof should finally be adduced, then all who read the evidence would easily be brought to salvation. This, however, is obviously not the way. Historical proofs have to do with the mind and critical reason; faith has to do with the whole man. We do not mean that faith is divorced from reason, for faith works through reason or in alliance with it. The complete divorce of the realms of reason and faith is another erroneous philosophical assumption of many modern men. But a complete identification of the two is equally wrong. Convincing the mind does not automatically mean commitment of the will. Intellectual proof does not necessarily lead to saving faith, although in some instances it does. Saving faith comes through the working of the Holy Spirit upon man's heart, his mind, and his will. The Holy Spirit may use intellectual proofs to bring about faith or he may use a simple proclamation of the Word, as illustrated even in New Testament times. In Athens, according to Acts 17:18, 31, Paul proclaimed the resurrection; but in I Corinthians 15:3-7 he cites witnesses to establish the fact of the resurrection, as even Bultmann recognizes (*Kerygma and Myth,* p. 39). Paul, however, is not here trying to prove the resurrection in order to bring men to faith in Christ. He is trying, rather, to convince believers of the fact of *bodily* resurrection, and names witnesses who can establish that the nature of Jesus' resurrection body is one which could actually be witnessed by mortal men.

Does it follow, then, that the resurrection of Jesus belongs to the realm of faith rather than of history? Can the resurrection be known only by faith rather than by historical evidences? The answer cannot be a simple yes or no, for God's redemptive acts involve events which, while they have occurred within history, yet contain meanings that transcend history. Insofar as an event is "historical," it can be established historically. When an historical event embodies a supra-historical meaning or significance, the latter can be known only by faith. But what can be said of an event which occurs within history but whose nature itself, like the resurrection, is supra-historical? We must conclude that such an event can be accepted only by faith, faith created by the Holy Spirit who uses historical witnesses. Evidences are not proofs which compel faith, but are instruments used by the Spirit to elicit faith.

If this thinking is correct, does it not follow that the faith of the first disciples was created by the Holy Spirit and not by the objective fact of the resurrection? This conclusion overlooks the very important fact that the disciples stood in a different relationship to the resurrection event than we do. They were in a position to experience the objective fact directly and thereby be brought to faith. We cannot do this. We cannot experience what they experienced. We are dependent upon witnesses. Furthermore, the modern man thinks in "historical" terms which are alien to the disciples. We must therefore analyze the problem in different categories than did the early Christians.

We are convinced that the only adequate and intelligible explanation for the disciples' resurrection faith is the fact of an objective bodily resurrection. We are further convinced that if one could evaluate all the possible "hypotheses" to find the one that best explains the rise of the resurrection faith, it would be that an objective bodily resurrection occurred. This would be a legitimate use of the inductive "scientific" method of testing hypotheses and accepting the one which best accounts for the most facts. However, the modern critical historian excludes this very possibility by his idea of what constitutes "historical" reality. He closes his mind to the possible hypothesis of an objective bodily resurrection. This is why we appeal to a different dimension, to that of faith. Faith does not have to do only with subjective "spiritual" realities; faith is the Spirit-imparted ability to recognize divine meanings in historical events, and also to recognize within history divine acts whose character transcends ordinary historical explanation. Such faith involves personal commitment. It is no mere rationalism. To believe in one's heart that God has raised Jesus from the dead is inseparably linked with confession of Jesus as Lord (Rom. 10:9) and with one's personal salvation. Not the understanding alone but the whole man is involved in such an act of faith.

It is often said that the resurrected Jesus appeared only to believers, and this statement is used to support the theory of the subjective nature of the appearances. The fact is, however, that the disciples were not *believers in the resurrection* until after something happened to create their faith. Furthermore, there is not the slightest evidence that James was a believer of any sort until Jesus appeared to him (I Cor. 15:7). Paul places himself among those who had seen the resurrected Lord, and who was brought to faith through this appearance.

To say that the resurrection can be accepted only by faith does not mean, therefore, that the resurrection is cut loose from history and relegated altogether to the realm of the subjective. Faith indeed belongs to the soul of man; but faith is reposed not alone in the invisible God but in the God who acts in history, in the God who raised Jesus from the dead. Thus faith, while not identical with historical proofs, nor dependent upon historical proofs, must be consistent with the historical evidences. While the facts of history do not compel faith, they are nonetheless relevant to faith.

Thus the early Church bore witness to the resurrection as an event which occurred in recent history, and this witness the Holy Spirit used to bring men to faith. Sometimes there is mere proclamation and witness; sometimes, as in I Corinthians 15:3-8, there is an appeal to evidences. We conclude, therefore, that the resurrection of Christ is a supra-historical event which took place within history. While it can be accepted and known only by faith which is engendered by the Holy Spirit through the proclamation of the Word, this proclamation makes use of historical evidences, for it proclaims an act of God in history for man's redemption.

VI. THE EFFECTS OF THE RESURRECTION

In conclusion we briefly mention a twofold effect of Christ's resurrection: present spiritual life and future bodily resurrection. The business of the Church is not that of proving *historically* the factualness of the resurrection; rather, it is that of proclaiming the resurrection that men may be brought into the experience of resurrection life. Since the resurrection occurred within history, however, it must be consistent with the "historical" events which can be established. The resurrection itself means that a new order of life—eternal life, the life of the age to come—has emerged within history. Jesus who rose from the dead outside of Jerusalem on Easter Sunday morning is still the Risen One who is on the "heavenward" side of the first act of the eschatological resurrection. Therefore we may even now, in this present evil age (Gal. 1:4), experience resurrection life, which is the life of the age to come. This is the meaning of dying and rising with Christ (Romans 6), of being raised from death into life (Ephesians 2), of knowing the power of His resurrection (Phil. 3:10). The Christian community is therefore an island of life in a world engulfed in death. It is itself a witness to the fact of eternal life. It should be displaying to dying men what it means to live, to be alive. It should ever embody in this death-beset age the life and powers of the age to come. The very character of the Christian community, if it displays the life which brought it into being, should beckon men to turn from death to find the life of the new age.

But this is not all. Even though the living Christ indwells us so that we are spiritually alive, yet our bodies are still dying (Rom. 8:10). As we have said, the resurrection life of Christ is experienced by believers in this age in the realm of the spirit; but, "if the Spirit of him who raised Jesus from the dead dwells in you, he who raised Christ Jesus from the dead will give life to your mortal bodies also through his Spirit which dwells in you" (Rom. 8:11). The bodily resurrection of Christ is the pledge also of the bodily resurrection of believers. Yet it is more than a pledge. It is, as we have seen, the "firstfruits," the first act of the eschatological fact of resurrection. Here is the ground of Christian hope.

This means that God is concerned not merely with man's soul but with his whole being. Bultmann is right in saying that the New Testament conceives of full human existence only in terms of bodily existence (*Theology of the New Testament,* New York, Charles Scribner's Sons, 1951, Vol. I, p. 195). If this is true, then redemption must include the redemption of the body as well as of the soul, or there is no hope for human immortality in biblical terms. Paul holds out the hope of such bodily redemption.

Christ's resurrection is the climax in Christian revelation. It tells us that the God who stands above history acts in history. It proclaims that God has acted in history to defeat the powers of decay and death which blight historical existence. It demonstrates that God has released a new life and power within history which transcends history even while operating within it; this new life, moreover, will someday deliver the whole historical process from the curse of decay and death and lift it to a level of existence beyond all present knowledge and imagination.

THE HOLY SPIRIT

✝

Robert Paul Roth

Robert Paul Roth is Professor of Systematic Theology at Northwestern Lutheran Theological Seminary, Minneapolis. He served as Professor in Luthergiri Seminary, Rajahmundry, India, in 1947-48; then as Professor of Philosophy in Augustana College; and in 1953 became Professor of New Testament and Dean of the Graduate School of Southern Lutheran Seminary in Columbia, South Carolina, serving there until 1961. He holds the M.A. degree from University of Illinois, B.D. from Northwestern Lutheran Seminary, and Ph.D. from University of Chicago.

14. Robert Paul Roth

THE HOLY SPIRIT

CHRISTIAN theology has regarded the Holy Spirit as the source and giver of life, the communicator of revealed truth, and the comforting helper and guide to loving conduct. It has been the work of the Holy Spirit not only to participate with the Word in creation but also in redemption. In this dual function the Spirit reveals both the nature of God and the nature and destiny of man. God acts as free, purposive person. We know ourselves as persons only because through the Holy Spirit we see ourselves in the image of the divine person. Contemporary theology has sometimes lost this biblical understanding either by seeking to know God on the model of impersonal force or by constructing God in the image of subjective human experience. A recovery of the full scriptural dimension in the theology of the Spirit will alert us to the presence of that person in the Godhead whose work is radical and sustaining, spontaneous and comforting, mysterious and revealing. A review of the teaching of the Spirit in both Testaments and in the history of the Church will aid in this recovery.

I. THE SPIRIT IN THE OLD TESTAMENT

To speak of the Holy Spirit in the Old Testament in the traditional Trinitarian sense immediately raises a serious question. How can we develop a doctrine of the Spirit from the religious legacy given to us in a body of literature that was used for centuries by a people who did not themselves develop such a doctrine? Why does the Jew read the Old Testament and remain unitarian in his concept of God? The answer must be in the new and special revelation which came after the Old Testament was compiled in the historical advent of Jesus of Nazareth. In the first place it must be shown that Jesus is the fulfillment of all that is fundamentally promised in the Old Testament. Only in this way can we read the Old Testament without falling into the error of gratuitousness. In the second place it must be shown that the same Spirit who was present in various ways throughout Israel's history is the agent who makes possible the Church's confession that Jesus of Nazareth is Christ and Lord. Here again we must not beg the question of the Trinitarian teaching in the New Testament, but we must clearly demonstrate that the revelation of Christ given us in the New Testament necessarily requires a personal view of the Spirit without denying basic monotheism.

We are saying that the confession of Jesus Christ as God and Saviour ineluctably involves the person of the Spirit in a relationship of equality with the Father and the Son. Our concern is not to develop a doctrine of the Trinity. This would go beyond the scope of this essay. Our concern is rather to present a biblical view of the Spirit, and to show that inasmuch as this view is personal a Trinitarian Godhead is implicit. To say that the Holy Spirit is a person in Trinity is to say that God is three in one. Given the Aristotelian categories of substance and accidents as basis for the Trinitarian formula, the statement that God is three in one gets into logical difficulties. If there are three substances they cannot be one substance. If Father is God and Son is God and Spirit is God, then Father, Son, and Spirit must be the same substance. But what is the difference between the three? The early church fathers devised the term "person" for this distinction. In Latin the word "person" means mask or face (Greek: *prosopon*). Does this mean that God is Father when He shows His Father-face and Son when He shows us the face of Christ? But how does this avoid modalism, the view that the Trinity is three modes of the one divine being? If a mode is an accidental property of a substance, it immediately becomes objectionable to say that the Father or Christ or the Spirit are accidental modes of God's being. Yet to say that the Father or Christ or the Spirit are persons in the modern sense of discrete, independent beings results in tri-theism. In order to avoid these logical difficulties, which stem only from definitions, perhaps it would be better to drop the Aristotelian categories and recognize the ultimate mystery of the Trinity as a fact of God experienced as a datum of salvation history.

"God is one" means, among other things, that He is unique. We wish to say that there is a God who has no equal in degree or kind, and of this God we may say meaningfully that He exists in three personal distinctions. But the term "person" as applied to the Godhead originally meant something quite different from what it has come to mean in modern usage. Exactly what it means to say that God is personal, or specifically that the Holy Spirit is a person of the Godhead, is the problem of this essay. We shall see that theologians expounding the doctrine of the Spirit have not always made it clear whether the Spirit is an animistic being or a dynamic force; whether the Spirit is an abiding presence or a special agent with intermittent functions; whether the Spirit is a distinct person in a "social Trinity" or a different face in a functional Trinity, whether the Spirit is objectively an aspect of God or subjectively the avenue of human response to God. Perhaps we shall not be able to answer all these questions, but it should be possible to discover what it means to speak of the divine person of the Spirit by examining what He does. Only by recognizing the personal nature of the Spirit can we understand the gift of the Spirit, for this is not a thing but the action of a person.

1. The Spirit is the Agent of God in Creation.

Genesis 1:2 says: "The earth was without form and void, and darkness was upon the face of the deep; and the Spirit of God was moving over the face of the waters." Immediately following in verse three we read: "And God said, 'Let there be light.'" C. K. Barrett says, "The *ruach elohim* was, along with the creative speech of God, the agent by which the present existing world was brought out of the inchoate primeval waste" (*The Holy Spirit and the Gospel Tradition*, London, S.P.C.K., 1954, p. 18). Spirit and Word are both agents of creation. The Hebrew word *merachepheth*, moving, suggests the brooding of a bird, but not, as in pagan mythology, over a primeval world-egg from which proceeded earth, sky, sun and moon. This implies that the germ of life was already in the egg. The biblical idea is that the abyss over which the Spirit broods is not potential life but chaos. The life is not in the chaos, or better, the void, the emptiness; it is in the Spirit.

In addition to the fact that the Spirit is the source of life and creativity and as such suggests personal power, the use of the word *ruach* has significant personal connotations. While the Greek word *pneuma* is neuter, the Hebrew word is feminine and in its most primitive usage means *breath*. Its use to designate wind seems to derive from animistic and anthropomorphic origins. If this is so a similar origin for its use to describe the agent of creation cannot be denied. Since all language about God and His work must ultimately be metaphorical it is to be expected that we should find an anthropomorphism here, but the fact that the word *breath* was chosen indicates a concern for a vital principle, for without breath there is no life. This alone would not affirm a personal quality for Spirit, but when the life-giving function of Spirit is coupled so intimately with the form-giving function of the Word as a single act of creation at least the beginning of a notion of a personal Spirit can be affirmed.

2. The Spirit is the Indwelling Power of Elect Men of God

In primitive Israelitic times certain heroes are described as being chosen for their special tasks because the Spirit of God dwells within them. Joseph is chosen by Pharaoh to be the prime minister of Egypt for this reason (Gen. 41:38). Moses selected Joshua because he was a man of the

Spirit (Num. 27:18). The Spirit of the Lord appears frequently in the book of Judges energizing men for heroic deeds of strength and cunning. When we come to the early schools of the prophets in the tenth century we find them claiming that their inspiration is due to the coming of the Spirit of the Lord upon them. Saul is described as being numbered among the prophets because the Spirit takes possession of him (I Sam. 10:5-13; 19:23, 24). When he is seized by the Spirit he falls into a trance, sheds his garments, and engages in a feverish dance. A pattern for the Spirit's activity seems to have been established, not unlike that which is still imitated by the whirling dervishes of Muslim mystic sects. The form of the ecstasy became an end in itself with the prophet deliberately seeking to lose himself so as to gain the psychic energy of the infused Spirit (Arnold B. Come, *Human Spirit and Holy Spirit,* Philadelphia, The Westminster Press, 1959, p. 126).

Perhaps it was precisely this attempt to control the Spirit which brought about the remarkable shift in Israel's history away from emphasis upon the Spirit to a less than warm proclamation of the Word. Although the activity of the Spirit was always unpredictable, from the beginning its sporadic manifestations could be seen to follow a meaningful purpose in the direction of a responsible goal. Such purposefulness is the mark of a person. When the divine purpose was violated by men who sought to manipulate spiritual energy according to repeatable patterns, the withdrawal of the Spirit was inevitable.

3. The Later Major Prophets Came with the "Word of the Lord" Rather Than the "Spirit of the Lord"

It has been observed that the newer prophets of the eighth and seventh centuries deliberately dissociated themselves from the earlier ecstatic prophets. In time the formula, "The word of the Lord came ...," replaced the older formula, "The Spirit of the Lord came...." (*ibid.,* p. 127). This was not because they depreciated the Spirit, nor because they thought themselves less capable of speaking prophetically to Israel. On the one hand they rejected the professionalism of the ecstatic mystics, and on the other hand because of their reverent knowledge of the Spirit they knew that they could not speak in His name. The Spirit was the presence of holiness. They knew this holiness was lacking in Israel. Not only was it lacking in the people as a nation but it was lacking also in the prophets themselves who were part of the corporate personality of Israel. Just as Israel had a solidarity in its destiny for holiness so also it had a solidarity in sin, and the prophets from Amos to Habakkuk conceived it to be their mission to bring a word of judgment upon this sin. Never was this icy condemnation without the warmth of promise in the background, but the sin of the people in confrontation with a holy God demanded stern speech.

4. Isaiah 40-66 Indicates the Return of the Spirit

In that portion of Isaiah which is commonly called Deutero-Isaiah the picture of a bereft nation is drawn against an uplifting promise of the return of the Spirit. The prophet recalls the old days under Moses when the Lord gave life and strength to Israel with His Spirit. Because Israel has rebelled, however, and become an enemy to God, the Lord must send His Word of judgment. Nevertheless God is gracious and He will comfort His people again with His Holy Spirit (Isa. 42:1; 61:1). Here is the history of salvation. The Spirit is the person of God who comes to comfort the creatures He gave life. Salvation is a purposive drama of cosmic dimensions played out upon a stage of linear time with a future eschatology. In the beginning the Spirit gave life. When in the course of time this life was spoiled, however mysterious the entrance of the spoiler, the work of the Spirit was to restore this life. Since there is no life without holiness, it is recognized that where holiness is absent there also the Spirit is absent. Salvation history then becomes the work of God in restoring holiness through the comfort (strengthening) of His Holy Spirit.

5. The Diverse Views of the Spirit in the Old Testament are Resolved Only in Personal Terms

In conclusion we may make the following observations. In the Old Testament the Spirit is the extraordinary and abnormal work of God, yet throughout the history of the covenant people we must recognize the universal presence of God in His Spirit. Israel is a people in whom the Spirit dwells. Although the Spirit occasionally acts in a wonderful way upon certain individuals, nevertheless. He is present at all times undergirding and strengthening the corporate life of Israel such that even their craftsmanship is acknowledged to be a gift of the Spirit (Exod. 31:1-5; 35:31). And in spite of this presence of the Spirit in things great and small we find stormy prophets reminding the people that the Spirit has left them. Furthermore the Spirit is the *presence* by which Israel lives currently, and yet under the guidance of the prophets and seers all the people look to the future when in the Day of the Messiah there will be a comforting outpouring of the Holy Spirit.

All these apparent contradictions can be understood only if we grant that the Holy Spirit is purposive, acting toward His creatures always in a personal way. He speaks, guides, gives gifts, abides as a comforting presence, comes as a future solace. None of these activities can be ascribed to an impersonal force. Their very contradictoriness is the mark of the mystery of the Person. A person comes and goes and cannot be mechanically controlled. His behavior is unpredictable and yet he can be seen to pursue a purposive goal. The Spirit of the Lord is such a Person working mysteriously and purposively in the drama of salvation.

II. THE SPIRIT IN THE NEW TESTAMENT

Compared with the numerous references to the Holy Spirit at Pentecost, in the life of the early Church, and in the letters of Paul, the Gospels say very little about the Spirit. Significantly the Spirit does figure in the Gospel narratives, however, in connection with (*1*) Jesus' birth, (*2*) His baptism, (*3*) His temptation and conflict with evil powers, and (*4*) His teaching of the Spirit as Paraclete.

1. The Spirit at Jesus' Birth

After centuries of a seeming dearth of the Spirit, suddenly at the birth of Jesus there is an abundant outpouring of His gifts and power. Zechariah is told by the angel of the Lord that he will have a son who will be filled with the Holy Spirit (Luke 1:15). Elizabeth was filled with the Spirit at the occasion of Mary's visit after the annunciation (Luke 1:41). Simeon was inspired by the Spirit when he came into the temple and recognized the child Jesus to be the long expected Christ (Luke 2:27). John grew and became strong in the Spirit as his father had prophesied under the power of the Spirit (Luke 1:67; 1:80). But especially wonderful is the presence of the Spirit at the conception of Jesus (Matt. 1:18, 20; Luke 1:35). Mary was found to be with child of the Holy Spirit. The Spirit came upon her and she was overshadowed by His power. Interestingly the same Greek word for overshadow (*episkiasei*) is again used by Luke to describe the Transfiguration experience of the disciples: "A cloud came and overshadowed them" (Luke 9:34). And as they were overshadowed a voice came out of the cloud, indicating the intimate connection between the revelatory activity of the Word and the power of the Spirit. That these two functions of the divine will should be found together in the advent of Jesus is of great importance, as we shall see, for our understanding of the virgin birth.

What is the meaning of the Spirit's activity in this conception of Jesus? Although there is no parallel instance of a virgin birth in the Old Testament it is clear that Matthew saw it as a fulfillment of Old Testament prophecy (Matt. 1:23 quoting Isa. 7:14). Moreover there is no comparable example of such a birth in pagan literature. In all the stories of miraculous births in Hellenistic and Oriental religious lore, impregnation is by some physical act of a snake or a thunderbolt or a stream of gold (Arnold Toynbee, *A Study of History*, Vol. VII, London, Oxford University Press, 1948-61). The utter uniqueness of this birth can be understood therefore only as the prophetic fulfillment of an activity already adumbrated in the Old Testament. This activity is nothing less than God's work as *Spiritus Creator*. The New Testament proclamation of the virgin birth is related to the Old Testament declaration of creation *ex nihilo* in which both Spirit and Word shared. Just as the Spirit was active at the foundation of the world, so the Spirit is declared to be active at its renewal. The entry of the Redeemer into the world to effect a new creation is seen to be the creative work of the Spirit, hence the birth of Jesus was recognized in this same faith to be by the over-shadowing power of the Spirit. Jesus' birth marks a new act of creation: "Unless one is born of water and the Spirit, he cannot enter the kingdom of God" (John 3:5). When the Word became flesh in Jesus for the purpose of recapitulating or restoring a lost creation, that which was holy took upon Himself that which was sinful. A sinner did not rise up to holiness, shedding his iniquity by the merit of his obedience, but rather the holy one of God cast aside His glory and assumed our sin. This coming of holiness into sinful flesh to effect a new creation is the work of the Spirit bringing God into the womb of Mary as a creative act itself and for the purpose of inaugurating a new creation of the entire cosmos.

2. *The Spirit at Jesus' Baptism*

The presence of the Spirit at the baptism of Jesus confirms what we have said about the work of the Spirit at His birth because here in the beginning of His public ministry the Spirit descends along with the un-leashing of the prophetic voice and the creation of the new kingdom is begun. The descent of the Spirit in the form of a dove is somewhat enig-matic to some scholars because it seems like a pagan notion. Bultmann argues that this report is a Hellenistic intrusion, that the Gospel accounts of the baptism are partially demythologized relics of Hellenistic traditions which are more purely preserved in the apocryphal Gospel of the Ebionites and the Gospel of the Hebrews (Rudolf Bultmann, *Theology of the New Testament*, Vol. I, New York, Charles Scribner's Sons, 1955, p. 131. Cf. also Rudolf Bultmann, *Primitive Christianity*, New York, Living Age, 1956, p. 197). The argument is easily refuted, however, when it is recognized that the Gospels cannot be interpreted by literature which is demonstrably later in origin (C. K. Barrett, *op. cit.*, p. 37).

It is quite clear that the work of John the Baptizer was Messianic because he was killed by Herod for being the leader of a revolutionary Messianism. And if John's baptism was Messianic we can understand that when Jesus submitted to it He understood it as the fulfillment of what John expected and prepared for. This was certainly a Semitic Messianism and not a Hellenistic folk myth. The connection between the Messianic Sonship and the descent of the dove may now be established inasmuch as the voice of heaven (*bath qol*) addresses Jesus as the Son of God in virtue of this installation as Messiah. The Messianic office involves the personal endowment of the Holy Spirit which it was believed would be poured out in the last days. The voice of the prophets had been stilled and the rabbis had to hear the *bath qol* only indirectly as the chirping of a bird or the moaning of a dove. But now this dove descends and the voice that is heard is a direct allusion to the prophetic word of Isaiah 42. Thus Jesus is elevated from the category of the rabbis to the level and authority of the prophets.

3. Jesus' Conflict with Evil Spirits

Next we read that in withstanding His temptation in the wilderness Jesus was led by the Spirit. Furthermore He vanquished the power of evil by the power of the Spirit: "But if it is by the Spirit of God that I cast out demons, then the kingdom of God has come upon you" (Matt. 12:28). Strangely when the demons recognize Jesus as Messiah He charges them to secrecy, as He does also with His disciples. This is because as a pneumatic person Jesus ran the danger of being put in the category of a charismatic healer along with others who performed similar miracles. Once His ministry was acknowledged to be Messianic the exorcisms take on great significance because they indicate that Jesus brings spiritual power to subdue the empire of the Adversary. The work of the Spirit is thus ambiguous. It was not simply a means of revealing Jesus' Messiahship; it was rather at the same time a revealment and a concealment. Hence we find at this point a characteristic mark of the Spirit which has major significance: He is a mystery who works to reveal through concealment. In the exorcisms some saw merely the magic of a thaumaturge and they were hardened against Jesus. Others who possessed the mystery of the Spirit could understand the true Messianic significance, but flesh and blood did not reveal it to them (Matt. 16:17).

4. The Spirit as Paraclete

Jesus re-established the voice of prophecy. He was the incarnate Word and the Word had spoken by the Spirit in the prophets. Like the prophets Jesus spoke with authority. He spoke in poetic form. He spoke with pneumatic traits such as were associated with visions of the prophets. He uttered predictions concerning His death and His return. He performed symbolic actions and dramatic parables as at the Last Supper. His eschatological teaching was of a radically ethical nature as in the prophets. He announced the reign of God as a preacher of repentance such that to accept Him is to accept God and to reject Him is to reject God. He not only declared the divine Word but He fulfilled that Word in Himself through His special mission to Israel. In all these respects Jesus was sent as a prophet, yet He does not speak of Himself as a profit. Again, as in the case of the miracles, the Spirit of prophecy is kept secret. Just as the miracles were ambiguous signs so the prophetic teaching of Jesus was a revelation in mystery, and all this is due to the nature of the Spirit which is both hidden and revealed. Sometimes Jesus is moved by human suffering compassionately to perform miracles as signs of the power of the Spirit which rests upon Him. At other times He sharply refuses to give signs. Sometimes His words are a saving comfort and at other times men fall away because His sayings are too hard. What He says and does shows forth a power (*dunamis*) which is available to all who see and hear, but the authority (*exousia*) for what He says and does is not openly manifest and is acknowledged only in the presence of the Spirit. The *dunamis* is thus the anticipated power of the Spirit but not the naked Spirit unimpeded by the veil of human and worldly relativity. Jesus was the Messiah, but He was not in any obvious sense identifiable with the end of the world as the Messiah was expected to be. Hence the paradox: the authority was there but always concealed. As Messiah Jesus was the bearer of the Spirit, but He kept His Messiahship secret because it was to be a Messiahship of suffering and death which only the Spirit could reveal to be a glorification of God. Openly He was a scandal, but secretly in the Spirit He was the glory of God.

What Jesus said and did was therefore not in His own authority as a man of Nazareth but in the authority of the Spirit sent from the Father. Thus He could distinguish Himself from the Spirit and speak of sending this Spirit after He is gone. In both the so-called Q source and in John we read of Jesus consoling His disciples with the promise of the Spirit as a friend who comes alongside to help (*paraklētos*) in time of persecution and when guidance is needed (Luke 12:12; John 16:7).

5. *The Spirit at Pentecost and in the Early Church*

At the resurrection of Jesus and especially after His ascension, as Jesus had promised, the presence of the Spirit was experienced in many remarkable ways by those whom He called. There was after Pentecost the warm, quickening, unifying *koinōnia* in the worshiping community of the earliest Christians. This communion and fellowship bound them together because they now knew themselves to be participants in the active passion of Christ's love for sinners. They lived by the same authority of the Spirit which authenticated His mission, and consequently they could perform the same kind of miracles. They gave expression to their conviction that the Spirit was present in the ritual gesture of the laying on of hands which had always been a sign of blessing and authority. Now they coupled the laying on of hands with water baptism because they recognized that something more than repentance and cleansing was taking place. As John had prophesied, with the coming of Jesus came also a baptism of fire and the Spirit, a regenerating baptism which brought the elect, through death to their old sinful natures, into a new life in the Spirit. The laying on of hands was not limited by any means to baptism, for the presence of the Spirit was affirmed at the commissioning of missionaries, at the healing of the sick, and at services of worship. Sometimes the Spirit was manifest in the peculiar phenomenon called speaking with tongues. Other times the Spirit was acknowledged in the prayers and prophetic preaching. The Spirit guided the missionary work of Paul, holding him back here and pushing him forward there. It is the Spirit that makes the living tradition which is the Church.

6. The Spirit in Paul's Writings

Paul speaks sometimes of the gifts of the Spirit and sometimes of the power of the Spirit, both of which appear at first to be mechanistic and impersonal.

When Paul speaks of the gifts of the Spirit it has been argued that the *Spirit* is personal but the *gifts* are a substantial grace which may be appropriated through the sacramental apparatus of the Church. This indeed is the interpretation which Augustine gave to Romans 5:5: "The love of God is infused into our hearts by the Holy Spirit." The Greek word *ékkechutai* was translated in the Vulgate by the Latin words *infusa est*, which conveyed the meaning that the Holy Spirit is the giver of spiritual substances which by sacramental infusion complete our being. From this was derived the famous motto that grace does not destroy nature but perfects it. Augustine took his cue from Socrates who had defined love (*erōs*) as the child of Want and Plenty. We find ourselves in existence to be empty, desiring to be filled. Being not yet real we strive for completion of our being. Being not yet good we strive for perfection. Hence love is the impulse within us to be filled with being and goodness.

Augustine defined *caritas* in terms of this Socratic love of divine reality and perfection. He distinguished *caritas* from *cupiditas* which is the lust for earthly unreality and evil. Thus when he read in Paul of the love shed abroad by the Holy Spirit, he thought of this love as a substantial gift which completes an otherwise imperfect nature.

But Paul nowhere speaks of Socratic love. The word he uses is *agapē*, and it means God's sacrificial, suffering love for sinners. Quite the opposite of seeking fulfillment, *agapē* "seeks not her own" (I Cor. 13:5). Furthermore this love is shed abroad and not infused. Grace is *favor dei*, not spiritual substance (Regin Prenter, *Spiritus Creator*, Philadelphia, Muhlenberg Press, 1953, p. 32). This means that the gift of the Holy Spirit is not a thing that can be mechanistically imparted through a structured sacrament. The gift of the Spirit is not a thing at all, but God's sacramental presence sealed by the elements (*arrabōn*) by which He brings the risen Lord Christ whom we celebrate with joy and thanksgiving (Eph. 1:13).

It is also through His personal presence, not by an impersonal gift, that the Spirit gives us access to God (*prosagōgē*) both through prayer and by the adoption of sons (Rom. 8:16; Gal. 4:6). Moreover, the gift of ordination in the ministry, as in the case of Timothy, must be understood as the personal presence of the Spirit charging him with a task to perform rather than the bestowal of an indelible, substantial character (I Tim. 4:14). And the equipment with which every Christian walks in righteousness (*dikaiosunē*) must be seen as the personal guidance of the Spirit. Qualities such as love, joy, patience, endurance, hope, faithfulness, gentleness, self-control (Gal. 5:22, 23; Rom. 5:4, 5) might easily be interpreted abstractly as substantial gifts of virtue, but when seen alongside the Spirit's gifts of freedom and life (Rom. 8:2, 11) it becomes clear that the Spirit for Paul is truly the Paraclete who walks alongside us and helps us to do works of love, joy, patience and the like.

A mechanistic view of the Spirit could still be maintained if He were understood as the source of energy rather than the giver of substances. The dynamism of the Spirit is amply illustrated in the teaching of Paul. The Spirit is the power that saves us in worship (Phil. 3:3), that unifies the Church (I Cor. 12:4), that guards and inspires our confession of faith (I Cor. 12:3), that guides our decisions (I Cor. 7:40), that intercedes for us in prayer (Rom. 8:26), that enables us to war against the flesh (Rom. 8:6; Gal. 5:17), and that gives us strength to walk in righteousness for sanctification (Rom. 8:4). But again such an interpretation would misunderstand the nature of the Spirit. It must be remembered that the Spirit is God's agent in both creation and redemption. Paul teaches that the same Spirit who was active in creation is effective in the resurrection of God's Son, and it is through this victory that the cosmos is released from bondage to decay (Rom. 8:19-23; I Tim. 3:16; Rom. 1:4, 8:11). The same Spirit who personally brooded with loving care at the beginning is now personally working with suffering sighs too deep for words. The Spirit neither dispenses impersonal gifts nor energizes His creation with impersonal power. He gives Himself. Only a person can spend himself and yet remain inviolate and uncontrolled. A substance can be disposed and power can be harnessed. The Spirit is free.

III. THE SPIRIT IN THE CHURCH

There are certain tensions and ambiguities in the nature of the Spirit which we have seen set forth in the biblical revelation. These tensions have manifested themselves throughout the history of the doctrine of the Spirit in the life of the Church. Sometimes the tensions have been clearly seen but resolved at the expense of one side or another of the truth. At other times the tensions have not been recognized or they have been explained away, and this has resulted in a perversion of the true nature of the Spirit.

1. Thus we have seen that the Spirit has been conceived *animistically* as an independent agent, a discrete, personal being which can take possession of a man and empower him to perform unusual and heroic deeds. This view has appeared from time to time in the history of the Church in such movements as those of Montanus, Joachim of Flora, the Enthusiasts of the Reformation period, and the Quakers of England. On the other hand, the Spirit has been conceived *dynamistically* as an impersonal force or energy which fills a man with power to walk in newness of life. This view generally prevailed throughout the life of the Church from Augustine to the Reformation. As we have seen, it developed from the substantial metaphysics of classic Greek philosophy which became the ruling though pattern of Scholasticism.

While a true biblical understanding will include both a general indwelling and an occasional visitation of the Spirit, it will also become clear that both these historical developments are separately erroneous. While the Spirit is discrete as related to His creatures, He is not an independent agent in the Godhead. His relation to us is interpersonal, but within the Godhead His relations may be said to be intrapersonal. Moreover, it is the nature of the Spirit's being personal never to violate the person of His creatures who have been made in the image of God. The ecstasy of the pneumatic is therefore difficult to distinguish from demon possession and must be subject to the most intense scrutiny of the Spirit-led Church as a whole. There is no room for individual aberrations in the name of the Spirit, but yet the same Spirit who comes in baptism and seals us for the new life to come also on special occasions visits specially chosen individuals for extraordinary tasks. But just as this special visitation is a personal leading of the Spirit and not an animistic possession, so also the general indwelling is a personal presence and not a mechanistic power.

This same duality manifested itself from time to time in opposing notions of the nature of the Church. Sometimes the Church was understood merely as a historical phenomenon, whether in the form of the hierarchical tradition of Rome or the folk Church of Protestantism. At other times the Church was seen as the eschatological congregation of the elect under the special guidance of the Spirit. Again it is just as wrong to identify the work of the Spirit with historical phenomena as it is to delimit the Spirit to an invisible order which is exempt from regulation and tradition. As Bultmann has said, Sohm was right in rejecting Harnack's definition of the Church as a historical religious society, he was right in saying that legal regulation contradicts the Church's nature, but he was wrong "in his failure to recognize that a regulative legal provision not only does not stand in opposition to the Spirit's sway, but may actually be the creation of the Spirit" (Rudolf Bultmann, *Theology of the New Testament*, Vol. II, p. 98). The Spirit works not only in special proclaimers of the Word but also in the entire worshiping community which is the Church.

2. Another perennial problem in the historic doctrine of the Spirit is the place of the Spirit in the Godhead. Within the grand tradition of those who uphold the Trinity there remains the quarrel between those who follow the Cappadocian Fathers (Basil and the two Gregories) and those who follow Athanasius. The Cappadocians said God is a Trinity and the mystery is that He is also One. They emphasize the distinctions between the Persons to such a degree that their modern adherents can even speak of a "social Trinity." There is no question of the Spirit being personal, but the unity of the three hypostases is an abstract, impersonal essence. For Athanasius, on the other hand, God is a unity and the mystery is in the threeness. The Persons of the Trinity are three modes of being of the one God, and distinctions between the modes blur. Thus the Spirit and the Son were both active in creation, the Father and the Son both suffer in redemption.

It seems from our biblical analysis that two things must be said concerning the historical formulation of this doctrine. While the biblical revelation provides the materials for the doctrine of the Trinity, the actual formulation was a Church product. Consequently we must ask (1) whether the words of the historical formulation mean the same today as they were intended at the time of their origin, and (2) whether the intended meaning can be supported by Scripture.

Arnold Come says quite bluntly: "It is absolutely misleading to refer in the contemporary scene to the three 'Persons' of the Godhead. For us today, 'person' unqualifiedly designates the unique, discrete, self-determining *subject*. The early church meant no such thing" (*op. cit.*, p. 144). Both the Greek word *prosōpon* and the Latin *persona* mean face or mask. Usage of masks in the theatre indicates that the word designated a character or a function and not a subject or an agent.

If the creedal meaning intended to convey this operational and functional designation for the Persons of the Trinity we must next determine whether such meaning is supported by the biblical revelation. Certainly the monotheism of both Testaments would require beginning with the unity of God and then proceeding to explain His threefoldness. Yet the threefoldness cannot be regarded as three divine attributes or as three departments in the divine essence. This would destroy the personal relationship in which God comes to us whether as Father, Son, or Holy Spirit. And here is at least a hint of the solution to our modern semantic problem. God in His Unity is Person in the modern sense of discrete subject, yet in His various functions He does not operate in a mechanical way but comes to us on all three levels of relationship as Person, *wholly Person,* in Father, Son and Holy Spirit. Perhaps this will point the way to a satisfaction of the Cappadocian concern for the personal quality of the three functions of the Godhead while at the same time retaining the Person of the God who is a wonderfully multifarious Unity.

3. At the time of the Reformation the biblical conception of grace as *favor dei* rather than spiritual substance was recovered. This entailed a view of the Spirit as the personal guide and quickener of life. When the Spirit gives His gifts He does not give things or qualities to possess. He gives Himself. We have discussed the implications of this both for the meaning of the Church and the sacrament. It involves a return to the biblical paradox of the *deus absconditus/deus revelatus*. It is precisely the nature of God as Spirit which necessitates our understanding Him as the God who reveals Himself to be unknown as an object of human intellect. Human knowledge names and manipulates, but through revelation God becomes known to man as free, mysterious Person. As with the wind no one knows whence the Spirit comes or whither He goes. The Spirit remains free and beyond human control. He possesses us; we do not possess Him. Yet the Spirit does not come immediately or directly, but always He is tied to the Word. This bondage of the Spirit is ultimately due to the unity of God. In His activity in history, however, because of the nature of time in its sequential order, there is always an interval, whether infinitesimally small or incomprehensively long, between the coming of the Word in open revelation and the comfort of the Spirit in secret confirmation (Regin Prenter, *op. cit.*). But the Word does not go out and return void (Isa. 55:11).

Søren Kierkegaard expressed the Reformation spirit accurately when he said the Spirit is the denial of direct immediacy. To hold God directly is the characteristic mark of an idol. It was this understanding of the freedom and the hiddenness of the Spirit which enabled the great Reformers to hold a biblical front against the papist doctrine of sacramental immediacy on the one hand and the enthusiast doctrine of spiritual immediacy on the other hand. While the one led to a cynical compromise with the world in its materialization of the Spirit, the other led to a gnostic escape from this world in its spiritualistic attenuation of the Spirit.

IV. THE MODERN REVISION AND THE RETURN OF THE SPIRIT

1. After the Reformation, perhaps due to a combination of Pietism and the Enlightenment, a completely new interpretation was given to the Spirit. The modern revision emphasized the subjective side of our God-relationship. According to Schleiermacher, true religion is the feeling of absolute dependence upon God. The Christian is the man who has the spirit to see the finger of God in every event and to respond to this awareness with a rush of emotion (F. Schleiermacher, *The Christian*

Faith, Edinburgh, T. and T. Clark, 1928, p. 52). The Spirit soon ceases in such a view to stand over against us as an objective person. Instead the Spirit becomes the subjective avenue of human response to God. This was a radically new departure, but when Christianity lost the uniqueness of a transcendent revelation, and when the Spirit became a subject of religious psychology rather than revealed theology, salvation became a matter of human possibility rather than a divine gift of grace.

2. In the current generation we have experienced a violent reaction against this modern subjectivism spearheaded at first by Karl Barth and then flanked by Rudolf Bultmann. Barth says all Christianity must begin with the Word of God and the Word is Christ. Man is inextricably caught in sinful existence desperately in need of a saving knowledge of God, but unable with all the resources at his command in this world to satisfy this need. Obviously there can be no subjective spirit in man capable of bringing him to God. All such approaches are relative and temporal, and no matter how magnificent the temporality, whether of the mind or the heart or the will, it is destined to death as is everything else in this world. Against this judgment stands the wholly-other God who comes in mercy with the revelation of his Word.

There is no possibility of knowing God in ourselves before He comes, but when the Word speaks to us in Christ the grace is given us to know. Hence Barth shifts all theology from the *analogia entis* to the *analogia relationis* (Karl Barth, *Church Dogmatics*, Vol. I/1, New York, Charles Scribner's Sons, 1936, pp. 353 ff.). Instead of deriving a doctrine of the Holy Spirit by examining the human spirit, he seeks to listen to Christ and learn from this hearing in faith who is the Spirit. The Spirit becomes known through the relation of His revelation to us. It is the nature of revelation itself that gives Barth his doctrine of the Trinity. If there is a revelation of God's Word in Christ, then there must also be One who reveals and One who is revealed. Thus if there is a Son who is the Word, there must also be a Father who speaks this Word and a Spirit that is the Son's and the Father's revealedness. The Spirit clearly in such an analysis remains over against us in the transcendent Godhead. The sentimentality of liberal theology is avoided. Barth furthermore, following his *analogia relationis,* declares that man is related to God through an I-Thou encounter which is derived from the self-encounter which takes place in God Himself between Father and Son. Yet Barth is at great pains to refute the old concept of the three Persons of the Trinity. Instead he affirms that the One God is Person in the contemporary use of the term while Father, Son, and Spirit are related as modes of the divine existence.

Two things must be said in criticism of this otherwise salutary return to biblical transcendence. The analogy of relations is not so free of human experience apart from revelation as Barth would have it. All

communication involves the same trinitarian relationship. Every word
spoken must have a father in the thought that conceives it. When that
word becomes flesh and is uttered in audible or visible means it remains
hidden until there is a common spirit of communication. If I think the
word *"Bagunara"* (a word of greeting in the Telugu language), even
though I give that word flesh by speaking it aloud, I cannot communicate
my meaning unless there is the mystery of a common spirit of language
between myself and the one I address. It seems that Barth's analogy of
relation has itself an analogy in the general being of communication.

Barth, of course, would maintain that communicability is possible
only because of the prior address of God to man. But at least in Barth's
statement of his position it appears that no room is made for man as a
person in himself. As Arnold Come has put this objection: "If Father
and Son are two modes of being of the same Person, and if God and man
are related in a way analogous to the relation of Father and Son, then
man is no subject or person in himself, over against the Person of God.
Rather, he is a mode of a Mode (Sonship) of God's being, i.e. of the
Person of God" (*op. cit.*, p. 85).

3. The full *reductio* of the new "revelation theology" came when
Rudolf Bultmann tried to explain the Christian faith entirely in terms
of the kerygma. The kerygma for him is simply the message that sinful,
dying men can be free from the frustrations of a doomed existence by
deciding against any of the given moments of history and for the gracious
Moment of Eternity. Jesus was the occasion for the revelation that such
freedom is possible for man. This decision for eternity does not mean
that man is now free from a future hell and safe for a future heaven.
These are only mythical expressions for the quality of damned and
saved conditions. The meaning of salvation is that a man comes to a
true self-understanding whereby he knows his limitations and accepts
his destiny. He does not deceive himself with attachment to any temporal
or earthly goods since he knows that all things on this plane pass into
the death of the past. Hence he does not project his salvation into a
mythical future which is, after all, only an object of his earthly wishes.
As a result Bultmann interprets the eschatological hope in the Bible to
be a present decision for a new quality of existence which is realizing
itself. In all his writing Bultmann says very little about the Spirit, but
when he interprets the Fourth Gospel he says: "For John Easter, Pentecost, and the parousia are not three separate events, but one and the
same" (*Theology of the New Testament,* Vol. II, p. 57). It is clear from
this that for Bultmann the resurrection of the Son, the descent of the
Spirit, and the return of the Son are all symbols which point to a single
reality. There should be no identification of the symbol with the reality,
since the symbol is mythical language which cannot be taken literally.
According to this view of realized eschatology and demythologized reve-

lation the Trinity is truncated. The Spirit and the Son of man are not distinguished. The so-called historical events which are reported in the Bible concerning the various activities of Son and Spirit are not to be understood, according to Bultmann, as real events at all. They are mythical ways of saying that God comes to us with the gift of deliverance from anxiety. No real redemption can be actualized in Bultmann's view, if by redemption we mean a new existence in a resurrection life eternally with God and proleptically experienced in the communion of the Church. Indeed there seems to be little room at all in Bultmann's expression of the Gospel for life in a worshiping community, for sacramental grace, for a mission guided by the Spirit.

4. While it was helpful, and indeed necessary, to counteract the subjectivism of liberal theology with a re-affirmation of the transcendence of revelation, the inadequacy of this reaction becomes manifest in its total lack of a doctrine of the Church, both militant and triumphant. A return to the biblical teaching of the Spirit seems to call for an understanding not only of the transcendence of revelation and inspiration but also the immanence of revelation and illumination in the personal guidance and strengthening of the Spirit as He works in the Church.

The Spirit calls us, but He does not only thereby effect an encounter which brings us knowledge of God. He also gathers us into the fellowship of holiness. We are elected to a mission. We are not just gathered because we have like feelings about God, nor because we share in a decision which relieves our common anxieties. We are gathered for a sanctified life in faith which charges us with the mission to suffer and sacrifice in love for our neighbor. It is the Spirit who calls, gathers, sanctifies, and sends us into the world to glorify God by edifying His Church. The same Spirit who made us in the beginning strengthens us in our redemptive task in the end. This does not only lend a new quality to our existence in some demythologized realized eschatology. It sets us on our way as pilgrims elected by God to travel in this valley of the shadow through suffering to a mountain of light. There is a quantitative dimension to salvation as well as a qualitative, and although this cannot be measured in space and time, it must be so represented in the history of our cosmic salvation because the purpose of God has a direction. The Spirit is God personally guiding us in this direction, coming alongside to help us, comforting us with His Word, and quickening us to holiness.

THE NATURE OF REGENERATION

✝

Robert D. Knudsen

Robert D. Knudsen is Assistant Professor of Apologetics at Westminster Theological Seminary, Philadelphia. He is author of The Idea of Transcendence in the Philosophy of Karl Jaspers *(1958). He holds the A.B. degree from University of California, Berkeley, the Th.M. from Westminster Theological Seminary, the S.T.M. from Union Theological Seminary, New York, and the Ph.D. from the Free University, Amsterdam.*

15. *Robert D. Knudsen*

THE NATURE OF REGENERATION

THE NEW TESTAMENT portrays the believer in Christ as having entered upon a new life. From a profound discouragement he had been born again to a living hope by the resurrection of Jesus Christ from the dead (I Pet. 1:3). By the incorruptible seed of the Word of God he had been quickened to a new life of obedience to the truth (I Pet. 1:23; Jas. 1:18). For the Gentile this had meant deliverance from the pagan worship of idols. For the Jew it had meant an independence of the false traditions of men. As a newborn infant the believer was to desire the unadulterated milk of the Word, that he might grow (I Pet. 2:2). From the lust which had formerly enthralled him, he was called into the sincere fellowship of the children of God in love.

This change was so definite that it had to be expressed in the sharpest contrasts. The believer has come out of darkness into the light, from bondage to the flesh with its desires to subservience to the Spirit. The change is so radical that the most important figure used to express it is the transition from death to life. The believer is said to have been reborn. He has been buried with Christ in baptism and has been raised together with Him to a new life (Rom. 6:4).

The ministry of our Lord Himself gives us insight into this new life in which the Christian participates. One of the most important passages in the entire Scriptures dealing with this new life is found in the discourse of Jesus with Nicodemus.

When Nicodemus came to Jesus, inquiring about the kingdom of God, he received a reply that was not at all what he had expected. Being a Pharisee, Nicodemus was himself a teacher. That he came to Jesus to

make an inquiry, not only for himself but also for his associates, itself
indicates a recognition of Jesus as a teacher and shows a readiness to be
instructed. This impression is strengthened as Nicodemus calls Jesus
Rabbi and recognizes Him as being a teacher who has been sent by God.
Jesus does not refuse this title, nor does He deny this recognition; His
reply simply breaks off the thread of Nicodemus' thought. His answer is
emphatic and abrupt, "Except a man be born from above, he cannot see
the kingdom of God" (John 3:3).

The manner in which Jesus replies to Nicodemus is instructive concerning the new life of the Christian in the kingdom of God. That Jesus
uses the figure of birth implies, altogether in agreement with the remainder of the New Testament, the radical nature of the new life into
which the Christian enters. The answer also points out the source and the
effects of this new birth.

I. THE RADICALITY OF THE NEW BIRTH

When one speaks of the radicality of the new birth, he can only mean
that this birth affects the root (radix) of human existence. The very
abruptness with which Jesus interjects His reply suggests this already.
Although Jesus did not refuse to accept the recognition that Nicodemus
gave Him, He does not teach Nicodemus in the sense of filling in lacunae
in his information or correcting shortcomings in his attitudes. His answer
does not appeal to anything that is within Nicodemus himself or that is
a fruit or accomplishment of his labors. What Jesus requires is not a
modification or a completion of something that is already present. He
demands no less than a radically new beginning, a new birth that has
its point of origin altogether apart from Nicodemus himself.

The biblical idea of the new birth has always had to meet the opposition of those who either denied the necessity of any change at all or who
denied that the required change was as radical as the Scriptures demanded. The early Church had to face the steady pressure of the culture
of the Hellenistic world, which had been strongly influenced by neo-
Platonism. For the neo-Platonist the soul of man was by nature divine.
At the outset this divine principle within man was obscured and he was
under the domination of the material world, which he experienced
through his senses. If one was to find God, he had to wrestle free of the
world, repressing all of his consciousness and will, and he had to turn
inward to his own deepest self. There he would find God, for at bottom
God and the soul are one. According to the neo-Platonist there was
indeed the necessity of a change; but this change was not a change in the
innermost being of man. The soul had to turn away from the world; but
it itself, being divine, needed no inner regeneration.

At the time of the Reformation the evangelical doctrine of grace had a bitter enemy in humanistic rationalism. Rationalism thought of man as having a pure spring of truth and goodness within himself, namely, his reason. It is not essential to rationalism to hold that everyone is rational as a matter of fact. It is necessary for rationalism to believe, however, that it is possible for a man, or for mankind in general, to rise by the power of reason above the irrationalities which cling to him and impede him. This process is one of bringing to expression to more or less degree what already belongs to man, what comprises his innermost selfhood. It is reason which is sovereign. Of itself it has the power to change man, dictating to the will what it should do. To be sure, it is necessary for the reason to disentangle itself from the shroud of the irrational; but the reason itself needs no regeneration. Because of the power of his reason man inherently has the ability to change himself.

Although it did not return to the position of the Bible, theological liberalism attacked several basic assumptions of rationalism and tried to make place again for regeneration. Schleiermacher, the father of modern theology, is said to have been the one who re-introduced the idea of regeneration into theology. In Schleiermacher the center of gravity has shifted away from the power of the individual understanding. What is now in the center is the divine life as it is manifested in Jesus Christ. In Christ there was a perfect consciousness of God. In His encounter with man, He works powerfully upon him, strengthening his weak and suppressed God-consciousness and making it dominant. Through man's encounter with Christ, someone outside of himself, a new religious personality takes hold. There is a break with the old situation, and there is the beginning of a new life of personal communion with God. Schleiermacher thought of regeneration as being this turning point, at which the old life breaks off and a new life begins. Nonetheless, for Schleiermacher regeneration is still nothing more than strengthening and making dominant something that is already present in man. The encounter with Christ only awakens the slumbering consciousness of the divine.

Among the contemporary theologians there has been a revolt against such positions, spearheaded by Karl Barth. It is particularly Barth who has stressed that Christian faith does not arise from within man. It is not a human possibility. The Christian life is something radically new, not being the expression of anything within man at all.

In this emphasis Karl Barth is one of the closest followers of Søren Kierkegaard. Kierkegaard taught, in his *Philosophical Fragments* (Princeton, Princeton University Press, 1936) that if Christian faith were a human possibility, Christ would be expendable. His significance would be no more than that of a teacher whose task was completed when the inner potential of his student had come to expression. Kierkegaard maintained, on the contrary, that Christ is the One who is absolutely significant for the believer, being the One who is his Saviour, changing him from the ground up.

Barth has taken a similar position. That which can spring up, and that which everywhere does spring up, from man's innermost being is religion. Far from thinking that religion is the link between man and God, however, Barth interprets religion as being a human attempt at self-justification before God, the odious effort to build a tower of Babel, a tribute only to human pride and illusion. The Christian faith is, according to Barth, not an extension or a continuation of religion; it is a judgment on man's religion, standing in direct opposition to it. For Barth, Christian faith is not a human possibility. Instead, it is the result of a radical change effected by the creative power of the divine Word.

For Barth, as for many contemporary theologians, God's Word is a saving power. That is to say, it is not the words of the Scriptures, written and codified, that constitute the Word of God. These words, as much as any words, are human, and confidence in them is a human, religious act. God indeed uses these words in revelation; but these words are not themselves the revelation of God. The Word of God is a saving power, employing human words but not identifiable with them. It encounters man and changes him completely, from trusting in human accomplishments to a life of faith. For Barth, therefore, wherever there is the Word of God, in the primary sense of the term, and not simply the human and fallible vehicle of that Word, there the saving power of God is manifest.

That this Word is the creative, saving Word of God means for Barth that it, unlike all human words, is not at the disposal of man. As soon as the Word of God is said to be written and codified, at man's disposal, it is a human work, a religious edifice, a token of man's unbelief and sinful arrogance. Barth does not accept therefore the traditional distinction between the Word of God, written, and the power of God in applying the Word to man's heart. The primary distinction in Barth's thinking is that between the powerful Word of God in salvation and the inadequate, erring, unbelieving words of men which are used as its vehicle of expression. The radical change which Barth demands must be seen in the context of the equally radical tension of the creative Word of God and sinful human religion.

From the foregoing it has become clear that the change theologians require of man if he is to see the kingdom of God runs no deeper than the depth of sinful corruption ascribed to him. If one holds that there is an inner core of human selfhood which remains uncorrupted, he may indeed say that a certain renovation is necessary; but he cannot speak of any radical need for regeneration.

It is because the Scriptures see man in his sinful state as being dead, dead in trespasses and sins, that they demand an equally radical regeneration, so radical that it is spoken of as being life from the dead. The Scriptures do not discover the seed of the new life within man himself; instead, the new life is what is implanted from a source which is not in man himself at all.

II. THE SOURCE OF THE NEW BIRTH

Jesus' discourse with Nicodemus also points out the source of the new birth. In His reply to Nicodemus, Jesus simply retorts that it is necessary to be born *anōthen* in order to enter the kingdom of heaven.

The word Jesus employs, *anōthen,* can mean "again" as well as "from above." It is grammatically possible that Jesus intended the word in the first sense. It was, to be sure, in this sense that Nicodemus understood Jesus' words. It is much more likely, however, that Jesus meant to convey the thought that one must be born from above, and that Nicodemus, interpreting Jesus' words in a fashion which was conformable to his own experience and spiritual state, took Jesus to mean that one must be born again in a physical sense.

The ensuing discussion between Jesus and Nicodemus lends weight to this interpretation. Nicodemus asks Jesus whether it is possible for one again to enter his mother's womb and be born a second time. Jesus' reply shows that this was obviously not what He intended. His further statements indicate, in addition, that He not only wanted to convey to Nicodemus the idea that one must be born again, but that He meant to indicate the source of the new birth, namely, that it is from above. Jesus says that unless one is born of water and the Spirit, he cannot enter the kingdom. Seizing upon the idea that Nicodemus himself had introduced, Jesus goes on to contrast the kind of birth which is observable to us, the birth of the flesh, with a birth of another kind, that of the Spirit. It is possible, He says, for the flesh to engender only that which is flesh, nothing more. But that which is born of the Spirit is spirit (John 3:5-6).

That Jesus refers to another kind of birth, from a different source, strongly suggests that He means by *anōthen* a spiritual birth from above, in contrast to the physical birth on the natural plane. This view is further supported by Jesus' subsequent use of the same word in verse 7, which is again immediately followed by a discourse on the Holy Spirit.

What Jesus teaches Nicodemus is that one cannot be a citizen of the kingdom of God unless he be born from above, born anew not by some agency belonging to terrestrial experience, but by the agency of the Spirit of God. The new birth comes from no observable source, neither in the person himself nor in his environment.

This point is further expanded by Jesus as He compares the operation of the Spirit to the movement of the wind. With the naked eye one can observe neither the wind's origin nor its destination. He can see only its effects. The same inscrutability and mystery attach to the Spirit in the work of regeneration. Like the wind the work of the Spirit is not observable. The new birth cannot be attributed to some observable cause. Neither can it be localized in some observable part of man's being. The operation of the Spirit is sovereign, independent of the will and the work of man, changing the entire man in a radical fashion. The one who has been regenerated belongs among those, "who are born not of blood, nor of the will of the flesh nor of the will of man, but of God" (John 1:13).

Summarizing the teaching of Jesus on the new birth, we can say the following. Regeneration precedes the conscious level of man. It is an act of God, through the agency of His Holy Spirit, renewing and restoring the sinful creature and putting him in a position where he can exercise faith and can respond to the gracious call of God to salvation.

Again, of the movements in contemporary theology, it is particularly the Barthian theology that with reference to regeneration has spoken of the freedom and sovereignty of the creative Word of God. God's Word is a saving word. The calling of God to the sinner is always effectual, as creative as God's fiat, "let there be light." The agency of the Spirit and of the Word are basically indistinguishable. Unlike other contemporary theologians, who would make regeneration prior to the Word, Barth fuses Word and regeneration into one indissoluble creative act of God. Regeneration is in and through the creative Word of God.

Such a position, which regards the Word of God as the instrument in regeneration, has within certain limits support from the Scriptures. The Scriptures indeed teach that regeneration is by the Word of God (I Pet. 1:23; Jas. 1:18). If one thinks of "word" in its usual sense as the medium of discourse, however, the question immediately arises concerning the relationship between the spoken or written word and the work of the Holy Spirit in regeneration. Is it the case that the Spirit works only in connection with and through the divine Word of God? Is it the case that the Spirit works before the hearing of the Word, opening the eyes and enlightening the understanding, so that the summons of God to repentance and faith can be heeded? Or is the position of some contemporary theologians correct, that the Word spoken of in these verses is not the simple spoken or written word itself but the creative Word of Christ, itself powerful to re-create the sinner?

One is not able to answer such questions simply in terms of the usage of the word "regeneration" in the Scriptures or in terms of a consistent usage of this word within the theology of the Reformation. The Scriptures themselves employ the terms respecting regeneration in a loose fashion. The Reformers also used the term "regeneration" in a broad sense, not clearly indicating by the use of the term itself its precise relationship

to the Word of God. It was common in the traditional Reformed theology, however, to distinguish between the use of the term "regeneration"
in a broader and less well-defined sense, as it is often used in Scripture,
and in a narrower, more theologically defined sense. In the first sense
regeneration includes not only the work of the Spirit but also the response
of man in repentance and conversion. It is also used of the final restoration and renovation of all things at the last time. In the narrower and
more theologically precise sense, regeneration was taken to refer to the
renovative and restorative activity of God in the heart of the sinner
which precedes the level of his conscious activity. In line with this usage
a distinction was also made between the call of God in a general sense,
as it goes forth to all men who come under the hearing of the Word, and
the effectual call of God, which indeed does not exclude the Word, but
whose effectiveness rests in the sovereign activity of the Holy Spirit,
irresistibly calling men to Himself.

As we have already come to expect, the theology of Barth has no room
for these distinctions. They either fall away entirely, or they are infused
with new meaning in terms of the particular foundation principles of
his theological thinking. According to Barth, God's calling is always
effectual. His Word is a creative word; it is always saving. The distinctions made by the traditional Reformed theology are replaced, as we have
seen, with a new fundamental distinction, between the creative, saving
Word of God, and the human expression of it in preaching and in theology, that is, where the use of words in human discourse is involved.

Because he takes this position Barth must tolerate such unbiblical
paradoxes as the following. The words of the Scriptures can be faulty,
and indeed they are all faulty human words, man's effort at self-justification; but God uses them nevertheless, in spite of their faultiness, as
the only vehicle of His divine revelation. The Word, the saving Word, the
Word of God, is a hidden word, as well as being a revealed word. The
Word of God employs the vehicle of the word of men, in which it is both
revealed and hidden at the same time.

The position of Barth might seem to be an improvement upon what
might appear to be artificial distinctions of traditional theology. It is
often regarded to be just that. There are certain considerations, however,
which throw grave doubt upon Barth's fusion of divine calling, regeneration, and the creative Word of God.

By now it should be very clear that Barth's view implies a certain conception of the Scriptures. The words of the Scriptures are regarded to be
the words of men, which are indeed used by the Word of God but
which are not to be identified with that Word. In taking this position,
Barth is consciously opposed to the traditional, orthodox view of the
Scriptures. He is also, we might add, at variance with the biblical understanding itself of the Word of God. For the writers of the New Testament,

the Old Testament, written and codified, was the Word of God. Christ Himself constantly appealed to the Old Testament, basing His arguments even upon minutiae of the Old Testament text. The apostle Paul, when speaking of the prerogatives of the Jewish people, referred to their advantage in having received the oracles of God (Rom. 3:1, 2). That the Word of God had been received and codified did not mean that it was dead. It was a living Word, received from the living God Himself. In his defense before the Jews preceding his martyrdom, Stephen speaks of the living oracles of God (Acts 7:38). Barth's position involves a devaluation of the trustworthiness and the authority of the Scriptures, making them only the fallible record, in human words, of the divine event of revelation.

The Barthian position also brings other substantial changes with it. If it is the case that there is no distinction between the Word of God in the peculiar Barthian sense and the regenerating activity of the Holy Spirit, if, in other words, all revelation is saving revelation and the divine Word is always a re-creating, saving Word, it is difficult if not impossible to hold that there is ever a simple, unambiguous word of judgment. Christ's judgment of Judas, that it were better that he had never been born, is of necessity an acute problem for Barth. It is almost unavoidable for one who takes the Barthian position to think that any divine word of judgment is somehow bound up with a divine word of salvation. Indeed, it is precisely this that Barth holds. Divine judgment can be seen only on the background of the divine word of grace and salvation.

The inadequacy of the Barthian view leads us to ask whether there is truly scriptural warrant for a definite distinction (though not a separation) between the energizing, quickening work of the Spirit of God in regeneration and the divine summons which is mediated through divine revelation. Such a distinction appears not only to be allowed but to be demanded by the Scriptures.

If due weight is given to the scriptural interpretation of the sinfulness of man, there is full reason to insist on the priority of the work of the Holy Spirit in regeneration. To a man who is dead in sin, bound by the fleshly mind which seeks its own righteousness and not the righteousness of God, the calling of God in Scripture and preaching is foolishness, unless there be a change of his heart and his spiritual apperception. The Scriptures do not ascribe this ability, as rationalism does, to man himself. It is ascribed to the power of the Holy Spirit, through whom the Son draws to Himself those who are His. Furthermore, no man comes to the Son, unless he is drawn by the Father (John 6:44). It is precisely the regard that the traditional Reformed theology had for the deadness and blindness of sinful man that led it to say that the divine act of regeneration preceded the response of man in faith to the call of the Gospel. It was regeneration alone that made this response of faith possible. Apart from it the natural man in his spiritual obtuseness would let the call of the Gospel go unheeded.

The idea that regeneration is prior to faith in and through the Word of God is not intended to deny the unity of the work of salvation, nor is it intended to set up a theory concerning the order of the psychological processes through which one passes as he becomes a child of God. It is unwise to expect that there will be a set order or pattern of human experiences in regeneration. According to what we have said previously, regeneration is not a psychical event at all. On the psychical level it can only be manifest in its effects, and then not in a rigidly definable pattern. The priority of the work of the Spirit in regeneration to any response on the part of man is the way in which the traditional Reformed theology expressed the sovereignty of God in salvation. Indeed, it is precisely this also that the Barthian theology wishes to express by its fusion of the Word, regeneration, and divine calling. It is highly questionable, however, whether the Barthian denial of a before and after, the denial of even a logical priority of regeneration, is scriptural. Instead, as we have seen, it appears to subject the scriptural data to a radical interpretation.

Although there is a before and after, a certain priority of the work of regeneration to the understanding of the Word, there is a true unity of the work of salvation. Regeneration may not simply be separated from the Word, nor from the effects which it produces in the life of the believer. Where there has been the regenerating power of the Holy Spirit, there is a subjective change in the person who has been regenerated. This change may not indeed be reflected immediately in active, articulate faith and confession of Christ, but it is inconceivable that the regenerating power of God not produce an effect. Furthermore, regeneration of God cannot be seen apart from the Word. Those who are regenerated are those who are the called of God. This call will also come to them through the preaching of the Gospel, by the instrumentality of God's messengers. The One who begins a good work in man will complete it to the end. Those who are called of God will come to faith and to confession of Christ in compliance with the summons of the Gospel.

III. THE EFFECTS OF THE NEW BIRTH

We have said that regeneration, being the sovereign work of the Holy Spirit, is prior to any response on the part of man. In regeneration man is passive. That this is the case is suggested already by the figure itself of the new birth. As it has often been said, one enters the kingdom of God as a child enters the world. When a man is born physically, he does not have anything to say about it. The identity of his parents, his hereditary gifts, and the time and the circumstances of his birth are altogether out of his control. In an analogous way this is also true of the new birth. According to the testimony of Christ Himself, the activity of the Holy Spirit is like that of the wind, mysterious and inscrutable, beyond the disposal of man. In the strict sense of the word regeneration is prior to faith in any explicit sense. It is prior to anything which belongs to the response of man to the gracious call of God, anything therefore which is on the order of repentance or conversion. It is by the sovereign operation of God that one is born from above and is enabled to respond to God's gracious call in the Gospel. To conceive this order in a different fashion, making regeneration in the narrower sense of the word dependent upon faith and conversion, is to leave altogether unaccounted for how man, dead in trespasses and sins, is to respond to the Gospel.

Although it is not dependent upon faith or conversion, it is true nevertheless that regeneration cannot be thought of apart from a subjective change in the one who has been reborn. It is not the case that the new birth can occur and then only later have an effect. Regeneration carries with it a subjective change, described in the Scriptures in great detail, and issuing in the sanctification and eventually in the glorification of the believer.

Regeneration is decidedly not a substantial union with God or the assumption of divine attributes. In regeneration the relationship between the Creator and the creature is strictly maintained. The Bible does not allow for mystical extravagances, such as the thought that the divine becomes human and that in the rebirth the human becomes divine. The Scriptures, however, describe regeneration as being in another fashion a partaking of the divine nature (II Pet. 1:4). One who has been regenerated is no longer impelled by the former lust of the flesh (I Pet. 1:14); he is spiritual (*pneumatikos*). He has escaped the corruption which attends the fleshly life (II Pet. 1:4) and he is in his innermost being impelled by the Spirit of God.

John 3:5 indicates the two sides from which regeneration must be viewed. It means, first of all, that there is a purging of the defilement of the heart. Second, it sets forth a re-creation of man in newness of life. These two aspects are portrayed when Jesus said that one must be born of water and the Spirit if he is to enter the kingdom of heaven. Very likely Christ alludes here to the two elements in Ezekiel 36:25, 26: "Then will I sprinkle clean water upon you, and ye shall be clean: from all your filthiness, and from all your idols, will I cleanse you. A new heart also will I give you, and a new spirit will I put within you: and I will take away the stony heart out of your flesh, and I will give you an heart of flesh."

Regeneration is presented in the Scriptures as involving a real change in the believer. Upon occasion the rich imagery of the Old Testament is employed in all its fullness to express the holiness of the new life, in contrast to the lust and the corruption that characterized unregenerate existence. The radicality and definiteness of this change are expressed in marked contrasts: that between lust and holiness, darkness and light (I Pet. 2:9), death and the resurrection to a new life (I Pet. 3:21, 24). Beforehand, one is not a citizen but a stranger to the kingdom of God; afterwards, he is a citizen of the kingdom (Col. 1:13) and a member of God's household.

The traditional Reformed view of regeneration saw the effects of regeneration manifested in a changed will, affections, disposition, inclinations. Using a Latin expression, they said that regeneration imparted to man a new *habitus,* so that whereas he was formerly inclined to evil he was now inclined towards the good. In his *Systematic Theology* (New York, Scribner Armstrong & Company, 1872), Charles Hodge describes this change in the following way: "In regeneration, therefore, there is a new life, communicated to the soul; the man is a subject of a new birth; he receives a new nature or new heart, and becomes a new creature. As the change is neither in the substance nor in the mere exercises of the soul, it is in those immanent dispositions, principles, tastes, or habits which underlie all conscious exercises, and determine the character of the man and of all his acts."

The traditional theology saw no conflict between the idea of man's radical depravity and the claim that regeneration implants a new *habitus* in man. Precisely Barth's view of the point of contact, however, brings him to a sharp rejection of the traditional Reformed position. As we have seen, Barth denies that Christian faith is an extension or a development of something that is already in man. Christian faith must come to man as something completely new from the outside. In making this claim Barth is formally in agreement with the Scriptures and with the traditional Reformed theology. The particular form his denial takes, however, hinders him from accepting the idea that there is a real change, in the sense of a change of qualities, in one who has been regenerated. His sharpest attacks are turned on the idea that the new birth imparts a new *habitus.*

To accept the traditional position means for Barth to have reverted to the idea that man can be something in and of himself, that he is a blessed possessor of something that has value in itself, apart from his relationship to God and his dependence upon Him.

For Barth the traditional Reformed position implies a denial of the very foundation of the Reformation confession, justification by faith. In the measure that the believer is thought to live by virtue of something he possesses, he lives by sight and no longer by grace through faith. There is an observable, describable principle within him that is supposed in a nearly mechanical fashion to issue in his sanctification.

There is for Barth, therefore, a tension between the Reformed view of justification and the idea of regeneration as it has traditionally been held in Reformed theology. The view of regeneration must be brought into conformity with the demands of justification as he conceives it. Indeed, there is a radical change as one becomes a Christian. This change, however, is in the first place a recognition that we have been justified by God through His free, sovereign grace. This change is most certainly not a change in *habitus,* in one's disposition, inclinations, etc. It is not that Barth denies altogether that there has been a subjective change, but the idea of what this change involves is modified to conform to his theology in general. Instead of being a change in *habitus,* the subjective change of which Barth speaks is a new openness or freedom towards God and one's fellow man. When one is thus open, one does not erect barriers between man and man, thinking of some as having new qualities implanted by the new birth and thinking of others as not having such qualities. This would be to make moral distinctions. For Barth, however, all moral distinctions are human work, being the product of man's effort to justify himself instead of being justified by God. On the moral level, we are all without distinction lost in sin, being unregenerate in our minds and wills. It is Christ who is preeminently the "new man," and it is only as we are in Him that we are liberated towards God and our fellow man.

Barth holds that the traditional view of the new birth clashes with the Reformational doctrine of justification by faith, in spite of the fact that the Reformers themselves saw no such conflict. The Reformers spoke with assurance of a real change effected in the regenerate by the grace of God. They were not even afraid to speak of grace as having been *infused,* if that was properly understood. What they indeed opposed was making the grace of God, and the resulting change within the regenerated, a meritorious basis for justification, as if God were to declare us to be righteous on the basis of anything within ourselves and not solely out of His free and unmerited favor. Justification, the righteousness of God through faith, was not dependent upon any subjective merit in the believer, not even a merit of supernatural origin.

Neither do the Scriptures themselves see a tension between justification by faith and a real change in the believer, involving his disposition, inclinations, etc. Nor do they regard such a change as being out of accord with the interests of the believer's sanctification. The Scriptures speak unabashedly in the highest terms of what has been wrought in man by the new birth, while they urge him at the same time to ever greater devotion and holiness. The actual condition of man as a new creation in Christ is simply regarded as carrying with it the demand to live accordingly.

Barth himself appears to recognize that for the Scriptures the very fact that one has been born again carries with it the demand that he live in conformity to its meaning and goal. Barth does not hold, as do some theologians, that regeneration must be counterbalanced by some critical principle external to it. It is all the more strange, therefore, that in the interest of denying the self-sufficiency of man over against God and His Word, Barth denies a change of *habitus* in the believer.

Barth is so concerned about the active nature of the believer's response to the Word of God that he cannot account for the organic language of the Bible, as it speaks about the continuity and the development of the new life in Christ. No amount of zeal to upset the idea that there is in man a principle having a quasi-independent existence can obscure the fact that the Bible speaks of a seed being implanted in man and remaining, so that he cannot sin, because he is born of God (I John 3:9).

As we have said before, the Bible is not at all conscious that there is a tension between this language and the equally biblical doctrine of justification by faith. Nor does it see here a tension between the believer's need to be constantly joined to Christ, as the branch to the vine. Indeed, the believer's new life has its only foundation in the work of Christ as the Redeemer, and it envisages as its goal complete conformity to His image.

IV. THE GROUND AND GOAL OF REGENERATION

The application of redemption in the believer must be seen against the background of the work of Christ for the believer in making provision for his redemption. Regeneration is altogether dependent upon what Christ has accomplished in His active and passive obedience as the mediator between God and man. The drama of Christ's mediatorship on the earth has its prologue in heaven, in the eternal counsels of God, as He covenants with His Son concerning the redemption that He is to accomplish. Regeneration is also understood only in terms of its ultimate intent and goal, that the believer be transformed into the image of Christ.

As Jesus speaks with Nicodemus, fixing the attention of His learned hearer on the source of the new birth from above, He is met with incomprehension. Thereupon Jesus remarks to Nicodemus that, being a teacher of Israel, he should have known these things. If he has not comprehended what Jesus has said about the new birth, which transpires here upon earth in the human heart, how will he then understand when Jesus proceeds to tell him of heavenly things, that which transpired in heaven as a prologue to this redemption upon earth? In spite of Nicodemus' incomprehension, however, Jesus proceeds to elaborate on this heavenly theme. The authority which He bears stems from the fact that it is He who has descended from heaven and who therefore has such a fellowship with the Father that the Father communicates these things to Him (John 3:11-13).

Thereupon Jesus begins one of the most famous discourses of the entire New Testament, speaking of the great love of God, whereby He sent His only begotten Son into the world, that whosoever believes on Him should not perish but have eternal life (John 3:16). Behind the sending of His only begotten Son stands the counsel of God, one of the heavenly things of which Jesus speaks. The sovereignty of the Spirit in regeneration must be seen against the background of the electing love of God. Those who are regenerated are elect in Christ before the foundation of the world (Eph. 1:4). He knows His sheep by name, and as they hear His voice they follow Him. That men must be born again if they are to enter the kingdom of God places us squarely before the biblical truths of election and predestination.

Regeneration is also connected with Christ's work of mediatorship. The Gospel does not disclose in man some spark of the divine, so he can ascend to God of his own power. The regeneration of the human heart depends entirely upon what Christ has wrought for man in His sacrificial death and in His triumphant resurrection. Christ Himself says that the sending of the Holy Spirit was contingent upon His ascension to the right hand of the Father. It was necessary that He go; but if He had to go away, He would send another Comforter. The outpouring of the Holy Spirit is by the authority and agency of the Son of God, and it is the expression of His saving power. The regeneration of man is possible only for God through the work of the Holy Spirit, giving birth to a new life.

Conformity to Christ is the destination and goal of the regenerating work of the Holy Spirit. Christ is the pattern and the norm of the Christian life: "Till we all come in the unity of the faith, and of the knowledge of the Son of God, unto a perfect man, unto the measure of the stature of the fulness of Christ. . ." (Eph. 4:13). The new life in Christ cannot have anything that is self-sufficient, independent of the exemplar, Christ Jesus.

Christ, however, is much more than an exemplar. Through His Holy Spirit He is the One who activates the Christian, making him conformable to His image. The older Reformed theology spoke of Jesus Christ as the *causa exemplaris* of the regeneration of His people. The believer in Jesus Christ may not think that this principle within himself, the seed which has been implanted, has any life in itself. It, and the entire life of the regenerated, which it forms, is nourished and sustained by this dependence upon Jesus Christ.

The conformity of the new creation to Christ Jesus also has its consummation in the final restoration of all things (Matt. 19:28). The Scriptures also call this final restoration a regeneration. This is a broader use of the term than the strict theological use we have been discussing. Nevertheless, even regeneration in the narrow sense of the work of the Holy Spirit in quickening the heart of man has within its purview this final restoration. Regeneration looks forward not only to the sanctification of the individual believer but also to the final restoration, when Christ shall have delivered up the kingdom and the Father shall be all in all.

————

The understanding of the scriptural doctrine of regeneration has profound implications for missions. The proclamation of the kingdom of God must not only speak of the saving work of Jesus Christ in making provision for the salvation of His own; it must also acquaint men with the inscrutable work of the Holy Spirit. It must provide for a proper understanding, both on the part of the missionary and on the part of the one who is evangelized, of the nature of the Spirit's work in salvation.

For the missionary, the sovereignty of the work of the Spirit makes indispensable the work of prayer. The missionary may not expect in terms of his own knowledge, wisdom, or labors, to accomplish the transformation of those to whom he speaks. In his missionary efforts he must always preach the Word in constant dependence upon the work of the Spirit, whose activity he cannot see but the effect of whose regenerative power will be discerned in the lives of those who respond to the call of the Gospel, often in a most unexpected fashion. The Scriptures are replete with the responsibility of the Christian in the work of missions; but whatever we do, the issue is finally that of the Holy Spirit, in His mysterious and indispensable work. The missionary can have an assurance, a source of courage and comfort, that in every place God has His own people, and that He will call His own to Himself in His own season.

The one who is evangelized must be brought to recognize that his salvation is all of God. Indeed, it is his responsibility to respond to the Gospel and to embrace it as it is tenderly offered to him. Nevertheless, even as he responds, he must realize that he does not come to Jesus Christ unless he is called of the Father. That this work in him is of the Spirit of God and not of man should also convict him of the wonder and the awefulness of that which is being worked in him, a realization that will also induce him to work out his own salvation with fear and trembling, as he knows that it is God working in him, both to will and to do of His own good pleasure. He must be humbled as he realizes that his salvation is not of himself, but that he is elected in Christ before the foundation of the world, that he should be conformed to Him in newness and holiness of life, and that together with the saints he is being built up as a living stone unto a holy temple to the Lord (Eph. 2:19-22).

THE NATURE OF FAITH

✝

Vernon C. Grounds

Vernon C. Grounds is President of Conservative Baptist Theological Seminary, Denver, which he formerly served as Dean from 1951-56. He holds the A.B. degree from Rutgers University, B.D. from Faith Theological Seminary, and Ph.D. from Drew University. He has written The Reason for Our Hope *(1944) and is a frequent contributor to religious magazines.*

16. *Vernon C. Grounds*

THE NATURE OF FAITH

Unique among world religions, Christianity assigns a distinctive to faith. So, for example, Gerhard Ebeling, professor of theology at Zurich, declares: "The decisive thing in Christianity is faith. . . . However confusing the manifold historical forms in which Christianity makes its appearance in the different centuries and different parts of the earth, the different nations and civilizations, the different confessions and personalities, however repulsive the contentions about faith, and however attractive only so-called practical Christianity may seem, nevertheless there cannot be the least doubt that Christianity itself has at all times and in all places regarded faith as constituting its essence. He who becomes a Christian has always been asked, do you believe?" (*The Nature of Faith,* London, Collins, 1961, p. 20).

In thus identifying faith with the essence of Christianity, Ebeling is echoing the famous American Calvinist, B. B. Warfield, who in a masterful article on the biblical meaning of *pistis* shows how in the New Testament this term evolves into "a synonym for 'Christianity'. . . . And we may trace a development," Warfield adds, "by means of which *pistis* has come to mean the religion which is marked by and consists essentially in 'believing.'. . . the idea of 'faith' is conceived of in the New Testament as the characteristic idea of Christianity" (*Biblical Doctrines,* New York, Oxford University Press, 1929, p. 483).

Our concern, therefore, is not with faith-in-general, faith *per se,* either as concept or phenomenon. Our concern is with Christian faith in particular and with Christian faith in its theological formulation. At once many issues, important and engrossing in their own right, are swept aside as irrelevant. Thus we shall not be considering faith, Christian or otherwise, epistemologically,[1] historically,[2] lexically,[3] apologetically,[4] polemically,[5] or psychologically.[6] Our attention will be focused rather on the analysis of faith made by Søren Kierkegaard, nineteenth-century litterateur, and the alleged father of existentialism. To evaluate Kierkegaard's views on this subject, however, we must first glance at the analysis of faith by Reformed theologians.

I. FAITH IN THE THEOLOGY OF PROTESTANT ORTHODOXY

Biblical religion in the Old Testament no less than in the New is a religion of faith. Such is Warfield's measured verdict: "The religion of the Old Testament is obviously as fundamentally a religion of faith as that of the New Testament. . . . its very essence consisted in faith, and this faith was the same radical self-commitment to God, not merely as the highest good of the holy soul, but as the gracious Saviour of the sinner, which meets us as the characteristic feature of the religion of the New Testament. Between the faith of the two Testaments there exists, indeed, no further difference than that which the progress of the historical working out of redemption brought with it" (op. cit., p. 484).

Whether in the Old Testament or the New, however, it is the Object

---

[1] John Hick in his *Faith and Knowledge* (Ithaca, New York, Cornell University Press, 1957) ably reviews the epistemology of faith.

[2] A standard work in this field is that of Stewart Means, *Faith: An Historical Study* (New York, The Macmillan Company, 1933).

[3] Warfield's article (op. cit.) is still unexcelled. The definitive contemporary study is that of Rudolf Bultmann and Artur Weiser in *Bible Key Words*, Vol. III (New York, Harper & Brothers, 1961), translated from Gerhard Kittel's *Theologisches Wörterbuch Zum Neuen Testament.*

[4] From an evangelical viewpoint nothing has yet replaced J. Gresham Machen's classic, *What is Faith?* (New York, The Macmillan Company, 1935).

[5] The major differences between Protestant Reformed and Roman Catholic concepts of faith are tersely stated by Auguste Lecerf, *An Introduction to Reformed Dogmatics* (London, Lutterworth Press, 1949), pp. 399-403. Franz Arnold, "The Act of Faith, A Personal Commitment," *Lumen Vitae* (Vol. V, No. 2-3, April-September, 1950, pp. 251-255), argues that the Roman Catholic position has been misunderstood and that faith in that tradition always meant "personal decision and confident trust." Cf., too, Jean Mouroux, *I Believe: The Personal Structure of Faith* (New York, Sheed and Ward, 1959); Romano Guardini, *The Life of Faith* (Westminster, Maryland, The Newman Press, 1961); Jerome Hamer, *Karl Barth* (Westminster, Maryland, The Newman Press, 1962); pp. 84, 85, 265-288.

[6] Cf. James Lindsay, *The Psychology of Belief* (London, William Blackwood and Sons, 1910); F. R. Tennant, *The Nature of Belief* (London, The Centenary Press, 1943); William Ralph Inge, *Faith and Its Psychology* (New York, Charles Scribner's Sons, 1910); Inge has been updated by W. S. Taylor, "Faith and Its Psychology," in *The Hibbert Journal*, Vol. LVIII, No. 3, April, 1960, pp. 237-248; Walter Houston Clark, *The Psychology of Religion* (New York, The Macmillan Company, 1958), pp. 219-239.

of faith, Warfield further observes, which—Who, to be more correct—imparts value to the act of self-commitment. "It is, accordingly, solely from its *object* that faith derives its value. This object is uniformly the God of grace, whether conceived of broadly as the source of all life, light, and blessing, on whom man in his creaturely weakness is entirely dependent, or, whenever sin and the eternal welfare of the soul are in view, as the Author of salvation in whom alone the hope of unworthy man can be placed. This one object of saving faith never varies from the beginning to the end of the scriptural revelation" (*ibid.,* p. 502).

In the New Testament, saving trust finds its object in Jesus Christ, presented as God the Redeemer. "Faith has ever terminated with trustful reliance, not on the promise but on the Promiser,—not on the propositions which declare God's grace and willingness to save, or Christ's divine nature and power, or the reality and perfection of His saving work, but on the Saviour upon whom, because of these great facts, it could securely rest as on One able to save to the uttermost. Jesus Christ, God the Redeemer, is accordingly the one object of saving faith, presented to its embrace at first implicitly and in promise, and ever more and more openly until at last it is entirely explicit and we read that 'a man is not justified save through faith in Jesus Christ' (Gal. ii.16)" (*ibid.,* p. 503).

In Scripture, then, far from being a simple human act, faith is the nexus of Christology, anthropology, hamartiology, soteriology, and pneumatology. To explicate faith—though fortunately not to exercise it!—a whole system of theology must be constructed.

To elucidate the relationship between the Object of faith and the subject of faith, Protestant dogmaticians of the seventeenth century resorted to Latin phrases and terms which have become a kind of doctrinal shorthand. *Fides quae creditur,* the faith which one believes, they set over against *fides qua creditur,* the faith by which one believes. *Fides historica,* faith as an impersonal agreement with the facts and propositions of Christianity, they distinguished sharply from *fides propria* or a personal acceptance of the Saviour; sometimes they made *fides salvifica* synonymous with *fides propria.*

Very commonly they stressed the three elements which in their opinion *fides propria* includes—*notitia, assensus,* and *fiducia.* Johannes Wolleb, author of *The Compendium of Christian Theology,* framed a classical definition of these elements. "*Notitia* is the apprehension of the things which are necessary to salvation. *Assensus* is that by which it is firmly believed, that the things transmitted by the Word of God are true. *Fiducia,* called *pepoithēsis* and *plērophoria* by the Apostle Eph. 3.12 (boldness and access in confidence through our faith in him) I Th. i.5 (our gospel came not unto you in word only, but in power and in the H. Ghost and in much assurance), is that by which each of the faithful applies the promises of the Gospel to himself" (cited in Heinrich Heppe,

Reformed Dogmatics, London, George Allen & Unwin Ltd., 1950, p. 530).

But in the Reformed tradition *fiducia* received an emphasis above and beyond either *notitia* or *assensus*. In other words, trustful self-commitment was viewed as the very essence of faith. As the sixteenth-century dogmatician Samuelis Maresius wrote, "Trust is the very form of faith as justifying and its noblest part" (*ibid.,* p. 534). Yet this emphasis on *fiducia* must not be construed to mean that knowledge and conviction were minimized: they were invariably assumed and as a rule expressly stated to be the foundations of trust. Karl Barth points out that for Old Protestantism or historic orthodoxy, faith as a mere and sheer voluntaristic *fiducia* was unthinkable. "To exclude from faith the element of *notitia* or *assensus,* i.e. the element of knowledge, to conceive of faith as pure trust, which is intellectually without form or, in view of its intellectual form, indifferent, has any kind of trust in any kind of thing, to make the object of faith problematical and to transfer the reality of faith to the believing subject, was a possibility of which we can say with certainty . . . that even in the early period of the Reformation none of its responsible leaders took it seriously for one single minute. . . . True, faith is first faith when it is *fiducia,* and *notitia* and *assensus* by themselves should not be faith at all but just that *opinio historica,* which even the godless may have. But how should it be *fiducia* without at the same time and because it is *fiducia,* being *notitia* and *assensus* too, *fiducia promissionis,* trust in the mercy of God which meets us as the *misericordia promissa,* i.e. in the objectivity of the Word, which has form and the form of the Word at that, and therefore in the faith that adopts it, the form of knowledge also, the form of conviction?" (*Church Dogmatics,* Vol. IV/1, Edinburgh, T. & T. Clark, 1956, pp. 268, 269).

Nevertheless, in opposition to the *fides historica* which they charged the Roman Catholic Church was teaching, Reformation Protestants insisted that *fides salvifica* must embrace trust, a response of will and heart, and that *fiducia* is indeed the crowning and dynamic element of faith. By this dogged insistence they again displayed their loyalty to Scripture; for as Warfield contends, biblical faith is never only *notitia* and *assensus;* it is "a firm, trustful reliance," "a vigorous act of commitment," "a profound and abiding disposition, an ingrained attitude of mind and heart towards God which affects and gives character to all their activities," "a trustful appropriation of Christ and surrender of self to His salvation," "an entire self-commitment of the soul to Jesus as the Son of God, the Saviour of the world" (*op. cit.,* pp. 471, 476, 478, 483, 500).

When faith in its full biblical significance is exercised—an exercise made possible not by some innate psychic endowment but by the effectual working of the Holy Spirit—then, so the entire Reformed tradition holds (cf. Heppe, *op. cit.,* p. 538), there results a state of assurance, *tranquilla possessio.* To quote another of the Protestant fathers, Franciscus Turrettinus, "The view of the orthodox is that the faithful may not only be certain of their faith and its truth and sincerity, a certainty not human and fallible but divine and infallible, which is yet greater or less according as faith itself is found to be firmer or laxer; but both may and ought to be certain of the grace of God and remission of sins, so far as in serious contrition for sins they do with true faith grasp the promise of free mercy in Christ, rest in it confidently and so render their hearts carefree" (*ibid.*, p. 536; cf. Hamer, *op. cit.*, p. 76, n. 57).

By the Spirit's witness the believer has a *certitudo salis,* a certainty of salvation; he knows himself to be among the *beati possedenti,* the blessed possessors of eternal life.

This is the concept of faith, biblically grounded and dogmatically formulated, which Protestant orthodoxy has always espoused.

II. FAITH IN THE THEOLOGY OF SØREN KIERKEGAARD

Sometimes curtly dismissed as an irrationalist, a brooding neurotic whose influence on philosophy as well as theology has been perverse,[7] Søren Kierkegaard is nevertheless a major influence in contemporary Christianity. Indeed, the Lutheran theologian, Martin J. Heinecken, thinks his influence can scarcely be exaggerated: "It is impossible to go back again beyond Kierkegaard. If what he said is understood, it means as violent an upheaval in theology as at the time of the Reformation.... Whether one is aware of it or not, the face of modern theology has altered because of Kierkegaard.... He marks a turning point in the history of Christian thought. No one can be a theologian today without coming to terms with the issues which Kierkegaard raised" (*The Moment Before God,* Philadelphia, Muhlenberg Press, 1956, pp. 17, 19). If Heinecken is even half right in his estimate, whatever Kierkegaard has to say on the subject of faith merits critical study.

Three comments seem to be in order, however, before we proceed. First, an unsystematic thinker who opposes any attempt to blueprint or strait-jacket reality, Kierkegaard never discusses dogma as such. Largely conventional in his orthodoxy,[8] he uses traditional doctrines as the background for aesthetic, ethical, philosophical, polemical, and

---

[7] A painful illustration is Walter Kaufmann, *From Shakespeare to Existentialism* (Boston, Beacon Press, 1959), pp. 161-183.

[8] Kierkegaard's essential orthodoxy is defended by Hermann Diem, *Kierkegaard's Dialectic of Existence* (London, Oliver and Boyd, 1959), pp. 81, 103; Libuse Lukas Miller, *In Search of the Self* (Philadelphia, Muhlenberg Press, 1962), Chapter V; and various authors in a brilliant collection of essays which supply a veritable handbook of Kierkegaard's references to faith, *A Kierkegaard Critique,* Howard A. Johnson and Niels Thulstrup, eds. (New York, Harper & Brothers, 1926), pp. 215, 223, 224, 226, 246, 255, 258. Hereafter references to this work will usually ignore individual writers and essays.

evangelistic writings. Yet in the prolific work of this non-professional theologian, a theology is certainly implicit. Second, Kierkegaard employs an amazing array of pseudonyms whose pronouncements must not be taken as his personal *dicta*. Third, Kierkegaard's ideas and formulations changed in some respects over the course of years (Johnson and Thulstrup, *op. cit.*, p. 201, n. 40). With these factors in mind then, we shall examine Kierkegaard's concept of faith.

    1. Had he been privileged to read Abraham Kuyper's *Encyclopedia of Sacred Theology,* Kierkegaard no doubt would have heartily endorsed this passage: "Nothing can ever be added to man by regeneration which does not essentially belong to human nature. Hence regeneration cannot put anything around us as a cloak, or place anything on our head as a crown. If faith is to be a human reality in the regenerate, it must be an attitude (*habitus*) of our human nature as such; consequently it must have been present in the first man; and it must be discernible in the sinner. . . . the pistic element is present in all that is called man" *Encyclopedia of Sacred Theology,* New York, Charles Scribner's Sons, 1898, p. 266).

    As Kierkegaard sees it, human nature is constitutionally *pistic;* hence he describes different kinds and levels of faith phenomenologically. Dividing existence into three spheres—the aesthetic, the ethical, and the religious, with the third of these subdivided into Religiousness A or non-Christian religiosity and Religiousness B or New Testament Christianity (this division is really a diagrammatic *schema*)—he shows that belief is operative in every mode and situation of life.

    In the aesthetic sphere, writes James Collins, "Faith signifies a man's immediate attachment to life, his animal conviction in the reality of the world and perhaps of its supreme principle" (Johnson and Thulstrup, *op. cit.*, p. 143). In the ethical sphere, faith, Collins says, is "The individual's confidence in the integrity and ultimate strength of his moral ideal or the social group's confidence in the practicality and humanness of its social aims" (*ibid.*, p. 146). Two types of faith function in the religious sphere, one the product of general revelation, the other born of special revelation. In the words of the Stigmatine scholar, Cornelio Fabro, Religiousness A is "the acme of human wisdom before Christ and was achieved by Socrates"; it "has God the ontological absolute as its object" (*ibid.*, p. 191). Kierkegaard, accordingly, does not rule out natural theology. Quite the contrary! He holds that "the *Theologia Naturalis* is truly the indispensable *Anknüpfungspunkt* for the reception of revealed religion" (*loc. cit.*).

    What catapults a man out of this "religion of immanence" into Christianity? The conviction of sin! (Søren Kierkegaard, *Training in Christianity,* Princeton, Princeton University Press, 1957, pp. 71, 72). Thus Kierkegaard's somewhat abstruse works, *The Concept of Dread* and *The*

Sickness Unto Death, are not merely psychological treatises: they are profound tracts on hamartiology. Evangelistic in thrust, they are calculated to arouse a desperate sense of guilt and need which only Jesus Christ can meet. Their purpose is to motivate the leap of faith, which is "a free intervention of the will" (Johnson and Thulstrup, *op. cit.,* p. 151). And Religiousness B is the true faith; indeed, "only Christian faith is considered by Kierkegaard to be faith in the strict sense" (*ibid.,* p. 165).

2. In virtually everything he says about faith Kierkegaard is concerned with its subjective rather than its objective character. Unfortunately, therefore, it is all too widely imagined that he shortsightedly or willfully suppresses the whole objective side of Christianity. Such is scarcely the case, however. A single passage will help to dissipate this misunderstanding: "Christianity exists before any Christian exists, it must exist in order that one may become a Christian, it contains the determinant by which one may test whether one has become a Christian, it maintains its objective subsistence apart from all believers, while at the same time it is in the inwardness of the believer. In short, here there is no identity between the subjective and the objective. Though Christianity comes into the heart of ever so many believers, every believer is conscious that it has not arisen in his heart. . . ." (*ibid.,* p. 235).

Judicious is Valter Lindstrom's appraisal: "Kierkegaard's thought is not, in fact, exclusively dominated by the argument in favor of subjectivity and against opinions that unduly emphasize objectivity. On the contrary, he tries to do justice to the objective element of Christianity whenever possible" (*ibid.,* p. 230).

But Kierkegaard lived in a day when Lutheran orthodoxy, to say nothing of Hegelian philosophy, magnifying the objective and suppressing the subjective, kept people from a vital relationship with Jesus Christ, the living Truth. *Fides quae* and *fides historica* had quite largely supplanted *fides qua* and *fides propria.* Christ as Person was shamefully ignored; only His insights were considered of value. Angrily Kierkegaard exclaims: "They have simply done away with Christ, cast Him out and taken possession of His teaching, almost regarding Him at last as one does an anonymous author—the doctrine is the principal thing, is the whole thing" (Kierkegaard, *op. cit.,* p. 123). Hence Kierkegaard sees no option except to supply a corrective: deliberately he overstresses subjectivity, *fides quo, fides propria* (Diem, *op. cit.,* p. 154). "There is no question of a dilemma between the subjective or the objective in the apprehension of religious content of revealed truth. This is the question: Should *emphasis* be placed on the doctrinal content as such, or on the personal assimilation of religious truth? What our age needs, without the shadow of a doubt, is a subjective thinker in the sense of the word" (cited in Hamer, *op. cit.,* p. 233).

His task is plain: he must help bring Christianity down from the realm of the abstract to the level of concrete experience where once again the Gospel will be meaningfully *pro me,* for myself as an existing sinner. "We must make effective the authority and inspiration of our example and pattern, in order to awaken at least a certain amount of respect for the religion of Christianity; in order to make it clear, to some extent, what it means to be a Christian, in order to transfer Christianity from the objective plane (the approach of learning, doubt, and chatter) to the subjective" (cited in Diem, *op. cit.,* p. 147).

This explains why Kierkegaard slights the *fides quae* or the *what* of faith, concentrating almost exclusively on its *quo* or *how.* "God himself is precisely this: *how* one relates himself to him. In the case of tangible and external objects, the object is something other than the way. Many ways are possible. One can perhaps hit upon an easy way, and so forth. In the case of God, *how* is *what*" (Johnson and Thulstrup, *op. cit.,* p. 171).

Defending his theology of faith, Kierkegaard in his *Journals* refers to Johannes Climacus, the pseudonymous author of the monumental *Concluding Unscientific Postscript,* which gives about fifty pages to the objective problem of Christianity and devotes its more than five hundred remaining pages to the subjective problem: "In all that is usually said about Johannes Climacus being purely subjective.... people have forgotten, in addition to everything else concrete about him, that in one of the last sections he shows that the curious thing is: that there is a 'how' which has this quality, that if *it* is truly given, then the 'what' is also given; and that is the 'how' of 'faith' " (*ibid.,* pp. 160, 161).

3. Kierkegaard's effort to summon back to the living Truth an orthodoxy bowing down before the shrine of objectivity no doubt inspires his well-known dictum, "Subjectivity is truth." "If subjectivity is truth, the definition of truth must at the same time contain a reflection of the reaction to mere objectivity, a recollection of that parting of the ways, and such allusions would suggest the tension of true inwardness. Here is such a definition of truth: *Objective incertitude, clung to and appropriated with passionate inwardness, is truth, the* highest truth that there can be, *for one who exists*" (cited in Diem, *op. cit.,* p. 39).

Misleading as this dictum may be, it does not brashly advocate an irrational voluntarism; it must not be brushed aside as nonsensical. Even the Roman Catholic critic, Jerome Hamer, defends Kierkegaard against the charge of "romantic subjectivism" (Hamer, *op. cit.,* p. 221). Kierkegaard is simply reminding us that man is more than a disembodied intellect. Man is a self whose essence is not a cool, detached, emotionless *ratio.* "The real subject," he insists, "is not the cognitive but the ethically existing subject" (*ibid.,* p. 221). Man, every man, is a flesh-and-blood individual; caught up in all the anxieties and ambiguities of life, he is faced with inescapable choices. Hence truth—not mathematical formulae or logical propositions but ethical and religious truth—remains an abstraction until it has been personally appropriated and incarnationally worked out. Affirmed intellectually, truth is often denied existentially. And therefore truth is really not truth *for me* until I affirm it inwardly, passionately, decisively—yes, existentially!

According to Kierkegaard, then, Christianity falls necessarily into the category of subjectivity. "Christianity is a spirit; a spirit is inwardness; inwardness is subjectivity; subjectivity is essentially passion, and in its highest form an infinite, personal, passionate interest in one's eternal happiness. As soon as the subjectivity is eliminated, and from subjectivity passion, and from passion infinite interest, there is no decision, neither in this problem, nor in any other. All essential decisiveness is rooted in subjectivity.... From the objective viewpoint, there are results everywhere, but nowhere are decisive results. This is a perfectly logical position, precisely because decisiveness inheres in subjectivity alone, essentially in its passion, *maxime* in personal passion, which is infinitely interested in its own eternal happiness" (*ibid.,* p. 245).

It follows, moreover, that faith, the organ for establishing the God-relationship through Jesus Christ, also falls necessarily into the category of subjectivity, and as such is distinct from knowledge. In point of fact, faith and knowledge are totally heterogeneous; when knowledge intrudes, when objective certainty is achieved, faith immediately evaporates. "If I am capable of grasping God objectively, I do not believe, but precisely because I cannot do this I must believe" (Johnson and Thulstrup, *op. cit.,* p. 199). In other words, as one of the greatest Scandinavian authorities on Kierkegaard, Eduard Geismar, suggests, subjectivity is Christianity's defense "against every merely intellectual assimilation, every attempt to regard it as something to understand or explain" (cited in T. H. Croxall, *Kierkegaard Studies*, London, Lutterworth Press, 1948, p. 129). And a merely objective relationship to Christianity, a pseudo-relationship of *notitia* and *assensus* without *fiducia*, is Kierkegaard's *bête noire,* a soul-destroying counterfeit of faith.

4. We can understand, therefore, why Kierkegaard rejects every attempt to ground faith on evidence. We can understand, too, his fierce polemic against an apologetic which requires history to substantiate and motivate faith.

Kierkegaard recognizes, to be sure, that Christianity is inescapably rooted in history. Indeed, he highlights this fact because the very historical character of the Gospel compels the exercise of faith. In a profound discussion Kierkegaard argues that history is the sphere of Becoming. When an event transpires, an event which was once a mere possibility, it issues out of the womb of non-being into actuality. Thus it is burdened with a twofold uncertainty. First, it might never have been;

logically we are at a loss to account for its emergence from non-being, regardless of what Hegel may claim to the contrary. Second, the way in which the event emerged might have been different: though we can grasp what has happened by sense or reason, we cannot grasp why and how it happened precisely as it did (T. H. Croxall, *Kierkegaard Commentary*, New York, Harper & Brothers, 1956, pp. 178-189). In brief we are unable to prove the necessity of any historical event, Hegel notwithstanding. In other words, history, a free process of becoming in time, rests upon an abyss of uncertainty. As Hermann Diem helpfully exegetes Kierkegaard's rather tortuous dialectic: "There is no means of knowing directly that the historical has come to be as the effect of a cause. It can be immediately realized how doubtful it must always be whether it has become thus by necessity or by a freely operating cause. This question cannot be decided by knowledge and the accompanying doubt cannot be argued away. If the historian supposes that what he immediately perceives is the effect of a certain cause and therefore might have been quite different, he is drawing a conclusion against which doubt must protest. In order to preclude this doubt, therefore, the statement must take the form not of a conclusion but of a decision. And for Kierkegaard this decision is *faith*.... Faith therefore is the means for the apprehension of the historical" (Diem, *op. cit.*, p. 62).

This basic uncertainty is compounded, furthermore, by other factors. In the first place, the most laborious research can never demonstrate that an event transpired precisely as it has been reported. At best history yields only a probability, an approximation. But rejoice! Kierkegaard exhorts. The impossibility of demonstration compels the exercise of faith. "What a piece of good fortune it is that this so desirable hypothesis, the supreme desire of critical theology, turns out to be an impossibility because even the fullest realization of its aim can only yield approximate results! And again how fortunate for the scholar that the fault is in no sense theirs! If all the angels united their efforts, they could still only afford us approximative conclusions, because in this matter we have only historical knowledge, that is, an approximation as our sole certitude" (*ibid.*, p. 91, 92).

In the second place, a devastating objection must be reckoned with. How can an event in time, an event inescapably befogged by uncertainty, furnish the sole and all-determining basis of eternal blessedness? In 1777 Gotthold Ephraim Lessing wrote a tract, "Concerning the Proof of Spirit and Power," which advances this thesis: "Accidental truths of history can never be the proof of necessary truths of reason" (Henry Chadwick, *Lessing's Theological Writings*, London, Adam and Charles Black, 1956, p. 53). Lessing inquires: "If on historical grounds I have no objection to the statement that Christ raised to life a dead man; must I therefore accept it as true that God has a Son who is of the same essence as himself? What is the connection between my inability to raise any significant objection to the evidence of the former and my obligation to believe something against which my reason rebels? If on historical grounds I have no objection to the statement that this Christ himself rose from the dead, must I therefore accept it as true that this risen Christ was the Son of God? ... to jump with that historical truth to a quite different class of truths, and to demand of me that I should form all my metaphysical and moral ideas accordingly; to expect me to alter all my fundamental ideas of the nature of the Godhead because I cannot set any credible testimony against the resurrection of Christ: if this is not a *metabosis eis allo genos,* then I do not know what Aristotle meant by this phrase" (*ibid.,* p. 53; cf. B. B. Warfield's incisive remarks "Christless Christianity," in *Christology and Criticism,* New York, Oxford University Press, 1929, pp. 318-320).

This is Kierkegaard's problem—except that from his standpoint the problem is a disguised blessing. The very difficulty compels the exercise of faith. So he remarks concerning his book, *Philosophical Fragments:* "That an eternal blessedness is decided in time through the relationship to something historical was the content of my experiment and what I now call Christianity ... To avoid distraction again, I do not wish to bring forward any other Christian principles; they are all contained in this one, and may be consistently derived from it, just as this determination also offers the sharpest contrast with paganism" (Johnson and Thulstrup, *op. cit.,* p. 214).

In the third place, how can a man living centuries after Jesus Christ achieve contemporaneity with Him? How can distance in time be obliterated? How can we experience the historical Figure as a living reality today? "Becoming a Christian in truth comes to mean to become contemporary with Christ. And if becoming a Christian does not come to mean this, then all the talk about becoming a Christian is nonsense and self-deception and conceit, in part even blasphemy and sin against the Second Commandment of the Law and sin against the Holy Ghost" (Kierkegaard, *op. cit.,* p. 68).

But how, the question persists, can a man living centuries later achieve contemporaneity with Jesus Christ? The very difficulty compels the exercise of faith, the same faith exercised by His first-century disciples who overcame the offense of the God-Man, Deity in time and flesh, the Creator incognito, the paradox which offended most of Christ's first-century contemporaries.

5. Not alone does the historical uncertainty of Christianity compel the exercise of faith; its logical absurdity, argues Kierkegaard, serves the same function.

This area of Kierkegaard's thought has been frequently misunderstood. Hence a consummate dialectician has often been labeled an irrationalist. One can sympathize with Kierkegaard's anger when some of his critics remarked that he had no interest in the bearing of thought upon faith. In his *Journals,* as Lindstrom tells us, Kierkegaard "points out that he had produced a wealth of pseudonymous writings, devoted to the investigation from various angles of the problem of belief, defining the realm of faith and attempting to determine its heterogeneity with respect to other spheres of spiritual life. And how had these investigations been carried out? With the aid of dialectic and thought. He goes on to claim that there is hardly a single writer who has thought about faith in such measure as he who has not been occupied simply by thoughtless speculation about individual dogmas. He claims that he, on the contrary, had really 'thought,' concluding that indeed one must first clarify the entire problem of faith" (Johnson and Thulstrup, *op. cit.,* p. 228).

Whatever one may conclude about Kierkegaard's view of the relationship between faith and reason, he cannot dismiss this dialectician as a bigoted voluntarist who flouts logic. An irrational retreat to *fiducia* is something Kierkegaard never advocates. "It is easy enough to leap from the irksome task of developing and sharpening one's intellect, and so get loud applause, and to defend oneself against all objections by remarking: 'This is a higher understanding.' The believing Christian both has and uses his understanding. By and large he respects what is human, and does not put it down to lack of understanding if anybody is not a Christian. But with regard to Christianity, here he believes against the understanding, and also uses his understanding in order to take care that he believes against the understanding" (cited in Croxall, *Kierkegaard Commentary,* p. 29).

It cannot be denied that by his constant underscoring of paradox and absurdity Kierkegaard invites criticism. The doctrine of the God-Man, he insists, is the absolute paradox: eternity's invasion of time is a fact at which reason balks. "Jesus Christ," he writes, "is the paradox, which history can never digest or convert into a common syllogism" (Kierkegaard, *op. cit.,* p. 33). How can an absurdity be reduced to a syllogism? And the idea of the God-Man, Kierkegaard contends, is literally absurd. "There is neither in heaven, nor on earth, nor in the depths, nor in the aberrations of the most fantastic thinking, the possibility of a (humanly speaking) more insane combination" (Johnson and Thulstrup, *op. cit.,* p. 210).

Inseparable from this absolute paradox, however, are other paradoxes. Original sin is such a paradox (*ibid.,* p. 216); so is the forgiveness of sins (p. 211); so, too, is the inspiration of Scripture (p. 217); so, once more, is the concept of Providence (p. 216). What is a paradox, after all, but a hopeless confusion of categories—like the unthinkable effort in the doctrine of original sin to take genetics, an element which belongs to the category of the physical, and merge it with guilt, an element which belongs to the category of the ethical (pp. 216, 217)? The supreme example of such confusion is the Incarnation, a dogma which seeks to fuse the incommensurables of time and eternity, deity and humanity, suffering and sovereignty! Kierkegaard calls the Incarnation "a folly to the understanding and an offense to the human heart" (p. 216), "a crucifixion of the understanding" (p. 217). With respect to the union of the predicates, God and man, in one hyphenated term, God-Man, he exclaims: "That which in accordance with its nature is eternal comes into existence in time, is born, grows up, and dies—this is a breach with all thinking" (p. 210).

There is reason, accordingly, why Kierkegaard is often branded an enemy of reason. But is he? Ontologically, at any rate, he votes for rationality, as a decent Christian is constrained to do. "The eternal essential truth itself is by no means a paradox, but becomes paradoxical through its relation to existence" (cited in Diem, *op. cit.,* p. 49). Epistemologically, moreover, Kierkegaard recognizes that the laws of logic must be obeyed. Logical nonsense, he maintains, is logical nonsense and may be logically exposed as such. The Christian is a believer, not a stupid simpleton. "Nonsense, therefore, he cannot believe against the understanding, for precisely the understanding will discern that it is nonsense and will prevent him from believing it" (Kierkegaard, *Concluding Unscientific Postscript,* Princeton, Princeton University Press, 1941, p. 504). And in at least one passage Kierkegaard asserts that "no self-contradiction" exists in the idea that "Christ was God in the guise of a servant" (Johnson and Thulstrup, *op. cit.,* p. 219).

How, then, does he define the absurd? It is a necessary category of thought, marking the boundaries beyond which reason cannot pass. "The Absurd is a category, it is the negative criterion for God or for the relationship to God. When the believer believes, the Absurd is not the Absurd—faith transforms it; but in every weak moment, to him it is again more or less the Absurd. The passion of faith is the only thing capable of mastering the Absurd. If this were not so, faith would not be faith in the strictest sense, but would be a kind of knowledge. The Absurd provides a negative demarcation of the sphere of faith, making it a sphere in itself. . . . the Absurd and faith—this is the like for like which is necessary if there is to be friendship and if this friendship is to be maintained between two such dissimilar qualities as God and man. . . . The Absurd is the negative criterion for that which is higher than human understanding and human knowing. The function of the understanding is to recognize the Absurd as such—and then to leave it up to each and every man whether or not he will believe it" (*ibid.,* pp. 182-184).

And what does Kierkegaard mean by paradox? He means essentially the same thing which he means by the absurd, a necessary category of thought. "Paradox is a category: everything turns on this point, really. People have been accustomed to talk thus—to say that one cannot under-stand such and such a thing does not satisfy science which insists on understanding. But it is this point of view which is wrong. One should say, rather, just the opposite: if *human* knowledge will not admit that there is something which it cannot understand, or, to speak more precisely, something about which it clearly realises that understanding is out of the question, then all is confusion. The problem for human knowledge is to see that there is something else. Human knowledge is normally in a hurry to understand more and more, but if it will at last take the trouble to understand itself, then it must frankly confirm the fact of paradox. Paradox is not a concession but a category, an ontological description expressing the relationship between a personally existent spirit and eternal truth" (Diem, *op. cit.,* p. 50).

In short, logic must "understand that faith cannot be understood"; it must acknowledge that "reasons can be given to explain why no reasons can be given" (Johnson and Thulstrup, *op. cit.,* p. 218). "If there is to be a science of Christianity," Kierkegaard affirms, "it must be erected not on the basis of the necessity of comprehending faith but on the basis of com-prehending that faith cannot be comprehended" (*ibid.,* p. 179).

One may argue, consequently, that Kierkegaard's position is not *contra rationem,* but rather *supra rationem.* This interpretation gains credence from what Fabro considers a pivotal passage in the *Concluding Unscien-tific Postscript:* "A true sentence of Hugh of St. Victor: 'In things which are above reason, faith is not really supported by reason, because reason cannot grasp what faith believes; but there is also a something here as a result of which reason is determined, or which determines reason to honor faith which it cannot perfectly understand' " (*ibid.,* p. 185).

Fabro also notes Kierkegaard's laudatory comment on the Leibnitzian distinction between "that which is above reason and that which is against reason" (*ibid.,* p. 187; cf. p. 209). But Martin J. Heinecken argues, on the contrary, that Kierkegaard sanctions no such distinction: he is not Leibnitz *redivivus.* To so interpret Kierkegaard is to misinterpret him grossly. Why saddle upon him the Thomistic philosophy which as a true son of the Reformation he abhors (Heinecken, *op. cit.,* pp. 346-355)?

In any event, this much is plain: the very nature of Christianity as a tissue of absurdity and paradox compels the exercise of faith. "Is it pos-sible to conceive of a more foolish contradiction than that of wanting to *prove* (no matter for the present purpose whether it be from history or from anything else in the wide world one wants to *prove* it) that a definite individual man is God? That an individual man is God, declares himself to be God, is indeed the 'offense' *kat echochen.* But what is the offense, the offensive thing? What is a variance with (human) reason? And such a thing as that one would attempt to prove! But to 'prove' is to demonstrate something to be the rational reality it is. Can one demonstrate that to be a rationality which is at variance with reason? Surely not, unless one would contradict itself. One can 'prove' only that it is at variance with reason" (Kierkegaard, *Training in Christianity*, pp. 28, 29).

Or as Kierkegaard concludes this whole matter: "The absurd is the proper object of faith and the only object that can be believed" (Hamer, *op. cit.*, p. 247).

Once faith has been exercised, however, the absurd loses its irrationality and paradox ceases to be a heavy burden for the intellect to carry. In the sphere of Christian experience, reached by a fiducial leap, "the absurd is not the absurd—faith transforms it" (Johnson and Thulstrup, *op. cit.*, p. 221). So Kierkegaard can affirm: "In the category of the Absurd, rightly understood, there is therefore absolutely nothing terrifying. No, it is precisely the category of courage and of enthusiasm. . . . And true faith breathes healthily and blissfully in the Absurd" (*ibid.*, p. 183).

6. Grounded on historical uncertainty and logical absurdity, faith is always accompanied by its sinister shadow, the possibility of offense, a violent revulsion of mind *and heart*. Offense is a scandal which impels a man, despite his need, to spurn the appeal of Jesus Christ, "Come unto me, and I will give you rest." "Just as the concept 'faith' is a highly characteristic note of Christianity, so also is 'offense' a highly characteristic note of Christianity and stands in close relation to faith. The possibility of offense is the crossways, or it is like standing at the crossways. From the possibility of the offense a man turns either to offense or to faith. . . . So inseparable from faith is the possibility of offense that if the God-Man were not the possibility of offense, He could not be the object of faith. So the possibility of offense is assumed in faith, assimilated by faith, it is the negative mark of the God-Man" (Kierkegaard, *Training in Christianity*, pp. 83, 143).

This is the crux of existence, the point of decision. And here, motivated by an infinite passion, the Christian turns his back on the offense and makes the leap of faith.

But the offense is not only or primarily intellectual in nature; it is primarily ethical. Recall Kierkegaard's statement that the incarnation is "an offense to the heart" (Johnson and Thulstrup, *op. cit.*, p. 216). Decision for Christ involves the surrender of autonomy, the practice of self-abnegation, a daily crucifixion. This is what intensifies the intellectual scandal. "It is not difficult for men to understand Christianity, but it is difficult for them to understand how much self-discipline and self-denial Christianity demands" (*ibid.*, p. 218). In fact, at bottom man's desire to remain his own master may account for his desperate clinging to the intellectual difficulties which can be marshaled against faith. "Christianity is not a matter of doctrines; all talk of its scandal from the doctrinal point of view rests on a misunderstanding. When people talk of the offensive aspect of the doctrine of the God-man, the doctrine of the Atonement, it means that they are weakening the shock of the offensiveness. No, the moment of scandalisation is connected either with Christ or with the fact that one is oneself a Christian" (cited in Diem, *op. cit.*, pp. 107, 108).

Or to quote Pascal as Kierkegaard does in his *Journals:* "It is so difficult to believe because it is so difficult to obey" (cited in Johnson and Thulstrup, *op. cit.*, p. 226, n. 17).

7. The exercise of faith makes the believer contemporaneous with Jesus Christ. It brings him into a vital God-relationship marked by "courage and enthusiasm." For all its demands, it banishes anxiety and gives peace. "Our Lord Jesus Christ did not bring a system of doctrine into the world, neither did He teach, but rather as a pattern demanded discipleship—and, at the same time, through the power of His atonement, drove, as far as possible, all fear out of the human soul" (cited in Diem, *op. cit.*, p. 147).

If Kierkegaard's own experience may be taken as illustrative—and his devotional writings as well—faith leads a sinful man into a loving fellowship with the transcendent God. "If, on some point or another, I have been mistaken, it remains nonetheless true that God is love. I believe this, and one who believes it is not mistaken. If I am mistaken, this will certainly become evident to me, I am sorry to say ... but God is love. We can say that He is love, He has been love, but not that He will be love; no, because the future would be too long for me to wait; He *is love*" (cited in Hamer, *op. cit.*, p. 236). How paradoxical it is, Hamer exclaims, that the thinker who accentuates the ontological and moral distance between God and man also magnifies His love—and evidently experienced it! (*loc. cit.*).

Yet according to Kierkegaard faith never becomes a *tranquilla possessio*. The believer does not enjoy security. Moment by moment he remains in a state of danger, haunted by the possibility of offense. He floats over a depth of 70,000 fathoms—buoyed up by what? By omnipotent arms or by his own psychic energy tirelessly repeating the decision of faith? Kierkegaard is no Pelagian, of course; but one wishes he were less ambiguous in announcing that faith is a divine gift rather than a human work.

III. AN ORTHODOX CRITIQUE OF KIERKEGAARD

How is this theology of faith to be appraised? What are its merits and liabilities? Does it mark a significant advance beyond traditional Protestantism?

1. Evangelicals are grateful for Kierkegaard's remarkable genius as a psychologist, a genius which he has focused lovingly and fruitfully on faith as a concept and a phenomenon. They gladly appropriate whatever deeper understanding of the God-relationship can be attained introspectively or scientifically. Yet in their opinion no psychology of Christian faith is possible. As a divine mystery, it ultimately defies human penetration, even the penetration of a Kierkegaard. Lovell Cocks speaks for evangelicals at this juncture: "There are certainly psychological states that accompany faith's verdict, and these the psychologist may describe. But when he calls his description a 'psychology of faith' we are bound to protest. So by virtue of its psychological continuity with the rest of our experience the act of faith cannot but occur in a context of 'religious experience,' of hopes and fears, doubts and assurances; these psychological states are not of faith's essence. And although the 'religious experience' of the 'twice-born' shows a certain typical structure and movement, it is still true that faith itself is not a succession of psychological states but an act of knowing whose psychical accompaniments may be quite unsensational and non-typical. The 'psychology of faith' may thus be as irrelevant to faith itself as the boredom or interest of the schoolboy to the truth of the geometrical proposition he studies and his ultimate apprehension of it" (H. F. Lovell Cocks, *By Faith Alone,* London, James Clarke & Co. Ltd., 1943, p. 72).

Hence, while evangelicals admire the acumen, subtlety, and depth of Kierkegaard's insight, they feel uneasy much of the time in reading these profound analyses of faith. Is this theology or is it psychology? If psychology, is it one more instance of love's labor lost? Perhaps not, however, if sophisticated unbelievers, challenged by a sophistication which exceeds their own and which is yet the servant of a childlike trust, are driven to make the leap of faith.

2. Evangelicals are grateful for Kierkegaard's refusal to classify Christianity as a mere species of the genus faith. He considers the Gospel and the experience it produces unique. He would, therefore, unquestionably challenge Gerhard Ebeling's statement, "Christian faith is not a special faith, but simply faith . . . when we simply speak . . . of 'the faith,' then we mean Christian faith, but with the implication that it is true faith, simply faith, just as Christian love is not a special kind of love, but true love, simply love" (Ebeling, *op. cit.,* pp. 20, 21).

By no means, Kierkegaard would reply! Christianity is precisely what Ebeling denies: it is a special faith. To catalogue it as just another specimen of faith-in-general or even as the highest example of faith-in-general is to deny the New Testament.

3. Evangelicals are grateful for Kierkegaard's attack on an intellectualized, rationalized, depersonalized belief which quite completely overlooks *fiducia,* reducing Christianity to a matter of dialectic, a philosophical affair that involves no existential commitment. Evangelicals are grateful for Kierkegaard's passionate advocacy of a trust which inspires the

believer to respond with his whole life. Only this emphasis, evangelicals are convinced, will keep orthodoxy from degenerating spiritually. Yet is this emphasis, while made by Kierkegaard with extraordinary effectiveness, something new or original? Is it not the emphasis of historic orthodoxy? Thus Warfield sums up Kierkegaard's entire polemic in a one-sentence definition of faith: "It is a movement of the whole inner man and is set in contrast with an unbelief that is akin, not to ignorance, but to disobedience" (Warfield, *op. cit.,* pp. 501-502).

4. Evangelicals are grateful for Kierkegaard's awareness of the objective ground of faith, its ontological and historical foundations, its sheer givenness, its theocentricity. Yet evangelicals wonder whether his entire approach is not overly anthropocentric, concentrating so exclusively on the subject of faith that faith's Object tends to become obscured. Hence evangelicals agree with Barth's criticism: "The objection against the underlying but all the more powerful presupposition of those modern doctrines of faith is in moral categories an objection against their arrogance. They rest on the fact that in the last centuries (on the broad way which leads from the older Pietism to the present-day theological existentialism inspired by Kierkegaard) the Christian has begun to take himself seriously in a way which is not at all commensurate with the seriousness of Christianity. They represent Christian truth as though its supreme glory is to rotate around the individual Christian with his puny faith, so that there is cause for gratification if they do not regard him as its lord and creator. From the bottom up we can neither approve nor make common cause with this procedure of modern doctrines of faith" (*op. cit.,* p. 741).

For all his stress on wholly Other, then, is Kierkegaard too anthropocentric? Barth thinks that he is, and the evangelicals concur.

5. While grateful for his struggle to correct an exaggerated objectivity, evangelicals fear that Kierkegaard's stress on subjectivity is just as exaggerated. Barth proves to be a discerning critic at this point also. In his *Church Dogmatics* he proclaims with a power equal to Kierkegaard's that unless Christianity becomes true *pro me,* true for an individual personally, it is abortively "untrue." To that extent Barth identifies himself with the thinking "of Pietism old and new, with that of Kierkegaard, with that of a theology like W. Herrmann's, and with that of the theological existentialism of our own day (so far as it can be seriously regarded as theological)" (*ibid.,* p. 755). At the same time Barth warns that an exaggerated subjectivism may, as in Kierkegaard, beget a warped and diminished Christianity. "It was an intolerable truncation of the Christian message when the older Protestantism steered the whole doctrine of the atonement—and with it, ultimately, the whole of theology—into the *cul de sac* of the question of the individual experience of grace, which is always an anxious one when taken in isolation, the question of individual conver-

sion by it and to it, and of its presuppositions and consequences. The almost inevitable result was that the great concepts of justification and sanctification came more and more to be understood and filled out psychologically and biographically, and the doctrine of the Church seemed to be of value only as a description of the means of salvation and grace indispensable to this individual and personal process of salvation. ... we will do well not to allow ourselves to be crowded again into the same *cul de sac* on the detour via Kierkegaard" (p. 150). Unhappy over the sub-orthodox elements in Barth's theology, evangelicals are happy to join with him in decrying a truncated Christianity which pivots everything on the individual's experience.

6. Evangelicals share Kierkegaard's negative stance with respect to demythologization. As an unflinching supernaturalist, Kierkegaard accepts miracles, especially the miracles of incarnation and resurrection. In this respect he is no forerunner of Rudolf Bultmann. But evangelicals suspect, as does Hermann Diem, that unintentionally Kierkegaard has served as a sort of John the Baptist for Bultmann. How? The sequence of faith, according to Kierkegaard, is this. A man decides to believe in Jesus Christ without any logical reason for doing so. On the basis of his own decision he discovers experientially that Jesus Christ is his contemporary with power to save. This experiential fact leads him to believe the historical fact recorded in Scripture concerning Jesus of Nazareth. This historical fact leads him in turn to believe the eternal fact that Jesus of Nazareth was God in the flesh. Hence Diem contends that according to Kierkegaard: "It is faith which through the existential fulfillment of the believer transforms a specific historical fact into a revelatory fact, and this change comes about through insight into the meaningfulness of that historical fact. Thus we have at last the figure of that Kierkegaard whom Rudolf Bultmann is said to have commented on in the form of an exegesis of St. John's Gospel" (Diem, *op. cit.,* p. 183).

Diem's study of the Kierkegaardian dialectic shows that like Bultmann, reversing the New Testament order, Kierkegaard puts faith before fact. And this is the evangelical's deepest objection to an existentialist theology. Fact must be the foundation of faith or faith has no foundation.

7. Evangelicals are grateful that Kierkegaard's discussion of faith and history brings to the fore perhaps the most crucial problem which Christianity faces today on the intellectual plane. This is a problem—or really a complex of problems—which requires untiring study, reflection and dialogue. But like Lessing, has Kierkegaard failed to stress sufficiently the true nature of the difficulty? Barth apparently penetrates to the very heart of this matter when he inquires whether the basic problem is actually that of historical distance. Is not Lessing's problem a protective smokescreen to hide the true problem? And what is that? The problem of decision! This is the problem which the sinner attempts to evade. He

dreads the shattering of his ego which he must suffer when confronted by Jesus Christ, the living Reality of the Saviour Who judges even while He offers forgiveness (Barth, *op. cit.*, pp. 288-293). Lessing's problem resolves itself into a matter of abandoning self-sufficiency, admitting sin, and accepting grace. In short, all the labored historical, philosophical, and logical objections to faith are ultimately a moral and spiritual problem. Kierkegaard, to be sure, perceives and says this. He fails, however, to trumpet it so ringingly as Barth does.

8. Evangelicals are grateful that Kierkegaard stoutly denies the impossibility of creating faith by any human proofs. It is Calvin, evangelicals recall, who states: "They are rash who would prove to unbelievers by arguments that Scripture is of God, for this cannot be known except by faith" (cited in Lecerf, *op. cit.*, p. 205). Evangelicals recall that Calvin also states: "Faith cannot be content with the witness of men, whoever they may be, if it is not preceded by the authority of God. But when the Holy Spirit has testified to us internally that it is God who is speaking, then we give some place to the testimonies of men in order to assure ourselves as to the certainty of the history. By the certainty of the history I mean the knowledge that we possess of the things which have happened either through having seen them ourselves or through having heard others speak of them" *(ibid.,* p. 228).

Evangelicals confess that no apologetic is able to create faith in a human heart. As Auguste Lecerf eloquently avers, only the Holy Spirit can do that: "If the Reformed Christian believes with absolute certainty in the historic appearance of Jesus the Christ, in the reign of Tiberius, in His crucifixion under a Roman procurator named Pilate, it is not on the evidence of a Josephus, a Tacitus or a Suetonius. The discussion of the texts of these authors can give no more than a certitude of probability, contested by scholars as well-informed and as competent as those who maintain the thesis of their historical reliability. . . . The facts of sacred history cannot become certain with a certainty of faith except on condition that, by His infinite power, through contact with the inspired texts or by the supernatural teaching of the Church, the Spirit of God renders present the past and puts on it the seal of His inner witness, the persuasive force of which is irresistible. It is only after the exercise of this divine pressure that the human reasons take on a convincing signification" *(ibid.,* p. 307).

In his repudiation of a rationalistic apologetic Kierkegaard fails to provide an adequate source and basis for faith. He neglects the all-sufficient source and the impregnable basis of faith—the witness of the Holy Spirit. Admittedly, he says: "There is only one proof for the truth of Christianity: the inner proof, testimonium Spiritus Sancti" (Johnson and Thulstrup, *op. cit.*, p. 173). But this appears to be a solitary reference, a glossly deficient comment of I John 5:9 (cf. the weak chapter on the Holy

Spirit in Croxall, *Kierkegaard Studies,* pp. 210-219). Eliminate or minimize the *testimonium Spiritus Sancti* and what is left once the utter failure of traditional apologetic has been exposed? Nothing remains but a choice between rational skepticism or sub-rational voluntarism. It is to this impasse that Kierkegaard brings Protestant theology. How, then, can we achieve a theological breakthrough? The overriding need is for a rehabilitation and development of the Reformation doctrine of the Spirit's testimony as the ultimate ground of faith. (A notable contribution is that of Bernard Ramm, *The Witness of the Spirit,* Grand Rapids, Michigan, Wm. B. Eerdmans Publishing Company, 1960.)

THE NATURE
OF JUSTIFICATION

✝

Lorman Petersen

Lorman Petersen is Professor of New Testament Interpretation at Concordia Theological Seminary, Springfield, Illinois. From 1956-62 he was Visiting Professor of Religion in Concordia Teachers College, River Forest, Illinois. He holds the B.A. degree from Concordia College, St. Louis, and the B.D., M.S.T., and Th.D. degrees from Concordia Seminary, St. Louis, and has pursued additional studies at University of Chicago.

THE NATURE
OF JUSTIFICATION

SOME churchmen are suggesting that the familiar terms "justify" and "justification" be jettisoned and substitutes be used in Christian teaching today because they are not understood by modern man. For example, a Christian college student is said to have written the following definition of the doctrine of justification: "Faith is the only way we can be acceptable to God and be true Christians. With faith we are able to please God and all our sins *are then overlooked* by God as a result of His grace." As a statement of justification as taught in the Scriptures this formulation is patently wrong. It also does violence to both the doctrine of God and Christ's atonement. And if it is typical of a large segment of church members, then much is to be desired in organized Christianity's communication of fundamental scriptural truths to present-day Christians.

When the Apostle Paul preached the doctrine of justification in the mission fields of the ancient Roman world it would seem that the idea of justification was readily understood by both "Greeks and barbarians, the wise and the foolish" (Rom. 1:14). To the troublesome Corinthians he simply wrote, "But you were washed, you were sanctified, *you were justified* in the name of the Lord Jesus Christ and in the Spirit of our God," and let it go at that (I Cor. 6:11). Even in his Epistle to the Romans, the longest and most forceful presentation of justification in the Bible, he does not pause to explain his terms to the converts but assumes his readers understood them. Is our modern world so different from St. Paul's or Luther's or Calvin's that these really simple terms are unintelligible to us? While this writer certainly does not oppose modern Bible versions or new methods of communicating the Gospel, he refuses to believe as yet that the old terms are outmoded or impractical.

Today words like "justify" and "justification" are often used differently from their original meaning. In present-day usage the justified man is an innocent man. Modern man uses the term to excuse his actions or to prove he was right in acting as he did, to vindicate himself either in principle or before the law. "I was justified in disciplining my son because he lied to me"; "The man was justified in killing the man because it was self-defense"; "Further investigation will justify your action" are typical statements. Used in this way the term has little in common with its prevalent meaning in Scripture. "Justify" and "justification" have always been legal terms, words used in the law courts. Do we not have courts of law today? Even if we assume that these terms are not used much in our courts in the biblical sense, does this mean they cannot be explained in terms of courtroom proceedings? After all, we still use terms like "pardon," "acquit," "render a decision," and "judgment." It is not merely a matter of semantics. These words are no more difficult than "hydromatic," "dragging," "egressing from a capsule," "thalidomide," or "I dig you." Often the content of the Gospel is the offense, not the terminology in which it is cached. Change the terms and the malady would still remain. It is mainly a matter of spelling out the old terms according to biblical usage.

A much more serious matter, in our opinion, concerns those modern theologians who change or obscure the biblical language, not because of semantics, but because of their own presuppositions. This is truly inexcusable, or unjustifiable, to use our term in the modern sense. If one honestly disagrees with another's statements, whether in the Bible or in any other book, he should state his disagreements instead of resorting to re-interpretation. This essay is an attempt, in humble fashion, to deal with both of these concerns—to explain the biblical teaching of justification in terms of the Scripture itself, and in doing so, to defend this precious doctrine against those whose formulations do not measure up to the biblical view.

I. JUSTIFICATION IN ST. PAUL

In his inspired teaching of God's revelation of salvation to sinful man, St. Paul used three picture words: "redemption," the setting free of a slave or prisoner by paying the price of liberation; "reconciliation," the restoration of peace between enemies, that is, of man's fellowship with God; and "justification," the acquittal of the sinner by the holy and gracious God. (All three terms appear in Romans. The Greek words are *apolytrosis* [redemption], Rom. 3:24; *katallagee* [reconciliation], Rom. 5:11; *dikaiosis* [justification], Rom. 4:25, 5:18; cf. Col. 1:14, Eph. 2:16, II Cor. 5:18-20. Galatians 3:13 throws light on the meaning of *redeem*, for there the Greek word is "purchase," or "buy out.") While the thrust of all three terms is basically the same, Paul's favorite term, especially in his Epistle to the Romans, was "justify" together with its related words.[1] In Romans he uses the idea of justification on "both sides of the ledger," as it were. That is, both in "justification by faith" and in "justification by works" the meaning of "justify" is the same. This fact contributes importantly toward a proper understanding of the term "justify." After the usual preliminary epistolary statements (Rom. 1:1-17), Paul launches into one of the most terrifying indictments of natural man ever recorded. Showing that sinful man can be saved only by justification is his method of presenting the doctrine. We note that the *idea of judgment* or *rendering a decision* is the *leitmotif* of his entire statement of justification.

In Romans 1:18-21, for example, Paul says that God has revealed His eternal power and deity in nature; from this revelation men form opinions about God. God gives this revelation, says Paul, "so that they are without excuse," that is, without defense when judgment comes. We read, further, that they rendered a judgment about God, for "although they knew God they did not honor him as God," but "they became futile in their thinking and their senseless minds were darkened. Claiming to be wise, they became foolish." On the surface it may seem that they were just ignorant idolaters. Actually, however, their judgment of God preceded their sin and idolatry; their actions betrayed their thoughts. At the same time, God rendered a judgment regarding them; three times it is recorded "Therefore God gave them up" (Rom. 1:24-28). Romans 1:28 specifically states "and since they *did not see fit* to acknowledge God, *God gave them up to a base mind* and to improper conduct." ("See fit" in Greek is *dokimazo* which means "to consider," "examine," or even "judge." "Base mind" is translated from *adokimos nous,* that is, God gave them over to a mind incapable of rendering correct judgments or opinions.) The Apostle concludes this part of the discussion by stating that "though they know God's *decree* [Greek: *dikaioma,* from same root as *dikaioo* "to justify"] that those who do such things deserve to die, they not only do them but *approve* those who practice them."

Paul continues his thesis of *judging* or *judgment* in chapter two of Romans. The man who *judges* another actually *condemns* himself, for he does the same things (Rom. 2:1-3). Romans 2:6-11 especially exemplifies this facet of justification. Revealed on the day of judgment will be the

---

[1] While the number of occurrences of redemption and reconciliation in the New Testament is small, we are confronted with numerous passages, mostly in Paul, in which *justify* and words of the same root appear. The adjective *dikaios* (just, or righteous) appears over eighty times; the noun *dikaiosyne* (righteousness) more than ninety times; the noun *dikaiosis* (justification) two times; the verb *dikaioo* (to justify) about forty times; the noun *dikaioma* (judgment, also decree) ten times; and the adverb *dikaioos* (righteously) occurs five times. Paul uses all these terms in Romans plus some compound forms. Note the "blood relationship" between *justify* and *righteousness* which isn't always apparent in English.

wrath of a holy God, stored up against every sinner. Since God's justice is righteous and perfect, He will award every man according to his works (Paul uses the compound *dikaiokrisia*, "righteous-judgment," again revealing how closely "judgment" and "justify" are connected). Paul says a judgment, a "justification" will be rendered for all men: eternal life to those who have done well, wrath and damnation to those who have disobeyed. The *verdict* will be as it should be, for there is no partiality with God. Then comes Paul's key and climactic verse, Romans 2:13: ". . . it is not the hearers of the law who are *righteous before God,* but the doers of the law shall be *justified."* Here Paul uses the term "justify" for the first time in Romans and does so in a context of law and judgment. Now in what sense are doers of the law righteous? Do they *become* righteous? Do they *make themselves* righteous? No, the Apostle says they are pronounced righteous *before God,* that is, in His sight, according to His divine opinion, judgment, or verdict. Paul is not teaching salvation or justification by works here; he is maintaining the basic principle of law and judgment involved in justification. No man can fulfill the law of God perfectly. Nevertheless, even if he could fulfill its demands, man would not thereby make himself righteous; but since it is God's law, only God could judge or pronounce man holy and righteous. Thus "to justify" in its first meaning is to render a judgment of guilty or not guilty. Later we will see that "justification by faith" specifically means to judge a man *not guilty,* that is, *to acquit the guilty rather than the innocent.* This is what Paul means by justification, God's acquittal of the sinner. In both Romans (3:20) and Galatians (2:16) Paul uses "justify" with the phrase "by works." In Galatians 2:16 the two phrases "justify by works" and "justify by faith" stand side by side. The former is only hypothetical, never possible. But the use of "justify" on both sides of the ledger gives an important insight into the meaning of the term.

This basic idea is exemplified in Romans 2:26: "So, if a man who is uncircumcised keeps the precepts of the law, will not his uncircumcision *be regarded as* circumcision?" Paul here uses a term which is closely related to "justify," namely, "to reckon" or "regard as." He is speaking of the true Jew as perceived *in God's sight.* A son of Abraham is an Israelite who is not merely circumcised but who also obeys the will of God. Contrariwise, a Gentile, or non-Jew, who is not circumcised but who does the will of God intrinsically is a true son of Abraham. To simplify this paradoxical thought, Paul says a man's uncircumcision is *regarded* or *counted as* circumcision. In other words, one thing is simply counted for another, or a person is regarded as someone he really is not. This is the basic, scriptural concept of justification.

II. NO MAN CAN JUSTIFY HIMSELF

Having established the principle of justification, Paul in Romans, chapter three, answers the next vital question: How is a man justified? How does he obtain a favorable judgment or acquittal? Misunderstanding sometimes occurs at this point because we commonly think of judgment as a negative concept, especially when speaking of divine judgment. But we should bear in mind that judging may be "not guilty" just as easily as "guilty," whether rendered by God or by man. God is always the judge, but is His verdict made on the basis of man's works or on his faith? The question ultimately is, can a man justify himself? We know Paul's answer. A man cannot gain justification for himself—this is a misuse of the biblical term. In the first place, since justification is a judgment, it is a decision made about a man by someone else. Secondly, after surveying all the possibilities among both Jews and Gentiles, Paul is forced to conclude that no man can gain acquittal by his works. If the Jew with all his advantages and "head-start" could not achieve justification, certainly no one else could. The verdict pronounced on man from God's universal courtroom is, "Every mouth is stopped [that is, if anyone protests God's decision] and the whole world is held accountable to God. For no human being will be justified in his sight by works of the law" (Rom. 3:19, 20).

III. JUSTIFICATION AND THE RIGHTEOUSNESS OF GOD

Where is there any hope then? Should man seek a different tribunal? Should he try to impeach the Judge? Can sinful man ever obtain a favorable verdict from this Judge? Is God's judgment always negative? Is there no acquittal? Paul pushes aside all these questions with one emphatic answer supplied by God: "Now the *righteousness of God* has been revealed *apart from all law,* namely, the righteousness of God through faith in Jesus Christ for all who believe ... they are justified by his grace as a gift" (Rom. 3:21). The revelation of God's wrath (Rom. 1:18) is answered by the revelation of His saving righteousness (the word for "righteousness" in Paul is *dikaiosyne,* easily seen to be akin to *dikaioo,* "to justify").

The well-known phrase "righteousness of God," as Paul uses it here and in Romans 1:17, is not an attribute of God but the activity of God in saving man. Paul borrowed this term from the Old Testament where it is "witnessed by the law and the prophets" (Rom. 3:21). In the Psalms and Isaiah it portrays God's grace in rescuing and delivering His people from their oppressors and their sin. Psalm 98:2, for example, is unmistakably clear: "The Lord hath made known *his salvation; his righteousness* hath he openly showed in the sight of the heathen." In Isaiah 56:1

we read, "Thus says the Lord: Keep justice and do righteousness, for soon *my salvation* will come and my deliverance be revealed." In Romans, Paul points out that this righteous activity of God is fulfilled in Christ; God saves men through the crucified Christ. To have this righteousness is to be justified. This fact is clearly shown in Romans 3:22, 25, 26, especially in the passage "the righteousness of God which is by faith in Jesus Christ" and in the words "whom God hath set forth to be a propitiation through faith in his blood, to declare his righteousness."

IV. JUSTIFICATION AND THE ATONEMENT

God's righteousness reminds us that we must pause to discuss Christ's atonement as it is tied up with justification. Justification cannot be separated from the atonement; indeed, justification rests upon it. The atonement explains "How can a just God acquit a sinner who remains sinful after he is justified?" Justification does not mean God "overlooks sin" or acts as if man were not a sinner. The sentimental view which many people hold of God makes Him simply a gracious old "grandfather" who winks at the sins of His "children." Such a view denies the integrity of the true God. No, God's holiness demands payment for sin and this penalty Christ paid in the atonement on the Cross. In justification God devised a plan whereby both His essential justice and His love as manifested in the salvation of sinners are given full due. By making Christ our Substitute, God preserved His own justice but at the same time achieved salvation for the sinner. It is unbiblical, therefore, to speculate whether God could or does forgive sins without Christ (Rom. 3:26).

In Romans 3:21-28 the "Holy of Holies" of the New Testament, Paul explains Christ's role in justification. Here all the great concepts involved in justification—the righteousness of God, faith, grace, redemption, propitiation—are linked in one majestic declaration. That sinful men "are justified by his grace as a gift *through the redemption which is in Christ Jesus,*" and that God "put forth [on the Cross] Christ as a propitiation through His blood [by his death]" are key statements in this passage. (The word "propitiation" is cumbersome but as yet no simpler word in English has been found which expresses the profundity of divine thought and action here. "Mercy seat" is next best but employs an entirely different metaphor. "Expiate" is inadequate because it does not go far enough and must be "re-loaded" with the biblical meaning.) God is involved in three ways in this atonement or act of propitiation: He is the Initiator, who first loved man; the Instrument or Means, who gave Himself in the incarnate Christ as the once-for-all sacrifice for sin; and He is the Object of His saving work, who satisfied His wrath and justice regarding sin through Christ's all-atoning sacrifice. Note how Paul expresses this in Ephesians 5:2, "Christ loved us and gave himself up for us, a fragrant offering and sacrifice *to God.*" Christ is at one and the same time Priest and Sacrifice. Similarly at one and the same time God satisfies Himself and forgives the sinner. Only in Christ does God justify the sinner by imputing Christ's perfect righteousness to the sinner who has none of his own. "For our sake he made him [Christ] to be sin who knew no sin, so that in him we might become the righteousness of God" (II Cor. 5:21).

Paul's discussion of justification and atonement in Romans culminates in the words, Christ "was put to death for our trespasses and raised again for our justification" (Rom. 4:25). God sentenced His innocent Son to punishment and death for man's sin. Since Christ completely fulfilled the law for man and suffered the punishment of his trespasses (Gal. 3:13), therefore God pronounced a loud "Well done!" upon Christ's work and raised Him from the dead to witness man's justification before the world. At the same time, says Paul, our justification was declared *because* of the Atonement. (The phrase "for our justification" is really *"because* of our justification," that is, because God had pronounced all men righteous as a result of His Son's perfect redemption or sacrifice He raised Christ from the dead. Note the close relationship of justification to other fundamental doctrines, namely, the Person of Christ and the Resurrection.) "The Scripture is clear that the wrath of God is visited upon sinners or else that the Son of God dies for them. . . . Either we die or He dies. But God 'commendeth his own love toward us, in that, while we were yet sinners, Christ died for us' (Rom. 5:8)" (Leon Morris, *The Apostolic Preaching of the Cross,* Grand Rapids, Wm. B. Eerdmans Publishing Company, 1955, p. 185. This is truly a significant study of the atonement and justification, extensive and fully documented, one of the best volumes to appear on our subject in many years).

V. UNIVERSAL AND PERSONAL JUSTIFICATION

Since Christ's all-atoning sacrifice covered all men's past, present and future sins, justification is universal. By raising His Son from the dead, God pronounced absolution upon the entire human race (I John 2:2). Many theologians call this *objective* justification. This does not mean universal salvation but rather universal grace and forgiveness. God pronounced all men righteous in Christ even though many men will not accept His forgiveness and many more will not even hear of it (Rom. 10:14-17). It means, too, that *our* sins were forgiven, even though we were not personally present. St. Paul discusses the relationship of universal justification and universal original sin as follows: "Therefore as sin came into the world through one man and death through sin, and so death spread to all men. . . . Then as one man's trespass led to condemnation for all men, so one man's act [Christ's] of righteousness leads to acquittal and life for all men" (Rom. 5:12, 18). This is why Paul says Christ "died for the ungodly," and "while we were yet sinners Christ died for us" (Rom. 5:6, 8). It is quite apparent that if God did not justify the ungodly, then man would be justified by works and there could be no justification by faith.

Universal justification is important for personal or subjective justification. If God had not justified all mankind the individual sinner might doubt he was included. Personal justification is simply this: when a sinner hears the Gospel and the Holy Ghost thereby works faith in his heart, then Christ's atonement becomes his and he personally accepts God's forgiveness. This experience makes him a Christian. But it should be remembered that universal or objective justification and subjective justification are not two separate acts of God. The latter is only the application of the former.

Universal and personal justification gives Christians tremendous impetus to believe the Gospel and to preach it to all men. God's love and Christ's work are of no avail to the individual sinner at all if he does not hear the Gospel. Unless the Gospel comes to condemned man and through it the Holy Spirit kindles faith and thus converts him to Christ, the Gospel is just as meaningless as if Christ had not risen. In such a case, man is yet in his sins (I Cor. 15:17). It is not enough to have the true doctrine of the Gospel; it must also be proclaimed (Rom. 10:14-17).

VI. JUSTIFICATION AS FORGIVENESS

Justification is really legal or courtroom terminology for the forgiveness of sins. The Lutheran Confessions consider justification above all else the forgiveness of sins and use the two expressions interchangeably (*Triglot Concordia,* The Symbolical Books of the Evangelical Lutheran Church, *Augsburg Confession,* Article IV, p. 45; *Formula of Concord,* Article III, 4, 7). Jesus illustrated this concept in His story of the Prodigal. St. Paul teaches it by quoting the great singer of Israel in Roman's 4:6, 7: "So David pronounces a blessing upon the man to whom God reckons righteousness apart from works." In the next verse he equates this reckoning with forgiveness: "Blessed are those whose iniquities are forgiven, and whose sins are covered." Note the series of terms the apostle uses in Romans to explain and develop the idea of justification: "Justify" (2:13), to "reckon" (2:26), to "forgive" (4:7), to "cover sin" (4:7), to "not reckon sin" (4:8). After a study of these terms and their various uses, it is difficult to mistake Paul's meaning of "justify." In effect, God says to the sinner: "I do not count your transgressions against you. My Son has paid the punishment of your sin. I forgive you your sin. I pronounce you righteous in My sight." Do we not also do this when we forgive someone who has transgressed against us? We say, as it were, "I do not hold your

sin against you. The sin is a part of history. I forgive you your sin, however, not because it is the thing to do, but because God has forgiven you
your sins and mine, too, imputing to us both the merits of Christ." This,
too, is the way our Lord Jesus taught us to pray, "Father, forgive us our
trespasses as we forgive those who trespass against us."

Justification as forgiveness also means that God's act of *imputation*
is a corollary of justification. It is both negative and positive: nonim-
putation of sin and imputation of righteousness. The merits of Christ
are imputed to the sinner; he is given a righteousness alien to him,
namely, Christ's righteousness, just as his sins are not imputed or counted
to him (II Cor. 5:19). The Lutheran Confessions teach this very plainly:
"The second matter in a mediator is, that his merits have been presented
as those which make satisfaction for others, which are bestowed *by divine
imputation* on others, in order that through these, just as by their own
merits, they may be accounted righteous. As when any friend pays a
debt for a friend, the debtor is freed by the merit of another, as though
it were by his own. Thus the merits of Christ are bestowed upon us"
(*Triglot Concordia, The Apology of the Augsburg Confession,* Art. XXI,
p. 347).

VII.   JUSTIFICATION BY FAITH

Now we are ready to speak specifically of *Justification by Faith,* to
which we alluded briefly under Personal Justification. Ask a Christian,
"What is the nature of justification?" and his first answer generally will
be, "Justification is by faith." Just how he comprehends the phrase is
something else again. Because they define *faith* differently, even learned
theologians present different views of justification. But the concept *by
faith* is just as vital as the term "justify" to properly understand the
nature of justification as taught in the Bible. Paul, for instance, in stating
the theme of Romans, stresses faith without using the term "justification": "The righteousness of God is revealed *through faith for faith*"
(Rom. 1:17). The Old Testament proof text he quotes (Hab. 2:4) emphasizes the nature and function of faith: "He who *through faith* is righteous
shall live." The close relationship between "righteousness" and "justification" is apparent. The Apostle emphasizes faith, however, as well as
"justify." The two terms go hand in hand; neither is meaningful or
even possible without the other. We read that "Abraham *believed,*" but
his faith is immediately linked to the words, "it was *reckoned to him*
as righteousness" (Rom. 4:3).

In the phrase "justification by faith," what exactly did the Apostle
mean by the words *by faith?* A reading of his letters reveals he usually
meant one if not both of two things: first, justification is justification
without works, without any merit or worthiness on man's part. For Paul,

faith and works in justification are mutually exclusive. No one can add to the atonement because Christ has done it all. Paul says this so often, the fact scarcely needs documentation. Familiar to all is Romans 3:27, 28: "Then what becomes of our boasting? It is excluded. On what principle? On the principle of works? No, but on the principle of faith. For we hold that a man is justified by faith apart from works of law." Secondly, Paul almost always considers faith *the instrument or means by which man accepts God's justification or forgiveness.* In Romans 1:16, 17, he says: "It is the power of God unto salvation *to everyone who believes";* it is revealed *"through faith for faith,"* and in Romans 3:22, 25: "The righteousness of God *through faith* in Jesus Christ *for all who believe";* "whom God put forward as an expiation by his blood, *to be received by faith."* Paul stresses this meaning of faith in his many repetitions of "by faith," "through faith," "believing in Jesus," and so forth. We see here, too, that faith is *faith in Christ;* it appropriates His work on the Cross, which is the basis of justification or forgiveness. If faith justifies, it does so only because it receives Christ. The righteousness of Christ is always intended for those who believe and all who believe receive this righteousness. Faith is the simple trust or confidence of the individual Christian that full forgiveness is bestowed for Christ's sake. Faith is something personal; each person must believe for himself, that is, rely on the promises of the Gospel. Faith is in no sense a moral achievement or ethical principle originating in man. If we call faith a good work, we do not mean that it merits favor or adds to Christ's work or influences God in justifying the sinner. While it is man who must believe, faith is really still God's work in man, for "no man can say that Jesus is the Lord but by the Holy Ghost" (I Cor. 12:3).

Faith, in general terms, may be said to be an act of the human intellect and will. *Saving faith,* however, is more than an intellectual believing the fact *that* God exists, that Christ died on the Cross, that God punishes sin, and so forth. *Saving faith* is believing *in* the Gospel, relying on Christ's merit, and *receiving* God's declared righteousness. This is what the Reformers meant when they stressed *sola fide,* by *faith alone.* While good works are not unwanted by God, they must be excluded entirely from influencing God's act of justification which is solely by grace, *sola gratia.* If justification is without works, and if God has justified sinners before they come to faith—as he did Abraham before he was circumcised —then faith's only role in justification is to receive the forgiveness offered by God in the Gospel. Man cannot merit forgiveness by faith. All he can do is take the Judge's word for it and walk out of the courtroom a free man, exceedingly grateful and humble. The Bible never says man is justified *on account of* faith, but *by* or *through* faith.

To summarize: Justification by faith is the just and loving God's pronouncement of unmerited forgiveness upon the unworthy sinner, and imputation to him of Christ's righteousness; this declaration of righteousness man accepts by faith, by believing in the promises offered in the Gospel. In justification by faith, God acts independent of man, and through Christ declares the whole world forgiven. The moment a man comes to faith and receives the righteousness won for him by Christ, this justification becomes his very own—God pronounces him justified, acquitted, free from the punishment of sin. This pronouncement is a judicial, a *forensic act,* that is, an act which takes place in a courtroom, as it were (Rom. 4: 4, 5).[2] This aspect of justification by faith is not difficult to understand; what staggers the human mind is to learn that God declares guilty men innocent, that is, He pronounces unrighteous sinners "not guilty as charged." This verdict they simply accept by faith. They have no righteousness of their own; it is imputed to them by faith. In their stead an innocent Person, Jesus Christ, is pronounced guilty, and guilty sinners go free. This is unlike the situation in secular courts where every effort is made to pronounce guilty men guilty and innocent men innocent. That God declares men to be what they are not and does so in strictest justice raises protests among many people. Such teaching they call "shocking doctrine," "unfair," "unjust," "impossible," "unworthy of God," "unethical," "immoral," "illogical," "mechanical," "magical," "a license to sin," "not fit for modern thinking man," "the devil's ethics," and so on, and try to formulate their own doctrine of justification. Justification by faith according to the Scriptures, however, is exactly as we have indicated; it may be paradoxical, but it is true, divine, reliable, comforting, saving.

What is more, justification by faith is always total and complete. There are no degrees of justification as in sanctification. When God justifies, a man is forgiven completely, and that not in a long drawn-out process but in an instant. All people are justified in the same way. By justification is not meant regeneration if this term is used to designate the entire life of Christian sanctification which follows the moment of conversion; nor is justification some psychosomatic or physical act which somehow transforms an evil man into a righteous person. No, justification is simply

---

2 "Godet goes so far as to say: 'As to *dikaioo* (to justify), there is not an example in the whole of classic literature where it signifies: *to make just*' (Romans, I, p. 157)." "The verb is essentially a forensic one in its biblical usage, and it denotes basically a sentence of acquittal" (Leon Morris, *op. cit.,* pp. 226, 260). "Justification is not a change in man's nature but a change in his standing before God. Instead of standing before God guilty and condemned, he stands acquitted, released, treated as if he had never been guilty. It is thus a forensic or judicial act" (*The Lutheran Cyclopedia,* edited by Henry E. Jacobs, New York, Charles Scribner's Sons, 1899). "Forensic" gets its meaning from the ancient Roman forum where the law courts were located and where much public discussion took place. The term thus involves the mental process of judgment.

God's pronouncement on the sinner by which he is declared innocent in the eyes of God. Justification by faith is complete and once-for-all; it involves nothing of injustice, since it is God who justifies man (Rom. 3: 26). If the Judge Himself has paid the debt, He has a perfect right to discharge the guilty person (Rom. 8:31-34). This free forgiveness He gives in the Gospel and the Sacraments; these means of grace are God's dynamic power to convey, present, and seal to us His forgiveness (Rom. 1:16; John 15:3; Gal. 3:27; I Cor. 6:11).

The Lutheran *Augsburg Confession* gives this concise definition of justification by faith: "Also they teach that men cannot be justified before God by their own strength, merits, or works, but are freely justified for Christ's sake, through faith, when they believe that they are received into favor, and that their sins are forgiven for Christ's sake, who, by His death, has made satisfaction for our sins. This faith God imputes for righteousness in His sight. Rom. 3 and 4" (*Triglot Concordia*, p. 45).

Dr. Henry Hamann strikes the proper note in his excellent treatises on justification: "If the forgiveness of sins is justification, then justification is first and foremost a declaring righteous. As little as the pronouncement of forgiveness is subjective in the one who is forgiven, so little is justification a process in the one justified. As forgiveness comes to a man from one outside of himself, so justification takes place outside of man. If outside of man, then in God. So justification is an *actus forensis*. This is the conclusion to which the identification of justification with forgiveness leads" (*Justification By Faith in Modern Theology*, St. Louis, School for Graduate Studies, Concordia Seminary, 1957, p. 5).

The Lutheran *Small Catechism* also spells it out very simply as follows: "We confess that we receive forgiveness of sins and are justified before God, not by our works, but by grace, for Christ's sake, through faith."

In summary, then, a scriptural definition of justification by faith must include these seven items: 1) God 2) justifies 3) sinners 4) by grace 5) for Christ's sake 6) through faith alone 7) for a new life here on earth and in heaven.

VIII. JUSTIFICATION BY FAITH IS CENTRAL

Justification by faith is the central and cardinal truth of the Christian religion. In both the Old and New Testaments it is the heart of all of God's mighty recorded acts. It is like the hub of a wheel from which extend all other doctrines of Scripture. Luther called it the "doctrine of the standing or the falling of the Church": "This article is the head and cornerstone of the Church, which alone begets, nourishes, builds, preserves, and protects the Church; without it the Church of God cannot subsist one hour" (*Luther's Works*, St. Louis Edition, XIV: 168).

This does not mean that all other doctrines originate in this central teaching; rather that it involves all the fundamental teachings of the Law and the Gospel and gives them meaning and importance. It makes of the Christian faith not a group of unrelated truths, one or more of which may be emphasized or changed or omitted to suit the individual, but rather, a system of divine Truth properly related in one harmonious whole. And since the Bible teaches that justification in Christ by faith is the center of revelation (I Cor. 2:2), this teaching tells us also that the Bible is not simply a collection of books by various authors having various ideas about God and His work, but is a cohesive unit. As the Bible's central doctrine, justification thus becomes the test or yardstick of theology. If someone is askew on the matter of justification, he will soon reveal himself to be wrong in some of the related doctrines and vice-versa. For example, if Christ is not God, how could He rise again? If He is not man, how could He die for man? If Christ was not man's substitute, how could God justify the sinner—for God could justify only the righteous man. If Christ did not satisfy God's wrath, where is God's justice *and* His love? If there is no forgiveness of sins, what do the sacraments offer and point to? If one denies that man is sinful, why bother with any or all of these doctrines? Whatever man may do or say, however, God is still there to judge or to save him (Luther: "Neither can anyone teach correctly in the Church or successfully resist any adversary if he does not maintain this article" [*ibid.,* p. 168]). Thus when either justification or any related doctrine is under attack, the Christian religion is being attacked. It is essential, therefore, that Bible students see the relationship of justification to all other doctrines of Scripture and that the Church pay strict attention to Scripture and to theology.

IX. JUSTIFICATION IN THE OLD TESTAMENT

Lest our Pauline emphasis be interpreted to mean that justification is only a New Testament doctrine or only "Pauline theology," we add a few paragraphs on justification in the Old Testament as well as on justification and Jesus. In reality, justification by faith is derived from the Old Testament but spelled out in greater detail in the New Testament. In both Hebrew and Greek the words "justify," "justification," "righteousness," and so forth, have a common background. The Septuagint, the early translation of the Old Testament into Greek and the Bible used by Jesus and the Apostles, uses the same Greek terms as the New Testament; we know, therefore, that St. Paul did not invent either the words or their contents. From his epistles we can see that Paul knew both the Hebrew and Greek Old Testaments very well.

Moreover, Paul often *quotes* the Old Testament as *proof* of justification. An example is Psalm 51:4, which he quotes in Romans 3:4, "That thou mayest be justified in thy words." Here "justify" is used of God and in the declaratory or forensic sense, since one can scarcely say that the holy and perfect God is in any sense "made righteous." After a thorough study of the concept of justification and related words in the Septuagint, Leon Morris concludes: "When we turn to those passages where the verb 'justify' occurs, there can be no doubt that the meaning is to declare rather than to make righteous" (*op. cit.*, p. 234). The crowning point of justification by faith in the Old Testament is Paul's use of Abraham; "For what does the *Scripture* [Old Testament] say? 'Abraham believed God, and it was *reckoned to him as righteousness*'" (Rom. 4:3). Several things are important in this verse: 1. Justification is reckoning or imputing to a man something he did not possess before, namely, righteousness before God. 2. God reckoned righteousness to Abraham entirely without merit on Abraham's part as seen by the fact that it took place long before Abraham was circumcised or before the Jewish law was given. 3. It was, therefore, justification by faith, because he received righteousness through simple trust in God's precious promise of the Messiah. 4. This led to his obedience to God so that by faith Abraham left the land of his fathers and went to a strange country (Heb. 11:8). The essential features of the doctrine of justification by faith are found in embryo in this single short Old Testament passage (Gen. 15:6). For this reason Paul selected this particular passage from those he could have used.

X. JESUS AND JUSTIFICATION

Did Jesus teach justification by faith? This is a crucial question, for it involves the four Gospels. The answer is clearly in the affirmative and is seen especially in our Lord's dealings with the Pharisees "who trusted in themselves that they were righteous and despised others" (Luke 18:9), and "who *justify yourselves before men,* but God knows your hearts" (Luke 16:14). That is, these men acquit themselves of all sin and guilt and attribute to themselves all righteousness (of the Law). Two examples suffice. In the parable of the Pharisee and the Tax Collector (Luke 18:9-14), Jesus quotes the tax collector, who had nothing to offer God as righteousness, as saying, "God be merciful [really, *be propitiated* for me] to me *a sinner.*" On this worst of sinners in the Jewish world, Jesus' judgment is that "this man went down to his house *justified* [acquitted in the sight of God] rather than the other." Another example is found in Jesus' story of the Prodigal Son (Luke 15:11 ff.). The picture or figure here is that of the family and not of the courtroom. The father (who represents God the loving Father) acquits a wayward and guilty son, forgives him, and reinstates him into the family without making any demands. Certainly the son had nothing to offer except to say "I'm sorry," but even his sorrow was not what caused the father to justify him; his father's love had forgiven him long before he came home. The elder brother did not understand the father's verdict because he was thinking in terms of works and worthiness. Our human reason—so like that of the older brother—does not comprehend this situation either, but here again we have an example of justification by faith without works. Thus our Lord teaches the same amazing grace of God in Christ which St. Paul articulates and expands so well in his epistles. Both Jesus and Paul preached this doctrine to both Gentiles and Jews because grace cuts across all lines and makes all men equal both in sin and in grace (Eph. 2: 1-22).

XI. JUSTIFICATION IN MODERN THEOLOGY

We now turn to those modern theologians who speak in terms of making the doctrine of justification "relevant to our modern world." Sorry to say, this doctrine has suffered at the hands of certain modern interpreters not unlike other fundamental teachings of the Scriptures. This may be attributed to several things. They may refuse to ascribe wrath to God and sin to man. They may regard the atonement as unjust and impossible. Or they may say that modern man cannot understand or accept the "old doctrine in its old form." Attempted "solutions" have ranged all the way from regarding the entire biblical revelation of salvation the myth of an ancient people to simply ignoring justification altogether. A favorite approach has been to re-interpret Paul to fit philosophical and anthropological presuppositions. Karl Heim, a well-known European theologian, can write an entire volume on the Lord Jesus Christ as "Leader" and completely ignore the teachings of justification and redemption. Regarding original sin, he asks: "Can man be held responsible for something on which he has never made a decision? . . . Can I be convicted of something for which I have not made a conscious decision?" (*Jesus the Lord,* Philadelphia, Muhlenberg Press, 1961, p. 111). In his excellent analysis of justification in modern theology, Dr. Hamann divides his entire treatment into these two major parts: "The Attack Direct: Justification is Regeneration"; "The Attack Indirect: Justification is Peripheral."

A leading example of those who delete justification and related teachings from the Christian witness is Rudolf Bultmann of Germany, who, unfortunately, has taken much of the theological world by storm in recent years. His method of demythologizing has led him to eliminate from the New Testament not only the so-called "three-story universe," but also all the saving acts of our Lord from the time of His incarnation to that of His Second Coming. "All of this is the language of mythology," says Bultmann, "and the origin of the various themes can easily be traced in the contemporary mythology of Jewish Apocalyptic and in the redemption myths of Gnosticism" (Rudolf Bultmann, *Kerygma and Myth*, ed. by H. W. Bartsch, trans. by Reginald H. Fuller, New York, Harper & Brothers, 1953, 1961). Regarding sin, the atonement, and justification, he has this to say: "Again, the biblical doctrine that death is the punishment of sin is equally abhorrent to naturalism and idealism. . . . And to attribute the human mortality to the fall of Adam is sheer nonsense, for guilt implies personal responsibility, and the idea of original sin as an inherited infection is sub-ethical, irrational, absurd. . . . The same objections apply to the doctrine of the atonement. How can the guilt of one man be expiated by the death of another who is sinless—if indeed one may speak of sinless man at all? What a primitive mythology it is, that a divine Being should become incarnate, and atone for the sins of men through his own blood! Or again, one might adopt an analogy from the law court, and explain the death of Christ as a transaction between God and man through which God's claims on man were satisfied . . . and it would make nonsense of all our ethical standards" (*ibid.*, pp. 7, 8. Faith for Bultmann is to "open ourselves freely to the future" p. 19).

Concerning the Cross of Christ, Bultmann writes: "This mythological interpretation is a mixture of sacrificial and juridical analogies, which have ceased to be tenable for us today. . . . Christ is crucified 'for us' not in the sense of any theory of sacrifice or satisfaction" (*ibid.*, pp. 35, 37).[3]

An example of New Testament re-interpretation is the work of D. M. Baillie of England. For him God's wrath is "the consuming fire of love." "Throughout the whole of this New Testament material there is no trace . . . of the idea that God's attitude to sinners had to be changed by the sacrifice of Christ from wrath and justice to love and mercy. . . . His wrath must not be regarded as something which has to be 'propitiated' but rather as being identical with the consuming fire of inexorable divine love in relation to our sins" (*God Was in Christ*, New York, Charles Scribner's Sons, 1948, pp. 186, 189, 198).

Another popular English theologian, C. H. Dodd, whose language and theology many English and Scottish theologians imitate, believes that justification is "vindication" (*The Epistle of Paul to the Romans*, in *The Moffatt New Testament Commentary*, New York, Harper & Broth-

---

[3] Julius Schniewind in "A Reply to Bultmann" writes, "Since its first appearance, Bultmann's essay has evoked a storm of indignant repudiation. He has been accused of eliminating all the facts of salvation. He has left us without a message for our Christmas, Good Friday, and Easter sermons" (*Kerygma and Myth*, p. 45). It should be noted, however, that Bultmann says that Paul teaches forensic justification. He says it is not a quality but a relationship. He does not say that this is his own personal theology, however (Rudolf Bultmann, *Theology of the New Testament*, Vol. I, tr. by Kendrick Grobel, New York, Charles Scribner's Sons, 1951, pp, 253, 272, 274). He also attempts to revive an obsolete English verb "rightwise" (Anglo-Saxon: *rihtwis* and *rihtwisness*) for "justify" and "righteousness," p. 253.

ers, 1938, pp. 10, 12, 13). Under Romans 1:16, 17, he states that righteousness means "to be in the right rather than to be righteous" and to justify means "to put in the right," and thus "to vindicate," or "give redress to" a person who has suffered wrong. He says a judge or ruler is thought of as "righteous" not so much because he observes justice but because he vindicates the cause of a person who has been wronged. "His righteousness is revealed in the 'justification' of those who are the victims of evil." Into this framework he also fits the atonement of Christ under Romans 3:21-25: "The rendering *propitiation* is therefore misleading, for it suggests the placating of an angry God, and although this would be in accord with pagan usage, it is foreign to biblical usage." The blood of Christ is "self-dedication to God" (*ibid.,* p. 55). While Dodd therefore defines faith in terms of regeneration, it is mainly a change of heart and its object is of little importance—it is not the receiving of righteousness nor is it directed toward Christ. "Faith is that attitude in which we rely utterly on the sufficiency of God ... to make room for the divine initiative" (*ibid.,* p. 15). In another volume, Dodd says the actual state of mind of the "justified" person is that "he has disowned, not merely certain evil practices, but his own guilty self. ... Outwardly, he is the same man he was ... but really the man is changed through and through by that act of self-committal, self-abandonment to God ... he is righteous in a fresh sense of the word" (*The Meaning of Paul For Today,* London, The Swathmore Press Ltd., 1920, p. 110). But we have already indicated that to make regeneration a condition of justification and to call it faith is to forget the phrase "not by works." Faith for Paul is the unconditioned and pure reception of Christ's earned righteousness and makes untenable any suggestion whatever that justification is in some way sanctification. It is astounding how this modern view approximates that of the Roman Catholic Church.[4]

Still another English scholar, Vincent Taylor, treats justification and the atonement in a similar way. He associates the concept with man's moral character: "When man so acts," says Taylor, "he has stepped out of the category of the godless, and can be accepted by God as righteous."

---

[4] The attempt to find righteousness in man unites some of these interpreters with Roman Catholicism regarding justification. Catholicism teaches that justification is a gradual process through life; faith is only the initial act. They speak of "infused grace." Rome has not changed her views through the years. The position criticized by the Reformers ("If anyone saith that by faith alone the impious is justified, in such wise as to mean that nothing else is required to co-operate in order to obtain the grace of justification, and that it is not in any way necessary that he be prepared and disposed by the movement of his own will, let him be anathema" [*Tridentinum,* Sess. 6, Can. 9. Cf. Cans. 11, 12, and 20]) finds place in the words of a modern Catholic, Jacques Maritain: "The first act (faith), the initial act of this life within us, is the act by which we freely open our minds to the truth of the word of God and deliver ourselves with love to the God of salvation" (*The Living Thoughts of Saint Paul,* New York, Longmans, Green & Co., 1942, p. 52).

"Christ's ministry is also sacrificial, not as a sin- or guilt-offering, but because He poured out His life in willing surrender for men ... and this makes Him the means of their penitent and believing approach to God" (*Forgiveness and Reconciliation,* London, Macmillan and Company, 1941, p. 64). In a volume entitled *A Man in Christ,* another scholar, James Stewart, maintains that union with Christ and not justification is central in the Christian faith: "The heart of Paul's religion is union with Christ. This, more than any other conception—more than justification, more than sanctification, more than reconciliation—is the key which unlocks the secrets of his soul" (*A Man in Christ,* New York, Harper & Brothers, 1935, p. 147). While his volume contains many splendid statements on reconciliation and the atonement, his emphasis, however, leads to an attack on justification itself. Stewart maintains that one endangers the atonement by making justification central. To do this, he says, makes the redemption of Christ something purely mechanical and magical, "altogether outside us, independent of our attitude.... it is certain such an idea of justification can only be gravely misleading" (*ibid.,* p. 152). Thus we see that even when expressed in scriptural terminology, modern views that rest on a personal emphasis or presupposition may warp a fundamental teaching. In Stewart's case, it can also be shown that the Pauline phrase "in Christ" has many other meanings than that of being united by faith with Christ.

A familiar theologian today is Emil Brunner. Given to differing statements about justification and the atonement at various times and in various books, he sometimes seems to believe that justification is forensic as Paul teaches and that Christ's death is a vicarious sacrifice for sinners. At other times these great doctrines appear to be unimportant to Brunner. He says in *The Mediator:* "God addresses man as just.... Just as the touch of the royal sword transforms a burgher into a noble, so the divine declaration of forgiveness raises the sinner into the state of righteousness.... Justification cannot be separated from the objective atonement, from the expiatory sacrifice of the Mediator" (*The Mediator,* Philadelphia, The Westminster Press, 1947, pp. 523 f.; note that he says something of the opposite in this same volume, p. 591). However, in *The Divine-Human Encounter,* he displays an astonishing negative attitude toward forensic justification: "People have believed ... that one must understand the message of justification by faith alone in the sense of the later orthodox doctrine of forensic justification. This interpretation can in no way be blamed on Paul" (*The Divine-Human Encounter,* The Westminster Press, 1945, p. 100). Brunner's recent commentary on Romans presents the subject in such "round terms" that his meaning is not always clear. The tone is negative, however. He states that justification is "God's bestowing declaration"; while God does not simply pass over sin, it is not righteousness which He bestows but rather, "unconditioned love." While God's grace, says Brunner, cost Him His Son, Christ died, not to become our righteousness, but as a proof of His righteousness. This would indicate that God forgives sin without Christ: "It is not as if God would have to be appeased first before he were able to turn his love towards men; neither the letter to the Romans nor the rest of the New Testament knows of a reconciliation whose object is God. . . . Jesus truly is the reconciler, but the performer of this reconciliation is solely God. The blood of Christ serves not for the removal but for the revelation of his punitive wrath on sins. . . . Justification by faith alone is therefore not a kind of 'as if,' but a divine creation" (*The Letter to the Romans,* The Westminster Press, 1938, 1956, 1959, pp. 30, 31). To say the least, this uncertain and confused interpretation of Romans 3:21-31—an oasis of salvation in the Scriptures —leaves us rather cold, comfortless, and uncertain. Some of the modern interpreters insist on turning these oases of God's Word into dry deserts. The doctrine of justification is so dehydrated that scarcely a drop of grace remains. This process can hardly be called making theology "relevant" for modern man; rather, it is a chipping away of doctrine through lifeless and enigmatic formulations of words.[5]

XII. THE SIGNIFICANCE OF JUSTIFICATION FOR MODERN MAN

A proper question might well be: Why is adamant loyalty to the doctrine of justification by faith as revealed in Scripture so necessary? Is this doctrine really relevant to modern man who lives under jet-filled skies in a furiously-paced space age? Is St. Paul, as Archibald Hunter asks the question, "an extinct volcano" who was morbidly interested in sin and critical of everything, including women? (*Interpreting Paul's Gospel,* The Westminster Press, 1954, p. 67). Men have labeled Paul the corrupter of Christianity, a hard-hearted man who took the simple "Gospel of the Fatherhood of God and the Brotherhood of Man" and turned it into an ugly drama of redemption through blood and antinomian injustice. They note that Paul never heard of Darwin, Freud or Dewey. How, therefore, can he have anything to say to men who fly into space and soon expect

---

[5] Luther, in his usual forward manner, complained of this error over four centuries ago. Under Galatians 3:10 he writes: "The sophisters do wrest and pervert this place after this manner, 'The just man doth live by faith': that is to say, by a working faith or formed (and made perfect) with charity; 'but if it be not formed with charity, then doth it not justify.' . . . They speak of faith formed (and made perfect) with charity, and make a double faith, that is to say, formed and unformed. This pestilent and devilish gloss I utterly detest" (*Commentary on St. Paul's Epistle to the Galatians,* Westwood, N.J., Fleming and Revell Company, 1953, pp. 251, 262).

to explore the moon? Furthermore, they ask, is not sin really only ignorance, something which can be cured by education and a better socialism? Is it not something man must simply endure on his way to goodness just as a butterfly must struggle in the cocoon before it gets its beautiful wings? While these are pertinent questions, the most important one is this: Is the scriptural diagnosis and cure for modern man *true* and *reliable?*

Modern man is in a serious predicament. This he knows. He also knows the predicament is of his own making. (Whether he traces evil back to Adam or looks around at his own generation, the answer is the same.) If we interpret the man in the street aright, we believe he is tired of being told by "learned men"—after two world wars and the threat of nuclear war—that this sorry state is all a delusion. It is very real and present and man realizes this fact as never before. But is not this hopelessness and helplessness of man the very predicament of sin of which Scripture speaks? He has been prepared, we also believe, to hear that rescue must now come, not from still further human schemes, but from the Divine, from outside himself and his environment. Is not this rescue, this divine solution in God through Christ, the doctrine of justification by faith that the Bible beseeches man to accept? This solution is God's revelation, and His only revelation of salvation, to man. It is His Word. It is always true, infallible, reliable. Paul states it well in his letter to the Corinthians: "We preach Christ crucified, a stumbling block to Jews and folly to Gentiles, but to those who are called, both Jews and Greeks, Christ the power of God and the Wisdom of God" (I Cor. 1:23). "And we impart this in words not taught by human wisdom but taught by the Spirit" (I Cor. 2:13; II Tim. 3:16, 17).

Just when modern man most needs it, justification by faith as revealed in Scripture can be the source of limitless spiritual and moral power (Rom. 1:16, 17). This doctrine does not leave him "hanging in mid-air" on some unethical sky-hook, as some have said. No, what is called the doctrine's greatest weakness is actually its greatest strength. Faith does not cast off Christian works but is the source and power of the greatest work of all, namely, LOVE. Luther said, "Good works do not make a good man but a good man does good works." When some suggested to Paul that a doctrine of salvation by faith and not by works implied "why not do evil that good may come?" (Rom. 3:8), his firm answer was "By no means! How can we who died to sin still live in it? Do you not know that all of us who have been baptized into Christ Jesus were baptized into his death? . . . so that we too might walk in newness of life" (Rom. 6:1-4). If we are wearing Christ's spotless robe of righteousness we want to keep it that way. If we soil it or drag it in the mud we demonstrate we do not want it or perhaps have not even accepted it. Thus, justification by faith means not only forgiveness of sins, but the gift of the Holy Spirit (Rom.

15:13).[6] Notice how Paul combines everything: "But you were washed, you were sanctified, you were justified in the name of the Lord Jesus Christ and in the Spirit of our God" (I Cor. 6:11). This Spirit dwells in man (I Cor. 3:16). He is the Spirit of Christ and is personal, active, powerful. He assists in prayer, He strengthens, sanctifies, reveals, and He guarantees eternal life. Paul experienced this power in his own justified life: "I can do all things in him who strengthens me" (Phil. 4:13). "I have been crucified with Christ; it is no longer I who live, but Christ who lives in me; and the life I now live in the flesh I live by faith in the Son of God, who loved me and gave himself for me" (Gal. 2:20). "If any man be in Christ, he is a new creature" (II Cor. 5:17). Compare I John 5:4.

Finally, only justification by faith can assure us of eternal life with God after death. It alone turns death into life and defeat into victory. All systems that use or imply works in any way or degree result inevitably in the wretchedness and tension of doubt. Those who trust in the doctrine of justification by faith need no longer be the "devil's martyrs." (In his *Commentary on Galatians* Luther used this pungent expression to describe those who worked harder trying to get to heaven by works than the wicked did in going to hell, only to end up in the same place.) When God says He has justified the ungodly, we know we are included. When He says "it all depends on faith, in order that the promise may rest on grace and be guaranteed to all his descendants" (Rom. 4:16), we know His grace is sufficient for all things. When He takes us from eternity to eternity in justification, "those whom he predestined he also called; and those whom he called he also justified; and those whom he justified he also glorified" (Rom. 8:30), we are comforted beyond human words. We need not rely on any man, not even on deceitful self. When God says that no one can be against us when He is for us (Rom. 8:31), that "He who did not spare his own Son" will give us all things with Him, we are lifted to the heights of certainty. When He says that acquittal is the only pronouncement on us in His courtroom of grace in Christ, because it is God who justifies and Christ who died and rose again (Rom. 8:33, 34), then we are translated into glorious ecstasy. We have the confidence of Paul himself, who said: "In all these things we are more than conquerors through him

---

[6] See Hunter, *Interpreting Paul's Gospel,* p. 108. Hunter is determined in his view that Paul's Gospel (salvation by faith) is as relevant today as it always was: "Nevertheless, if I understand St. Paul aright, it is the third view of the Cross—the view which sees the death of Christ as an expiatory sacrifice for sin—which dominates Paul's thought. It seems to me, indeed, that to do justice to his view, we must also include in it those elements of truth for which the old 'juridical' theory of the Atonement stood" (p. 91). He is not willing to push aside the theology of fathers, either: "Our forefathers, whose theological systems we dismiss so light-heartedly as out of date, at least saw the human problem and understood the divine solution. And whatever word we may adopt to replace 'justification,' it is the duty of all who preach and teach the Gospel today to emphasize the truth for which it stands" (p. 87).

who loved us. For I am sure that neither death, nor life, nor angels, nor principalities, nor things present, nor things to come, nor powers, nor height, nor depth, nor anything else in all creation, will be able to separate us from the love of God in Christ Jesus our Lord" (Rom. 8:37-39).

Modern man, like ancient man, needs this truth, this power, this certainty offered by God in justification by faith. At this point of doctrine where all truth and salvation are at stake, we Christians dare not give an inch.

THE NATURE
OF SANCTIFICATION

✝

Warren C. Young

*Warren C. Young is Professor of Christian Philosophy at Northern
Baptist Theological Seminary, Chicago. He is author of* A Christian
Approach to Philosophy *(1954). He served as President of Evangelical
Theological Society in 1958. He holds the A.B. from Gordon College,
A.M. and Ph.D. from Boston University, where he served in 1945-46 as
Borden Parker Bowne Fellow.*

18. *Warren C. Young*

THE NATURE
OF SANCTIFICATION

CONTEMPORARY theologians like to discuss the nature of Christian faith in paradoxical terms. It may not be amiss, then, to call "sanctification" the "impossible possibility," for God's standard of holiness for us, "you shall be holy, for I am holy" (Lev. 11:44, 45; I Pet. 1:16), is indeed humanly impossible to fulfill.

If, after an abundant, long life of service, a saint like Paul confesses to be still striving for perfection, then surely we should be concerned about our far greater shortcomings. Satisfied? Impossible! Yet, through Christ, we have the ever present possibility of experiencing this seeming impossibility of sanctification.

Since perfection is found in Christ alone, our hope of perfection is likewise found only in Him and rests on the scriptural teaching of the believer's union with his Saviour and Lord. Through Christ the human spirit, regenerated and justified, can become one with Christ and a member of His body. This union with Christ is the cornerstone of reconciliation. It supports and sustains the entire Christian life from regeneration to glorification (Eph. 2:20-22; Rom. 7:4; John 15:1-10; I Cor. 6:15-19). Further, this union with Christ is neither natural nor metaphysical in nature, but is totally and exclusively spiritual, vital, and mystical (cf. A. H. Strong, *Systematic Theology*, Philadelphia, Judson Press, 1907, p. 795 ff.; E. H. Palmer, *The Holy Spirit*, Grand Rapids, Baker Book House, 1958, p. 90).

Union with Christ is inseparable from regeneration, for as his spirit is born again by the Holy Spirit (John 3), the believer becomes a new person. This newness of life cannot occur apart from the supernatural and spiritual experience of regeneration.

373

As a new person in Christ the believer now stands in a new relationship to his Creator and Redeemer and is said to be "justified." That is, justification is the standing given by God to the regenerated sinner who by faith has appropriated the redemptive work of Christ. This *sola fide* doctrine, justification by faith alone, was the great plea of the Reformers over against the teaching of Rome. Regeneration involves subjective newness of life whereby the believer enters objective newness of position in Christ.

Sanctification concerns the believer's new life in view of his new position. Does this sanctification make a difference? Are Christians really unique because they are sanctified? Would programs of evangelism and missions really mean anything if they stopped short of sanctification? Nietzsche once said, "Christians must show me they are redeemed, before I will believe in their Redeemer." Jesus Himself said, "Let your light so shine before men, that they may see your good works and give glory to your Father who is in heaven" (Matt. 5:16; cf. Phil. 2:14-16).

In Reformation thought sanctification means the growth and development of that new life which began with the believer's regeneration and his union with Christ. The fulfillment or eschatological goal of this new life begun here on earth is glorification in the life to come. As popularly expressed, we *are* saved (justification), we are *being* saved (sanctification), and we *shall be* saved (glorification). To accomplish this complete reconciliation of sinners to Himself God sent His son to provide full and perfect atonement which the believer appropriates by faith through the work of the Holy Spirit.

I. WHAT IS SANCTIFICATION?

The primary reference to sanctification concerns God Himself. In the Old Testament the term emphasizes His separateness and unapproachableness because of His unique distinction from and relationship to His creation. Holiness, then, belongs to everything pertaining to God.

On this basis anything which is separated from the world and consecrated unto God is holy. For this reason the same term was used to denote sacred days, seasons, objects, or even persons separated unto God. In the same sense the nation Israel was to be sanctified or set apart.

This formal usage of the word carries over into the New Testament. We read that Jesus was consecrated or sanctified for His mission in the world (John 10:36; 17:19). And in his epistles Paul designates Jesus' followers as "saints," although moral perfection is not thereby ascribed to them. That is why Paul calls the Corinthians "saints" while, at the same time, he rebukes them for carnality (I Cor. 1:2; 3:1-3).

The ethical use of the term sanctification is never absent from the Old Testament, although, in the early period, its formal use predominates.

A strong ethical emphasis is found in the prophets. God desires man's pure and sanctified heart far more than formal sacrifices or "sanctified" offerings (Isa. 1:11; 1:16, 17; Hos. 11:1; 6:6) . To belong to God is more than a mere formality; it involves an inner life that is ethical, spiritual, and consecrated to God.

In the Synoptics Jesus uses "Sonship" to express the idea of purity. To be a "son" is to share in Christ's spirit (Matt. 5:43-48; Mark 3:35). While Paul uses the word "saint" to show this Sonship, his delineation of ethical transformation is not confined to this one term. His entire epistles breathe with the very spirit of the new life in Christ. In fact, the phrase "in Christ" has often been called Paul's motto. It is the sanctified life that is the life "in Christ" (Eph. 4:13; Rom. 12:1; II Cor. 5:17).

The full meaning of sanctification comes only by awareness that it is a personal relationship, a personal fellowship with the Father through Christ. This is essentially a positive experience that develops through increasing oneness with Christ. The ultimate goal of the sanctified life is complete surrender, that is, we no longer seem to live by our own resources but live through the Christ within us (Gal. 2:20).

This complete oneness of the new life in Christ is no isolated or monastic existence. And, while prayer, meditation, worship, and many spiritual disciplines are in order to refresh this relationship, fullness of the life in Christ expresses itself best in consecrated service. Monasticism was surely no hallmark of the apostles.

II.   APPROACHES TO SANCTIFICATION

1. Reformed. The Reformation placed great emphasis on justification by faith. This stress was proper since Luther's revolt centered on salvation by works as taught and practiced in the Pre-Reformation Church.

It was perfectly natural, then, that Rome should bitterly attack the *sola fide* teaching of the Reformers. At the heart of the attack, practically speaking, was the doctrine of sanctification. Rome asked, Where is the new life to be found in the *sola fide* doctrine? Were not the Reformers teaching that one could be justified and yet remain a sinner?

Rome teaches that God's saving grace is at work in man and that it begins in sanctification. Since the natural man is incapable of leaving his sinful state or of meriting salvation, God imparts His own grace to him, which permits the sinner to be saved. This sanctifying grace comes from the merit of Christ. This merit of Christ is at the disposal of the Church and is made available to man through the sacraments. God's grace remits original sin, imparts righteousness, and carries with it the promise of ultimate perfection. Certain merits may also be obtained additionally through the good works of the sanctified believer.

In Roman Catholic thought the process and goal of holiness is called justification, inasmuch as sanctification, that is, the making just of the sinner by infusing the grace of God, has already occurred. Since justification is the process whereby the sinner is made righteous, it is really indistinguishable from sanctification.

According to the Roman Catholic position, the Reformers were teaching simply justification. No wonder Rome asked and is still asking, if the sinner is justified, where is the new life?

Rome's position also explains its personal attack on Luther. Luther, it was argued, could not overcome the lusts of the flesh and, to free himself therefrom, he devised an ingenious view of salvation. Since man is justified by faith alone, Luther sees man as freed from the guilt of sin, but not from its corruption. In other words man may be justified by faith in Christ and yet be a depraved sinner. He could, it seems, said Rome, be fully justified, but not one whit sanctified! It is hardly correct to assume, of course, that Luther stopped with Romans 1 and never bothered to read passages like Romans 6:1-2.

Despite the criticisms of Rome, the Reformers certainly did teach sanctification. Indeed it is the *sola fide* doctrine of Reformed thought which properly incorporates and explicates sanctification. Unless the work of God begun in us in regeneration continues in sanctification, then all our subsequent activity is but self-edification. Unless the life initiated by faith continues by faith through the ongoing work of Christ, it degenerates to mere moralism. This moralistic understanding of the new life of the believer was the essential error of the liberal conception of sanctification.

If we are justified by faith, is not this enough? When the sinner is declared "not guilty" by God, why should we desire anything else? (Col. 1:13, 14). The answer is simple. We do not stop with justification by faith because the Scriptures do not stop here. After Paul speaks of our justification by faith in Christ (Rom. 3:9-11), he immediately goes on to discuss the growth of the new life (Rom. 12). Christians are admonished to perfect the holiness they have in Christ (II Cor. 7:1). They are admonished to throw off the fruits of the flesh (Gal. 5:19), and to develop the fruit of the Spirit (Gal. 5:22). Many Scripture passages call the believer to total purity and perfection (Jas. 2:14; 1:26; I John 3:15, 18; Heb. 12:14). Indeed God's will for us is our sanctification (I Thess. 4:3).

Just as truly as both justification and sanctification are taught in Scripture, just so truly are they to remain unseparated in experience. Both operate by faith, and both are rooted in the Cross of Christ. When we move from justification to sanctification we do not leave the area of faith. Should sanctification ever function apart from faith, it would be merely the work of the self in the justified man. Such work is, then, his own work and is untouched by faith in God's redemptive work in

Christ and by Christ's work in him. Sanctified deeds, on the other hand, are never our own, but always the work of Christ in and through us.

This fact is evident both in God's work with Israel and the continuation of His work in the Christian Church. In the Old Testament holiness is often associated directly with obedience to the divine law; in the New, it is grounded in God's mercy as revealed in the justifying work of Christ (Deut. 13:1-4; I Cor. 6:15; 6:19, 20). Because the believer is justified and in Christ, what else can he do but manifest the life within? The New Testament Christian lives in obedience to God just as truly as the Old Testament saint, but his obedience is always rooted in the redemptive work of Christ. The Christian walks obediently because he is in Christ. Contrary to the Catholic view, where sanctification is a cooperative work between God's infused grace and man's action, the Reformers' teaching realigned sanctification with faith and demonstrated their inseparable bond.

In spite of the Reformers' efforts to avoid separating justification and sanctification, the danger which Rome saw in the *sola fide* teaching has sometimes been very real. Accepting justification by faith alone without also recognizing the apparent necessity of showing forth the fruit of the Spirit sometimes characterizes the lives of believers. Although it is difficult to understand how one can be justified and not, at the same time, manifest sanctification, at least to some degree, the possibility of such shortcoming is ever present in Christian experience. It is quite possible to "assume" and to "claim" justification by faith in Christ without ever giving practical evidence that verifies this claim. The problem, in fact, has been so real and acute that certain theologians, like the late Baptist professor, W. T. Connor, called for a radical rethinking of the whole position (*The Gospel of Redemption*, Nashville, Tenn., Broadman Press, 1945).

Connor reminds us that God not merely justifies the sinner, but regenerates him as well; the sinner receives both new standing and new life in Christ. Paul's teaching on justification, says Connor, should not be viewed as legal or forensic, as ordinarily taught in Protestant theology. Paul, he feels, used a legal term, but gave it new content that describes "a vital experience, not just a forensic act" (*ibid.*, p. 174). "Paul is thinking about the justified man as enjoying peace with God, as rejoicing in hope, as having the love of God shed abroad in his heart, and as enjoying life, eternal life, here and now. He is thinking of these blessings as coming to the justified man as a direct result of his justification. And when we say as a direct result of his justification, we do not mean a result beyond justification and distinct from it, but rather something involved in justification itself" (*loc. cit.*). In Romans 6-8 Paul presents not something in addition to justification but an explanation of what justification involves. Life in the Spirit is a privilege inherent in justification and not an adjunct to it. "To be justified, then, is to be in Christ Jesus; . . . it is to have a new life . . . all the blessedness of the life of the Spirit belongs to the justified man" (*ibid.*, pp. 175-176). Justification is never to be thought of as "a forensic transaction in which a man is declared righteous without being made so." Connor protests, therefore, against "a judgment favorable to the sinner but a judgment that did not change the sinner's character nor bestow spiritual life."

Connor makes it clear, however, that he is not advocating a return to the Roman position which espouses a gradual or progressive justification instead of something completed at the very inception of the new life (*ibid.*, pp. 177 ff.). Connor pleads for a view of justification which involves more than simply legal standing, a view that includes also evidence of the new life.

While scholars commend Connor's ambition to solve the problem, many may feel his attempted solution was wrong. It would be better to stress that sanctification begins with regeneration and justification, they insist, than to try to show that Paul used "justification" in a broader sense. But even more unfortunate, they feel, is the amount of lifelessness in evangelicalism, which warrants such efforts to face and improve the situation. The presence of so-called "justified" but "lifeless" Christians is a sad commentary on the Church, but it often results from a distorted emphasis on the *sola fide* doctrine. As G. C. Berkouwer and others have pointed out, however, the Reformers actually sought to prevent this kind of erroneous emphasis (Berkouwer, *Faith and Sanctification*, Grand Rapids, Wm. B. Eerdmans Publishing Company, 1952. This is the best work to appear on the subject in recent years. See especially Chapter IV).

The very real existence of the problem that prompted men like Connor to seek a solution shows the danger in separating sanctification from justification. As we have noted, some sectors of evangelicalism erred on the side of lifelessness. Liberalism, on the other hand, fell prey to moralism. According to this view, justification was often accomplished by simply willing to be in moral sympathy with God. Sanctification became a product of the will, the voluntary development of latent personal resources. In liberal thought justification, then, became self-salvation and sanctification moralism.

While liberalism was emphasizing the development of the spiritual life through self-edification, elements of evangelicalism took refuge in a distorted emphasis on "eternal security" that made sanctification more or less unnecessary. Berkouwer rightly points out that sanctification is not something that occurs merely in the subconscious life but that it "must be the redemptive touch of faith on all our life" (*ibid.*, p. 12) .

Although there are obvious points of difference between Barthian and evangelical theology, in the matter of sanctification Barth stands with the Reformed tradition (*Church Dogmatics*, Edinburgh, J. & J. Clark,

1958, Vol. IV/2, pp. 499 ff.). He agrees that sanctification is always the work of Christ in the believer; he thus has no use for moralism or self-edification as found in liberal thought. We are in Christ through participation in His exaltation. We attain new freedom and power by the work of the Holy Sirit within us. Although Barth notes that terms like regeneration, renewal, and conversion, might describe what is involved in sanctification, he has no desire to give up the word "sanctification" for it emphasizes that sanctification is the work of God in us. It is God alone who sanctifies.

Sanctification does not follow justification as a second work of God in man. Rather God's work in man is one single action. Barth disallows a doctrine of mere positional justification that shows no evidence of the new life. At the same time justification is not to be swallowed up in sanctification, nor sanctification in justification. Each is distinct but not to be isolated from the other. There is no justification without sanctification, nor sanctification without prior justification, and both are accomplished by faith in Christ. While Barth may have stated his position in extreme terms at times, this emphasis, as Berkouwer suggests, grows from a desire "to avoid lapsing into independent human activity" (*op. cit.,* p. 122).

Before leaving this phase of our study we must also consider the matter of the law, for the Reformers were charged with antinomianism. Extended discussion is not necessary, however, since the function of the law in relation to the Gospel has been made abundantly clear many times. The Reformers were well aware of the law's function and validity; grace, they knew, is never an excuse for setting aside man's legal and moral requirements under God. Luther recognized three basic functions of the law: (a) to maintain external order; (b) to induce sinners to recognize their guilt; and (c) to direct the lives of believers. Properly understood there is never any conflict between law and the spontaneity of the new life in Christ. He who lives in Christ lives by law, for he lives a life of spiritual obedience. Paul reminds us that faith does not detract from the law but rather confirms it (Rom. 3:31). Faith opens our eyes to the law's true function. In Christ we are released from the bondage of the law that we may delight in it. Faith merely emphasizes our freedom—our freedom in bondage to Christ. As John has stated, when the Son frees us, we are free indeed (John 8:36). Berkouwer summarizes exceedingly well the theme of our discussion as follows: "The linkage between faith, sanctification, and law has never been more brilliantly high-lighted than by Paul: 'For we are his workmanship, created in Christ Jesus for good works, which God afore prepared that we should walk in them' (Eph. 2:10). It appears that in his reasoning Paul is here pushing to this one goal: that we should walk in good works. This conclusion is the more surprising because the context is exhaustively concerned with the sovereign grace of God in Christ Jesus. The initial point of discussion was the transition from a false faith to the true faith, a transition exclusively founded upon the mercy of God (Eph. 2:4). 'For by grace have ye been saved through faith; and that not of yourselves, it is the gift of God; not of works that no man should glory' Eph. 2:8, 9). At this point Paul brings up the good works of those who are God's workmanship, God's poems, and says, to our amazement, that God prepared these works. The path of good works runs not from man to God, says Paul, but from God to man. Salvation is by grace—good works included" (*ibid.*, p. 191). In other words, those who are sanctified by faith do the works of obedience.

In conclusion, we cannot overemphasize that any teaching of justification which stops with merely a positional change, and does not recognize the simultaneous change in the inner life is foreign to the Scriptures and to Reformational teaching. When the sinner is justified, he receives new life by the Spirit, a new life that, at the same time, the Spirit begins to sanctify. If one is truly in Christ, it is unthinkable to assume that Christ is not also in him. If one is in Christ, obedience and growth are demanded by an inner compulsion. Further, the believer is enabled to do what he could never do by himself (Gal. 2:20). By faith our lives are hid in Christ (Col. 3:3, 17).

2. *Perfectionism.* This view of sanctification is of great significance in some areas of evangelical thought. And the reasons for its presence in the Church are not to be dismissed lightly. What place has sin in the life of one who is in Christ? What have we who are justified to do with sin? We are told to be holy, even as our God is holy. Is not full sanctification in this life, then, a real possibility?

Certainly no one can properly deny that the goal of perfection is clearly set before us in the Scriptures. The problem is, however, is this goal attainable here and now? Most of the Church has traditionally taught the impossibility of perfection in this life. We present here, however, the Wesleyan view of Perfectionism as stated by one of its best exponents, the late Nazarene scholar H. Orton Wiley.

According to Wiley, while God saves us by an act of regeneration, this act removes only part of our sin. Not to leave the believer in the state of positional salvation without full cleansing, God brings to the Christian a "second" blessing, a second work of grace, which is the baptism of the Holy Spirit. Through this further operation sin is completely eradicated. The baptism of the Holy Spirit follows water baptism and is for Christians only, according to Wiley's understanding of Matthew 3:11, 12. "Nothing can be more evident than that (a) the baptism with the Holy Ghost effects an internal and spiritual cleansing which goes deeper than John's baptism. One was for the remission of sins, the other for the removal of the sin principle. (b) This baptism is applicable to Christians only, not to sinners. (c) The separation is not between the tares and the wheat, but between the wheat and the chaff, or that which clings to it by nature.

Sinners are never regarded as wheat, but always as tares. (d) The wheat thus separated, will be gathered into the garner and preserved; the chaff will be burned, or destroyed with unquenchable fire. The chaff referred to here is not the wicked, but the principle of sin which cleaves to the souls of the regenerate and which is removed by Christ's purifying baptism" (*Christian Theology,* Kansas City, Mo., Beacon Hill Press, 1953, Vol. II, p. 444). As seen from Wiley's treatment here, as well as of other biblical passages, theological exegesis supplies a basic difference between the Reformed and Perfectionist views of sanctification.[1]

According to Wiley distortion of the doctrine of sanctification came as a reaction to the Catholic view of justification. As a result, the Reformers laid special stress on a tendency which, in turn, gave rise to various theories of imputation. The same overemphasis carried over into sanctification, namely, that both justification and sanctification are provided for the believer as the gift of the covenant of grace. The work of Christ *in* us was slighted in favor of His work *for* us. The Reformers, with their unique emphasis on Christ's substitutionary atonement for us, held to "a belief in the imputation to Him of our sins, and to us of His righteousness for our justification and for our sanctification also, in so far as it applied to the cleansing from guilt" (*ibid.,* p. 453). Since sin cannot really be done away with in the Calvinistic system, it is necessary to admit that it still remains. What actually happens is that sin is not imputed to the justified believer and therefore is not laid to his account. The believer has a kind of sanctified standing in Christ, but his actual condition is still sinful. Sin is not abolished as a principle or a power, but instead, Christ's righteousness is imputed as a substitute for his sin. Inbred sin is covered or hid by Christ's righteousness. While sin is repressed in the regenerate person so that it no longer reigns, it is, nevertheless, still present. Sanctification in this non-Wesleyan view is the process of bringing the believer

---

[1] This fact is very evident from Wiley's exegesis of two key passages. Romans 12:1-2: Nothing can be clearer than (a) that this exhortation is addressed to those who were at the time Christians; (b) that an appeal to the mercies of God would mean nothing to those who had not already experienced His pardoning grace; (c) that the sacrifice was to be presented holy, as initially sanctified by the cleansing from guilt and acquired depravity; (d) that it was to be acceptable, that is, those who presented it must have been justified; all of which the apostle deems a reasonable service. In the second verse it is admitted, (e) that there remained in the hearts of the believers, a bent toward worldliness, or a bias toward sin; (f) that this tendency to conform to the world was to be removed by a further transformation, or a renewal of their minds; and (g) that they were thereby to prove, or experience, the good, and acceptable, and perfect will of God. II Cor. 7:1: Regeneration, as we have seen, is the impartation of a life that is holy in its nature; and concomitant with it, is an initial holiness or cleansing from guilt and acquired depravity. Now this holiness already begun is to be perfected by the cleansing at a single stroke from inbred sin, and brings the soul to a constantly existing state of perfected holiness. This cleansing applies to the body as well as the soul (*ibid.,* pp. 445, 446).

into subjection to the life of imputed righteousness; it is progressive and perfected only at death when the believer is glorified.

The Perfectionists consider this teaching erroneous and dangerous. "Anything which falls short of an actual cleansing from all sin or the death of the 'old man' is anti-Wesleyan and anti-scriptural," writes Wiley (*ibid.*, p. 454). Sanctification is *imparted* and not merely *imputed* holiness; it is an act, not a process. "Entire sanctification is provided by the blood of Jesus, is wrought instantaneously by faith, preceded by entire consecration; and to this work and state of grace the Holy Spirit bears witness" (*ibid.*, p. 467).

This cleavage among evangelicals between the Reformed or Calvinist and the Wesleyan concepts of sanctification is unfortunate. Most Calvinists, as well as others standing in the Reformed tradition, would agree with the late Professor L. Berkhof, who says that in the light of Scripture the Perfectionist position is "absolutely untenable" (*Systematic Theology*, Grand Rapids, Wm. B. Eerdmans Publishing Company, 1949, p. 539).

A basic point of tension is the definition of "sinlessness." The old phrase "freedom from sin," has been superseded by expressions like "freedom from all known sin," "entire consecration," or "Christian assurance." Reformed theologians often feel that the very meaning of "sin" has been thereby weakened. Sin becomes more an act of the will than a state of man's being in revolt against God. Some would ask, has the standard been lowered in order to assure the attainment of "perfection"?

Another problem is the very practical matter of human experience. Who, either in the Scriptures or in the history of the Church, has ever attained perfection this side of heaven? Even the most saintly Christians have denied any such realization. No matter how high we climb the stars still elude our grasp. However, the more basic question is whether the Scriptures teach the possibility of such attainment.

Biblical references to the universality of sin are plentiful. No one is without sin (I Kings 8:46; Eccles. 7:20; Jas. 3:2; I John 1:8). Even the saints, although sometimes referred to as perfect, are represented always as people who have sinned, who have fallen short; none personally claims to have reached perfection. Toward the close of his earthly career, Paul was still "following after" and "striving toward" the goal of perfection (Phil. 3:12-14). The Scriptures everywhere set forth God's holiness, as revealed to us in Christ, as the standard of ultimate attainment. Being holy, God certainly could not be expected to present a goal any lower or any less than one of complete holiness. Faith in Christ is always the means of reaching this goal. Through Him, Christians are called on to endure to the end; by constant perseverance they shall be ultimately saved from the reality of sin. We are saved, we are being saved, and we shall be saved. As Berkouwer notes, the justified sinner remains a sinner to the very end of his earthly career. However, this fact does not exclude the possibility of his making progress.

Sanctification depends on its orientation to justification. A merely man-made morality that results from one's justification is never to be substituted for true sanctification. Constant renewal of life comes not by our own strength but always by operation of the Holy Spirit within us. Sanctification is possible only because of this Presence constantly indwelling us (Gal. 2:20). The Romanists and Perfectionists notwithstanding, Reformation thought has always emphasized that sanctification is a real, changing experience. Justification without the inception of sanctification is just as impossible as sanctification in an unregenerate and unjustified person. "Genuine sanctification—let it be repeated—stands or falls with this continued orientation toward justification and the remission of sins," writes Berkouwer (*op. cit.,* p. 78).

3. Existentialism. In recent years we have heard much about the return to a biblical theology and perspective by theologians who have more or less revolted against liberal idealism. Does their movement involve also a return to the biblical idea of sanctification? Although the final volume of Paul Tillich's *Systematic Theology* has not yet appeared, the nature of his emphasis is fairly clear from the second volume and other works. Tillich understands theology in terms of symbols. Truths such as Christ's deity and incarnation, which evangelicals have always insisted are real, Tillich interprets symbolically. The heart of the Christian message he presents in the expression "Jesus as the Christ." What Tillich means is that the ideal we associate with the Christ came into existence in the man Jesus. Since the "New Being" came with Jesus, He is called the Christ. Our loyalty as Christians to the New Being centers, then, not in the divine-human person, but in a principle, the principle of *agape* or love. Wherever love is manifested in the world, there is the Christ. The meaning of John's Gospel is "that the truth which liberates is the power of love, for God is love" (Tillich, *The New Being,* New York, Charles Scribner's Sons, 1955, p. 74). The New Being is found anywhere in history where there is an acceptance of Jesus as the Christ, that is, of the principle of love. Participation in the New Being of the Christ is what constitutes justification. For Tillich this takes place within the individual through some kind of psychological transformation. In his natural state man is estranged from his true being. Finding the New Being means the end of this estrangement. By commitment to the New Being which Jesus brought as the Christ, man becomes adjusted to reality or is "saved." "To experience the New Being in Jesus as the Christ means to experience the power in him which has conquered existential estrangement in himself and in everyone who participates in him" (*ibid.,* p. 125). Salvation is best understood as "an healing and saving power through the New

Being in all history" (*ibid.*, p. 167), and "in some degree all men partici-pate in the healing power of the New Being" (*loc. cit.*).

For Tillich sanctification is the New Being progressively overcoming the distortions of man's existence in both religious and secular history. Sanctification is "the process in which the power of the New Being trans-forms personality and community, inside and outside the Church" (*Existence and the Christ*, Chicago, University of Chicago Press, 1957, pp. 179, 180).

Reinhold Niebuhr likewise insists on the symbolic interpretation of biblical truths. Biblical concepts are to be taken seriously but not literally; they are symbols rather than facts. Niebuhr builds his system more on an existential analysis of the self than on biblical teachings. This analysis leads him to postulate the *imago dei* or image of God in man to be man's original righteousness (*justitia originalis*), or simply his conscience. The essence of this law written in man's heart is *agape* or love. Since the full-ness of the revelation of love has come into history through Jesus, He is the Christ.

Niebuhr's view of redemption requires no relationship to the Jesus of history, but only to the symbol of the Christ (*The Nature and Destiny of Man*, New York, Charles Scribner's Sons, 1941, 1943, Vol. II., pp. 109, 110n.). Love or the "hidden" Christ is the original righteousness God has given to all men. As man grasps this truth he may be converted or re-deemed (*ibid.*, pp. 103 ff.). Salvation or justification does not involve a transfer of Christ's merit but merely a comprehension of the meaning of "Christ" in history. Christianity, then, is not so much Christ as *agape*.

Sanctification is this "Christ" in us and means some kind of self-trans-formation as we grasp and appropriate love in our personal lives. There is no Holy Spirit within to lead, guide, and transform us. "Christ lives in me" means that at last I have caught the "agape" spirit. Christ is the sanctifying agent for both Tillich and Niebuhr but their "Christ" is the principle of love, not the divine-human person of biblical revelation.

What concerns us at this point is how the teaching of men like Tillich and Niebuhr differs from that of the old liberalism. Despite the termi-nology is not this more recent system, in the last analysis, just another kind of self-edification or moralism? If "Christ" is merely symbolic, then the heart of the Gospel has evaporated and all theological terms become symbols of what happens through our own resources and our own strength. Thus the reality of the Gospel is reduced to a mere experience of psychological transformation and ethical betterment. A symbolic Christ has no grace to sanctify us. Imitating a human Jesus, according to this view, himself in need of sanctification, cannot sanctify us. We cannot even be sure that Jesus is necessarily the final expression of love, for liberalism considers history flexible and relative. May not a still greater than "Christ" perhaps yet come?

III. GOAL OF SANCTIFICATION

Paul reminds us that growth is the goal of the new life in Christ. In every way we are to grow up into Him (Eph. 4:15). The believer is to perfect his holiness (II Cor. 7:1); he is to follow after peace with all men (Heb. 12:14), and grow in grace (II Pet. 3:18). The believer is not to leave everything to God's outworking, however, any more than he is to expect to do everything for himself. While he believes that all growth depends on Christ, he presses on to exercise his faith. Berkouwer suggests four steps to Christian growth: (a) increasing knowledge of our own sinfulness, (b) increasing earnestness in seeking remission of sin and the righteousness of Christ, (c) prayer to God for the grace of the Holy Spirit and a constant endeavor to be renewed more and more after the image of God, and (d) the eschatological prospect of perfection (*op. cit.*, p. 109).

For the Christian sanctification means working out his own salvation with an ever growing sense of dependence on God's grace. This experience should develop an increasing sense of humility; for, in the last analysis, the believer can do nothing of himself. It is to the credit of theologians like Barth and Niebuhr that they have spoken out fearlessly against self-righteousness, both of the individual and of the Church. No Church can do God's will by giving mere lip service to God's sanctifying grace.[2] Indeed one of the greatest dangers in the ecumenical movement of our day is that quite unconsciously churches may substitute the power of bigness for the power of the Holy Spirit.

A word concerning the practical aspect of sanctification may not be amiss. Far too often in modern Church life worldliness is equated with specific activities. Christians who engage in such pursuits are "worldly" while those who refrain are "sanctified." Thus a new type of monasticism results as Christians separate themselves into groups whose character is determined by abstinence from "unsanctified" activities. At the same time such Christians may engage in other types of worldliness which are not recognized as such because they are not so catalogued. Spirituality is not a matter of "things," but rather of one's attitude toward "things." Sanctification is neither determined nor achieved by external activities, but always stems from the believer's attitude and relationship toward God.

The essential nature of sanctification lies in imitating Christ. This means more than spending time in prayer; it involves also imitating Christ in act and in deed. While the sanctified life must be one of prayer, dedication, and worship, it must also be realized amid everyday activities. It is just as possible to lead a sanctified life in the arena of

---

[2] See, for example, Niebuhr's criticisms of the Roman Catholic Church in his article, "The Pope's Domesticated God," in *The Christian Century*, Jan. 18, 1950.

social and political affairs as in a monastery. Indeed, the active life of
service in the spirit of Christ is more sanctified than a secluded, passive
existence. It is unfortunate that isolation often has been mistaken for
sanctification.

In brief, sanctification is the ultimate spiritual goal of the new life in
Christ. It is the work of Christ in the believer who by faith appropriates
the life Christ has given him. Sanctification takes place in a Spirit-
regenerated life which is justified because it by faith has accepted the saving
work of Christ. Neither in the Scriptures nor in properly interpreted
Reformation thought are sanctification and justification ever treated
separately or divided. As Calvin once wrote, "Christ therefore justifies no
one whom he does not also sanctify" (*Institutes*, III, XVI, 1; quoted by
Berkouwer, *op. cit.*, p. 130).

The essential impact of the term "sanctification" is ethical; the sanctified life is one which manifests the loving spirit of Christ and which is
fully yielded to the control of God's will. The sanctified life is continually
being transformed by the Holy Spirit; it is the life "in Christ."

While Christians differ in their concepts of sanctification, the idea of
continuous growth toward ultimate perfection in the glorified life seems
most scriptural. While the Apostle Paul prays that the perfect life be seen
in all Christians, yet in his letters he admonishes believers to growth
and progress. Sanctification involves the entire span of the Christian
life, not just a particular period or moment, although every moment
counts. God's work in us and our own appropriation thereof are coexten-
sive with the whole earthly life of the believer. While sanctification
expresses itself in human ways, it is above all the work of the Spirit within.
As Palmer so clearly summarizes, sanctification is (a) primarily the work
of the Holy Spirit to bring about our victorious life in Christ; (b) the
Spirit working within and not moralism, for the Spirit affects the very
being of man; (c) the power that transforms man's entire being—his will,
emotion, and understanding; (d) a gradual work toward perfection; and
(e) a work completed in the life to come (*op. cit.*, Chapter VIII). The
indwelling presence of Christ by His Spirit is the only means to this new
and sanctified life.

We began our discussion by citing God's requirement of holiness for
every believer. We close by stating how to attain this fullness of the salvation experience: "To them [the saints] God chose to make known ... this
mystery ... *Christ in you, the hope of glory*" (Col. 1:27).

THE NATURE
OF THE CHURCH

✝

William Childs Robinson

*William Childs Robinson is Professor of Historical Theology at Colum-
bia Theological Seminary (Southern Presbyterian), Decatur, Georgia.
He is author of* The Certainties of the Gospel (*1935*), What is Christian
Faith? (*1937*), Our Lord, An Affirmation of the Deity of Christ (*1937*),
The Word of the Cross (*1940*), Christ, the Hope of Glory (*1945*), Christ,
the Bread of Life (*1950*), *and* The Reformation: A Rediscovery of Grace
(*1962*). *He holds the A.B. from Roanoke College, A.M. from University
of South Carolina, B.D. from Columbia Theological Seminary, Th.M.
from Princeton Theological Seminary, and Th.D. from Harvard University.*

19. *William Childs Robinson*

THE NATURE
OF THE CHURCH

By bringing denominations into discussion with one another, the ecumenical movement has encouraged a renewed consideration of the doctrine of the Church. Moreover, out of the current milieu has emerged a realization that church dogmatics is a discipline distinct from those of the natural and social sciences. Christian faith derives its concept of the Church from God's dealings with His people as seen in the light of His Word. This chapter discusses the meaning of the Church, her history, her ministry, and her mission.

I. THE MEANING OF THE CHURCH

The meaning of the Church is indicated first of all by definition of the term *Church* and then by observing the distinguishing marks and essential relations which reveal her true nature.

Etymology

Our word *church,* like its cognate forms, *kirche, kerk, kirk,* comes from the Greek adjective *kuriakon,* used first of the house of the Lord, then of His people. The New Testament word *ekklesia* designates a public assemblage summoned by a herald (Acts 19:32, 39, 40). In the Septuagint, however, it means the assembly or congregation of the Israelites, especially when gathered before the Lord for religious purposes. Accordingly, *ekklesia* in the New Testament means that congregation which the living God assembles around His Messiah Jesus. In other words, the Church is the spiritual family of God, the Christian fellowship created by the Holy Spirit through the testimony to the mighty acts of God in Christ

Jesus. Wherever the Holy Spirit unites worshiping souls to Christ and to each other, there is found the mystery of the Church.

The Definition of the Church

More fully stated, the one Church of God is not an institutional entity; rather, she is a supernatural entity in process of growth toward the world to come. She is the risen and ascended Lord's sphere of operation. All her members are in Christ and are knit together by a supernatural kinship. All their gifts and activities originate in Christ, continue His work by the power of the Holy Spirit, and are co-ordinated by Christ to a culmination in the final goal. In the age to come, therefore, the Church will appear as one people of God united before the throne in one congregation as the one celestial city, the new Jerusalem.

The Marks of the Church

By His Spirit and by His Word (Isa. 59:21) the Lord brings and keeps His people in covenant fellowship with Himself. His voice is heard in the proclamation of His Word and His acts are seen in the administration of His sacraments. Accordingly, God's Word and sacraments together with prayer and praise are the marks of the visible Church, the means whereby the Holy Spirit brings individuals to personal faith and nourishes believers in the corporate worship of the Christian community. As God's people receive His promises, He forgives their sins and seals them with His sacraments for the world to come.

II. THE NATURE OF THE CHURCH

The Apostle Paul speaks of the whole realm of believers and of each local group as "the church"; he uses this term for a household of believers as well as for larger gatherings. Thus it is not the addition of churches which constitutes the whole Church, nor is the whole Church divided into separate congregations. But wherever the Church meets she exists as a whole, she is the Church in that place. Any particular congregation represents the universal Church, and through participation in the redemption of Christ mystically comprehends the whole organism of which it is the local manifestation.

The separate terms, "the church of God," and "the churches in Christ" reach their full, combined expression in "the churches of God ... in Christ Jesus" (I Thess. 2:14). This phraseology indicates that the truly significant features of the Church are her relationship to God and to Jesus Christ.

As to her relationship to God, the Church is a fact established by God. This is His supernatural act. According to the consentient testimony of both the Old and the New Testaments, the Church is not a man-made myth but a God-given fact. The same God who spoke the word of promise to ancient Israel also speaks the word of fulfillment to the Christian congregation. As the Father reveals the Son, so the Messiah builds His Church (Matt. 16:17, 18; 11:25-30). The three miracles at Pentecost manifest God's direct action in establishing His Church. The New Testament speaks of the Church as God's building, His planting, His vineyard, His temple, His household, His olive tree, His city, and His people. It describes her ministers as the gifts either of God (I Cor. 12:28), of the ascended Christ (Eph. 4:11), or of the Holy Spirit (Acts 20:28). Paul recognized the priority of the Jerusalem church not because of the personal importance of the individuals who composed it, but because this fellowship of men and women was the assembly of God in Christ. That is, he recognized the fact of God's action and did not treat it as a matter of mere human speculation.

Just as the Church is a fact established by God, so she is the place where God acts for our salvation. Here the risen Lord encounters men and changes them from rebels against their Maker into children of their heavenly Father, thereby bringing them from enmity into peace. It pleases God by the foolishness of the *kerygma* to save those who believe (I Cor. 1:21). The Gospel is the power of God who saved us and called us to faith (Rom. 1:16; 15:16 f.; II Tim. 1:8). We observe the outward functioning of the Word and the sacraments with our bodily senses; it is no less important to contemplate God's activity in the Church with the ear and the eye of our faith. Preaching becomes more effective when it calls men to behold God working for them than when it scolds them for not serving Him. "God, the Creator of heaven and earth, speaks with thee through His preachers, baptizes, catechizes, absolves thee through the ministry of His own sacraments" (Luther). While the sacrament is being administered, Christ is more active in giving Himself and His blessings to the believer than the minister is in distributing the bread and the cup to the communicants. The Reformers speak of the Sabbath as the day in which we are to rest from our labors that *God may work* in us. As God generates believers by the preaching of the Word of Christ, and nourishes them by the sacraments of His grace, so faith beholds the face of the Lord in the Church of the living God.

God's acts in the Church are in Christ Jesus. Adequate recognition of Jesus as the Messiah and of God's mighty acts in Him establishes the integral relation of the Church to her Lord. The King-Messiah and the people of God belong together. As the shepherd implies the flock, as the hen gathers her chickens under her wings, as the vine has many branches, the body its several members, as the foundation supports its building, as the Servant justifies many, as the Son of Man represents the saints of the Most High, as the King implies the kingdom, so the Messiah has His twelve and the Lord His Church. Jesus spoke of "my church" and of "my flock," and these are linked in Acts 20:28. These several lines of parallel thought thus support Jesus' infrequent use of the word *church* (Matt. 16:18; 18:17).

Following His exaltation, we are all baptized by the one Holy Spirit into the one body of Christ; here each believer is given a special function to fulfill in Christ's body. Christ is the Church since the Church is His body; at the same time Christ is distinct from the Church because while she is the body He is her Head, and also her Lord, her Judge, and her Bridegroom. Her life, her holiness and her unity are in Him.

The Church is the bride awaiting Christ her Bridegroom (Mark 2: 19, 20; II Cor. 11:2; Rom. 7:1-6, and especially Eph. 5:25-32 and Rev. 19-21). Christ loved the Church and gave Himself for her. Having cleansed the Church by the washing of water with the Word, He is now sanctifying her that He may present her spotless for the marriage feast of the Lamb. Within the heart of Christ's bride there should ever be, therefore, a great longing for the hour when all shadows shall flee before the flaming of His advent feet.

III. THE HISTORY OF THE CHURCH

The story of the Church is the account of God's activity in history. Indeed, the existence of the Church reveals the gracious heart of God. The Father chose His eternal Son to become the Saviour of sinners, the Messiah of the whole Israel of God. In Him God chose a people for His own possession and called individuals into this fellowship. This one people of God includes the patriarchs, the congregation of ancient Israel, Jesus and His disciples, the primitive community of His resurrection ministry, and the Christian Church.

For the people of God, the Old Testament period was a dispensation of promise, that of the New Testament one of fulfillment. Jesus Christ revealed not a new God, but a new way of worshiping the same God. In the Old Testament it is "the whole assembly of the congregation of Israel" (Deut. 31:30) who hear the law (Deut. 4:10; 9:10; 18:16; Acts 7:38), who sacrifice the passover lamb (Exod. 12), whom God redeems from Egypt (Exod. 15:13, 16; Psalm 77:15; 74:2; Acts 20:28), with whom God makes the covenant at Sinai (Exod. 33-35), for whose sins expiatory sacrifices are provided (Lev. 4 and 16), and who as a holy nation are to praise God (Exid. 19:6; Hos. 2:23; Psalm 22:22; cf. Heb. 2:12; I Pet. 2:9, 10). Other New Testament passages similarly recognize a unity with the Old Testament people of God (Matt. 8:11; Rom. 11:16-28; I Cor. 10:1-4). The Old Testament Messianic expectation includes the formation of a faithful new Israel. The God of the Old Testament so speaks in Christ that the New Testament Church is the fulfillment of the Old Testament congregation.

The several steps in forming the new Israel of God include the calling of the disciples to gather as sheep about their shepherd, the confession of Peter, the Last Supper, the Cross and the Resurrection, Pentecost, and the sending out of the apostles as eyewitnesses of the Resurrection. Jesus bound the disciples, not to the Torah of the rabbis nor to the ideas of a Socrates, but to Himself. To this fellowship that centered in God's saving self-revelation in the Messiah, Jesus gave the *kerygma,* the Lord's Prayer, and, following the Last Supper, the sacraments with common praise. He taught a distinct code of conduct on such matters as divorce. He trained authoritative teachers. The Master and the Twelve had a common purse in the hands of a treasurer.

God's dealings with men are marked first by a narrowing and consequent deepening of the channel of revelation that its blessing may become world-wide. Thus He dealt first with the human race, then with the nation of Israel; later with the remnant thereof, and even further, with the few pious families from which came John, Jesus, and the first disciples. When the Good Shepherd was taken from their midst, all the disciples forsook Him and fled, leaving only one person, the Saviour who died on Calvary for the sins of the world as the Israel of God. But God raised up from the dead our Lord Jesus Christ and sent that Great Shepherd of the sheep to regather the flock. At the appointed mountain over five hundred met Him, at Pentecost three thousand were converted, and daily the Lord continued to add those who were being saved.

On the basis of the preparation in the Old Testament and in Jesus' ministry, the exalted Christ poured forth the Holy Spirit at Pentecost to constitute the assembled fellowship as the Church of God. The Spirit anointed, christened, sealed every member of that gathering. Then in order to bring the Gospel to the Gentile world, God established a new missionary center in Antioch, called a new voice, that of the Apostle Paul, and approved a new name for His people, namely, that of Christian.

From heaven the Spirit went forth to establish the Lordship of Christ among believers and to be the life and guide of the Church until her exalted Saviour should return. The presence of the Spirit of Christ was the inner stimulus of the fellowship. From the very beginning, however, alongside this inner stimulus were certain definite outward forms of proclamation (*kerygma*) and moral instruction (*didache*), the ordinances of baptism and of the Lord's Supper, and the authority of the apostles as the ministers ordained by Christ. At Pentecost there was the coming of the Spirit like a rushing mighty wind. There was also the Word of God in its written form as Peter cited it from Joel and the Psalms, the Word preached by the one hundred and twenty and by Peter, and the Word incarnate and ascended Jesus Christ who poured forth what was seen and heard. The Book of Acts records the work of the Spirit as He guides each apostle and fills the Church with spiritual gifts. At the same time, Acts portrays the fellowship of believers continuing in the apostles' doctrine, in the breaking of bread, and in taking wise counsel for just distribution of alms by the diaconate. Throughout the history of the Church the reciprocal interaction of this inward power and outward direction has been essential to a healthy church life. Where the inward work of the Spirit has been forgotten, the external forms have yielded to formalism, scholasticism, rationalism, carnal security, and a timeless metaphysics. Where the Word, the sacraments, and ministration have been neglected and only the inner aspect has been magnified, the Church has drifted toward unbalanced subjectivism, unregulated mysticism, and even to fanaticism.

Some enthusiasts so emphasized the sovereign freedom of the Spirit that they severed the relationship between the mission of the Spirit and the historical Jesus. Traces of this danger are indicated in the New Testament, for example, I Corinthians 12:3, I John 4:2,3, perhaps Revelation 2:15, 20, Ephesians 4:20, 21. The effect of more extreme forms of enthusiasm, such as Montanism and Joachimism, has been to supersede the historical revelation of Christ with the dispensation of the Spirit. The maintenance of the *filioque* clause in the Western churches has helped preserve the indissoluble connection between the mission of the Spirit and the work of the incarnate Christ. "Where the Holy Spirit is sundered from Christ, sooner or later He is always transmuted into quite a different spirit, the spirit of the religious man, and finally the human spirit in general" (Karl Barth, *Church Dogmatics,* New York, Charles Scribner's Sons, 1956, Vol. I/2, p. 251; cf. George Hendry's *The Holy Spirit in Christian Theology,* Philadelphia, The Westminster Press, 1959, p. 68). The Spirit was to come, not to speak of Himself, but to show us the things of Christ and to glorify Him (John 16:13-24). Similarly, the apostles preached not themselves but Christ Jesus the Lord (II Cor. 4:5).

Certain "liberal" scholars posit a fluid situation in the period that followed the apostolic age, and suggest a state of mild anarchy in the Church. A more careful examination of the data shows that Christians considered themselves a new race (*To Diognetus, The Preaching of Peter, Barnabus*) and members of the Catholic Church that existed wherever the living Christ was present (Ignatius, Polycarp). They regarded their faith as a holy deposit given by the apostles who had received it from the Lord, to be expressed in an ecclesiastical life with liturgy, discipline and subjection to the ministers God had set over them. The Apostle Paul considered disciples such as Timothy and Titus as his representatives who then in turn would be succeeded by the presbytery in every Church (cf. P. Batiffol, *Primitive Catholicism,* London, 1911, pp. 164-197).

The alleged "free and easy" period when "organization did not matter" is a figment of modern imagination (cf. A. J. Mason in *Early History of the Church and the Ministry,* edited by H. B. Swete, London, 1921, p. 43; John Lawson, *A Theological and Historical Introduction to the Apostolic Fathers,* New York, The Macmillan Company, 1961, pp. 48-51). *The First Book of Clement* was written to strengthen an already existing church order that had a duly appointed ministry and that used a specified liturgy. It considers this accepted ministry which continued from the time of the apostles as essential to the peace of the Church. The figure of the Church as a building, found in the New Testament (Matt. 16:18; I Cor. 3:10; Eph. 2:20, 21; Rev. 21:14; I Pet. 2:4-6) and in the Apostolic Fathers Hermas (*Similitudes* 2) and Ignatius (*Ephesians* ix.1), indicates a continuing external structure but implies also that the foundation has been laid once for all time. While there is a continuing ministry from the time of the apostles, only those who have seen the resurrected Lord are authentic apostles (Acts 1:22; I Cor. 9:1).

Because of *First Clement*'s insistence on a continuous, divinely ordained ministry, and because of the *Didache*'s stress on baptism, of Ignatius' magnifying the bishop, presbyters and deacons, and of Hegesippus' historical research, the external forms which embodied the inner treasure of Christ's living presence by His Spirit were more carefully shielded from temptations to jealousy and schism, and from the dangers of persecution and heresy. Carried forward by such apologists as Justin Martyr and such theologians as Irenaeus, this movement led to a magnifying of concrete tests for apostolic truth. The baptismal creed crystallized into the rule of faith, or the Apostles' Creed. The apostolic Scriptures of the New Testament were added as an accretion to the already existing canon of the Old Testament to form one Bible. The bishop of each Church founded by an apostle was exalted as the holder of the apostolic office competent to decide on the validity of oral traditions.

Concern of the medieval Church to preserve the faith petrified in the Dark Ages into papalism, curialism, scholasticism, ceremonialism, and sordid worldliness; a whole array of saints and intercessors shut out believers from the one Mediator between God and man. The Reformation was "the rediscovery of the Holy Spirit" as the dynamic presence of God in Jesus Christ "under the veil of the preached Word" (H. A. Oberman, in *Harvard Divinity School Bulletin,* October, 1961). For Luther, "God's Word is an instrument and tool through which the Spirit works" (*W.A.,* III. 672-674, *Tischreden*). "Now the Word is seen as an instrument in the hands of the Spirit by which the merits of Christ are given or the Church sanctified, and then it is seen as an instrument in the hands of the Triune God by which the Spirit is given" (R. Prenter, *Spiritus Creator,* Philadelphia, Muhlenberg Press, pp. 124, 256).

On the basis of Isaiah 59:21, Calvin insists on an inviolable union and a mutual connection between the Word and the Spirit in God's concrete revelation of Himself to fallen man (*Institutes* I.vi, vii, ix), and likewise weaves together God's ministries through His Spirit and by His Word in creating and sustaining man's faith (III.i, ii).

If this Reformation balance was obscured in later orthodoxy, and in the age of the Enlightenment, something of it was recovered in the spiritual awakenings of the eighteenth century. An evangelical like Charles Simeon of Cambridge stressed the Word but not apart from the inner working of the Spirit: "It is not the Word that does good, but the Holy Ghost by the Word. . . . It is not the knowledge of the Word that benefits but the knowledge of Christ in the record" (H. D. McDonald, *Ideas of Revelation, 1700-1860*, London, The Macmillan Company, 1959, citing both Simeon, pp. 234, 235, and Wesley, p. 245 f.). While Simeon emphasized the adequacy of the Word used by the Spirit, his friend and older contemporary, John Wesley of Oxford, stressed the activity of the Spirit who uses the Word (*loc. cit.*). God the Holy Spirit bears witness with our spirits that God the Father is our Father through the merits of God the Son.

In the revival of more recent years, when only the Church lifted a banner against Hitler's National Socialism, Karl Barth on the Continent emphasized both the objective revelation in Jesus Christ the Word and the subjective revelation in the Holy Spirit. He warned, too, against confusing the one with the other or of neglecting either phase (Karl Barth, *Church Dogmatics* I/2, *Die Protestantische Theologie im 19. Jahrhundert*, pp. 422-424).

From my own revered mentor, William M. McPheeters, come these words concerning the ministry of the Church: "O if our ministers could only realize the utter reasonableness of doing what the Apostles did: *Preach the Word, and pray the Holy Spirit to bless it.*"

IV. THE MINISTRY OF THE CHURCH

The one essential ministry of the Church, therefore, is the ministry of her Lord and Saviour Jesus Christ. As Hebrews and Revelation indicate, the focus of Christian worship is the Lamb in the midst of the throne, the High Priest ever interceding at the heavenly altar of prayer.

Since Jesus Christ is the same yesterday, today and forever (Heb. 13:8), it is He who has preserved the Church in the centuries past and who will maintain her in the years to come (Luther, *W.A.*, 54.470). Neither Satan nor all his cohorts abroad in the world can ever destroy the Church (Matt. 16:18), for she is founded upon the Christ reigning at the right hand of God (Calvin, *Institutes* II.vi.2; II.xv.3).

At this point conservative Reformation thought breaks with the radical or left-wing movements of the sixteenth century. The latter assume a declension or decease of the Church, perhaps at the time of Constantine, which necessitated a complete restitution of the Church. Anabaptist logic requires this so-called Christian Primitivism (cf. E. H. Littell, *The Anabaptist View of the Church*, Boston, The Beacon Press, 1958; "Christian Primitivism," in *Encounter*, 1959:31). Already as early as the twelfth century Peter the Venerable answered the attack on family baptism. He showed that for five centuries churches in Europe had practiced exclusively infant baptism and hence, according to these sects, there had been no Christians at all. But if there were no Christians, there was no Church; if there was no Church, there was no living Christ.

While the conservative Reformers accepted their Catholic baptism, they labored to reform and to restore the existing Church to the biblical pattern of the Church. Some contemporary interpreters of the Scottish Reformation emphasize the element of the true Church's continuity; others stress the element of her restoration in the Protestant movement (contrast J. Bullock, *The Kirk in Scotland*, 1960, p. 132, with J. H. S. Burleigh, *A Church History of Scotland*, New York, Oxford University Press, 1960, p. 177). Roman Catholics in France maintained that evangelicals were Anabaptists who held that there had been no Church for a millennium or who had forsaken the only true, that is, the Roman Catholic Church. Calvin rejected both charges and wrote Francis I that the Church's essence is distinct from her form and may exist with little or no visible form. In fact, the true form of the Church is not best demonstrated or preserved by the external splendor of papal worship but is distinguished, rather, by the faithful preaching of the Word and the proper administration of the dominical sacraments.

By Christ's heavenly ministration all of God's people have access to the throne of grace. The New Testament Church has no chancel separating the clergy from the laity. All of the flock are God's heritage (clergy), a royal priesthood, a people (laity) for God's own possession (I Pet. 2:9; 5:2, 3). Through the merit and intercession of the great High Priest (I Pet. 2:5; Hebrews; Rev. 1:5) every believer is a priest and prays both for himself and for others. God uses this priesthood of all believers to choose those whom He has equipped and called (Acts 20:28; I Cor. 12:28; Eph. 4:11) to be ministers of the churches (Acts 1:15-25; 6:2-6; 13:2, 3; I Tim. 3:1-10; Tit. 1:5-9). Likewise each officer and member is to receive grace from the Head of the Church and use it for the communion of the saints (Eph. 4:1-16), that the body may grow up into all things in Christ.

In keeping with the Son of Man's own mission not to be ministered unto but minister and to give His life a ransom for many (Mark 10:45), our Lord calls upon His disciples not to lord it over others but to be the servants of all (Mark 10:42). Every office in the Church is to be more a ministry than an exercise of leadership. The authority Christ gives to a pastor is vested not in him personally but in his office, or rather, in the Word of God which he is commissioned to administer. The non-Reformed Western Church believes her chief bishop is endowed with infallible teaching authority and with supreme legislative and juridical powers. The Reformed churches, however, consider the power of the Church to be ministerial rather than magisterial and declarative rather than legislative; in other words, the Church has authority to declare, to administer, and to enforce the law of Christ, the King and Lawgiver, as set forth in His Word (cf. Matt. 15:6-9; Isa. 29:13; Acts 4:19; 5:29). That is, ecclesiastical action has divine sanction only as it serves Jesus Christ in submission to His Word (cf. Karl Barth, *The Faith of the Church*, New York, Meridian Books, 1958, p. 146; *Church Dogmatics*, I/2, p. 540; *Book of Church Order*, Presbyterian Church, U.S., 1961, I-3). The Church does not exist for the ministry, but the ministry for the Church. "The ministry of the Church is related to the ministry of Christ in such a way that in and through the ministry of the Church it is always Christ Himself who is at work nourishing, sustaining, ordering, and governing His Church on earth" (T. F. Torrance, *Royal Priesthood*, Edinburgh, 1955, p. 37).

As under-shepherds Christ appointed first of all the apostles who had companied with Him through His ministry and who were eyewitnesses of His resurrection. Then by the apostolic *kerygma*, God brought those who had not seen Jesus personally into a like precious faith. The apostles represent Christ directly and speak with the authority He has conferred; there is no access to Him which detours around the apostolic witness to Christ. They preached Christ Jesus as Lord and themselves servants for Christ's sake (II Cor. 4:5). The Church belongs to Christ, and the apostles belong to the Church, not the Church to them (I Cor. 3:22). Lest anyone should think the apostles baptized in their own name, it was their custom to have associates perform the rite of baptism (Acts 10:47 f.; I Cor. 1:13-17).

After the apostles came the prophets; they brought words from God concerning the practical problems of life and were responsible to the Church. Then there were evangelists with the gift of winning men to Christ by the Gospel, and teachers who instructed believers in Christian living. Local congregations had a plurality of officers: elders to oversee the work and conduct of the Church, and deacons to distribute to the necessities of saints. Women assisted in this latter service.

V. THE MISSION OF THE CHURCH

The Lord Jesus Christ is the sun around which the whole mission of the Church revolves. In public worship the risen Redeemer encounters His people; in evangelism the Saviour calls men to Himself. Proclaiming God's law announces Christ's lordship, and Christian nurture feeds and disciplines His flock. Ministering to the needs of men continues the work of the Great Physician.

In this vast work and witness of the Church, Jesus Christ must be her Lord and her only King. Her task is to obey His will and to proclaim His sovereign reign, for God has established Him upon that throne typified in David's rule (Isa. 9:6, 7; Luke 1:26-35; Acts 2:25-36). He has been enthroned at God's right hand that He may give repentance and remission of sins (Matt. 28:18; Acts 5:31). Through His intercession, believers have access to the throne of grace and obtain mercy and help in every time of need. Every mercy received from Christ, every comfort of the Spirit, every assurance of the Father's love testifies to the praise of God's glorious grace. And the Church is this witness: the concrete evidence of the grace of the Lord Jesus Christ, the love of God, and the communion of the Holy Spirit (II Cor. 13:14).

THE NATURE
OF LAST THINGS

✝

Harold B. Kuhn

Harold B. Kuhn is Professor of Philosophy of Religion in Asbury Theological Seminary (Methodist), Wilmore, Kentucky. He has traveled to West Germany and Austria summer after summer to engage in a ministry to refugees from Communist countries. He holds the A.B. degree from John Fletcher College, S.T.B., S.T.M. and Ph.D. degrees from Harvard University, and has pursued post-doctoral studies at the University of Munich.

THE NATURE
OF LAST THINGS

Preceding chapters have scored the point that when a man commits himself to personal faith in Jesus Christ and to the precise core of Christianity's redemptive message, he commits himself also to a great deal with respect to the larger context of general truth. He becomes involved in broader delineations of his faith which influence his total life outlook. It was not without point that James Orr, over a half century ago, called his classic book *The Christian View of God and the World.* In confronting us at the crossroads of life, the Christian Scriptures are not only notably contemporary, but they also have much to share about the future.

Others writers have discussed the origins of things, God's activity in history, and the divine purpose in the present. Our discussion deals with the future things of the Christian message, with "things to come." While intensely personal in purpose and direction, redemptive truth also concerns itself with reconstructing and re-ordering of man's world and society. The New Testament declares that the Lord is building His Church; it assures us also of a day in which righteousness shall fill the earth "as the waters cover the sea."

Eschatology, to use the technical term for the study of Last Things, has a twofold aspect. It investigates the matter of life after death by discussing questions like the survival of personality and memory, the conditions of rewards and punishments, and so on. It relates also to certain cosmic events, which the Scriptures indicate are yet future, and which will affect the entire universe.

In the past fifty years, evangelical scholarship has concerned itself increasingly with the second aspect of eschatology. And the shock of two

World Wars has tended to interest many liberals in the cosmic meaning of current events. They have had to investigate the New Testament with fresh seriousness, and to re-examine the validity of much they once considered final and indisputable.

Our study will present, first, the biblical basis and the content of the historical Christian doctrine of Last Things. Second, it will investigate some sub-Christian views of eschatological teaching. Finally, it will indicate the relevance of eschatology for us in meeting the demands of daily life in the present dynamic world situation.

I. THE HISTORIC CHRISTIAN VIEW OF LAST THINGS

Historic Christianity has constructed its view of eschatology around the four principles of Futurism, Discontinuity, Divine Intervention, and Adventism.

Futurism

The Old Testament prophets continually scanned the skies for signs of a future "Day of the Lord." They never regarded the present either as final in time or as final in meaning. Sometimes they found it necessary to correct current interpretations of the expression "Day of the Lord" (for example, Amos 5:18). In the same spirit Malachi (4:5) reminds Israel of a coming "great and dreadful day of the Lord." The New Testament adopts the terminology of the prophets, as seen in Matthew 24:36, Mark 13:32, and so forth. (G. R. Beasley-Murray, *Jesus and the Future*, London, The Macmillan Company, 1954, pp. 130, 135). The "Day" was regarded as future, one determined and controlled by God the Father.

Much has been written about Christ's relationship to the events that will mark the end of the age. And it is evident that Christ indeed associated His return to this world with these events (Matt. 24:30). He made it clear, however, that He Himself did not know the precise time of His return, and of the final enactment of future events (Mark 13:32). This fact suggests at least that Jesus voluntarily limited the exercise of omniscience at this point. Whether or not His statement indicated "an unconditional ignorance as to the time of the end" is a question of interpretation (Beasley-Murray, *ibid.*, p. 262).

We readily admit that our finite, limited knowledge makes difficult our full understanding of futuristic elements in Scripture. Our natural curiosity seeks to know *when* and *how*. While revelation does not leave us wholly in the dark at these points, it is not explicit about all details concerning God's plans. Nonetheless we must stress that, just as the Gospel promises individual and personal redemption for the believer here and now, so also it promises a future unfolding of God's redemptive purposes for society and for man's environment.

We often hear it said that Christianity refers too much to a future time, that it promises "pie in the sky." Christians, similarly, are criticized for being so concerned with the future that they have no dynamic social concern for present needs. This charge is not altogether unwarranted. At the same time, hope is an essential ingredient in any empirical system that faces the tension between the ideal and the real, the *ought* and the *is*.

It is significant that the very system (Marxism) which so vehemently attacks Christianity at this point has its own element of futurism. Even the modest goal of an apartment with running water for every family in the U.S.S.R. is promised at least two decades from now (an escape clause allows further deferment, should conditions of military preparedness or military action thus require). This may be a short-term kind of futurism, but it requires sacrifices even of those who themselves will never see its fulfillment. They, too, must live in hope!

Futurism, with its implied corollary of a *decisive* type of providential action in the "times to come," is a challenge to the contemporary way of thinking. For a century Western thought has been largely interpreted in terms of an evolutionary framework which has assumed a unilinear and gradual, presumably upward and progressive, course of events. This perspective has conditioned vast areas of Western scholarship in such a manner that it resists any suggestion of some future intervention by God whereby He will decisively fulfill his purposes. Such an intervention seems a scandal to the evolutionist—a threat to his entire *Weltanschauung*. That this intervention will supersede the usual "single-line" progression of events suggests the second basic principle in the historic Christian concept of Last Things, namely, discontinuity.

Discontinuity

Under Futurism we noted that historic Christianity challenges much of contemporary thought by believing that some future event will crucially—and the word *crucially* is important—fulfill God's plan for man and for His world. This suggests a perspective which anticipates a future departure from the pattern of events which is customarily regarded as established and perhaps predetermined. Unfortunately the word "evolution" has been used so imprecisely that one really needs a term that more exactly delineates what the past century has meant by its use of this word. Basically considered, evolution assumes that the universe is so constructed that its events move along in unilinear fashion without abrupt breaks or gaps. In other words, the underlying principle of evolution is continuity.

Scripture, on the other hand, amply teaches that the regularity of progression which marks much of the life of our world does not in itself guarantee the achievement of the ultimate *telos* or goal toward which the universe moves. Rather, the Bible teaches that the world will experience a pattern of events in sharp deviation from the usual operations of the cosmos. God Himself will enter actively into the affairs of men. Events will unfold which are qualitatively different from those commonly observed. Human affairs will be interrupted. Nations will be brought into subjection and subservience to the Son of Man. Knowledge of the glory of the Lord shall cover the earth as the waters cover the sea. Peace will come to reign forever.

Modern man salutes many of these objectives. His perplexity centers, not so much upon their statement, but on the manner in which they are to be achieved. Even sensitive humanists laud the values which biblical eschatology envisages, but are inclined to lift an eyebrow at the suggestion that they are to be brought to realization by supernatural action. Within the past century we have seen unprecedented scientific and technical progress. Vast areas of new knowledge have radically transformed our mode of life. Such attainments have engendered great expectations: if man has achieved such rapid progress during a relatively brief segment of history, what may he not accomplish in a few more centuries?

Great expectations have characterized not only the secular scientists at the turn of the present century; many alert and eager Christians as well felt that a parallel achievement in the life of the Church might be forthcoming, whereby man's complex of ethical and spiritual problems could quickly be solved by means of an unprecedented, sweeping proclamation of the Gospel. In a positive way, this feeling motivated the Student Christian Movement and inspired its slogan—to evangelize the world in one generation. Less evangelical movements felt that the Church's impact on the twentieth century must be made chiefly in the areas of politics and economics.

These proposals were generally optimistic, for they grew out of a buoyant and vigorous era. But their advocates failed to recognize that the forces foundational to today's world were vastly more complex than they supposed. On the one hand, Christian missions moved ahead as in no period in modern history. But this advance, particularly of missions—which actively entered such areas as medicine—brought unexpected consequences. The conquest of communicable diseases, especially among children, precipitated population increases in Asia, Africa, and South America that percentage-wise outstrip any advances which the Church can make.

Later we shall note how many liberal theologians responded to the optimism evoked by the technological progress of our century. For the moment we observe only that the dream of inevitable progress also penetrated the thinking of the Church. Prominent leaders, for a period at least, felt it expedient to abandon the biblical element of discontinuity which Christian supernaturalism clearly implies, and to adjust their theology to what they considered the demands of modern man.

Divine Intervention

Closely related to the principle of discontinuity is the scriptural emphasis on the divine invasion of history at the end time. We must remember, at the outset, that the Christian view of Last Things is first and always associated with the facts of the Redeemer and of His *parousia* (appearing). In regard to the events usually called "apocalyptic" it is significant to recall that over nineteen centuries ago, the Eternal Son entered the stream of human history when Omnipotence in swaddling clothes invaded our earthly life. Eternity wrapped in a boy's curiosity walked the streets of Nazareth. The Creator of heaven and earth plied a carpenter's trade. The Joy of Heaven became the man of sorrows. The One going about doing good became the Man on the Cross. The Eternal One entered history, to die one day on the brow of Skull Hill. It is this same Jesus who at the end of the age will intervene finally and definitely to bring all things into subjection unto Himself. And His first invasion of our common life laid the foundation for His final conquest of all things.

This bold assertion should not be advanced without careful thought. Unfortunately, some may never have thought through the profound implications which the concept of divine intervention has for the mind of our time; in consequence they have not sought a point of contact with the non-Christian mentality in terms of which this idea could be addressed meaningfully to it. It must be borne in mind, however, that however well it may be expressed, this future which the Christian Scriptures promise for man and his world will scarcely be palatable to modern man, enamored as he is with his own cherished planning.

Adventism

It would be wrong to avoid the term "Adventism" because of its association with the name or distinctive teaching of some religious sect. Actually, the New Testament abounds in predictions and promises that our Lord, now ascended to the right hand of God, will once again physically visit the arena of human activities. Obviously men will assess such an event in various ways, according to their world outlooks. Later we will note some of the "modern" approaches to advent passages in the New Testament. For the moment, we concern ourselves especially with the views of evangelical Christians.

A high view of Scripture, both as to origin and as to final authority, is basic for true believers. In our discussion we take this position for granted as typical evangelicalism. It is not surprising that where this attitude toward the Christian revelation has persisted, devout men and women have cherished our Lord's promise to return with utmost serious- ness and with deep reverence. This promise finds most explicit expression in the words of Jesus, "I will come again, and receive you unto myself" (John 14:3) and also in the words of the messengers at the ascension, "This same Jesus ... shall so come, in like manner ..." (Acts 1:11). It is not surprising that Christ's return should be called the "blessed hope" (Titus 2:13). The early Church regarded it thus, and in view of the promised unrolling of the scripturally foretold pattern of events, emphasized the need of living in a spirit of constant expectancy. Writers in the first three centuries of the Church likewise gave earnest thought to those events which should cluster about the Advent of our Lord. Men like Irenaeus, Justin, and Tertullian pondered the presence of oppressive dictatorships and sought to understand them in terms of the Antichrist and of his de- struction at Christ's return.

The attitude of the Church to our Lord's promised return has varied throughout the centuries, particularly since the legal imposition of Chris- tianity by Constantine during the fourth century. The more the Church was geared to secular social, economic, and political programs, and the more its leaders aligned the Church with visible institutions of one kind or another, the more it lost interest in the advent of Christ. The same pattern of declension was true of the centuries which followed the Protestant Reformation. When one reviews the course of history, he is amazed to see the degree to which this "hope" has been pushed in the background, as the Church came to identify herself with assorted kinds of worldly prog- ress-programs and with the power-structures of modern times.

This does not mean that since the Reformation the Church has totally ignored the *parousia* of Christ. There have been times when reverent churchmen vigorously pressed for evangelizing the world, while at the same time they lifted into prominence the message of the advent of Christ. There were, for example, devout evangelicals during the eight- eenth and nineteenth centuries who espoused what is popularly known as *postmillennialism*. This view, in brief, teaches that the earnest and dedi- cated efforts of the Church can bring about a world-wide devotion to the Christian Gospel. When the world has been conquered by the Gospel, then the Lord will return to claim His Kingdom and will establish a thousand years of peace under Messiah's reign. This view preserves the sense of moral dualism which is a part of evangelicalism; that is, it recog- nizes that this world is a battleground of evil forces, and that the com- pletion of its reconstitution depends on the coming of Someone from outside its processes.

This postmillennial view seemed satisfactory at a time when local and geographical units were relatively small, and when wars were limited affairs. Even dedicated Christians accepted the view that the building of the Kingdom was basically a quiet and "regular" process which resulted from inner forces at work in men's lives, and which operated as a gentle, transforming agent within the social structure. In our century, however, political and scientific changes have overwhelmed our world with such staggering speed that thoughtful persons have begun to see that certain things are transpiring on the earth which are quite beyond any visible human control. From the general consternation over world events has come a quest by Christians of all levels of maturity of instruction in scriptural references to the return of the Son of Man who will "cut short the work in righteousness."

Another way of interpreting Last Things is a system called *amillennialism.* As the term suggests, amillennialism considers some of the Scriptures (notably the Book of Revelation) which speak of the return of Christ and of His millennial reign on the earth to be of figurative, rather than literal, interpretation. Those who champion this view emphasize the folly of trying to construct exact numerical time systems from Scripture, and note that such literalism too frequently leads to absurdities. Amillennialists recognize that human history has a purpose; they believe it is God who will solve the ultimate problems of history, that He alone holds the secret to the consummation of the age.

Another approach to eschatology is known as *premillennialism.* Its advocates, like the postmillennialists, believe that the Scriptures predict a thousand years of peace under the power and rule of the Son of God, when the nations shall be governed with a rod of iron, and there shall be no more learning of war. They agree, also, that it is the Church's duty to promote evangelization of the world with all speed and vigor, not with a view to ushering in the Kingdom, but rather in obedience to the New Testament command.

Premillennialism, moreover, tries to face the entire range of predicted events which the New Testament seems to indicate will antedate and lead to the consummation of the age. It notes, for example, the preparatory signs of the advent; it believes that the end-time will be a period of great distress on the earth, a time when men grope for solutions, but without success. It believes there will be a special dealing by God with the Hebrew people, by which they may be led to resettle in their ancient land. Premillennialism feels that rising international lawlessness and increasing manipulation of technical civilization by "strong men" will herald the end-time. Not all followers of this system agree on all eschatological details. Some hold that at the beginning of the Great Tribulation—a time which will manifest a final and massive demonstration of the powers of Antichrist, the man of sin—the Church will be translated into heaven. Others feel the Church will be called upon to endure a portion of this testing period; still others believe that she will continue on the earth until the Lord returns to reconstitute all things and to inaugurate the thousand years of peace.

The common denominator of these adventist views—a-, post-, and pre-millennial—is the belief that the Son of Man Himself shall return visibly to the human scene to bring in a New Day. Each view is a distinct philosophy of history. Of the three, postmillennialism is the most optimistic, premillennialism the least so. All avoid the tendency to equate the Kingdom of God with any temporal institution, and all refuse to equate history with nature. All are forced to reject and repudiate the Marxist heresy, namely, that history is simply the outworking of materialistic forces which operate relentlessly (guided and shaped, of course, by the Communist party) to produce a classless society, a utopian "kingdom on earth."

Thus far we have sketched the historic Christian view of Last Things, structured on the principles of Futurism, Discontinuity, Divine Intervention, and Adventism. We have noted that the Christian message implies a characteristic philosophy of history; it necessarily involves a special way of viewing human events and of understanding history. It has been observed, further, that to articulate the message of her Lord, Christianity must interact with the stark facts of history and their display of human depravity in our day. Such a view forthrightly accepts the fact of sinful man's inadequacy, and recognizes his need for divine assistance if God's ultimate purpose for human history is to be realized.

II. THE TWENTIETH-CENTURY REVOLT AGAINST ESCHATOLOGY

Adherents of postmillennialism, many of whom at the turn of the century were evangelical in outlook, tended to shift their view in one of two directions. Some moved to premillennialism. Others identified themselves with a theological trend usually called the "liberal-modernist" movement. This latter schema was supported by men of varying backgrounds whose thinking involved many facets and differed in many details. Briefly stated, the liberal-modernist theology sought to reinterpret the Gospel message in terms of modern presuppositions. That is, it sought to give theological support to the motif of continuity, to the almost limitless confidence in the inevitability of human progress, and to the fashionable expectation of the systematic elimination of social ills by human efforts.

Basic to the liberal-modernist reinterpretation of the Christian message was the axiom that whatever may have been the nature of the historic Christian message, today's world requires theological adjustment and restatement of the *kerygma* or Gospel preaching, in terms familiar to men of scientific outlook and conforming to man's confidence in himself as essentially good. Such accommodation meant reorienting the biblical emphasis on the radical nature of human sin, and on the need for man's consequent personal reconciliation to God. In place of Christ's redemptive work, emphasis was assigned to His moral and social teachings, and to the hope of a new heaven on earth to be achieved within the present time by scientifically acceptable means.

From this perspective, biblical eschatology seemed like some kind of theological excrescence, something to be eliminated or explained away. From 1890 onward, liberal scholars therefore expended much effort to this end. Traditional eschatology was disparaged as pessimistic and as implying lack of confidence in man. The prospect of any supernatural operation of God in this world was written off as "unscientific" and hence unthinkable. Those who expected such divine intervention were regarded as indolent persons who lacked either the will or the vision to do their part in bringing about the "Beloved Community." The positive program of the liberal-modernist movement involved cooperation with "an Eternal Creative Good Will," with a striving Deity who, as "one of the facts" that help establish good upon the earth, vitally needs man's assistance in the fulfilling of the creative process (Eugene W. Lyman, *The Experience of God in Modern Life,* New York, Charles Scribner's Sons, 1918, p. 82).

Something like a bombshell fell on this liberal-modernist movement, however, with the appearance in 1906 of Albert Schweitzer's *The Mystery of the Kingdom of God* (New York, Dodd, Mead & Company, 1914), and in 1910 of an English edition of his monumental work, *The Quest of the Historical Jesus* (New York, The Macmillan Company). The latter struck a devastating blow at those theologians who centered their emphasis only on the moral teachings of Jesus, rather than on those teachings of our Lord which deal with personal redemption and with Last Things. In a word, Schweitzer showed that eschatology is not merely an incidental feature of Jesus' thinking and teaching; rather, His message was oriented to His expectation of a supernatural and catastrophic coming of the Kingdom. In Schweitzer's own words, to remove this element of eschatology made Jesus be "to our time a stranger and an enigma" (*The Quest of the Historical Jesus,* New York, The Macmillan Company, 1948, p. 399).

In referring to the conventional and convenient Jesus as portrayed by such "liberal-minded" theology, Schweitzer wrote: "The Jesus of Nazareth who appeared as the Messiah, proclaimed the morality of the kingdom of God, established the kingdom of heaven upon earth and died in order to consecrate his work—this Jesus never existed. It is a figure sketched by Rationalism, enlivened by Liberalism, and dressed up by modern theology in the clothes of historical science" (*The Mystery of the Kingdom,* p. 26).

Schweitzer's works were read with something like passive hostility in Germany, although English theologians received them with extreme seriousness. In the United States, most liberal-modernist thinkers showed little interest in Schweitzer's negative comments, so long as history seemed to uphold their optimistic position. They disliked Schweitzer's radical concept of "interim ethic" which he held applicable only to the brief time span which Jesus allegedly expected between His earthly ministry and the final and ultimate inauguration of the Kingdom (*The Quest of the Historical Jesus*, pp. 340 ff.). Critics felt this view did violence to the gradualism which they insisted that Jesus had proclaimed as the methodology of the Kingdom.

It needs to be said, however, that for all its impact upon the liberal-modernist tradition, the effect of Schweitzer's work was negative insofar as historic Christianity was concerned. Schweitzer asserted (correctly, we think) that Jesus believed the present age would end catastrophically. But Schweitzer also asserted (incorrectly, we think) that our Lord's teachings at this point must be interpreted wholly in terms of imminence; that is, that Jesus asserted that the Kingdom must be ushered in quickly. Schweitzer implies, consequently, that Jesus was a misguided enthusiast mistaken with respect to the true facts. Such a concept is, of course, entirely incompatible with a high view of the Person of our Lord.

For three decades after the appearance of Schweitzer's epoch-making book, the liberals in America sought to bring in the Kingdom by projecting wide-scale political and social reforms. From its outset this program had serious limitations. Chief among them was a deficiency of insight into the question of human evil, or more specifically, into the problem of sin. More than the shock of one World War was needed to lay bare the shallowness of easy programs of social sanctification. These schemes hoped to conquer human greed merely by moral persuasion, or by advocating collectivist schemes, and particularly in the 1930s by co-operating with movements which advocated government ownership and/ or operation of major industries, the elimination of the profit motive, and "a deliberate calm attempt at national planning." This emphasis led some clergymen to align themselves with organizations of the "United Front" type, which paraded as "progressive" and which seemed notoriously unable to prevent infiltration, and in some cases domination, by communists.

Very few of those who later discovered that they had fraternized with subversively-tainted organizations were, in the long pull, personally disloyal to their country. Being perhaps politically and economically naïve, a number were deceived concerning the true nature of some of these groups. It is lamentable that they lent the support of their names to organizations which proved to be hostile to values basic to our American heritage. Most of them were not prolonged victims of deception.

At the end of World War II, man found himself face to face with social and political problems which he could scarcely have foreseen a generation before. Massive forces had flaunted both their desire and their ability to wipe the memory of God from the face of the earth. They had openly advocated a program of fraud, treachery and subversion to destroy freedom (which liberal thinkers have always professed to cherish) on the earth, and especially to destroy the free governments of the West. These forces now emerged from the war apparently bent on making good their threats. It is remarkable that from 1917 to 1935 these threats were passed off by "liberals" as mere trifles which would be laid aside when the U.S.S.R. took her place among the nations. By 1947 most of these illusions were swept away by the realities of the Cold War.

These facts dealt hard blows to the ruling optimism of liberal-modernist theology, as it sought to accommodate itself to the modern mood. The desired "kingship of God"—which was to ensue as the power of nationalism was broken, as the social struggle between classes was resolved, and as society was reconstructed on new and spiritual principles (Eugene W. Lyman, *The Meaning and Truth of Religion*, New York, Charles Scribner's Sons, 1933, pp. 438 f.) seemed more remote than ever. Hope for "the achievement of a spiritual universe" through utilizing all the "resources of creative love and wisdom" (*ibid.*, p. 456) seemed doomed; actual conditions of the times only mocked the thirst which had been created among sensitive and idealistic persons by the preaching of a gradually evolving utopia on earth. This frustration of hopes by the realities of the world situation caused some thoughtful persons to ponder with new seriousness the meaning of biblical references to future catastrophic events associated with the *parousia* of the Lord and the perfecting of His kingdom. More specifically, the development of thermonuclear devices of the kiloton-range turned thoughtful men to consider seriously those passages of Scripture which formerly seemed incongruous to the modern mind. The fantastic capabilities of modern explosives give many descriptions in the Book of Revelation fresh sharpness and frightening credibility.

While older liberalism had considered the scriptural meaning of Last Things difficult at best and scandalous at worst, a changed attitude overtook the younger scholars, even those whose early orientation and academic training had been within the liberal-modernist tradition. The theology which for some decades had tried to adapt to the mind of modern man, by 1950 was being called seriously into question. Professors discovered that far from being repelled by such subjects as eschatology, their students were finding such teaching rather exciting!

During the past decade all whose teachings had been related to the liberal-modernist theological tradition have had to make readjustments and compromises in their theology. It will be instructive, therefore, to survey some of the post-liberal attempts to deal with the question of Last Things and to compare the statements of our Lord about the *eschaton* with what some scholars consider acceptable to the mid-century man.

Professor Werner Georg Kümmel of Marburg gives an excellent overview of recent treatments of eschatological teaching. As the first of these treatments he lists the work of Albert Schweitzer. We have noted previously that Schweitzer claims that in accordance with the Jewish apocalyptic spirit, Jesus announced the imminent occurrence of the events marking the end of the age; these He is alleged to have expected in His lifetime, and later to have connected with His death (*Verheissung und Erfüllung*, Zurich, 1957, Introduction).

Dr. Kümmel's second reference is to C. H. Dodd. In developing his view of "Realized Eschatology," Dodd seeks to eliminate the futuristic element in our Lord's teaching; he considers it a misunderstanding by the early Church of Jesus' real intent. This misunderstanding presumably resulted from the early Christians' orientation in the Jewish apocalyptic and caused them to overlook Christ's emphasis on realizing the hope of the kingdom here and now. That is to say, because of the type of Judaism from which most of the first believers came, the early Church was considered so excessively futuristic in outlook that it could not comprehend the kingdom-teaching of our Lord. Dodd interprets such passages as Mark 1:15 ("The time is fulfilled, and the kingdom of God is at hand....") to mean that, in Jesus' opinion, the kingdom of God had now arrived with His ministry. Futurism thus becomes irrelevant, and Dodd clearly implies that Jesus intended to engender no hope of a *parousia*. For Professor Dodd such questions as "When shall these things be?" have no significance. He says: "In reality, time-measurement is irrelevant here. An absolute end to history, whether it be conceived as coming soon or late, is no more than a fiction designed to express the reality of teleology within history" (*The Apostolic Preaching and its Developments*, New York, Harper & Brothers, 1949, p. 82).

Professor Kümmel notes a third example of attempts to explain away New Testament eschatology. This is exemplified by G. Delling who, in his volume, *Zeitverständnis des Neuen Testaments*, denies the significance of time in Jesus' thinking. Kümmel points out that this is a sophisticated argument; it rests upon critical analyses of time which are a product of our modern thinking and which are still open to grave doubt. He notes further, that all such attempts to discount the true biblical teaching of eschatology rely, not merely upon variant interpretations of certain New Testament passages, but also upon differing appraisals of the original evidence for the validity of Jesus' own message. These appraisals, in turn, rest upon differing assumptions concerning the possibilities of the supernatural in general (*loc. cit.*).

The treatment of time in this connection is usually in terms of what is called an "existential" interpretation. Professor Delling holds that Jesus' message did not lend itself to formulation in keeping with our normal temporal sequences (*Zeitverständnis des Neuen Testaments,* 1940, pp. 102 ff.), and that the question of nearness or remoteness in time is really of no concern. In similar vein, M. Meinertz considers the Kingdom of Heaven as both timeless and beyond time (*Theologie des Neuen Testaments,* 1956, Vol. I, p. 37). Dr. Kümmel notes that such interpretation violates correct exegesis of the Gospels, and undermines confidence in the factual accuracy of the New Testament record (*op. cit.,* Chapter IV).

In America the view of the essentially transcendental and existential quality of redemptive time is usually associated with Reinhold Niebuhr. In volume two of the 1939 Gifford Lectures he speaks of cultures "where a Christ is not expected" and of other cultures "where a Christ is expected." Classical cultures, he says, are among those "not expecting a Christ" because the "sovereignty to which man must be subordinated is not the kind which is partly hidden and may be expected to be more fully revealed" (*The Nature and Destiny of Man,* London, Nisbet & Company, 1948, Vol. II, p. 15). On the other hand, a culture "where a Christ is expected" characteristically looks forward to the culmination of history and the vindication of God through the triumph and the vindication of the righteous of all nations" (*ibid.,* p. 33). But Niebuhr leaves us in the dark as to whether or not *time,* in relation to this culmination of history, is something akin to time as we know it. In his chapter, "The New Testament Idea of the End" (pp. 299-309) he suggests that if such a "symbol" as the Second Coming of Christ is taken literally, "the dialectical conception of time and eternity is falsified and the ultimate vindication of God over history is reduced to a point in history" (p. 299).

He suggests, therefore, that the coming of the kingdom is something which occurs in a realm above history; he feels that "super history" is something transcendental which our minds cannot really comprehend. There are symbols, he says, such as the return (*parousia*) of Christ, the last judgment, and the resurrection (*ibid.,* pp. 300 f.) which try in a limited way to express this super-historical level of time in which the Kingdom is to come. But Niebuhr regards these terms as symbolic only, and contends that they yield no knowledge which we can properly express in terms of events in empirical time. Thus, for Niebuhr, eschatology is reduced to little more than a study of poetic concepts which offer nothing corresponding to our usual understanding of history, be it in terms of past, present, or future.

In similar manner Professor Amos N. Wilder holds that Jesus left the future to God on the premise that the only language that could adequately describe the kingdom was transcendental language. Therefore, when Jesus spoke on the subject at all, He used "suprahistorical" terms, with the result that in the New Testament "the apocalyptic event in the future is essentially of the character of myth . . ." (*Eschatology and Ethics in the Teaching of Jesus*, New York, Harper & Brothers, 1950, rev. ed., p. 182). But how then, we would ask, can the promised reign of righteousness come in this world? In the most elemental terms the existential answer would seem to be that parallel to man's realm of empirical history is a level of "redemptive history" or "parahistory," wherein God is working to accomplish His purposes. These purposes are largely hid from man's view: even the lifting of the veil (*apocalypsis*) is partial and ambiguous. The only way this "redemptive history" can in any sense be rendered intelligible to us is by the use of the semantic device of the future tense. This *future* is not, however, a future in the usual sense; rather, it designates what is "existentially" futuristic but essentially timeless.

The existential interpretation of future things takes a slightly different and undoubtedly more devastating form in the thought of Rudolf Bultmann. He discusses this question in Chapter III of the 1955 Gifford Lectures under the title *The Presence of Eternity* (New York, Harper & Brothers, 1957). His treatment of Last Things depends on his concept of "myth" and on his declared necessity to demythologize the Christian message. He traces the idea of Last Things to myths concerning the end of the world that are extant both in the ancient and modern worlds (*ibid.*, pp. 23 ff.). After showing how myths presumably became "historicized," particularly in Hebrew apocalyptic thought (p. 34), Bultmann concludes that the real meaning of the New Covenant is simply that *"The new people of God has no real history, for it is the community of the end-time, an eschatological phenomenon. How could it have a history now when the world-time is finished and the end is imminent!"* (p. 36).

Bultmann follows the same thinking in his work *Jesus Christ and Mythology* (New York, Charles Scribner's Sons, 1958). He admits that eschatology was integral to Jesus' teaching (p. 13). But he maintains that historic Christianity expresses the substance of Jesus' message at this point in mythological form, that is, in "mythical" categories such as *Parousia* and *Second Coming*. In Bultmann's view, these have no relevance for the intelligent modern man. He says, "Modern men take it for granted that the course of nature and of history, like their own inner life and the practical life, is nowhere interrupted by the intervention of supernatural powers" (p. 16). According to this view, the task of the theologian is to separate the central core of truth in the Gospel as embodied in the New Testament from the "mythical" wrappings which surround it. This requires demythologizing, a process which does not involve the elimination of myth, but simply a reinterpretation of it (p. 18).

The crucial question we would ask of Bultmann is this: precisely what is left of the Gospel when demythologizing has occurred? More specifically, what remains of the biblical teaching concerning Last Things? He says: "We must, therefore, say that to live in faith is to live an eschatological existence, to live beyond the world, to have passed from death to life . . . This means that the eschatological existence of the believer is not a worldly phenomenon, but is realized in the new understanding" (*ibid.*, p. 81). It seems clear that in Bultmann's frame of reference the entire futuristic and adventist thrusts of the Christian message vanish into a kind of semantic gnosticism. If he is correct in his thinking, then the Christian is merely wasting his time and wearying himself in looking for a New Heaven and a New Earth.

III. ELEMENTS INTEGRAL TO THE CHRISTIAN HOPE

So far we have sketched both the essential features of the historic Christian view of Last Things and some representative attempts to accommodate Christian eschatology to modern thought, particularly to the antisupernaturalism which has typified the age of science. Now we shall delineate those factors considered vital in the present evangelical understanding of eschatology.

Much of the disparity between the historic Christian and current accommodated thinking on Last Things depends on one's view of the inspiration and authority of Scripture. Usually any tendency to explain away a literal intervention of God in the *eschaton* goes hand in hand with disbelief in the historical accuracy of Holy Writ, for the Bible clearly affirms in the affairs of the world a final activity of God which is distinguishable from His general providential activity. Neither the fact of a final and authoritative revelation nor the thought of an eschatological termination of human affairs is appealing to the modern man. As Edmund Schlink reminds us, "Against this proclamation of its end, the world defends itself by means of its own hopes" (address given at the opening of the Second Assembly of the World Council of Churches in Evanston, Aug. 15, 1954, quoted in *Christian Century, Vol. LXXI*, No. 34, Aug. 25, 1954, p. 1002). In other words, a high degree of correlation exists between the acceptance or rejection of the final authority of the Scriptures and the acceptance or rejection of the possibility of a literal eschatological culmination of the present age in terms of the advent of the ascended Lord of History.

The evangelical believer usually states the problem of eschatology as follows: How shall I as an individual view this matter of Last Things? To this consideration we now direct our closing discussion.

In the first place, Christian eschatology reflects a frankly dualistic view of man and of history. That is to say, it reckons realistically with the question of evil, both in individuals and in the expression of man's common life in history. Each of us, of course, would prefer some type of monistic perspective that does not demand a dramatic and vigorous revision and resolution of life. Since life confronts us, however, with the stark realities of sin, of suffering, and of death, any system that hopes to win the allegiance of ethically sensitive men and women must come to grips with these problems. This Christian eschatology does; it manifests its realistic nature both by its pronouncements about the demonstrated truth of these inescapable facts, and by its insight into God's ultimate and final triumph over all evil. An integral part of this triumph, a vital element in its rationale, is the eschatological action of God in history.

We have seen how social monism motivated the social gospel movement, how the radical quality of evil was adjusted to the mood of the times, and how, in consequence, eschatology came to be regarded as superfluous. We have traced the inherent instability of such thinking, and can only conclude that no other alternative is possible except a frankly super-naturalistic concept of Last Things. The movements espoused by C. H. Dodd or Reinhold Niebuhr or Rudolf Bultmann seem to be systems of expediency, half-way houses which offer the Christian no valid confidence for the future. They offer no hope, no prospect of an overruling Hand in the affairs of mankind, as we face the mounting forces of self-destruction that would overwhelm us. Transcendental "parahistory" or "demythologized" New Testament teaching offers no anchor whatever in a world like ours.

The Christian doctrine of Last Things answers to the believer's deep desire to see a resolution of the problem spawned by the gaping dualism of human moral history. The sensitive Christian responds with delight to the promise that "in the dispensation of the fulness of time" the Father shall gather together in one all things in Christ. He is deeply aware that the natural world also yearns for this final reconstitution, for this final recapitulation of all creation in Christ. When the centrifugal forces of the Fall shall be reversed, and its tragic consequences neutralized, then, and only then, shall man's spirit finally be at rest.

Stated more popularly, the Christian doctrine of Last Things meets the believer's yearning for that time when the kingdoms of this world shall become the Kingdom of our Lord and of His Christ. This hope to see evil dethroned and the petition fulfilled ("Thy Kingdom come, thy will be done on earth, as it is in heaven") characterizes every truly regenerate heart. As members of Christ's Body, we live in tension, yea in distress, so long as we see all things not yet put under His feet.

Those events, therefore, which cluster around the End of the Age (the *eschaton*) constitute the Christian's hope. Ever since the first century of our Christian era, the Church militant has looked for the final regathering of all things in Christ. Especially in troubled and threatening times she has turned her thoughts toward an Eternal Kingdom where evil will be overthrown, and where mankind's divinely-kindled hope, the desire of the ages, will be fulfilled. Other-worldly as it may seem, this hope concerning Last Things has characterized the Church in the best chapters of her history. And it has been the Church, in whose eyes this vision has been the most vivid, which has borne with fortitude even the greatest persecutions, and which has been willing to suffer untold risks in witnessing for her Lord.

The historic Christian view of Last Things, therefore, fulfills a deep need among those who, in honestly facing the yawning dualities of our world, have been mocked by the shallow promises and unfulfilled hopes of non-eschatological programs. While Christian eschatology does not profess to satisfy all our questions about events of the last days, it does impress anyone who is disposed to take the matter of divine revelation seriously that it has something vital to say. It offers the bold proposal that God Himself will speak the last word in history. Further, to the sensitive Christian it offers a satisfying fulfillment of his reverent anticipation of Prince Immanuel's universal and righteous rule. Finally, this message supplies vital encouragement for the Christian's daily walk, particularly as he lives in the tension between the empirical *now* and the expectation which the Holy Spirit has awakened in his heart for the glorious *then*.

It is no secret, of course, that for many years earnest Christians have differed in their views about the millennium and about the order in which end-time events will occur. This chapter has not tried to delineate the varying interpretations of eschatology within the historic Christian faith. In all honesty one must recognize that legitimate and explainable differences of opinion may indeed surround such matters. The basic and major thrust of biblical teaching seems clear and commonly shared, however, namely, that as the present age reaches its close, there will come a final, conclusive expression of "the mystery of iniquity," that will be marked by the emergence of Antichrist. Great distress will overtake mankind as these happenings draw near. But the Blessed Hope will sustain the Church, whatever the trials may be that she is called to endure. The climax toward which all these events shall point will be the personal return of the Risen and Ascended Christ. Then once again the earth shall feel the tread of His sacred feet. Then all things shall be brought into subjection under Him.

Could anyone in 30 A.D. have read Joel 2:28-32, and therefrom have systemically charted the events of Acts 2? Yet when the glories of the Day of Pentecost were unrolled, Peter could say, *"This is that* which was spoken by the prophet Joel ..." So, too, when the last trumpet shall have sounded and details of the Last Things shall have been unfolded, the Church Triumphant shall say, "This is that glorious event! This is that Blessed Hope!"

A SELECT
BIBLIOGRAPHY

I-III. EVANGELICAL THEOLOGY

L. Berkhof, *Systematic Theology*. Grand Rapids: Wm. B. Eerdmans Publishing Company, 1946. (*Reformed*)

G. C. Berkouwer, *Studies in Dogmatics,* fifteen volumes (of which eight have been translated from Dutch into English). Grand Rapids: Wm. B. Eerdmans Publishing Company. (*Reformed*)

Carl F. H. Henry (ed.), *Basic Christian Doctrines.* New York: Holt, Rinehart and Winston, 1962. (Interdenominational symposium)

———, *Fifty Years of Protestant Theology.* Boston: W. A. Wilde Company, 1950. (Survey)

H. D. McDonald, *Theories of Revelation: An Historical Study, 1860-1960.* London: Allen & Unwin, 1963. (Survey)

E. Y. Mullins, *The Christian Religion in Its Doctrinal Expression.* Philadelphia: The Judson Press, n.d. (*Baptist*)

Roger Nicole, "Theology," in *Contemporary Evangelical Thought* (Carl F. H. Henry, ed.). Great Neck, N.Y.; Channel Press, 1957.

Francis Pieper, *Christian Dogmatics,* 3 volumes. St. Louis: Concordia Publishing House, 1950. (*Lutheran*)

L. B. Smedes, *The Incarnation: Trends in Modern Anglican Thought.* Kampen, The Netherlands, 1953.

IV. THE NATURE OF GOD

Herman Bavinck, *The Doctrine of God.* Grand Rapids: Wm. B. Eerdmans Publishing Company, 1951.

G. C. Berkouwer, *The Providence of God.* Grand Rapids: Wm. B. Eerdmans Publishing Company, 1952.

Carl F. H. Henry, *Notes on the Doctrine of God.* Boston: W. A. Wilde Company, 1948.

Carl F. H. Henry, *Personal Idealism and Strong's Theology*. Wheaton, Illinois: Van Kampen Press, 1951.
J. Gresham Machen, *Christianity and Liberalism*. New York: The Macmillan Company, 1925.

V. THE NATURE OF REVELATION

G. C. Berkouwer, *General Revelation*. Grand Rapids: Wm. B. Eerdmans Publishing Company, 1955.
Charles Hodge, *Systematic Theology*, 3 volumes. New York: Scribner, Armstrong and Company, 1872.
Addison H. Leitch, "General and Special Revelation," in *Basic Christian Doctrines*. New York: Holt, Rinehart and Winston, 1962.
A. H. Strong, *Christ in Creation and Ethical Monism*. Philadelphia: The Judson Press, 1899.
B. B. Warfield, *Revelation and Inspiration*. New York: Oxford University Press, 1927.

VI. THE NATURE OF THE BIBLE

Carl F. H. Henry (ed.), *Revelation and the Bible*. Grand Rapids: Baker Book House, 1958.
P. E. Kretzmann, *The Foundations Must Stand*. St. Louis: Concordia Publishing House, 1936.
James I. Packer, *"Fundamentalism" and the Word of God*. Grand Rapids: Wm. B. Eerdmans Publishing Company, 1958.
F. Pieper, *Christian Dogmatics*, Vol. I. St. Louis: Concordia Publishing House, 1950.
J. A. O. Preus, *It is Written*. St. Louis: Concordia Publishing House, 1962.
Benjamin B. Warfield, *The Inspiration and Authority of the Bible*. Philadelphia: Presbyterian and Reformed Publishing Company, 1948.

VII. THE NATURE OF THE PHYSICAL UNIVERSE

Percy Bridgman, *The Logic of Modern Physics*. New York: The Macmillan Company, 1928.
W. C. Dampier-Whetham, *A History of Science*. New York: The Macmillan Company, 1931.
Ernest Nagel, *The Structure of Science*. New York: Harcourt, Brace & World, 1961.
Henri Poincare, *The Foundations of Science*. New York: The Science Press, 1913.
Bernard Ramm, *A Christian View of Science and Scripture*. Grand Rapids: Wm. B. Eerdmans Publishing Company, 1954.
J. W. N. Sullivan, *The Limitations of Science*. New York: Viking Press, 1933.

VIII. THE NATURE OF MAN

G. C. Berkouwer, *Man: The Image of God*. Grand Rapids: Wm. B. Eerdmans Publishing Company, 1962.

John Calvin, *Institutes of the Christian Religion*. Editor, J. T. McNeill. Translator, Ford L. Battles. Philadelphia: The Westminster Press, 1960.
H. Dooyeweerd, *In the Twilight of Western Thought*. Studies in the Pretended Autonomy of Philosophical Thought. Philadelphia: The Presbyterian and Reformed Publishing Company, 1960. Chapter VIII, "What is Man?"
J. Gresham Machen, *The Christian View of Man*. Grand Rapids: Wm. B. Eerdmans Publishing Company, 1947.
James Orr, *God's Image in Man and Its Defacement in the Light of Modern Denials*. Grand Rapids: Wm. B. Eerdmans Publishing Company, 1948.

IX. THE NATURE OF SIN

James Oliver Buswell, Jr., *Sin and Atonement*. Grand Rapids: Zondervan Publishing House, 1936.
J. Gresham Machen, *The Christian View of Man*. Grand Rapids: Wm. B. Eerdmans Publishing Co., 1947.
John Murray, *The Imputation of Adam's Sin*. Grand Rapids: Wm B. Eerdmans Publishing Company, 1959.
James Orr, *Sin as a Problem Today*. New York: Eaton & Mains, 1910.
Benjamin B. Warfield, *Studies in Augustine and Tertullian*. New York: Oxford University Press, 1930.

X. THE NATURE OF REDEMPTION

Thomas J. Crawford, *The Doctrine of Holy Scripture Respecting the Atonement*. Edinburgh: Blackwood, 1874 (second edition).
Leon Morris, *The Apostolic Preaching of the Cross*. London: Tyndale Press, 1955.
John Murray, *Redemption, Accomplished and Applied*. Grand Rapids: Wm. B. Eerdmans Publishing Company, 1955. Reprint in paperback form.
————, *The Atonement*. Philadelphia: Presbyterian and Reformed Publishing Company, 1961.
George Smeaton, *The Doctrine of the Atonement as Taught by Christ Himself*. Edinburgh: T. & T. Clark, 1871 (second edition). Reprint, Zondervan Publishing House, 1953.
————, *The Doctrine of the Atonement as Taught by the Apostles*. Edinburgh: T. & T. Clark, 1870. Reprint, Zondervan Publishing House, 1957.
Benjamin Breckinridge Warfield, *The Person and the Work of Christ*. Philadelphia: Presbyterian and Reformed Publishing Company, 1950. Several articles in this collection are relevant here. They are reprints from the earlier volumes *Biblical Doctrines* and *Studies in Theology*, published by Oxford University Press in 1929 and 1932.

XI. THE NATURE OF HISTORY

Earle E. Cairns, "Philosophy of History" in *Contemporary Evangelical Thought* (Carl F. H. Henry, ed.). Great Neck, N.Y.: Channel Press, 1957.
Kenneth Scott Latourette, "The Christian Understanding of History," in *American Historical Review*, Vol. LIV, January, 1949, pp. 259-276.
Philip Schaff, *What is Church History? A Vindication of the Idea of Historical Development*, translated from the German by J. W. Nevin, Philadelphia, 1846.
C. Gregg Singer, "An Approach to a Theological Interpretation of American History," in *The Westminster Theological Journal*, Vol. XX, November, 1957, pp. 26-45.
————, "The Meaning and Goal of History," in *Christianity Today*, Vol. IV, Nos. 12, 13, 14, March 14, 28, April 4, 1960.

XII. JESUS OF NAZARETH

Günther Bornkamm, *Jesus of Nazareth*. London: Hodder and Stoughton, 1960. A "post-Bultmannian" portrait.
Alfred Edersheim, *The Life and Times of Jesus the Messiah*. New York: E. R. Herrick and Co., 1883 (first edition). Reprinted in 1956 by Wm. B. Eerdmans Publishing Company, Grand Rapids. A classic work.
Adam Fahling, *The Life of Christ*. St. Louis: Concordia Publishing House, 1936. A conservative presentation, somewhat over-harmonized.
James M. Robinson, *A New Quest of the Historical Jesus*. London: SCM Press, 1959. The current situation and the "post-Bultmannian" quest.
Albert Schweitzer, *The Quest of the Historical Jesus*. New York: The Macmillan Company, 1961 (reprint of 1910 edition).
Ethelbert Stauffer, *Jesus and His Story*. London: SCM Press, 1960. Based primarily on the Gospel of John and "new sources."

XIII. THE RESURRECTION OF CHRIST

William Milligan, *The Resurrection of Our Lord*. New York: The Macmillan Company, 1927.
Richard Niebuhr, *Resurrection and Historical Reason*. New York: Charles Scribner's Sons, 1957.
James Orr, *The Resurrection of Jesus*. Cincinnati: Jenning & Bryan, n. d. (1909).
A. M. Ramsey, *The Resurrection of Christ*. Philadelphia: Westminster Press, 1946.
W. J. Sparrow Simpson, *The Resurrection and Modern Thought*. London and New York: Longmans, Green & Company, 1911.

XIV. THE HOLY SPIRIT

Karl Barth, *Church Dogmatics*, I/1. New York: Charles Scribner's Sons, 1936.

C. K. Barrett, *The Holy Spirit and the Gospel Tradition*. London: S.P.C.K., 1954.

Come, Arnold B., *Human Spirit and Holy Spirit*. Philadelphia: The Westminster Press, 1959.

G. S. Hendry, *The Holy Spirit in Christian Theology*. Philadelphia: The Westminster Press, 1956.

Regin Prenter, *Spiritus Creator*. Philadelphia: Muhlenberg Press, 1953.

XV. THE NATURE OF REGENERATION

G. C. Berkouwer, "The Genesis of Sanctification," *Faith and Sanctification*. Grand Rapids: Wm B. Eerdmans Publishing Company, 1952.

Stephen Charnock, *The Complete Works of Stephen Charnock*, B.D. Edinburgh: James Nichol, 1965, Vol. III, pp. 7-335.

Charles Hodge, "Regeneration," *Systematic Theology*. New York: Scribner, Armstrong, and Company, 1877, Vol. III, pp. 3-40.

John Murray, *Redemption Accomplished and Applied*. Grand Rapids: Wm. B. Eerdmans Publishing Company, 1955.

Benjamin B. Warfield, "On the Biblical Notion of Renewal," *Biblical Doctrines*. New York: Oxford University Press, 1929, pp. 439-463.

XVI. THE NATURE OF FAITH

While not all evangelical, these works furnish a very representative appraisal of Kierkegaard's religious views:

James Collins, *The Mind of Kierkegaard*. Chicago: Henry Regnery Company, 1953.

Hermann Diem, *Kierkegaard's Dialectic of Existence*. London: Oliver and Boyd, 1959.

Eduard Geismar, *Lectures on the Religious Thought of Søren Kierkegaard*. Minneapolis: Augsburg Publishing House, 1938.

Martin J. Heinecken, *The Moment Before God*. Philadelphia: Muhlenberg Press, 1956.

Libuse Lukas Miller, *In Search of the Self*. Philadelphia: Muhlenberg Press, 1962.

Denzil G. M. Patrick, *Pascal and Kierkegaard,* Volumes I and II. London: Lutterworth Press, 1947.

J. M. Spier, *Christianity and Existentialism*. Philadelphia: The Presbyterian and Reformed Publishing Company, 1953.

S. U. Zuidema, *Kierkegaard*. Philadelphia: Presbyterian and Reformed Publishing Company, 1960.

XVII. THE NATURE OF JUSTIFICATION

Henry P. Hamann, *Justification by Faith in Modern Theology*. St. Louis: School for Graduate Studies, Concordia Seminary, 1957.

Archibald M. Hunter, *Interpreting Paul's Gospel*. Philadelphia: The Westminster Press, 1954.

Joh. Ph. Koehler, *Commentary on the Epistle of Paul to the Galatians*. Milwaukee: Northwestern Publishing House, 1957.

Leon Morris, *The Apostolic Preaching of the Cross*. Grand Rapids: Wm. B. Eerdmans Publishing Company, 1955.

John Murray, *The Epistle to the Romans* (Chapters I-VIII), *The New International Commentary on the New Testament*. Grand Rapids: Wm. B. Eerdmans Publishing Company, 1959.

Uuras Saarnivaara, *Luther Discovers the Gospel*. St. Louis: Concordia Publishing House, 1951.

XVIII. THE NATURE OF SANCTIFICATION

G. C. Berkouwer, *Faith and Sanctification*. Grand Rapids: Wm. B. Eerdmans Publishing Company, 1952.

A. J. Gordon, *The Ministry of the Spirit*. Philadelphia: The Judson Press, 1949 reprint.

International Standard Bible Encyclopaedia, "Sanctification."

E. H. Palmer, *The Holy Spirit*. Grand Rapids: Baker Book House, 1958.

XIX. THE NATURE OF THE CHURCH

R. Newton Flew (ed.), *The Nature of the Church*. New York: Harper & Brothers, 1952.

R. B. Kuiper, *The Glorious Body of Christ*. Grand Rapids: Wm. B. Eerdmans Publishing Company, 1958.

D. G. Miller, *The Nature and Mission of the Church*. Richmond: John Knox Press, 1957.

A. Schlatter, *The Church in the New Testament Period* (translation). London: S.P.C.K., 1955.

K. L. Schmidt, "Ekklesia," in *Theologisches Wörterbuch zum Neuen Testament* III, 1933. Translation, *Kittel's Bible Key Words*, I, J. R. Coates, ed., New York: Harper & Brothers, 1938.

Ed. Schweizer, *Church Order in the New Testament* (translation). Naperville, Illinois: A. R. Allenson, 1961.

XX. THE NATURE OF LAST THINGS

G. R. Beasley-Murray, *Jesus and the Future*. London: The Macmillan Company, 1954.

Archibald Hughes, *A New Heaven and a New Earth*. Philadelphia: Presbyterian & Reformed Publishing Company, 1958.

George Eldon Ladd, *The Blessed Hope*. Grand Rapids: Wm. B. Eerdmans Publishing Company, 1956.

—— *Crucial Questions about the Kingdom of God*. Grand Rapids: Wm. B. Eerdmans Publishing Company, 1952.

—— *The Gospel of the Kingdom*. Grand Rapids: Wm. B. Eerdmans Publishing Company, 1959.